Accountability without Democracy

This book examines the fundamental issue of how citizens get government officials to provide them with the roads, schools, and other public services they need by studying communities in rural China. In authoritarian and transitional systems, formal institutions for holding government officials accountable are often weak. The state often lacks sufficient resources to monitor its officials closely, and citizens are limited in their power to elect officials they believe will perform well and to remove them when they do not. Not surprisingly, governmental public goods provision in these places is often poor. Half of the villages in China, for example, lack paved roads and running water.

The answer, Lily L. Tsai finds, lies in a community's social institutions. Even when formal democratic and bureaucratic institutions of accountability are weak, government officials can still be subject to informal rules and norms created by community solidary groups that have earned high moral standing in the community. These solidary groups establish and enforce public obligations that everyone in the community – officials as well as citizens – is expected to follow. This argument builds on existing theories of social networks and social capital, but in contrast to many existing social capital arguments that emphasize trust and cooperation, the book focuses on the importance of moral authority and the moral obligations that these social networks generate.

Lily L. Tsai is an assistant professor of political science at the Massachusetts Institute of Technology (MIT). Her research for this book received the Best Field Work Award from the American Political Science Association Section on Comparative Democratization in 2005. She has written articles in *Comparative Economic and Social Systems* (Jingji Shehui Tizhi Bijiao) and the *China Journal*. Two of her articles appear in edited volumes by Elizabeth Perry and Merle Goldman and by Lei Guang. Professor Tsai graduated from Stanford University with honors and distinction in English literature and international relations. She received an M.A. in political science from the University of California, Berkeley, and a Ph.D. in government from Harvard University in 2005.

Cambridge Studies in Comparative Politics

Other Books in the Series

Lisa Baldez, *Why Women Protest: Women's Movements in Chile*
Stefano Bartolini, *The Political Mobilization of the European Left, 1860–1980: The Class Cleavage*
Mark Beissinger, *Nationalist Mobilization and the Collapse of the Soviet State*
Nancy Bermeo, ed., *Unemployment in the New Europe*
Carles Boix, *Democracy and Redistribution*
Carles Boix, *Political Parties, Growth, and Equality: Conservative and Social Democratic Economic Strategies in the World Economy*
Catherine Boone, *Merchant Capital and the Roots of State Power in Senegal, 1930–1985*
Catherine Boone, *Political Topographies of the African State: Territorial Authority and Institutional Change*
Michael Bratton and Nicolas van de Walle, *Democratic Experiments in Africa: Regime Transitions in Comparative Perspective*
Michael Bratton, Robert Mattes, and E. Gyimah-Boadi, *Public Opinion, Democracy, and Market Reform in Africa*
Valerie Bunce, *Leaving Socialism and Leaving the State: The End of Yugoslavia, the Soviet Union, and Czechoslovakia*

Continued after the Index

Accountability without Democracy

SOLIDARY GROUPS AND PUBLIC GOODS PROVISION IN RURAL CHINA

LILY L. TSAI

Massachusetts Institute of Technology

CAMBRIDGE UNIVERSITY PRESS
Cambridge, New York, Melbourne, Madrid, Cape Town, Singapore,
São Paulo, Delhi, Dubai, Tokyo, Mexico City

Cambridge University Press
The Edinburgh Building, Cambridge CB2 8RU, UK

Published in the United States of America by Cambridge University Press, New York

www.cambridge.org
Information on this title: www.cambridge.org/9780521692809

First published 2007

A catalogue record for this publication is available from the British Library

Library of Congress Cataloguing in Publication Data

Tsai, Lily L., 1975–
Accountability without democracy : solidary groups and public goods
provision in rural China / Lily L. Tsai.
p. cm. – (Cambridge studies in comparative politics)
Includes bibliographical references and index.
ISBN 978-0-521-87197-6 (hardback) – ISBN 978-0-521-69280-9 (pbk.)
1. Municipal services – China. 2. Social institutions – China.
3. China – Rural conditions. I. Title. II. Series.
HD4710.T73 2007
320.8′40951–dc22 2006035959

ISBN 978-0-521-87197-6 Hardback
ISBN 978-0-521-69280-9 Paperback

For my parents, Huei Chu Tsai and Cheng Kween Lee

Contents

List of Figures page x
List of Tables xi
Acknowledgments xv

1 GOVERNANCE AND INFORMAL INSTITUTIONS OF ACCOUNTABILITY 1
2 DECENTRALIZATION AND LOCAL GOVERNMENTAL PERFORMANCE 27
3 LOCAL GOVERNMENTAL PERFORMANCE: ASSESSING VILLAGE PUBLIC GOODS PROVISION 60
4 INFORMAL ACCOUNTABILITY AND THE STRUCTURE OF SOLIDARY GROUPS 86
5 TEMPLES AND CHURCHES IN RURAL CHINA 120
6 LINEAGES AND LOCAL GOVERNANCE 148
7 ACCOUNTABILITY AND VILLAGE DEMOCRATIC REFORMS 187
8 THE LIMITATIONS OF FORMAL PARTY AND BUREAUCRATIC INSTITUTIONS 228
9 CONCLUSION 251

References 271
Appendix: Additional Notes on Survey Sampling and Data Analysis 287
Index 341

List of Figures

1.1.	Surveyed provinces	*page* 22
1.2	Selection of provinces	22
2.1	Number of villages with government debt	48
3.1	Total government expenditures on public goods by province	63
3.2	Provincial variation in village income per capita and public goods provision outcomes	83
5.1	Provision of public goods in villages with and without temples	131
5.2	Provision of public goods in villages with and without churches	133
6.1	Number of villages with ancestral hall reconstruction since 1979	156
6.2	Provision of public goods in villages with and without lineage groups	165
7.1	Provision of public goods in villages with good and poor implementation of grassroots democratic institutions	214
8.1	Provision of public goods in villages with and without performance contracts	248

List of Tables

2.1 Number of administrative units in the Chinese government (2003) *page* 29
2.2 Distribution of villages by reliance on informal sources of revenue 45
2.3 Distribution of villages by size of village government debt relative to 2000 government revenue 51
2.4 Distribution of villages by village government expenditures relative to 2000 government revenue 52
2.5 Distribution of villages by salary level of village officials in 2000 55
3.1 Measures of the dependent variable: village provision of public goods 75
3.2 Variation in government investment (in yuan) 77
3.3 Variation in paved roads 78
3.4 Variation in paved paths 78
3.5 Variation in classrooms unusable during rainy weather 78
3.6 Variation in years since the construction or last major renovation of the village school building 79
3.7 Variation in probability of running water 79
5.1 Comparing temple-dominated villages and church-dominated villages 138
6.1 Number of villages with only household kinship institutions, by province 154
6.2 Distribution of villages with collective lineage ritual activities 155
6.3 Distribution of villages with lineage-organized services 155

6.4 Distribution of villages with specific lineage institutions 155
6.5 Comparison of willingness to contribute to public projects 168
6.6 Comparison of social trust 168
6.7 Comparison of confidence in and relevance of village government 170
6.8 Comparison of Jiangxi villages by key variables 171
6.9 Comparison of Hebei single-surname villages by key variables 178
7.1 Comparison of Fujian villages by key variables 199
7.2 Comparison of Hebei villages by key variables 202
7.3 Comparison of Jiangxi villages by key variables 203
7.4 Descriptive statistics on interference in the preelection process 205
7.5 Summary statistics on interference in the preelection process 206
7.6 Descriptive statistics on implementation of voting institutions 206
7.7 Descriptive statistics on implementation of VRA institutions 210
7.8 Comparison of willingness to contribute to public projects among people with different assessments of elections in their village 224
7.9 Comparison of willingness to contribute to public projects among people with different assessments of the importance of villagers' representative institutions 225
A3.1 Intercorrelations (*r*) among indicators of village governmental provision of public goods 297
A3.2 Economic factors and public goods provision in rural China: all five economic factors in the same model with all controls (SUR). Missing data are multiply imputed 298
A5.1 Descriptive statistics 300
A5.2 Village governmental provision of public goods and the existence of a temple manager, with all controls (SUR). Missing data are deleted listwise 302
A5.3 Village governmental provision of public goods and the existence of a temple manager, with all controls (SUR). Missing data are multiply imputed 304
A5.4 Village governmental provision of public goods and the percentage of households participating in temple 306

reconstruction, with all controls (SUR). Missing data are deleted listwise 306
A5.5 Village governmental provision of public goods and all solidary group measures, with all controls (SUR). Missing data are deleted listwise 308
A5.6 Village governmental provision of public goods and all solidary group measures, with all controls (SUR). Missing data are multiply imputed 310
A5.7 Village governmental provision of public goods and the existence of a village church, with all controls (SUR). Missing data are deleted listwise 312
A5.8 Village governmental provision of public goods and the existence of a village church (SUR). Missing data are multiply imputed 314
A5.9 Village governmental provision of public goods and the existence of church reconstruction, with all controls (SUR). Missing data are multiply imputed 316
A5.10 Village governmental provision of public goods and interaction between temple and church groups (SUR). Missing data are deleted listwise 318
A6.1 Village governmental provision of public goods and village lineage groups, with all controls (SUR). Missing data are deleted listwise 320
A6.2 Village governmental provision of public goods and different types of lineage groups (SUR). Missing data are deleted listwise 322
A6.3 Village governmental provision of public goods and different types of lineage groups (SUR). Missing data are multiply imputed 324
A6.4 Village governmental provision of public goods and interaction between villagewide lineage groups and village temple groups (SUR), with all controls. Missing data are multiply imputed 326
A7.1 Village governmental provision of public goods and the additive score of implementation of village democratic institutions (SUR). Missing data are deleted listwise 328
A7.2 Village governmental provision of public goods and the index of implementation of preelection institutions (SUR). Missing data are deleted listwise 330

A7.3 Village governmental provision of public goods and the index of implementation of voting institutions (SUR). Missing data are deleted listwise 332
A7.4 Village governmental provision of public goods and the index of implementation of villagers' representative institutions (SUR). Missing data are deleted listwise 334
A7.5 Village governmental provision of public goods and interaction between village democratic institutions and village temple groups (SUR). Missing data are deleted listwise 336
A7.6 Village governmental provision of public goods and interaction between village democratic institutions and villagewide lineage groups (SUR). Missing data are deleted listwise 338

Acknowledgments

It is a great pleasure to acknowledge the many people who have contributed to this book.[1] First and foremost, I would like to thank the members of my doctoral committee: Elizabeth Perry, Grzegorz Ekiert, Robert Putnam, and Theda Skocpol. I have been very privileged to have such an extraordinary group of scholars as advisers.

This book would not have been possible without the scores of people in China who generously shared their time and experiences to help me understand the complexities of Chinese society. I owe especially large debts of gratitude to Fang Yan, Ma Rong, Su Peiyou, Xiao Tangbiao, and Hu Rong. Much of the fieldwork would not have been possible without their assistance. I am also deeply grateful to Chen Silan, Lai Hairong, Niu Weihong, Zhao Shukai, and Zhou Xiaohong.

Special thanks are due to Margaret Levi for her support of this book and to Jorge Dominguez for all his incisive comments and eminently practical suggestions over the years. Suzanne Berger, Frances Hagopian, Chappell Lawson, Daniel Posner, and Susan Rose-Ackerman also merit special thanks for their critical readings of the entire manuscript. At various stages of the project, conversations with and feedback from Eva Bellin, Adam Berinsky, Thomas Bernstein, Melani Cammett, Andrea Campbell, Adam Chau, Jim Clem, Sarah Cook, Deborah Davis, Bruce Dickson, Michael Foley, John Gerring, Merle Goldman, David Goodman, Emily Hannum, Jennifer Hochschild, Yasheng Huang, Gary King, Atul Kohli, David Laitin,

[1] Portions of chapters appear as Lily Tsai, "The Struggle for Village Public Goods Provision: Informal Institutions of Accountability in Rural China," in *Grassroots Political Reform in Contemporary China*, ed. Elizabeth J. Perry and Merle Goldman (Cambridge: Harvard University Press, 2007), and are printed here with permission of Harvard University Press.

Steve Levitsky, Lianjiang Li, Xiaobo Lu, Roderick MacFarquhar, Melanie Manion, Devra Moehler, Emerson Niou, Kevin O'Brien, Jean Oi, Albert Park, Roger Petersen, Susan Pharr, Benjamin Read, Elizabeth Remick, Scott Rozelle, Tony Saich, James Scott, Mark Selden, Minggao Shen, Tianjian Shi, Vivienne Shue, Dorothy Solinger, Edward Steinfeld, Kellee Tsai, Jon Unger, Ashutosh Varshney, Wang Xu, Wang Zhenyao, Rob Weller, Lynn White, Dali Yang, and several anonymous reviewers were all extremely valuable. Over the last two years, I have also benefited greatly from the stimulating intellectual communities at MIT and the Harvard Academy, and for that, I am extremely grateful.

Financial and institutional support for this research were provided by the Department of Political Science and the School of Humanities, Arts, and Social Sciences at MIT; the Harvard Academy; the Hauser Center for Nonprofit Studies at Harvard University; the Fulbright Scholar Program; the Research Center for Rural Economy of the Ministry of Agriculture in China; Nanjing University; and the Weatherhead Center for International Affairs at Harvard University.

At Cambridge University Press, I would like to extend sincere thanks to Lew Bateman for his enthusiastic support of this project. I am also deeply grateful to William Tilden, Chunping Han, Pengyu He, Matthew Amengual, Meg Rithmire, David Prout, and especially Nathan Cisneros for their assistance in preparing the final manuscript. Thanks also to Daniel Posner for suggesting the title of the book, to Kathy Kwack for the cover design, and to Andy Saff for his editorial assistance.

Some debts go far beyond the scope of this project. I have been extraordinarily lucky to have Stephen Tsai, the Coe family – Franny, James, Shelby, and Sophia – Scott Roberts, Tiphaine Lam, and Richard Chen in my life. I am deeply thankful to them.

No one has contributed more on a daily basis to this project than Edward Young. He has tirelessly provided critiques of countless drafts, and his observations continually illuminate the world for me in new and various ways. My life is incalculably richer for his presence in it.

Finally, and above all, I am indebted to my parents, Huei Chu Tsai and Cheng Kween Lee. They have worked unbelievably hard and sacrificed a great deal to give me the luxury of the best education possible. I owe them more than I can say. Their extraordinary accomplishments are and always will be a source of inspiration and an example to emulate. This book is dedicated to them.

1

Governance and Informal Institutions of Accountability

In the winter of 2001, I boarded a bus that would wind its way westward from the sunny, prosperous city of Xiamen on the coast of Fujian province in southern China, through the mountains that make up 90 percent of Fujian and across the border into the only slightly less rugged terrain of Jiangxi province. After this fourteen hour trip, I disembarked in Ganzhou, a city of a quarter of a million people and Jiangxi's only major urban center in the south. From Ganzhou, I hopped on a minibus for the last seventy kilometers of my journey to the villages of High Mountain and Li Settlement. A friend in Xiamen, hearing that I wanted to investigate the performance of local governments in less developed areas of rural China, had suggested I visit her relatives in these two neighboring villages.

Both villages, she said, were poor and agricultural. Most families survived only by sending someone to nearby Guangdong province to find work, and even with the four thousand yuan (about U.S.$500) that a migrant worker might send home every year, the income per capita in these villages was still only half that of the national average. Most houses were still constructed from clay soil pounded into large blocks. Small windows cut into the walls of houses lacked glass panes to keep cold air out. Political reforms had been slow to take root in these areas. Unlike the highly touted villages in suburban Xiamen that had carefully implemented central government directives to establish elections for village officials, grassroots democratic reforms in High Mountain and Li Settlement remained "just for show." Officials at the township level, just above the villages, determined to protect their ability to extract heavy, illegal levies on villagers, typically brought the ballot box personally to each household. Not surprisingly, villagers in High Mountain and Li Settlement reported that voting for someone other than the "recommended" candidate was very difficult.

Located right next to each other, with similar economic, geographical, and political conditions, High Mountain and Li Settlement sounded from my friend's description like they would be virtually identical. After struggling into each village with heavy bags, however, it was clear that they were not. High Mountain's roads were muddy, rutted, and poorly maintained. When it rained, people simply had to get off their bicycles and push them through a sticky mire of dirt and dung. If temperatures then dropped below freezing, as they often did during the winter, the bicycle tracks hardened permanently into a crazy quilt of ridges and furrows. In contrast, Li Settlement's village government had turned the main village road into a beautifully paved thoroughfare wide enough for two cars to pass each other. Officials in Li Settlement had even taken the trouble to construct drainage channels running on either side of the road to facilitate water runoff and slow the wear and tear on the concrete. The difference in roads between the two villages was, in short, startling.

I had come to Jiangxi to compare local governance in poorer areas with local governance in wealthier areas such as Xiamen, but I found myself confronted with vast differences in communities with the *same* level of economic development. Why were Li Settlement's roads so much better than High Mountain's roads? It was not because Li Settlement was more industrialized or because Li Settlement's government collected more revenue. It was also not because Li Settlement had free and fair elections that allowed citizens to hold village officials accountable for their performance. Nor did the village operate under a conscientious township government that monitored village officials to make sure they provided citizens with needed public services.

Back in Xiamen, I also discovered that villages with similar levels of economic development could have significantly different provision of public goods and services. West Gate and Three Forks, two neighboring villages I visited regularly while based in Xiamen, were the polar opposite of the villages in Jiangxi but very similar to each other in terms of economic development and the implementation of democratic reforms. Both West Gate and Three Forks were extraordinarily wealthy. It was not unusual for village governments in this area to control upward of a million dollars in public assets. West Gate and Three Forks have benefited enormously from the industrialization and foreign investment that Xiamen has attracted as a Special Economic Zone (SEZ). In contrast to High Mountain and Li Settlement, where three-room tamped-earth houses were the norm, residents of West Gate and Three Forks have built two- and three-story houses covered in shiny pink and white tiles with blue-tinted windows.

Villagers in West Gate, as we might expect, enjoyed a high level of public services provision. West Gate officials arranged for streetsweepers and trash disposal services. A few dirt roads remained, but most of West Gate's roads and footpaths were paved in concrete. Some were even lined with rudimentary sewers, and leftover concrete had been used to construct several village basketball courts.

In Three Forks Village, however, public goods provision was just the opposite. Surprisingly, Three Forks resembled the poor Jiangxi village of High Mountain far more closely than it did its neighbor, West Gate. The Three Forks village government did not lack for funds, yet the only thing that officials had constructed in the last few years was a large village government office building for themselves, complete with a paved parking lot and electronically automated gate. What pavement there was ended at the gate of the government compound; beyond, a dirt road with deep potholes led into the rest of the village. Like the officials in the poorly performing Jiangxi village of High Mountain, village officials in Three Forks plundered the village coffers rather than funding public services. We would be hard pressed to say that public goods provision in Three Forks was significantly better than public goods provision in High Mountain.

So how could there be such dramatic differences in governmental performance and public goods provision between villages located right next to each other? In Jiangxi province, High Mountain and Li Settlement are both poor with poorly implemented democratic and bureaucratic institutions of accountability – yet Li Settlement somehow manages to fund and organize public projects. In Fujian province, West Gate and Three Forks are both wealthy with well-implemented democratic and bureaucratic institutions – yet only West Gate's officials provide public goods and services conscientiously. Villagers in the poorly performing villages would of course have been better off moving next door to the well-performing villages, but state regulations made changing one's registered residence very difficult.

Given the resource scarcity and weak formal accountability that plague many local governments in China and other authoritarian and transitional systems, it is perhaps not that surprising that officials in High Mountain or Three Forks provide little in the way of public services. Low investment in public goods and services is the default case in rural China. Villages with high investment are in the minority. But what makes Li Settlement and West Gate so special? Why do officials in these communities act more responsibly even when they have no fear of being voted out of office or of being punished by higher-level officials? In fact, why would any government official who is not held accountable by citizens through democratic mechanisms or by higher-level officials through bureaucratic mechanisms bother to provide more than the minimal level of public services needed to prevent widespread citizen protest?

The answer to this puzzle, I argue, lies in the recognition that government officials may be subject to informal rules and norms that are unwritten and unauthorized by the state, yet established by social groups and enforced by the communities of which they are members. When the individuals in office are embedded in the social networks of their communities, they may still feel obligated to provide public goods because it is what their church, temple, ethnic, or community group expects them to do and they know that fellow group members can use the group's norms and networks to punish them if they fail to do so.

This book demonstrates that in authoritarian and transitional systems such as China – where the state finds it difficult to supervise local officials and democratic mechanisms of accountability, such as elections, are weak or nonexistent – governmental performance and public goods provision may still be good when officials are embedded in what I call "solidary groups" – groups based not only on shared interests but also on shared moral obligations. Li Settlement in Jiangxi and West Gate in Fujian have villagewide solidary groups based on religious and lineage obligations. Their neighbors High Mountain and Three Forks lack such groups. When government officials participate in solidary groups that are open to everyone in the locality they govern – when the social structure "fits" with the structure of the state, and social boundaries overlap with political ones – *social* norms and obligations can reinforce or even substitute for the *public* obligations and responsibilities of officials and citizens that the state is supposed to establish and enforce. When elections, government audits, and other formal institutions fail to motivate officials to respond to public concerns, the norms and obligations established by solidary groups can act as *informal institutions of accountability* – rules and norms that were not officially authorized or intended to enable citizens to hold officials accountable for providing public services but which do so nevertheless. This book shows that informal institutions can account for why local governments with the *same* level of economic development or the same kinds of formal institutions can vary so widely in their levels of public goods provision. If we look only at economic factors or formal institutions without delving further into the social structure and informal institutions of a locality, the behavior of government officials in places like Li Settlement and West Gate can appear inexplicable or even irrational.

Local Governance and Public Goods Provision

No matter how efficiently governments carry out other activities – decision making, budgetary planning, and information collection, for example – we do not think of them as performing well unless they also provide us with a modicum of basic public goods and services.[1] The provision of public goods and services is an essential element of governmental performance. We want our governments to provide roads, clean water, national defense, and other necessary goods and services that we have trouble producing on our own. In this book, I use the term "public goods and services" (at times, abbreviated to "public goods" or "public services") to refer to products that have what economists call "positive externalities" for the public – that is, they benefit everyone or almost everyone in society regardless of whether people pay for them or not.[2] Because excluding people from goods such as roads and national defense is costly once they are produced, few people will volunteer to pay for them since they can be enjoyed for free. Nor do profit-driven businesses have any reason to produce them. Without the government to make sure we all pay our share through taxation, these public goods and services would be in short supply.

[1] For a discussion of other dimensions of governmental performance, see Robert D. Putnam, *Making Democracy Work: Civic Traditions in Modern Italy* (Princeton: Princeton University Press, 1993), 65; Jennifer Widner, "States and Statelessness in Late Twentieth-Century Africa," *Daedalus* 124, no. 3 (Summer 1995), 131–7.

[2] This use of the term "public goods" differs from "pure public goods," which economists define as having two essential qualities: nonexcludability (people cannot be excluded from consuming the good once it has been produced) and nonrivalry (once the good has been produced, each person can enjoy its benefits without diminishing the benefits of others). The term "positive externalities" is typically used to refer to benefits of *material* welfare that can be enjoyed by individuals who do not pay for them; however, some services, such as universally affordable health care, can also be considered "public services" in the sense that they provide benefits to the *moral* welfare or well-being of people in societies that have a strong social consensus on "universal service obligations," or services that the public has a moral obligation to provide to all individuals. For a discussion of the concept of public services, see M. Krajewski, *Public Services and the Scope of the General Agreement on Trade in Services* (Geneva: Center for International Environmental Law, 2001).

Practically speaking, the provision of public goods and services matters deeply for the quality of people's lives everywhere. Politically speaking, how states provide public goods and services has major ramifications for the development of state institutions and state legitimacy. Rulers justified the building of the earliest states through preparations for war and the provision of national defense.[3] Since only effective provision of public goods and services can legitimize a state's existence, states that extract resources from their populations without providing adequate services in return (Haiti, Nicaragua, and Georgia being just some of the more egregious examples) must resort to rule by force, and even then, find it difficult to construct stable institutions.

Unfortunately, not only are predatory states that force citizens to pay their taxes but neglect to deliver the goods all too common, but even states that try to provide the goods and services people need are foundering in their efforts.[4] As more states adopt decentralization programs that shift much of the burden for providing public goods from the central state to local governments, these problems are increasingly concentrated at the local level. Reformers in many developing countries of Latin America, Africa, and Asia grapple with local officials who squander state resources by dispensing private goods to their clients and supporters. In some places, local governments simply lack sufficient resources. Privatization and the dismantling of the enterprise-based welfare system in formerly state-socialist systems such as Hungary and Bulgaria have led to revenue shortfalls in the funding of education, health care, public housing, and social insurance.[5] In the United States and Western Europe, fiscal federalism throughout the twentieth century has created competition between local governments to cut tax rates, resulting in declining public goods provision.[6] Unfunded mandates

[3] See Charles Tilly, "Reflections on the History of European State-Making," in *The Formation of National States in Western Europe* (Princeton: Princeton University Press, 1975), 74.

[4] The *World Development Report 2004* amasses a variety of data to show that government provision of public services in developing countries as well as for poor people in countries with higher levels of economic development is inaccessible, unaffordable, unresponsive to citizens' needs, and of poor quality in terms of materials, technical expertise, and corruption in the delivery process. They argue that public services provision suffers from stagnant productivity and a lack of evaluation and innovation. World Bank, "Making Services Work for Poor People," in *World Bank Development Report 2004* (Washington: World Bank, 2003).

[5] See Jon Elster, Claus Offe, and Ulrich Preuss, *Institutional Design in Post-Communist Societies* (Cambridge: Cambridge University Press, 1998), 245–6.

[6] See W. Oates, "An Essay on Fiscal Federalism," *Journal of Economic Literature* 37, no. 3 (1999), 1134; A. Breton, *Competitive Governments: An Economic Theory of Politics and Public Finance* (Cambridge: Cambridge University Press, 1998); A. Case, J. Hines, and H. Rose,

for social service provision further burden cash-strapped state governments in the United States. Fiscal decentralization in Russia has strengthened the incentives that local officials have to waste and embezzle funds for public goods provision.[7]

In few places are these issues more salient than in rural China. Fiscal decentralization in the reform period has given village governments primary responsibility for funding and organizing the construction of roads within villages, drainage systems, irrigation works, sanitation and trash disposal services, primary school facilities, and community recreational facilities.[8] The state now expects village officials to fund administrative expenses and public goods and services almost solely through the resources available in the village itself. Redistribution across provinces and localities is extremely limited, and funds for village government expenditures are not a regular part of the state budget at any level of government.[9]

Because of the tremendous variation in the performance of village governments, contemporary rural China provides an ideal setting to examine the factors that affect the quality of local governance. Local officials have so much discretion in policy implementation that both citizens and researchers often refer to policy *making* by local officials rather than policy implementation.[10] Some village governments provide citizens with outstanding public

"Budget Spillovers and Fiscal Policy Interdependence: Evidence from the States," *Journal of Public Economics* 52 (1993), 285–307; H. Ladd and J. Yinger, *America's Ailing Cities: Fiscal Health and the Design of Urban Policy* (Baltimore: Johns Hopkins University Press, 1990). See also B. Cigler, "Challenges Facing Fiscal Federalism in the 1990s," *PS: Political Science and Politics* 26, no. 2 (1993), 181–6.

7 The fiscal arrangements in Russia do not increase local government revenue when the tax base is increased. Local officials therefore have no incentive to promote economic growth in their communities but have strong incentives to waste or steal funds for public goods. See E. V. Zhuravskaya, "Incentives to Provide Local Public Goods: Fiscal Federalism, Russian Style," *Journal of Public Economics* 76, no. 3 (June 2000), 337–68.

8 In this book, I use the term "village government" to include both the village Party branch and the village committee. Chapter 2 discusses the structure of village governments in greater detail.

9 Redistribution and intergovernmental transfers are likely to increase with the recent tax reforms piloted and implemented since 2001.

10 Such high levels of local autonomy may be changing. Policies since 2002 have showed trends toward administrative and fiscal recentralization. The abolition of the agricultural tax in 2006 has necessitated increased central transfers. Localities have also experimented with practices such as *shuang daiguan*, in which townships take control of village accounts, leaving village officials with only a bare minimum in circulating funds. For a brief description, see Jean Oi, *State Responses to Rural Discontent in China: Tax-for-Fee Reform and Increased Party Control* (Washington: Woodrow Wilson International Center for Scholars, March 2003); Zhongyang Gu, "Trial on Substitution of Villages by Townships in Fiscal Management

goods and services; other village governments provide nothing at all. These dramatic differences in village governmental performance across localities are an important problem in their own right to the 800 million people who live in the Chinese countryside, but the extensive variation in governance and local economic and political conditions within the same country also presents us with something akin to a "natural laboratory." This strategy holds certain macroconditions constant (such as political ideology, national policy, and regime type) while allowing to vary particular factors that existing theories suggest are important for governance and public goods provision. Finally, both villagers and village officials remain strongly tied to the village community. With very few exceptions, village officials all come from within the village. Moreover, at the time of this study, it was still very difficult for villagers to free themselves from their home village completely and move to other places permanently.[11] These conditions thus allow us to isolate the impact of key *local*-level factors on local governmental performance.

Explaining the Performance of Local Governments

What might these key factors be? One school of thought highlights *economic development and processes of "modernization."* Political scientists such as Seymour Martin Lipset and Adam Przeworski have emphasized the importance of increasing levels of wealth in creating the conditions for more effective and more responsive government.[12] Research in development studies argues that good governance and economic development constitute a "virtuous cycle" – good governance fosters economic development and higher incomes, which in turn lead to demands for better governmental performance.[13] As localities industrialize and incomes rise, people not

in Xingtai (Xingtai 'cuncai Xiangdaiguan' Toushi Wenlu)," *People's Daily (Renmin Ri Bao)*, October 23, 2005; Junjie Han, "Supervision of Villages' Fiscal Issues by Townships: Hindrance or Promotion of Villagers' Self-Governance? (*Cuncai Xiangjian: Shi zu'ai Haishi Cujin Cunmin Zizhi?*)," *China Youth Daily (Zhongguo qingnian bao)*, October 22, 2003.

11 Rural migration for work, however, has increased dramatically, and future reforms are expected to release villagers completely from their responsibility for taxes on the plots of land assigned to them by their home village.

12 S. M. Lipset, "Some Social Requisites of Democracy: Economic Development and Political Legitimacy," *American Political Science Review* 53 (1959), 69–105; A. Przeworski and F. Limongi, "Modernization: Theories and Facts," *World Politics* 49, no. 2 (1997), 155–83.

13 Recent statistical analysis by D. Kaufman and A. Kraay constitutes a notable exception. They present findings that show a lack of evidence for a positive effect of incomes on the

only want better infrastructure and more services, but they become more capable of mobilizing themselves politically to make these demands effectively. Local governments, for their part, should also have more resources to fund higher levels of service provision. In China, as rural industrialization accelerated in the late 1980s and early 1990s, particularly along the coast, Jean Oi and others observed wealthy villages where officials used revenue windfalls to provide villagers with free water and electricity, subsidies for education, as well as new schools, movie theaters, and community centers.[14]

But looking at the four preceding village case studies suggests that local governmental performance and public goods provision may not be automatically correlated with economic development. The case of Li Settlement showed that wealth and industrialization were not necessary conditions for good public goods provision, while the case of Three Forks suggested that even villages with high levels of economic development could have poor public goods provision.

Why might public goods provision *not* be correlated with how wealthy a community is? The contrast between Three Forks' dirt roads and the shiny new office building for its officials provides part of the answer: *nothing guarantees local governments with more resources will actually use those resources for the public good.* Something has to give local officials a sense of obligation to the public and hold them accountable for meeting their obligations. Higher-level officials or citizens themselves must have ways in which they can monitor local officials to make sure that they fulfill their public responsibilities. What might some of these ways be?

This question brings us to a second school of thought about governmental performance and public goods provision that focuses on *formal institutions*. When investigating how state officials are held accountable for their behavior, political scientists often look first within the formal organization of the state. Are there adequate *democratic* mechanisms such as free and fair elections and legislative assemblies that enable citizens to elect officials they believe to be responsive and responsible and to vote these officials out of office when their expectations are not met? Or are there top-down *bureaucratic* institutions that enable higher-level officials in the state to supervise lower-level officials and make sure they are doing their job? These formal institutions govern the government and keep officials

quality of governance. See Kaufmann and Kraay, "Growth without Governance," *Economia* 3, no. 1 (2002), 169–229.

[14] Jean Oi, *Rural China Takes Off* (Berkeley: University of California Press, 1999), 79–80.

from abusing their powers. Max Weber's classic statement on bureaucracy stresses the "supervision of lower offices by the higher ones" and the centrality of formally designated job responsibilities and obligations to "modern officialdom."[15] In a more modern formulation, Terry Moe's analysis of bureaucratic organization draws on "principal-agent models" – models of relationships in which "the principal" (such as an employer) hires an "agent" (or an employee) to choose actions that benefit the principal's interest.[16] Formal institutions such as bureaucratic performance reviews at fixed intervals and auditing systems help higher-level officials (who can be considered "principals") monitor and supervise lower-level officials (the "agents"). Meritocratic selection and promotion, long-term career rewards, training programs, and selective recruitment from elite social groups encourage the formation of bureaucratic norms emphasizing loyalty, trust, and corporate identity, thereby fostering a sense of duty among bureaucrats to put collective goals above individual ones and, ideally, making the state capable of "transcending the individual interests of its private counterparts."[17]

Models of bureaucratic accountability seem particularly appropriate for authoritarian systems such as China. In China we have seen central elites successfully mobilize village officials to extract agricultural surplus, most notably during the disastrous developmental policies of the Great Leap Forward, and to carry out draconian policies of birth control. During the 1990s, both Chinese and Western scholars argued that bureaucratic performance contracts requiring local officials to meet state-mandated targets for economic development, public goods provision, and policy implementation imposed heavy administrative and financial responsibilities. These responsibilities spurred local officials to levy (and allowed them to justify) unsustainably high levels of taxes and fees on villagers.[18] Since 1999 the central government has stated in numerous directives that rural public goods provision and infrastructural development should be prioritized.[19]

15 Max Weber, *Wirtschaft und Gesellshaft* (Tubingen: Mohr, 1922), 650–78.

16 T. Moe, "The New Economics of Organization," *American Journal of Political Science* 28, no. 4 (1984), 739–77.

17 Peter Evans, *Embedded Autonomy: States and Industrial Transformation* (Princeton: Princeton University Press, 1995), 12.

18 See Thomas Bernstein and Lu Xiaobo, *Taxation without Representation in Contemporary Rural China* (New York: Cambridge University Press, 2003); Justin Yifu Lin et al., *The Problem of Taxing Peasants in China* (Beijing: Beijing University, China Center for Economic Research, June 2002), 29.

19 A more detailed elaboration on the need for rural infrastructural development can be found in "Ideas on Several Policies on Further Strengthening the Work in the Countryside and

Governance and Institutions of Accountability

Theories of democratic accountability have also become increasingly popular with scholars studying reforms in China. In the eighteenth and nineteenth centuries, Mill and other political philosophers came to the conclusion that representative democracy could provide "accountable and feasible government." In a democracy, citizens would be capable of and responsible for "controlling the business of government."[20] In democratic models, citizens – rather than higher-level officials – become the "principals" supervising local officials. As with top-down bureaucratic institutions, bottom-up democratic institutions ideally create incentive systems that motivate government officials to act in the public interest, punishing them when they pursue their own private interests at the expense of the public interest and rewarding them to make pursuing the public interest in their own interests as well. In the case of China, the central government, recognizing its limited ability to supervise grassroots officials, instituted popular village elections in the late 1980s, hoping to make villagers responsible for monitoring and sanctioning village officials when they failed to provide adequate public goods and services. Their rationale was the same as that of most normative theories of democracy: that elections and other representative institutions would encourage better governmental performance by creating incentives for officials to respond to citizen demands, increasing the transparency of government, and promoting a stronger sense of civic duty among citizens and officials.

Improving Comprehensive Productive Capacities of Agriculture by the Central Committee of the CCP and the State Council (*Zhonggong zhongyang guowuyuan guanyu jinyibu jiaqiang nongcun gongzuo tigao nongye zonghe shengchan nengli ruogan zhengce de yijian*)," approved on December 31, 2004. The most systematic and comprehensive central document concerning rural public goods provision and infrastructural development is "Several Ideas on Promoting Development of the New Socialist Countryside by the Central Committee of the CCP and the State Council (*Zhonggong zhongyang guowuyuan guanyu tuijin shehuizhuyi xin nongcun jianshe de ruogan yijian*)," approved on December 31, 2005. State directives reaffirming the state's commitment to improving the educational system include the 1993 "Guidelines for the Reform and Development of Education in China," jointly issued by the CCP Central Committee and the State Council; the "Action Plan for Educational Vitalization Facing the 21st Century," formulated by the Ministry of Education and ratified by the State Council in early 1999; and the "Decision on the Deepening of Educational Reform and the Full Promotion of Quality Education," jointly promulgated by the CCP Central Committee and the State Council in June 1999. See "Basic Education in China: A Survey of the Development of Basic Education," China Education and Research Network, www.edu.cn/20010101/21775.shtml.

20 J. S. Mill, "Considerations on Representative Government," in *Utilitarianism, Liberalism, and Representative Government* (London: Dart, 1951), 229–30.

Yet if we return to our four village case studies in mountainous Jiangxi and coastal Xiamen, we see that theories focusing on formal bureaucratic and democratic institutions cannot account for their variation in governmental performance and public goods provision. Li Settlement in Jiangxi enjoys good governance despite a lack of democratic and bureaucratic mechanisms for holding village officials accountable, while governmental performance and public goods provision in Fujian's Three Forks are deplorable despite well-implemented elections and regular performance evaluations by higher levels. Officials from the township government supervising both West Gate and Three Forks in Xiamen frequently visit the village government to see how everything is going. They pride themselves on organizing model village elections, having hosted a number of American election observation groups. Both bureaucratic and democratic institutions of accountability are equally well implemented in West Gate and Three Forks – yet only West Gate has good governance. As with economic development, formal institutions of bureaucratic and democratic accountability do not seem to have a major impact on village governmental performance and public goods provision.

Solidary Groups and Informal Accountability

The solution to this puzzle emerges when we shift our attention from formal institutions of accountability to *informal* ones. Even when local officials have nothing to fear from elections or sanctions from higher levels of the state, they can become enmeshed in community obligations and norms established by solidary groups such as temples, churches, and lineages – collections of individuals engaged in mutually oriented activities who share a set of ethical standards and moral obligations. Religious groups, philanthropic groups, and public advocacy groups are good examples of solidary groups. Groups based primarily on conviviality such as bowling leagues and birdwatching clubs and groups based primarily on shared interests such as manufacturers' associations are less so.

The model of informal accountability – specifically, the informal accountability of government officials – presented here is simple. Even when formal accountability is weak, solidary groups can offer moral standing as an incentive to officials for performing well and providing public goods and services responsibly. Within solidary groups, members who are seen to meet or exceed the group's moral obligations and ethical standards will be thought of and publicly praised as good people. Being thought of as a particularly good person can be very useful for accomplishing a variety of political, social, and economic objectives. For local officials, higher moral standing can be an important source of soft power. A community with a solidary group that can increase the ability of officials to attain moral standing can give officials an extra incentive to provide public goods.

I call the norms and obligations provided by solidary groups *informal institutions of accountability*. Formal institutions of accountability such as elections and performance contracts are formal in the sense that they are officially authorized for the purpose of holding officials accountable. The norms and standards provided by solidary groups can be defined as *informal* institutions of accountability because they evolved or were created to maintain the solidarity of a social group and were not officially authorized or intended to enable citizens to hold government officials accountable – but do so nevertheless.[21]

Solidary groups such as lineages and temples facilitate the conferral of moral standing by providing a set of standards for awarding moral standing and by organizing public activities and opportunities for people to demonstrate and publicize that their behavior adheres to or even surpasses these standards. Officials may have numerous kinds of objectives and motivations – personal gain, self-respect, promotion, effective implementation of state policies, and so on – but moral standing can be a potential resource for achieving any of these.

To provide informal institutions that enable citizens to hold local officials accountable for public goods provision, solidary groups have to have two particular structural characteristics. First, they must be encompassing, or open to everyone under the local government's jurisdiction. Examples of encompassing solidary groups might include citizens' groups that monitor town planning decisions in the United States, parish churches in nineteenth-century England (Morris 2000), and villages *harambees* or self-help organizations in Kenya (Miguel 2004). Second, solidary groups must be *embedding* in that they incorporate local officials into the group as members. Not all encompassing solidary groups are embedding. English

[21] This definition is similar to the one employed by Gretchen Helmke and Steven Levitsky. The concept of "informal institution," as Helmke and Levitsky point out, should be distinguished from the concept of "nonstate" institution. Institutions such as clientelism govern behavior within the state but are informal, whereas institutions that govern nonstate actors such as political parties and business corporations are widely considered formal. See Helmke and Levitsky, "Informal Institutions and Comparative Politics: A Research Agenda," *Perspective on Politics* 2, no. 4 (2004), 727.

parish churches are often embedding since local officials are likely to attend church services and identify as members of the congregation. In contrast, citizen watchdog organizations in the United States, which are designed to monitor and challenge government in an adversarial relationship, may encompass a particular town or municipality but are unlikely to embed officials into the group as members.

In localities with encompassing and embedding solidary groups, citizens and officials are more likely to share a common set of ethical standards and moral obligations. Members of clans, churches, fraternal organizations, and other solidary groups have strong obligations to their groups. In solidary groups, members are judged according to the group's standards of what constitutes a good person and a good member. Members of church congregations thus feel compelled to contribute something when the donation basket is passed around. Members of clans are commended for siding with fellow members in disputes with outsiders. Group activities and dense social networks also provide ample opportunities for individual members to publicize their exemplary behavior. Churches hold services and publicly ask for volunteers to help with church activities. In rural China, lineage members are expected to attend group rituals of respect for shared ancestors. These collective gatherings help publicize who is deserving of moral standing in the community.

One fundamental solidary obligation is doing one's fair share to contribute to the group. Members of the group are expected to do what they can to contribute to the group as a whole. When the boundaries of a solidary group overlap with the administrative boundaries of the local government, embedded officials have a strong *social* obligation to do what they can to contribute to the good of the group. One obvious thing they can do is to make sure that local government funds are used on public goods provision. Because under these conditions the group and the public are the same, officials in localities with encompassing and embedding solidary groups can earn moral standing for providing public goods. Under these conditions, officials who choose not to use public funds on public goods will be seen not only as bad officials but bad group members. Officials in localities with encompassing and embedding solidary groups thus have an extra incentive to provide public goods and services to their jurisdictions.

Under these conditions, solidary groups can provide an extra incentive for officials to invest public funds in public goods provision. Not all officials will necessarily prioritize the pursuit of moral standing. But for those that lack other kinds of political resources such as funding, coercion, or useful connections outside their locality, moral standing can be a crucial resource and powerful incentive.

Let me emphasize that this model of informal accountability is intended to address the specific problem of *governmental* provision of public goods and services. Governmental public goods provision requires solutions to two different problems: free-riding and governmental accountability. First, there is the classic free-rider collective action problem of getting citizens to contribute their share to the provision of a collective good. Each resident wants better roads in the village, but each resident also prefers to free-ride on the contributions of others and benefit from the roads after they are constructed rather than pay his share. If this problem is solved, there is still a second problem: once public funds are in the hands of government officials, citizens have to figure out how to get officials actually to use them on public projects. If formal democratic and bureaucratic institutions are weak, as they often are in rural China, local officials may be likely to act on incentives to use public funds for purposes other than public goods provision – investment in industry, putting friends on the government payroll, or lining their own pockets.

Solidary groups can help alleviate both of these problems. The literature on social capital and civil society is rich in theories about how social norms and networks can overcome the first problem. Like other social groups that promote dense social networks, solidary groups can potentially reduce free-riding by strengthening group sanctions, promoting social trust, improving skills of cooperation, and encouraging attitudes and habit of cooperation or shifting tastes from particularistic interests ("how can I get richer?") to more community-oriented concerns ("how can our neighborhood be improved?").[22]

[22] See, for example, Putnam, *Making Democracy Work: Civic Traditions in Modern Italy*, 173–4; Carles Boix and Daniel Posner, "Social Capital: Explaining Its Origins and Effects on Government Performance," *British Journal of Political Science* 28, no. 4 (1998), 686–93; Robert Bellah et al., *Habits of the Heart: Individualism and Commitment in American Life* (Berkeley: University of California Press, 1985). On the impact of social fragmentation and particularistic tastes for public goods and services, see A. Alesina and R. Baqir, "Public Goods and Ethnic Divisions," *Quarterly Journal of Economics* 114, no. 4 (1999), 1243–84. One mechanism for changing people's "tastes" from individual goals to collective objectives is through what James Coleman calls "bounded solidarity." Coleman notes that when individuals identify strongly with their group, they may show altruism that is limited to their fellow group members. This mechanism can be an important way of overcoming free-rider problems. James Coleman, *Foundations of Social Theory* (Cambridge: Harvard University Press, 1990).

The focus of the model presented in this book, however, is on the second problem: holding government officials accountable for funding and organizing public goods and services. In political systems with weak formal accountability, it is unclear how voluntary associations, interest groups, or other types of social organizations generally considered indicators of civil society and social capital can reliably hold government officials accountable without formal political institutions – either corporatist or pluralist – to give these groups a guaranteed role in the political decision-making process.[23] Existing theories of civil society and social capital typically posit that social groups can help improve governmental performance and responsiveness by increasing the social trust and political skills of citizens that help them to organize and voice their demands more effectively.[24] But in political systems where group articulation of interests is illegal or repressed, better organizing and voicing can have an impact only through demonstrations and protest.

The contributions of a theory of informal accountability thus lie in the identification of informal, non-electoral mechanisms that give citizens leverage over officials and a voice in the political decision-making process on a day-to-day basis, which is likely to be more effective than protest for reliable and stable governmental provision of public goods and services. When officials belong to solidary groups that encompass or are open to all the citizens under their jurisdiction so that the boundaries of the group coincide with the boundaries of the local government, then the collective good promoted by the solidary group becomes synonymous with the public good of the citizenry. In a town where everyone goes to the town church, the mayor who provides public services is fulfilling his duties toward his or her congregation as well as his or her jurisdiction. Obligations to the group become obligations to the public. Those who choose to be part of the solidary group have access to the group's moral authority as long as they fulfill their obligations to the collective. When officials are embedded in

[23] As Alejandro Portes has noted, levels of social capital are often equated with levels of associational involvement and civic participation and measured by indicators such as newspaper reading and membership in voluntary associations. Alejandro Portes, "Social Capital: Its Origins and Applications in Modern Sociology," *Annual Review of Sociology* 24, no. 1 (1998), 1–24.

[24] Boix and Posner discuss five possible models of how social capital might lead to government effectiveness, but all of these models assume that government officials have a preference for public goods provision or that there are preexisting institutions – democratic or otherwise – that hold government officials accountable for providing public goods provision. Boix and Posner, "Social Capital," 686–93.

the group, they can earn moral standing and use the group's resources to elicit compliance from citizens with state policies. But if they fail to meet the ethical standards of the group, citizens not only can sanction them but also deny them access to moral authority and the group's resources. In this way, the solidary group's institutions become informal institutions of accountability.

The social groups that the model of informal accountability identifies as beneficial to governmental performance can therefore differ significantly from the ones identified by theories of civil society and social capital. The category of solidary groups can include groups that are supposedly "traditional" – clans, tribes, temple groups, community festival groups, and community self-help groups – as well as groups considered "modern," such as public advocacy groups, philanthropic organizations and charities, and environmental groups. By focusing on the importance of shared moral obligations and ethical standards, the model of informal accountability draws our theoretical and empirical attention to the fact that so-called traditional groups continue to be an active and integral part of communities that are integrated into the global economy and global information networks.

This book also argues that in places where formal accountability is weak, it is the groups that embed government officials that have a positive impact on local governmental performance, not the groups that are autonomous from the state. Theories of civil society stress the necessity of an autonomous sphere of voluntary associations capable of challenging and checking the power of the state. But, as others have also observed, autonomy from the state is not always a good thing. Like Peter Evans, I find that embeddedness, not insulation, of the state enhances governmental performance. Evans points out that good governance results when embeddedness is combined with a state that has high levels of corporate coherence and norms of solidarity.[25] I argue that good governance can also result when embeddedness is combined with *social groups* that have high levels of corporate coherence and norms of solidarity. These kinds of social groups can be especially important in transitional systems, where states may be fragmented and formal institutions for establishing shared obligations between officials and citizens, such as constitutions and laws, may be weak.

The causal mechanisms that the model of informal accountability posits as linking embeddedness to good governmental performance and public

[25] Evans, *Embedded Autonomy*.

goods provision also differ from the ones highlighted by existing theories of social capital. The social capital literature suggests that social networks can facilitate the flow of information between state and societal actors, which can increase trust between them.[26] Higher levels of trust can facilitate higher levels of cooperation, which can lead to better governmental public goods provision, especially if public projects require inputs from both citizens and government. Informal accountability does not rely primarily on increased communication and information but on how solidary groups increase the incentives of government officials to provide public goods and services by offering them the prospect of increased moral standing. Increased moral standing can be a powerful incentive by benefiting government officials personally and helping them accomplish state tasks. Increased moral standing leads not only to greater trust in government officials but higher levels of *deference* to government officials.

Moral standing, in other words, is a form of soft power.[27] In places where people lack formal political power or economic resources, moral authority and soft power can make an enormous difference. Even in wealthy consolidated democracies, moral authority can still be an important political resource. Psychologists Tom Tyler and Peter Degoey have found that confidence in the moral character of authorities has a larger and more statistically significant effect on eliciting citizen compliance than confidence in their abilities or performance.[28] This book begins to explore the ways in which actors acquire moral authority and soft power and the conditions under which moral authority and soft power become important political resources, but it also strongly suggests that more research is needed.

This book is about the accountability of government officials. Solidary groups that match the political structure of local government can provide informal institutions that reinforce and sometimes even substitute for the public duties and obligations that laws and other state institutions are supposed to set for officials and citizens. To do so, groups must be based on

[26] See, for example, ibid.; Peter Evans, *State-Society Synergy: Government and Social Capital in Development* (Berkeley: International and Area Studies, 1997); Valerie Braithwaite and Margaret Levi, eds., *Trust and Governance* (New York: Russell Sage Foundation, 1998).

[27] Joseph Nye, "The Changing Nature of World Power," *Political Science Quarterly* 105, no. 2 (1990), 177–92.

[28] Tom Tyler and Peter Degoey, "Trust in Organizational Authorities: The Influence of Motive Attributions on Willingness to Accept Decisions," in *Trust in Organizations*, ed. Roderick M. Kramer and Tom Tyler (Thousand Oaks: Russell Sage Foundation, 1995), 331–56.

some shared set of ethical standards and moral obligations, but these obligations can be based on any number of things – kinship, patriotism, religion, humanist values, and so forth. The kind of moral glue that holds them together does not matter – only the fact that there is such glue and the configuration in which they are glued together. As we will see, it *is* possible to have accountability without formal democracy if you have the right kind of social groups.

Overview of the Book

The empirical context of this study is rural China. To give us a foundation for our inquiry, the book opens with a bird's-eye view of the political and institutional context in which Chinese village governments operate. Chapters 2 and 3 assess how dramatic economic and political reforms and decentralization programs have affected local governance and public goods provision over the last two decades. Chapter 2 outlines the basic institutional arrangements for the provision of local public goods. It also explores whether decentralization has increased government efficiency and responsiveness in the way that many scholars and policy makers have argued it would. Chapter 3 assesses the provision of public goods and services in rural China since 1949, formulates specific strategies for assessing village governmental public goods provision, and presents previously unavailable statistics on village public goods provision gathered in 2001 through an original survey of 316 villages in four provinces. These data show that localities, even at the same level of economic development, vary immensely in how well they provide public goods and services.

Explaining this variation is the focus of the book's remaining chapters. Chapters 4 through 6 form the heart of the book and suggest that this variation is best accounted for by the model of informal accountability. Chapter 4 elaborates this model and then uses examples drawn from rural China to illustrate how the model's mechanisms work in a particular empirical context. Chapters 5 and 6 explore the plausibility of the model by using a powerful combination of quantitative survey data and qualitative in-depth case studies to examine the link between the performance of local governments and the social institutions in their communities. On the one hand, the survey data allow us to assess whether this model can be generalized to a large number of cases. On the other hand, the in-depth case studies allow us to trace exactly how different kinds of social groups affect local governance differently. Taken together, these analyses strongly suggest that villages with villagewide solidary groups that incorporate the participation of local officials are more likely to have better governmental performance and public goods provision than villages without these groups.

In Chapter 5 we look at village temples and churches, two kinds of encompassing solidary groups prevalent in rural China, and compare the effects they have on village governmental public goods provision. The comparison hinges on a crucial difference: temples typically embed local officials in their activities, but churches, which are more strongly discouraged by the state, typically do not. In Chapter 6, we turn to a different kind of comparison. Whereas Chapter 5 compares communitywide solidary groups that vary in their embeddedness of local officials, Chapter 6 compares solidary groups that vary in scale and in their overlap with units of local government. In the chapter we look at lineages – another common type of solidary group in rural China – and compare lineage groups that do and do not encompass entire administrative villages. *Villagewide* lineage groups encompass the entire village, and their boundaries are the same as the village's administrative boundaries. In contrast, *subvillage* lineage groups incorporate only part of the people in an administrative village, while *intervillage* lineage groups encompass people from multiple administrative villages.

These chapters suggest that informal institutions of accountability are important for village public goods provision, but would formal ones be any better? Any discussion of village governance in China would be incomplete without considering the recent grassroots reforms implementing elections for village officials and other democratic institutions such as villagers' representative assemblies. We often assume that democratization is good for governmental accountability. Chapter 7 evaluates this assumption empirically using a combination of statistical analysis and case study evidence. Finally, in Chapter 8, we evaluate whether formal Party and bureaucratic mechanisms intended to enable higher-level officials to supervise lower-level officials have had any impact on village governmental public goods provision.

Data

When looking at grassroots institutions and microprocesses, one of the most difficult tasks is to decide what information we need to provide a deep understanding of local governance and public goods provision that is broadly generalizable and not just limited to a few isolated cases. On one hand, looking at many different localities within the same country has a major advantage in that it is like working in a laboratory of sorts. The researcher can hold certain conditions constant – such as regime type, political ideology, or history – while focusing on the effects that other factors might have on the outcome of interest: governmental performance and public goods provision. The huge range of regional variation in rural China makes it ideal for this kind of study, but it also requires a great deal of effort to collect information on a large number of different localities. On the other hand, to develop a deep understanding of how local institutions influence political behavior, it is also necessary to learn how actual villagers and officials interact with one another on a day-to-day basis in actual communities. Only by dedicating a substantial amount of time to immersing ourselves in the life of a community can we hope to gain even a modicum of trust sufficient for frank discussion with community members about the motives and meanings implicit in their social interactions. In short, my objectives for this book called for both breadth and depth in data collection and analysis.

I thus adopted the following solution: a unique multipronged strategy combining qualitative data from in-depth case studies with quantitative data from a broad statistical survey, both of which covered a variety of regions in rural China. I collected extensive case study and survey data over twenty months of fieldwork conducted between 1999 and 2002. I focused my village-level fieldwork in four provinces: Shanxi, Hebei, Jiangxi, and Fujian. I selected these provinces to reflect important regional differences between north and south China and economic differences between coastal and interior provinces. Figure 1.1 shows the surveyed provinces outlined in black. Provinces are shaded according to their rural income per capita. Darker provinces have higher rural income per capita. Coastal and inland regions differ significantly from each other in terms of economic development, and north and south China vary greatly in terrain, institutional history, and social organization. Figure 1.2 shows how the surveyed provinces vary along these two macrodimensions.

First, I focused on developing a deep understanding of everyday village politics and governance. During this stage, I gathered information through extensive on-the-ground observation and interviews from a single set of villages over a six-month period. During this period, I was based in Xiamen, a coastal city in Fujian province, and repeatedly visited four villages in the area almost every week (as well as villages in other parts of Fujian on an itinerant basis) to observe community interactions and village politics and interview villagers and officials. Through these visits, I discovered a wealth of different social groups and institutions that often dominated village life.

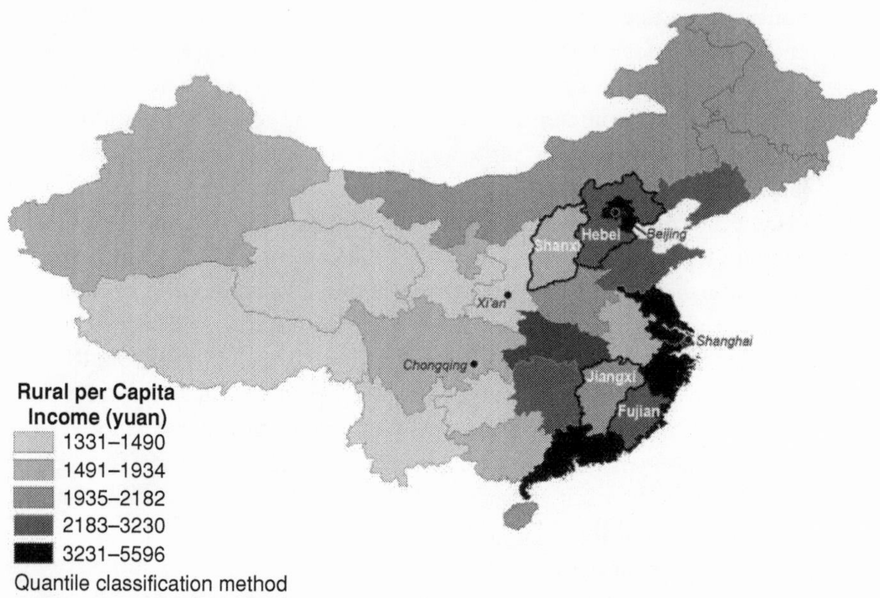

Figure 1.1. Surveyed provinces.

		Level of economic development	
		Low	**High**
Geographical location	**North**	Shanxi	Hebei
	South	Jiangxi	Fujian

Figure 1.2. Selection of provinces.

My time in Xiamen coincided with the round of village elections held in 2000, so I was also able to observe closely every stage of the election process – through all the preparations, nominations, and balloting – and to follow the aftermath of the elections. By continuing to visit the same villages regularly for several months after the elections, I developed a deep understanding of how state and societal actors interact in village elections and grassroots political processes and how democratic reforms affect village governance and public goods provision.

The next problem was the lack of statistical data on Chinese villages. I now had a basic understanding of political and social interactions at the village level, but it was based primarily on observations in only four villages. I needed data that would allow me to make generalizations about village governance and public goods provision for a broad range of villages. Official Chinese statistics have never included data on the provision of public services at a level as low as the village, and few studies of rural governance have systematically addressed the provision of public services.[29]

I thus designed an original village survey to collect previously unavailable data on village-level provision of public services and a wide array of village conditions. In 2001 I conducted this survey in 316 villages sampled from Shanxi, Hebei, Jiangxi, and Fujian provinces. The survey looked at objective and subjective indicators of the quality of village public goods such as roads, schools, water, electricity, sanitation, and agricultural infrastructure; funding sources for village public goods; village public finance; personal characteristics of village officials; township–village relations; village democratic institutions; and community social institutions. As a foreign scholar working in China, I was exceptionally fortunate to have complete control over the design of the questionnaire and the survey sampling.

Within each of the four provinces, a random stratified sample of about eighty villages was selected. These eighty villages were located in two counties, which were selected in a way to provide me with instrumental variables in order to solve potential problems of endogeneity during statistical analysis. To conduct the survey, I trained a group of Chinese graduate and undergraduate students as enumerators. All of us traveled to each of the eight counties and presented references from Chinese academics and researchers to the county government. After obtaining permission to carry out research in the county, I selected eight townships through a random stratified sampling procedure (with stratification by official income per capita). A county official then accompanied me and my research team of Chinese university

[29] In what is perhaps the only major study on rural public finance, Christine Wong looks at five village cases. See Christine Wong, "Rural Public Finance," in *Financing Local Government in the People's Republic of China*, ed. Christine Wong (Hong Kong: Oxford University Press, 1997b), 167–212. A recent study by Xiaobo Zhang and his colleagues draws on survey data collected from villages within a single province, Jiangsu. See Xiaobo Zhang et al., "Local Governance and Public Goods Provision in Rural China," *International Food Policy Research Institute* (July 2002), 1–22.

student enumerators to each of the townships, where I then selected five villages in each township through a similar procedure (again with stratification by official income per capita).[30] Each township government then contacted the village governments in their jurisdiction to notify them that a couple of students would be visiting them to do academic research. The combination of official approval from the local government and our obvious status as students helped secure the willing cooperation of our respondents. In each of the sampled villages, enumerators interviewed one or more village officials in order to fill out village-level survey questionnaires about village conditions. I coded and checked the results nightly with an assistant while in the field.

Relative to data collected for surveys that are commissioned or associated with government offices or government-affiliated research institutions, data from this survey are likely to be substantially more accurate. When asked, for example, for the village's "official" income per capita and "real" income per capita, most village officials were perfectly comfortable reporting different figures. Only 14 percent, in fact, reported the same figures. Village officials were also comfortable reporting interference (even by themselves personally) in the preelection process even though such interference goes against official state regulations and also constitutes a failure to implement officially required procedures for voting and the operation of villagers' representative assemblies. The high level of frankness among the survey respondents about even potentially sensitive topics can be largely credited to the highly skilled administration of the survey by the student enumerators, most of whom had grown up in villages themselves and were pursuing degrees in agricultural economics, sociology, and related disciplines. The students were extremely adept at establishing rapport with the village officials they were interviewing and often referred to circumstances in their own villages to put the respondents at ease. Respondents were also clearly informed about the purely academic nature of the survey, and all survey administrators clearly identified themselves as students.

Not only did these data provide important information on the state of village public goods provision in rural China, but they also were invaluable in identifying broad patterns and generalizable relationships in village governance, and isolating and measuring the effects of specific factors on village public goods provision.

[30] In townships with fewer than five villages, all the villages were surveyed. These townships account for why there were 316 rather than 320 villages in the sample.

The final step was to find out whether specific factors really affected village governmental performance in the ways that my initial observations and statistical findings suggested. To check whether these findings really made sense in a variety of different cases, I put together a set of in-depth case studies of villages selected from the same four provinces in which the survey had been conducted. Each case study of a village represents repeated visits totaling between two and twenty days of research, during which I lived either in the village or somewhere nearby. (Names of people and localities in the book have been changed to maintain interview confidentiality.) The interviews with current village officials, past officials, officials at higher levels, and ordinary villagers that I did for these case studies allowed me to do several things that I could not do with the survey data. Like the survey, the case studies were designed to evaluate and isolate the impact of the primary explanatory factors of interest so they allowed me to evaluate different theories in terms of the factors these theories identified as critical for governmental performance and public goods provision. But the case studies also allowed me to assess whether different theories identified the correct causal mechanisms through which particular factors affect governance. The detailed case studies provided invaluable evidence on the causal processes that underlie the correlations identified by statistical analysis. They allowed me to make inferences about interaction effects between different explanatory variables and to gather more observations of the implications of the theories being tested.

Qualitative data were especially important in this project because little systematic information in either Chinese or non-Chinese sources existed on the processes by which public goods are financed and organized in rural China or on the role of community, religious, and lineage institutions in these processes. Gathering data through case studies helped to trace the evolution of a village's institutions and understand how these institutions were shaped by interactions within the local historical and cultural context. These data allow us to examine how state and nonstate institutions coexist through mutual negotiation and accommodation and to compare how different institutions emerge from different contexts.

The theoretical arguments developed in this book are not intended to account only for the case of local governance in China but to draw attention to the *interactions* between informal and formal institutions, social structures and state structures, and social boundaries and political boundaries in ways that improve our understanding of governmental performance and public goods provision in many other places. Improving governmental performance is not simply a matter of reforming moribund formal institutions. Instead, we need to assess the existing informal institutions and understand how formal and informal institutions complement or conflict with one another. We also see that good governance does not simply emerge as a natural consequence of economic development. Nor does good government have to be a luxury. In the following chapters, we see that good government is not just something that everyone should be able to afford, but something everyone *can* afford.

2

Decentralization and Local Governmental Performance

Before we can evaluate the performance of local governments, we must first understand what their responsibilities are and how financial and administrative responsibilities are allocated among different levels of government. To provide a backdrop for the book's analysis of village governmental public goods provision, this chapter briefly sketches the broader institutional context in which local governments operate.

Examining these institutional arrangements inevitably brings us up against one of the central dilemmas of governance: what is the best way to divide up responsibilities for public goods provision among different levels of government? Proponents of decentralization argue that local governments should have primary responsibility for providing public goods for the citizens under their jurisdiction. They have more information about what citizens really need and want. When local governments are responsible for providing roads, schools, and other services, citizens know exactly whom to blame when something goes wrong. Competition for tax revenue, moreover, can keep local officials on their toes since taxpayers can always move to another locality that provides better public services more cheaply.[1]

[1] Classic elaborations of these arguments include Charles Tiebout, "A Pure Theory of Local Government Expenditures," *Journal of Political Economy* 64, no. 5 (1956), 416–24; Wallace Oates, *Fiscal Federalism* (New York: Harcourt Brace Jovanovich, 1972); idem, "An Essay on Fiscal Federalism," 1120–49; Geoffrey Brennan and James Buchanan, *The Power to Tax: Analytical Foundations of a Fiscal Constitution* (New York: Cambridge University Press, 1980); James Buchanan, "Federalism as an Ideal Political Order and an Objective for Constitutional Reform," *Publius* 25, no. 2 (1995), 19–81; Barry Weingast, "The Economic Role of Political Institutions: Market-Preserving Federalism and Economic Development," *Journal of Law, Economics, and Organization* 11, no. 1 (1995), 1–31.

China's extraordinary economic growth over the last few decades seems to suggest that decentralization in this case has been a success story. But counter to what optimistic theories of decentralization predict, problems of local governmental accountability and fiscal mismanagement have also increased.[2] Decentralization programs in China, as in many other countries, have increased unfunded mandates for public goods provision for all local levels – all levels below the central government but especially the lowest levels. To compensate for these unfunded mandates, the central government has enabled and at times even encouraged local governments to generate revenue through a variety of locally determined, sometimes informal non-tax channels. Since these revenues from channels such as local levies and informal loans are not recorded in the official state budget, higher levels find it extremely difficult to make sure these funds are actually used on public goods. We will see that given the state of public finance at the village level and other local levels of government, any examples of responsible provision of public goods by local governments would actually be highly surprising.

The Basic Structure of Village Government

What is the basic structure of local government? Under China's one-party system, institutions of the state and of the Chinese Communist Party are

[2] More cautious theorists of decentralization include Jonathan Rodden and Susan Rose-Ackerman, "Does Federalism Preserve Markets?" *Virginia Law Review* 83, no. 7 (1997), 1521–72; Jonathan Rodden, *Hamilton's Paradox: The Promise and Peril of Fiscal Federalism* (Cambridge: Cambridge University Press, 2005); P. Bardhan and D. Mookherjee, "Decentralization, Corruption, and Government Accountability: An Overview," in *Handbook of Economic Corruption*, ed. Susan Rose-Ackerman (Northampton: Edward Elgar, 2005), 305–28; H. Cai and Daniel Treisman, "State-Corroding Federalism," *Journal of Public Economics* 88, no. 3 (2004), 819–43; Judith Tendler, *Good Government in the Tropics* (Baltimore: John Hopkins University Press, 1997), 599–617. Scholars of China have also observed negative effects of decentralization policies in China. See, for example, A. Young, "The Razor's Edge: Distortions and Incremental Reform in the People's Republic of China," *Quarterly Journal of Economics* 115, no. 3–4 (2000), 1091–1136; S. Poncet, "Measuring Chinese Domestic and International Integration," *China Economic Review* 14, no. 1 (2003), 1–21; Justin Lin, Ran Tao, and Mingxing Liu, "Decentralization and Local Governments in China's Economic Transition," in *Decentralization and Local Governments in Developing Countries: A Comparative Perspective*, ed. Pranab Bardhan and Dilip Mookherjee (Cambridge: MIT Press, 2005); Dong-Hua Chen, Joseph P. H. Fan, and T. J. Wong, "Do Politicians Jeopardize Professionalism? Decentralization and the Structure of Corporate Boards" (2002); Martin Dimitrov, "The Dark Side of Federalism: Decentralization and the Enforcement of Intellectual Property Rights (IPR) Laws," paper presented at the Annual Meeting of the American Political Science Association, Chicago, 2004.

Table 2.1. *Number of Administrative Units in the Chinese Government (2003)*

Level of Government	Number of Units
Central government	1
Provincial-level	31
Municipalities and prefectures	333
County-level	2,861
Township-level	44,067
Administrative villages	678,589

Source: 2004 Statistical Yearbook, National Bureau of Statistics, Beijing, China.

tightly intertwined from the central government at the very top all the way down to the village at the very bottom. The Chinese party-state thus consists of six different levels of government: central, provincial, prefectural or municipal, county, township (formerly known as the commune), and village (formerly known as the brigade).[3] Table 2.1 lists the number of administrative units at each level of government as of the end of 2003. In this book, I refer to all levels of government below the center as "local" government, although this chapter's observations about local government generally become increasingly more applicable as the level of government becomes lower.

Village officials are responsible for collecting state taxes, enforcing state directives such as the birth control policy, and providing village public goods and services. They have almost complete formal authority and discretion over issues within the village community. Not surprisingly, villagers clearly consider village officials indisputably formal agents of the state. Within the village government, officials typically work together as one group, although village governments are officially divided into two formal organizations: the village Party branch and the village committee. Officials on the village committee are supposed to be elected by villagers in direct elections, whereas officials in the village Party branch are appointed by the party-state.[4] Each organization typically has three to five positions, depending

[3] Although the central government officially considers villages to be "self-governing organizations" run popularly by village residents, in practice the state's formal ruling apparatus extends all the way down to the village level.

[4] Officially, village Party branch members are elected by villagers with Party membership, but in practice, they are typically vetted by the township Party committee. According to Article 5 of the Regulations on the Work of Organization at the Rural Grassroots Level of the

on the size of the village population and local regulations.[5] In theory, a village head chairs the village committee, which usually also has a deputy head and accountant. Other possible committee positions include a public security officer and a representative to the state-organized women's federation. A village Party secretary chairs the village Party branch, which also has a deputy secretary and other general Party branch members. Village Party branch members are appointed by the Party committee in the township and approved through a vote by the village's Party members. In the villages where I conducted fieldwork, village committee and village Party branch members generally met and made decisions about village affairs together.

More often than not, the two organizations consist of largely the same people. In many places, higher-level officials continue to control village election procedures and administration. In these places, the members of both the village committee and the village Party branch are vetted by higher levels. In other places, localities are experimenting with linking the village committee election to the Party branch election. In these cases, the same person may be both Party secretary and village head. Conversely, when the existing Party secretary loses an election for village head, village Party members may decide that he should not continue as the Party secretary.[6] Another reason that many localities encourage villages to have at least some

Chinese Communist Party issued February 13, 1999, members of the village Party branch should be elected by an assembly of Party members in the village. However, according to Article 30 of Chapter 5 of the revised version of the Constitution of the Chinese Communist Party, approved on November 14, 2002, the Party secretary and deputy Party secretary of the village Party branch are subject to approval by higher-level Party organizations. As one village Party secretary in the Xiamen area of Fujian observed: "True, the township is supposed to 'guide' us, but does that mean I'm allowed to ignore what they tell me to do? No. For example, if they want us to demolish a house or even a factory building to appropriate the land for the use of the state, can I say no, we won't demolish it?" Others have observed that the appointment or election of officials to the village Party branch can be responsive to input from villagers. Susan Lawrence, for example, has noted that in some places when village Party members meet after village committee elections to elect a village Party secretary, they may decide that someone who has lost the village committee election should not be the village Party secretary. Susan V. Lawrence, "Village Democracy," *Far Eastern Economic Review* 163 (January 27, 2000), 16–17.

5 According to Article 9 of the Organization Law of Village Committees, approved on November 14, 1998, the village committee consists of three to seven members, including the village head, vice-head, and other committee members. A village Party branch can be established if there are three or more Party members in a village.

6 Lawrence notes, "if the newly elected village-committee chairman is a party member, he is a natural candidate to take over as party secretary." See Lawrence, "Village Democracy," 17.

of the same people serving concurrently on both the village committee and Party branch is to reduce public expenditures on wages for unnecessary village officials. Finally, most villages simply have a limited pool of people who are skilled enough and respected enough to become village officials.

The Provision of Local Public Goods in Rural China

So who is responsible for what? As a general rule, each level of government has been responsible for funding and organizing all the local public goods and services for citizens residing under their jurisdiction. Intergovernmental transfers may, of course, increase dramatically as the abolition of agricultural taxes in 2006 leads to new fiscal arrangements, but during the period of this study (1999–2002), funding allocated from higher levels was minimal. Fiscal decentralization has allowed local governments to keep any revenues in excess of a preset amount they are required to deliver upward, but it has also meant that local levels of government cannot expect much in transfers from higher levels. Villages have thus been responsible for constructing and maintaining all the roads, bridges, irrigation, and water infrastructure within the village as well as the village primary school building (which every village had until the state began to permit mergers of schools in 2001).[7] Townships have been responsible for funding roads connecting villages to the township seat and sometimes, depending on local policies, for roads connecting villages to each other. They have also provided township medical clinics and junior secondary schools intended for all the residents in the township (although the cost and location of township clinics and schools make them harder for villagers who do not reside in the township seat to access) as well as local radio and TV broadcast stations, electricity infrastructure, and local police. Public goods and services for residents in the township seat such as water and sanitation have also been under their jurisdiction. Similar principles applied to counties that fund roads connecting township seats to the county seat, county hospitals, and senior secondary education as well as various other countywide services.

In short, localities have had heavy expenditure responsibilities for public goods provision. According to one report in 2001, county and township

[7] In the Decision on the Reform and Development of Basic Education by the State Council, issued on May 29, 2001, rural primary schools and junior middle schools located close to each other were encouraged to merge with each other as long as the merged schools remained accessible to students.

governments paid for 70 percent of budgetary expenditures for education and about 55 percent of budgetary expenditures for public health.[8] The probability of higher-level subsidies decreases with each level down. Although provincial governments and municipalities, which oversee large areas, sometimes have surplus revenue to allocate as subsidies to counties, county and township governments, which draw on much smaller and often more homogeneous tax bases, have usually had much smaller margins.

Villages, at the very bottom of the hierarchy, have been expected to be largely self-financing. Until recently, they have not received any regular budgetary allocations from above. Village expenditures – on public projects or otherwise – were supposed to be funded primarily from revenue generated within the locality. Since all subsidies to village governments were ad hoc, the minority of villages that relied on subsidies from higher levels lived a kind of hand-to-mouth existence. Out of the 316 villages that I surveyed in 2001, 59 percent reported that they did not receive any funding from higher levels of government in 2000. Another 23 percent reported that funding from higher levels made up less than half of their total revenue in 2000.

Even the meager funding that is available from higher levels often does not get allocated to the localities that need them the most. Most state subsidies from higher levels take the form of ad hoc earmarked funds for special policy initiatives, such as poverty alleviation programs or the state education program mandating nine years of primary and secondary education.[9] These earmarked funds often require local governments to meet high "matching contribution" requirements, which eliminate the neediest localities from consideration. Successfully obtaining these funds also depends to a large extent on one's personal connections with higher-level officials. Local governments put together proposals to apply to higher levels for these funds, but competition is fierce and the playing field is not level. A village head in western Fujian stated bluntly:

Whether or not you get money from the township after you write up an application for a public project depends on whether there are good connections (*guanxi hao*) and good feelings (*ganqing hao*) between you and the township Party secretary. If you simply wait for the township to give you money, you might have to wait until

[8] World Bank, *China: Provincial Expenditure Review* (Washington: World Bank, December 11, 2001), 5.

[9] See Albert Park et al., "Distributional Consequences of Reforming Local Public Finance in China," *China Quarterly*, no. 147 (1996), 764–6; World Bank, *China: Provincial Expenditure Review*, 5.

the next century, and if you depend on the government levels above that, you'll starve.[10]

Another official in an eastern Fujian village commented, "If you don't know who to talk to and you don't know the procedures, then you can't make the deals you need to develop the village."[11]

Even when the state tries to target needy localities, the lack of formal institutions for allocating state funds makes the process unreliable. In some places, state funds are transferred informally between levels of government through the "adoption" of needy localities by higher-level government bureaus. Provincial and county governments are sometimes encouraged by higher levels to assign their individual government bureaus and offices (units such as the county auditing bureau or the county civil affairs bureau) responsibility for assisting needy localities in funding public expenditures. In northern Fujian, for example, where the state has officially designated "poverty districts," each county government bureau is responsible for looking after one or two villages (*baocun*) in a poverty district. County government bureaus are informally expected to juggle their budgets and eke out enough funding for one public project in each village per year using their own resources.

Sometimes villages get lucky. One village Party secretary observed, "Whichever villages get adopted by the civil affairs bureau or the transportation bureau are happy (*minzheng ju, jiaotong ju gua nali, nali jiu gaoxing*) because those bureaus have money."[12] In Mountain View county of Hebei province, villages that are particularly poor or that suffer from conflict between village officials are assigned to different county departments for a year. County departments are expected to offer their assigned villages administrative and financial support. In 1997, for example, Mountain View's civil affairs bureau gave 110,000 yuan out of its funds to help an isolated

[10] Interview with male village head, western Fujian province, February 23, 2001. All interviews for this book were conducted in confidentiality, and the names of the interviewees are withheld by mutual agreement.

[11] Interview with former production team Party secretary, eastern Fujian province, November 18, 2000. Han Jun also finds in his study of twelve villages in three provinces that higher levels of government provide almost no subsidies to village governments. Han Jun, "Public Finance Crisis in Chinese Counties and Towns: Performance, Causes, Impact and Measures: Case Studies of Xiangyang County of Hubei Province, Yanling County of Henan Province, and Taihe County of Jiangxi Province," International Conference Report on Rural Public Finance (Beijing: Rural Development Institute, Chinese Academy of Social Sciences, 2002).

[12] Interview with male village Party secretary, northern Fujian province, October 18, 2001.

village in the hills drill new wells and repair roads. In addition to allocating them funds out of their own budgets, county bureaus also help their assigned villages obtain funds earmarked for particular projects – although once obtained, the funds are not necessarily used for their designated purpose. Another village in Mountain View that was assigned to the county inspection bureau for three years was able to access over 20,000 yuan in environmental improvement funds (*shengtai gongcheng kuan*), which they used to drill new village wells.[13] In Shanxi province, retired government officials in an old revolutionary district have formed an association to raise funds for rural development (*lao gemin qu jianshe chu jinhui*).

In some villages, these informal arrangements have worked out well, but in others these arrangements do not produce any useful outcomes and are merely for show. Higher-level officials can coopt these arrangements for their own benefit. In Fujian province, one village official noted of the adoption system by higher-level bureaus: "The *tuanwei*, supervision bureau, planning committee, or the general office of the county Party committee, however, has no money and no power. All these offices just come down to the village to visit and eat [at the village's expense]."[14] One village in southern Shanxi with a severe water shortage problem was assigned to the director of the district agricultural bank, who had to fulfill his required service to a grassroots unit (*dundian ganbu*). The bank director allocated them some funds that allowed them to drill a new well and considered his job done, but because the funds were not enough to buy a transformer to provide the well's pump with the correct voltage, the well was basically useless.[15]

The biggest problem with these arrangements is that they are not officially mandated, and villages cannot rely upon them. County departments can always ignore the villages to which they are assigned. The new Party secretary in one Hebei village noted that the county departments assigned to them simply refused to do anything for them because of factional conflicts within the village.[16] While these informal intergovernmental transfers certainly have some positive effects, there is nothing to guarantee that transfers are distributed equitably or effectively. In many places, they simply peter out over time.

[13] Interview with former head of county civil affairs bureau, eastern Hebei province, April 25, 2001.

[14] Interview with male village official, northern Fujian province, October 18, 2001.

[15] Interview with male village official, southwestern Shanxi province, April 19, 2001.

[16] Interview with male village Party secretary, eastern Hebei province, May 2, 2002.

Funding from higher levels of the state is not only meager and unreliable, but allocated funds may be siphoned off before they ever reach the designated recipients. Even when a needy village manages to obtain a grant from above, whether it is through adoption by a higher-level bureau or through personal connections, the village may receive only a small fraction of what it was originally allocated. Because of administrative decentralization, each level of government deals with and supervises only the level directly beneath it.[17] Grants from above therefore pass through the hands of officials at every level of government between the funding level and the recipient level. Although a subsidy may be designated for a particular village or township, officials at each level take a cut as an "administrative fee." As a result, the amount of funding that finally reaches the recipient village is typically much smaller than what was originally allocated.

Mountain View county in Hebei provides a typical example. Mountain View's county government convened a meeting to notify all townships about money available from the state environmental projects (*guojia shengtai gongcheng*) fund for developing mountainous areas (*shanqu kaifa*) and reforestation (*tuigeng huanlin*). Townships in Mountain View then convened the villages in their jurisdiction to notify village officials and urge them to apply. One village Party secretary in this county explained to me that although the areas for which the funds were allocated were actually south of them, the township and Mountain View county governments were eager for them to apply because each level of government took a portion of any state subsidies obtained by one of their villages. "All the information and funds pass through the county and the township, so we don't know how much they actually take (*women bu zhidao tamen lao duoshao*)."[18]

Decentralization and the Provision of Local Public Goods

Localities in China have not been able to rely on grants from higher levels to fund public goods and services. Optimistic theories of decentralization, however, see this as a good thing. These theories argue that decentralization encourages good governance and public goods provision. Local governments are likely to have better information than higher-level governments about what citizens need and want and thus more likely to provide

[17] See Kevin O'Brien and Li Lianjiang, "Selective Policy Implementation in Rural China," *Comparative Politics* 31, no. 2 (January 1999), 167–86.

[18] Interview with male village Party secretary, eastern Hebei province, May 2, 2002.

appropriate public goods.[19] Decentralization may also increase accountability and transparency. When authority for public goods provision is decentralized to local governments, citizens are clear on whom they should hold responsible and able to target the right actors when sanctioning poor performance.[20] Finally, local authority over taxation and expenditures may foster healthy competition among local governments. Local governments have strong incentives to provide good public services since they are competing with each other for tax revenues from firms and individuals who move to the places with the best policies and public services.[21]

In many ways, China seemed well positioned to enjoy these benefits. Unlike countries in Africa, where experiments with decentralization have only created local extensions of central administration, or variations in federalism in Latin America, where federal governments continue to provide most of the state revenue, decentralization in China has resulted in a significant and substantive devolution of decision-making power and fiscal authority and has been accompanied by dramatic economic growth.[22] China's impressive economic performance has prompted Barry Weingast and others to characterize its political system as "market-preserving federalism," a comprehensive type of decentralization that, they argue, makes sustained economic growth possible.[23] Jean Oi has attributed the rapid rural industrialization that fueled much of the economic growth in the 1980s and early 1990s to the fiscal decentralization reforms of the 1980s granting local governments rights to any economic surplus they generated, thereby providing strong incentives to invest in local enterprises.[24] Edward Steinfeld has noted

19 See, for example, Oates, "An Essay on Fiscal Federalism," 1120–49.

20 See, for example, P. Seabright, "Accountability and Decentralisation in Government: An Incomplete Contracts Model," *European Economic Review* 40, no. 1 (1996), 61–89.

21 See Tiebout, "A Pure Theory of Local Government Expenditures"; Weingast, "The Economic Role of Political Institutions."

22 Dele Olowu, "Local Institutes and Development: The African Experience," *Canadian Journal of African Studies* 23, no. 2 (1989), 201–31; Barry Weingast, *The Theory of Comparative Federalism and the Emergence of Economic Liberalization in Mexico, China, and India* (Stanford: Hoover Institution, 2000).

23 Weingast and his colleagues argue that market-preserving federalism satisfies five conditions: (1) a hierarchical structure of governments with delineated domains of authority; (2) subnational governments with primary authority over the local economy; (3) a central government with the authority to police the common market; (4) hard budget constraints for all levels of government; and (5) an institutionalized allocation of political authority. Ibid. See also Gabriella Montinola, Yingyi Qian, and Barry R. Weingast, "Federalism, Chinese Style: The Political Basis for Economic Success in China," *World Politics* 48, no. 1 (October 1995), 50–81.

24 Oi, *Rural China Takes Off.*

that in localities lacking large state-owned enterprises, fiscal decentralization encouraged local governments to promote rural enterprises by giving them hard budget constraints.[25]

It is not clear, however, whether decentralization has been such a good thing for local governance and public goods provision in rural China. Village governments rarely have the resources to supply all the public services they are responsible for providing. Although a very small percentage of villages have industrialized sufficiently to provide generous levels of village infrastructure and social welfare services as part of a "redistributive local state corporatism,"[26] most villages lack successful enterprises or significant tax bases that generate enough revenue to cover all of their expenditure responsibilities. In these places, decentralization has given villages responsibility for public services that require more investment than they can afford, limiting them to only the revenues they can generate within their jurisdiction and reducing subsidies from above that could help make up shortfalls.

Unfunded Mandates and Informal Institutions of Local Public Finance

In exchange for assigning localities these unfunded mandates, the central government has given local governments the freedom to develop sources of revenue that are not supervised closely by higher levels of government. Knowing that they cannot possibly finance a significant level of public goods provision in all of China's nearly one million villages, the central government has permitted local governments to develop what we might call informal institutions for funding public expenditures – informal because the creation of these local institutions or rules for raising revenue do not require explicit authorization from above. Such institutions include loans, the rental and sale of local government assets, and locally established levies, fees, and fines. In fact, as long as they are not violating existing regulations, local officials have been allowed to raise funds using whatever means they have. The informal nature of these local arrangements shields them from the monitoring of higher levels – reporting requirements for these "extrabudgetary funds" are not strict or clearly defined. But nor

25 Edward Steinfeld, *Forging Reform in China: The Fate of State-Owned Industry* (Cambridge: Cambridge University Press, 1998), 228–47.

26 Oi, *Rural China Takes Off*, 79–80; Oi notes that "redistributive local state corporatism" is limited to "highly industrialized villages."

are they protected by official state recognition and legitimization – at any moment, higher levels of government can decide to make them explicitly illegal.

This extrabudgetary funding, which Christine Wong and Richard Bird broadly define as resources that are managed directly or indirectly by administrative branches of the government outside the normal budgetary process, is not taken into account by the state when "weigh[ing] expenditures against one another, or against increased revenue" in the formulation of the state budget.[27] Officially, local governments have no tax autonomy, and the central government assigns them taxes with set rates and bases.[28] In reality, however, "virtually all levels of government," Wong and Bird note, "down to municipal districts and villages . . . have the capacity to exact payments under various names from local businesses and residents."[29] Justin Lin and his colleagues argue that it is precisely the ambitious targets set by the central government for public services provision and policy implementation at the local level that have allowed local officials to justify their collection of unofficial fees and levies:

> [G]iven a central government regulation, the implementation and administrative costs entailed cannot be fully observed by higher-level government. In this case, local government may easily over-charge peasants in the name of implementing the central government regulation to increase local revenue, expand local bureaucracy by excessive staffing, and promote personal consumption by corruption of local officials.[30]

Informal institutions of local finance, of course, are nothing new. The current situation has numerous historical parallels. Pierre-Etienne Will and R. Wong have described local institutions of informal grain lending in

[27] Christine Wong and Richard Bird broadly define extrabudgetary funds as "all resources managed directly or indirectly by administrative branches of the government outside the normal budgetary process." As Wong and Bird note, the term "extrabudgetary funds" (*yusuanwai zijin*) as used within China has a narrower definition and refers to fees and funds that are not taxes or budgetary items but which are authorized by some government body. Christine Wong and Richard Bird, "China's Fiscal System," in *The Great Transformation: China's Economy since Reform*, ed. Loren Brandt and Thomas Rawski (New York: Cambridge University Press, forthcoming), 19–21.

[28] Ibid., 18.

[29] Ibid., 23.

[30] This relationship holds regardless of whether the taxation rate is defined to include all state agriculture-related taxes and local township and village levies, only the local township and village levies, or only those local township and village levies that are not legitimated by government regulations. Lin et al., *The Problem of Taxing Peasants in China*, 29–44.

the Qing dynasty.[31] Prasenjit Duara has observed that in the early twentieth century, the Chinese state was unable to develop formal bureaucratic institutions of accountability quickly enough to keep up with "the entrenchment of the informal apparatus of extraction."[32] In the early 1950s, the state allowed local governments to add surtaxes to the state agricultural taxes. Various government regulations capped these surtaxes at between 7 and 20 percent of the state tax, but Bernstein and Lu report that in the worst areas, informal levies amounted to as much as 560 percent of the formal state tax.[33] During the Maoist period, village-level brigade and team officials sometimes also borrowed informal loans from private individuals or from other production teams with the implicit and sometimes explicit support of their immediate superiors.[34]

The elimination of agricultural taxes in 2006, however, may eventually have a dramatic effect on informal institutions of local finance and extrabudgetary funds. The central government has estimated the reforms will eliminate a total tax burden of 120 yuan (about U.S.$15) per capita.[35] The hope is that the elimination of state agricultural taxes will also entail the elimination of locally determined fees and levies. In theory, budgetary transfers will replace informal sources of local government revenue and the state will recentralize fiscal authority. The actual effects of the reform, however, remain to be seen.

Informal Institutions of Public Finance at the Village Level

In some sense, all revenues at the village level are extrabudgetary since villages are not considered an official level of government and village revenues and expenditures are not included in the official state budget. It is perhaps more useful to think in terms of *formal* institutions of local public finance – rules for raising revenue that are explicitly regulated and approved by the

[31] In some counties, county administrators allowed local chiefs to receive group loans on behalf of individuals although there was no guarantee that individuals would actually receive any of the grain. See Pierre-Etienne Will and R. Wong, *Nourish the People: The State Civilian Granary System in China, 1650–1850* (Ann Arbor: University of Michigan, Center for Chinese Studies, 1991), 178–93.

[32] Prasenjit Duara, *Culture, Power, and the State: Rural North China 1900–1942* (Stanford: Stanford University Press, 1988), 74–5.

[33] Bernstein and Lu, *Taxation without Representation in Contemporary Rural China*, 24–5.

[34] Jean Oi, *State and Peasant in Contemporary China: The Political Economy of Village Government* (Berkeley: University of California Press, 1989), 119–21.

[35] Minister of Finance Jin Renqing, quoted in *Zhongguo qingnian bao (China Youth Daily)*, December 30, 2005.

state – and *informal* institutions of public finance – rules for raising revenue that local officials have not been authorized to make (though they have not been explicitly banned from doing so either).

This distinction would make local township and village levies (also known as *tongchou tiliu* or *santi wutong*) below the state-mandated cap of 5 percent of township income per capita – local taxes, in effect if not in name – formal institutions of local public finance.[36] In practice, however, it can be difficult to discern exactly what constitutes formally authorized revenues and what is actually informal. Since it is villages and townships themselves that calculate the local income per capita, it is difficult to know whether local levies and fees are in fact above or below the 5 percent cap.[37] Villagers also often pay far more than 5 percent of their income since the income of wealthy residents in the township seat helps inflate the income per capita reported for the township.

Data from the survey, for example, showed that in 2000 villagers on average paid 2.5 percent of the official village income per capita reported to the township and that only 5 percent of villages in the survey had tax rates of over 5 percent of reported village income per capita. When, however, village officials were asked what the "actual" (*shiji*) village income per capita was, the average tax rate for villagers rose to 3.9 percent. Moreover, 28 percent of villages had tax rates of over 5 percent of the actual village income per capita. The highest tax rate reported was 17 percent. While most villages seemed to have tax rates that were relatively reasonable as a percentage of actual village income per capita, a significant number of villages were levying taxes that were quite high.

As we can see, tax rates change substantially depending on whether township and village levies are calculated as a percentage of reported income per capita or actual income per capita. Because of this self-reporting, local officials in effect set local tax rates and define tax bases without official authorization from above, which has resulted in the "creation of a quasi-tax

[36] According to the Law on Agriculture passed in 1993, the combined payment of formal township and village levies (often referred to as *santi wutong*, the "three retentions and five unifieds," or *tongchou tiliu*) was capped at 5 percent of the average net per capita income of inhabitants in the township for the preceding year. Bernstein and Lu point out that this cap is frequently misinterpreted to apply to the entire tax burden of farmers, for example, including the state agricultural tax. See Bernstein and Lu, *Taxation without Representation in Contemporary Rural China*. See also Xiande Li, "Rethinking the Peasant Burden: Evidence from a Chinese Village," *Journal of Peasant Studies* 30, no. 5 (2003), 45–74.

[37] See also Qinglian He and Xiaonong Cheng, "Rural Economy at a Dead End: A Dialogue on Rural China, Peasants, and Agriculture," *Modern China Studies* 67, no. 3 (2001), 10.

system which is increasingly beyond the central government's control, and whose structure of fees and charges is extremely chaotic, nontransparent, and often inequitable."[38]

Localities varied widely, but villagers in many places also paid other charges and fees in addition to township and village levies. Charges for public goods and services included heavy ad hoc fees or apportionments (*tanpai*) levied on each person when local officials decided to pave a road or build a new school. User fees included what could be exorbitant charges for mandatory licenses and certificates such as marriage certificates or building permits, the widespread school-related fees, and surtaxes added to the price of electricity or tap water. According to Lin et al., marriage certificates in some regions cost a quarter of a farmer's average annual net income. In some places, local governments imposed heavy penalties for such violations as unapproved pregnancies or unapproved building construction, or even minor infractions in order to generate more revenue.[39] Students were often asked to pay, on top of tuition fees, school water and electricity fees, library fees, laboratory experiment fees, and so on.

If we add on other charges and fees that townships and villages levied per person to the amount villagers paid in so-called township and village levies, in 2000 40 percent of villages in the survey had local tax rates that were more than 5 percent of the actual village income per capita. The average local tax rate for villages in the survey was 5.1 percent, and the highest tax rate reported was 24 percent.

Allowing localities to create extrabudgetary funds and informal institutions of public finance over the years threw open a Pandora's box, since almost by definition these institutions were out of the direct control of higher levels. Between 1990 and 1995, the total amount of taxes and levies paid by the average villager increased 18 percent annually, double the growth of per capita income in the same period.[40] Farmers in some regions paid tens or even hundreds of fees on top of what they paid in state-sanctioned taxes.[41] Many individual administrative departments also levied their own fees in addition to the fees levied by their level of government

[38] Wong, *Financing Local Government in the People's Republic of China*, 13.

[39] State Planning Commission internal report, 2000, as cited by Lin et al., *The Problem of Taxing Peasants in China*, 8.

[40] He and Cheng, "Rural Economy at a Dead End," 10, citing "Obstacles to Improving Peasants' Purchasing Power," *Economic Times of China*, November 20, 1998, p. 3.

[41] Bernstein and Lu, *Taxation without Representation in Contemporary Rural China*.

in general.[42] These informal fees were set, collected, and recorded outside of the local government's official budget in each individual department's account book, which was "disposed by the units themselves."[43] Some government bureaus that were particularly successful at developing extrabudgetary revenue had their budgetary allocations taken away entirely and were left to rely solely on extrabudgetary funds.[44] Little attempt was made to coordinate among departments to make sure that the total number of fees levied on villagers was not excessive.

Throughout the 1990s, state directives seeking to curb local tax burdens had little effect, but rural tax and fee reforms since 2000 have made more progress. A circular issued by the State Council in February 1990 called on local officials to reduce peasant burden, specified the levies and charges that were permitted, restricted the total amount of township and village levies to 5 percent of local income per capita, and authorized the Ministry of Agriculture to examine all local government regulations and abolish those that contradict the circular. Local levies continued to rise, however, and farmer protests increased. In many places, however, local officials continued to charge fees that the central government had outlawed.[45] As of 2002, various state ministries had promulgated thirty-seven formal directives reducing and restricting taxes and fees levied on rural residents, with little success.[46]

[42] The finance department of each level of government oversees the budgets of all departments at that level. At the township level, for example, the township finance department supervises the budgets of all of the township government's departments. Fees levied by the township government as a whole are recorded by the township finance department. In addition to these general fees, however, individual township government departments often have leeway to levy their own fees independent of the township finance department.

[43] Han, "Public Finance Crisis in Chinese Counties and Towns," 4. Some of the local levies and user fees are legally defined, and the state requires local governments to report them, although local governments have discretionary power over their use. This category of fees is often referred to as "extrabudgetary funds." Other charges and informal revenue are completely outside the formal state accounting system. These are often referred to as "self-raised funds." See Park et al., "Distributional Consequences of Reforming Local Public Finance in China," 767–9.

[44] He and Cheng, "Rural Economy at a Dead End."

[45] Dali L. Yang, *Calamity and Reform: State, Rural Society, and Institutional Change since the Great Leap Famine* (Stanford: Stanford University Press, 1996), 209–10. See also Bernstein and Lu, *Taxation without Representation in Contemporary Rural China*; Li, "Rethinking the Peasant Burden," 45–74; Lu Xiaobo, "The Politics of Peasant Burden in Reform China," *Journal of Peasant Studies* 25 (1997), 113–38; Li Lianjiang and Kevin O'Brien, "Villagers and Popular Resistance in Contemporary China," *Modern China* 22, no. 1 (1996), 28–61.

[46] Lin et al., *The Problem of Taxing Peasants in China*, 3.

The rural levy card, an institution established by the central government to increase transparency and reduce arbitrary taxation, perversely helped local governments to impose levies that were not officially sanctioned. Township and village governments were required to list all their levies on a card handed out to each villager. Local officials, however, took advantage of the level-by-level transmission of information to doctor the information on official state regulations received by villagers. Villagers thus often paid local levies, believing that fees listed on the levy card must be formal and state-mandated, when in fact many localities included informal, unauthorized charges such as "joint defense security fees," "farm machinery maintenance fees," or "fees for village broadcasts" that contravened official regulations.[47] Local governments met attempts to correct this problem with intense resistance. In Jiangxi province, one magazine publisher produced a supplement in 2000 compiling a collection of all the central government's official documents on agricultural policies to help peasants understand what fees are mandatory and what fees are arbitrarily collected by local authorities. Not surprisingly, local authorities condemned the supplementary issue as a "reactionary publication," and the editor-in-chief was ultimately forced to leave town.[48]

After limited success in restricting unofficial local levies through numerous directives, the central government initiated a pilot program to eliminate state agricultural taxes in 2000 and expanded this program throughout the country in 2003. Since pilot rural tax reforms were disseminated throughout the country in 2003, burdens have lightened by as much as 30 percent.[49] Yu Jianrong found that only 1.9 percent of sixty thousand phone calls of complaint to a national media bureau between August 2003 and June 2004 involved disputes over agricultural taxes and fees.[50] According

47 He and Cheng, "Rural Economy at a Dead End," 8.

48 Ibid., 12–13. Increasingly, rural residents can draw on forms of legal aid and paralegal aid provided by state-licensed "basic-level legal workers" and self-trained "barefoot lawyers" who help fellow rural residents make use of the state court system. See Benjamin L. Liebman, "Legal Aid and Public Interest Law in China," *Texas International Law Journal* 34, no. 2 (1999), 211; idem, "Lawyers, Legal Aid, and Legitimacy in China," in *Raising the Bar: The Emerging Legal Profession in East Asia*, ed. William P. Alford (Cambridge: Harvard Law School, 2004), 311–55.

49 See Zhang Xudong and Liu Yangyang, "Remarkable Achievement in Pilot Tax and Fee Reform in Rural China (*Zhongguo nongcun shuifei gaige shidian chengguo xianzhu – jianfu yu 30%*)," *Xinhua Network*, July 6, 2004.

50 Disputes over land were the most frequently mentioned complaint. See Zhao Ling, "Major Shift in the Focus of Farmers' Petition to Rights: From Disputes over Taxes and Fees to

to news reports, these reforms helped to reduce unofficial local surtaxes and levies added to collection of the state agricultural tax by as much as 30 percent.[51] It remains to be seen whether the elimination of all agricultural taxes in 2006 will also eliminate the problem of unofficial fees and surtaxes levied by local governments.

In addition to unauthorized levies, fees, and fines, however, village governments in some places have also raised informal revenues by renting and selling public assets under their control. Localities that succeeded in establishing profitable industrial sectors benefited from the contracting fees and rental fees paid by their formerly collective enterprises. As Tony Saich has observed, "rather than frowning on commercial activity, local governments are positively encouraged to use state assets to raise funds to cover the management and operational costs."[52] County governments sold urban residence permits to generate revenue.[53] Some local governments ran prostitution rackets through the hotels and karaoke bars they operate.[54] Other local governments, desperate for revenue and saddled with unprofitable enterprises, simply sold off their assets, thereby "draining the pond to catch the fish."[55] Profits from these sales were of course only a one-time source of income. As one county official in Shanxi noted: "Village officials used to do big public projects by selling off collective assets – tractors, tractor stations, public buildings. Now they sell land contracts but these are also one-time things (*yicixing*) since contracts are for thirty to fifty years. The only way left for most villages is to coerce illegal fees from villagers."[56]

By 2000, informal institutions of public finance were extremely widespread among villages in the survey. Table 2.2 shows that 27 percent of the surveyed villages reported that they relied *entirely* on revenue generated from sources other than official township and village levies. The average

Petitioning for the Right to Land (*Nongmin weiquan zhongxin zhongda bianhua: cong shuifei zhengyi dao tudi weiquan*)," *Nanfang Zhoumo* (Southern Weekend), September 2, 2004.

51 See ibid.; Zhang and Liu, "Remarkable Achievement in Pilot Tax and Fee Reform in Rural China."

52 Tony Saich, "The Blind Man and the Elephant: Analysing the Local State in China," in *On the Roots of Growth and Crisis: Capitalism, State, and Society in East Asia*, ed. L. Tomba (Rome: Annale Feltinelli, 2002), 83.

53 Park et al., "Distributional Consequences of Reforming Local Public Finance in China," 770.

54 Saich, "The Blind Man and the Elephant," 85.

55 Chinese version of He and Cheng, "Rural Economy at a Dead End." See also World Bank, *China: Provincial Expenditure Review*, 5.

56 Interview with assistant bureau chief, county civil affairs bureau, southwestern Shanxi province, April 19, 2001.

Table 2.2. *Distribution of Villages by Reliance on Informal Sources of Revenue*

Level of Reliance on Informal Sources	Percentage of Villages
All revenue from informal sources	27
More than half from informal sources	32
Less than half from informal sources	30
None from informal sources	11

amount of village government revenue coming from informal, non-official sources was 58 percent. Only 11 percent of villages reported that they had no informal sources of revenue and relied entirely on the village portion of township and village levies for their expenditures.

Reassessing Decentralization

Many scholars have focused on the positive aspects of fiscal decentralization in China, which is often interpreted as a successful response to the needs of a marketizing economy. Justin Lin and Zhiqiang Liu's econometric analysis shows that fiscal decentralization has improved economic efficiency and stimulated economic growth.[57] Barry Weingast and his colleagues argue that China exemplifies what they call "market-preserving federalism." They contend that decentralization – which results in a hierarchy of governments that have clearly delineated and strongly institutionalized powers, local governments that have primary authority over the local economy, a national government that has the power to police the common market, and hard budget constraints for all levels of government – creates conditions that foster markets, protect competition, and prevent arbitrary intervention in market exchanges by government actors.[58] Oi argues that fiscal decentralization has fueled economic growth in China by giving local governments strong incentives to invest in rural township and village enterprises (TVE). Fiscal decentralization gave local governments the right to keep any economic surplus they were able to generate. After delivering the set amount of revenue owed to the central government, local governments could keep the remaining portion for themselves. This arrangement gave

[57] Justin Yifu Lin and Zhiqiang Liu, "Fiscal Decentralization and Economic Growth in China," *Economic Development and Cultural Change* 49, no. 1 (2000), 1–21.

[58] Weingast, *The Theory of Comparative Federalism and the Emergence of Economic Liberalization in Mexico, China, and India*; see also Montinola et al., "Federalism, Chinese Style."

local governments strong incentives to promote local economic growth by making productive investments that would increase flows of revenue into the public coffers under their control.[59] Throughout the 1980s and 1990s, local governments invested heavily in rural enterprises that generated government revenue in the forms of profit remittances, taxes, and contracting fees. Between 1995 and 2000, TVEs produced more than half of China's industrial value-added and profits and contributed 30 percent of the gross domestic product (GDP).[60]

A Darker Picture of Decentralization

But economic growth and industrialization do not necessarily lead automatically to better governance and public goods provision. Fiscal decentralization may have generated the conditions for rapid economic growth and rural industrialization, but it has also led to the deterioration of local governance and public goods provision in several ways. First, decentralization has reduced funding from higher levels while increasing the responsibilities that local governments have for public goods provision. Second, the central government's decision to allow localities to develop informal sources of revenue to meet expenditure needs for public goods provision has created a large area of local public finance over which they have little control. Higher levels have little power to make sure that revenues generated through informal institutions of local public finance are invested in public goods provision. Moreover, because higher levels (and citizens) cannot get accurate information about the levels and sources of local government revenue, they cannot determine the real level of public goods and services that a local government can afford, which means they cannot assess accurately how well the local government is really performing.

The development of extrabudgetary funds and informal institutions of local public finance has had several consequences. Until the late 1990s, when TVEs were privatized, there was little to stop local officials from diverting resources away from public goods investment and toward investment in industrialization. By giving village officials strong incentives to invest in industrialization, decentralization reduced their incentives to fund public

[59] Oi, *Rural China Takes Off.*

[60] Carl Riskin notes that between 1979 and 1997, the real output of TVEs grew by an average of more than 20 percent per year. C. Riskin, *Rebuilding Effective Government: Local-Level Initiatives in Transition* (Bratislava: United Nations Development Program, 2000), 3–4.

goods and services that had minimal short-term returns. If, as Oi has argued, village officials were residual revenue-maximizers, there was little reason for them to fund repairs of the village school building or construct running water infrastructure for household use since these investments were "nonproductive" by their standards.

Decentralization and Local Governmental Debt

The strong incentives to invest in TVEs also had a negative impact on funding for public goods provision when TVEs went bankrupt, draining public coffers and leaving local governments with high levels of debt. In places that lacked market access, proximity to large cities, sources of investment, and a stock of entrepreneurial skills[61] – and even in many places that had these advantages – overly eager officials made bad investments.[62] During the 1990s, TVEs in many places failed, sometimes leaving local officials with impossibly high debts.[63] As Justin Lin and his colleagues observe, "in the mid-1990s, many local governments, driven by budget incentives and TVE development mandates set by upper level governments... borrowed huge amount [sic] of funds from local banks... and initiated a wave of TVE investment frenzy, which turned out to be huge amount of debts at township and village level [sic]."[64]

Villages with village government enterprises in the survey were more likely to have higher levels of debt than villages without enterprises. On average, a village with village government enterprises had about half a million yuan (about U.S.$62,500) more debt than a village without enterprises,

61 Bernstein and Lu point out that these conditions are not distributed equally across the countryside. Bernstein and Lu, *Taxation without Representation in Contemporary Rural China*, 10.

62 Debt at the township level is an especially large problem, in large part because township officials are transferred every few years and expect to be working somewhere else when the loans they borrow come due. (Thanks to Elizabeth Perry for this observation.) Based on a national study of eighty-one counties, Yu Jianrong has estimated that the average township government debt is about 11 million yuan. Jianrong Yu, *Township and Village Autonomy: Basis and Path (Xiangzhen Zizhi: Genju He Lujin)*, June 2002, 119.

63 Yuan Peng and Xiaoshan Zhang, "Problems and Challenges Encountered in the Development of TVEs," *Review of Economic Research (Jingji Cankao Yanjiu)*, no. 28 (2001), 28–40; Wen Lu, "Problems during the Process of TVE Reforms," *Journal of Agricultural Economy Research*, no. 1 (1998), 18–21; Russell Smyth, Jiangguo Wang, and Quek Lee Kiang, "Efficiency, Performance and Changing Corporate Governance in China's Township-Village Enterprises since the 1990s," *Asian-Pacific Economic Literature* 15, no. 1 (May 2001), 30–41.

64 Lin et al., "Decentralization and Local Governments in China's Economic Transition," 14.

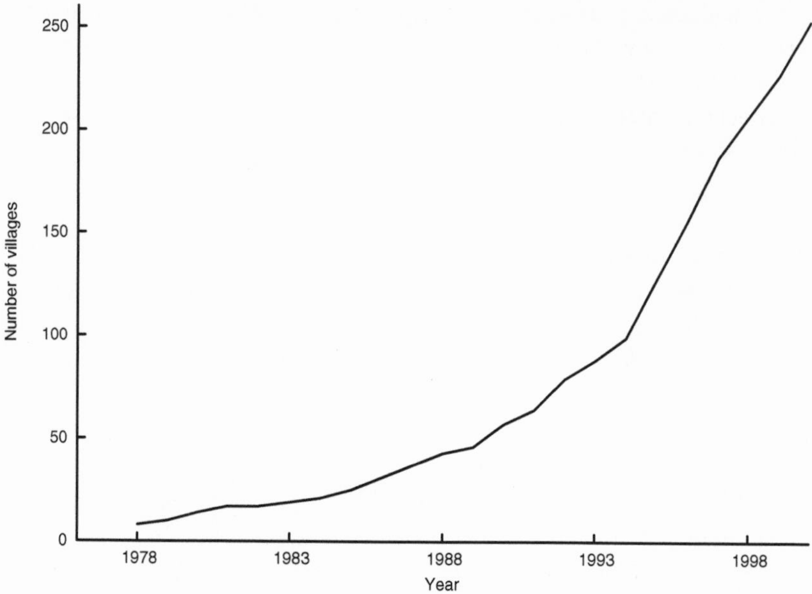

Figure 2.1. Number of villages with government debt.

all other things being equal.[65] Data from my survey of 316 villages suggest that the problem of village government debt took a turn for the worse around 1995 and 1996 (see Figure 2.1).[66] The total number of villages in the survey with government debt rose from eight in 1978 to eighty-eight in 1993. Between 1993 and 1997, the number of villages with government debt more than doubled, jumping from 88 to 187 villages.

The Case of New Brook Village The case of New Brook Village in northeastern Hebei province vividly illustrates the financial mess that can result when village enterprises fail. In total, the village government's debt is over 15 million yuan. When I interviewed the Party secretary in the spring of 2002, the village had just received another notice from the bank urging payment for 500,000 yuan of the principal coming due. Village officials observed that the bank did not even bother to bill them for interest anymore.

[65] Statistically significant at the .01 level. Effect robust to the inclusion and exclusion of various controls.

[66] See Russell Smyth, "Recent Developments in Rural Enterprise Reform in China: Achievements, Problems, and Prospects," *Asian Survey* 38, no. 8 (August 1998), 784–800.

New Brook's problems started in the mid-1990s when the village government ran several village enterprises, the largest of which was a concrete factory. At the peak of their success, the village's collective enterprises employed a total of 230 villagers (out of about 500 households). Village officials did not expect to have any problem paying off the 3 million yuan borrowed from the rural credit cooperative to establish the factory. In 1996, they were so optimistic that they borrowed another 4.8 million yuan to expand the factory. A year later, however, the concrete factory ran a deficit of 1.3 million yuan. After several more years in the red, the village government decided to cut its losses and contracted the factory to an outside individual in 2000.

Because of the concrete factory fiasco, the village government now owes 8 million yuan to the local bank and rural credit cooperative, 4 million yuan in loans borrowed from private individuals and unpaid wages, and 3 million yuan to the concrete factory's suppliers. In addition to these debts, the village government owes numerous smaller debts. In 1991, it borrowed 99,000 yuan to start a flour mill, and in 1992 it borrowed 98,000 yuan to run an agricultural machine station. On both loans the village government paid the yearly interest until it ran out of money in 1999. It still owes the entire principal on both loans. Another 40,000 yuan is owed in unpaid wages to villagers who worked in the village's experimental mechanized agriculture project and villagers who were hired to rebuild the village school, and 80,000 yuan is owed in unpaid wages to eight village officials. The village government is also contesting a debt of 20,000 yuan transferred over from the county electricity bureau. The county electricity bureau told the villagers they would be paid for the labor they contributed to the renovation of the village's electricity grid and then unilaterally transferred the responsibility over to the village government.

It seems unlikely that New Brook Village will ever have enough money to repay all of its debts, to say nothing of funding public projects. As a final irony, formal institutions of local taxation have been extremely difficult to reinstitute after the village government abolished them in 1992, thinking that the concrete factory would continue to provide them with plentiful revenue. Now villagers are collectively supposed to pay 70,000 yuan per year in township taxes and 70,000 yuan per year in village taxes, but village officials say that they have to bargain intensively with villagers to get them to pay.

The Extent of Local Government Debt New Brook Village is by no means alone. When township and village enterprises seemed like the key to economic prosperity, local governments borrowed heavily from local banks to invest in rural industry. In 1992, state grain procurement agencies gave out 6 billion yuan in IOUs to farmers after banks had illegally diverted money from their agricultural procurement accounts to loan money, often to local governments, for industrial investment.[67] Local governments also borrowed capital held by state-owned enterprises and from individual government agencies and funds originally earmarked for other uses such as grain bureau subsidies or family planning funds.[68] Albert Park and his colleagues discuss one county that borrowed 1.25 million yuan from the Agricultural Bank to cover its deficit in 1992 and another county that borrowed 6.8 million yuan from thirty different government offices within the county, including education funds from the county education committee and funds for afforestation from the county forestry bureau.[69]

Village governments have also borrowed from private individuals. To pay for repairs to the village's dikes, officials in one Hebei village borrowed 60,000 yuan from individual villagers in 1999 at a yearly interest rate of 10 percent to supplement a 60,000 yuan loan from the rural credit cooperative at a yearly interest rate of 8.4 percent.[70] In another Hebei village, village officials have been unable to collect township taxes from villagers, so they have borrowed money each year from individual villagers. So far, the village government has made arrangements with fifteen villagers who borrow money from the rural credit cooperative using their savings accounts as collateral. The village government pays the bank's interest rate (between 6 and 7 percent) plus an additional 10 percent on these loans. Between 1995 and 2000, the village government racked up a debt of 350,000 yuan, not including interest.[71]

In places where village governments are responsible for collecting township taxes from villagers, when villagers refuse to pay their township taxes, village governments simply default on delivery of the taxes and accumulate debt. A study of one county in Hubei found that 47.8 percent of village

[67] Andrew Wedeman, "Stealing from the Farmers: Institutional Corruption and the 1992 IOU Crisis," *China Quarterly*, no. 152 (December 1997), 807.

[68] Park et al., "Distributional Consequences of Reforming Local Public Finance in China," 770.

[69] Ibid., 770.

[70] Interview with male village Party secretary, eastern Hebei province, May 3, 2002.

[71] Interview with male village Party secretary, eastern Hebei province, May 2, 2002.

Table 2.3. *Distribution of Villages by Size of Village Government Debt Relative to 2000 Government Revenue*

Size of Debt	Percentage of Villages
No debt	22
Less than 2000 government revenue	37
1–10 times 2000 government revenue	34
10–100 times 2000 government revenue	6
More than 100 times 2000 government revenue	1

government debt in the county consisted of back taxes for which township governments held village governments responsible. Over 80 percent of the villages were in debt, and the average debt for village governments in the county was 1.6 million yuan. Two other counties included in the study also had village governments with large public debt. The average debt for villages in one county in Jiangxi province, where 96 percent of the villages were in debt, was 48,000 yuan, and the average debt for villages in one county in Henan, where over 80 percent of the villages were in debt, was 124,000 yuan.[72]

Although 60 percent of the villages I surveyed had manageable levels of debt or no debt at all, about 40 percent had such large debts that it seems unlikely they would ever be able to pay it off, much less have the resources to fund public projects. Among villages with debt, the mean debt in 2000 was 225,369 yuan (about U.S.$28,000). In Table 2.3 we see that 41 percent of villages reported that the size of their village government debt exceeded the total government revenue in 2000. Seven percent of the surveyed villages reported that their debt was more than ten times the total government revenue in 2000. These figures are not surprising when we consider patterns of village government expenditure. As Table 2.4 shows, 45 percent of village governments spent more than their total revenue in 2000. Fifteen percent spent more than *twice* their total revenue.

Borrowing among different levels of local government has created byzantine patterns of local government debt. In one Hebei village, it is unclear whether the village government owes the township government money or the township owes the village. Both parties agree that the village government owes the township 190,000 yuan in back taxes for 1995 to 2000. In 1997, the village government borrowed 60,000 yuan, part of which went

72 Han, "Public Finance Crisis in Chinese Counties and Towns," 20.

Table 2.4. *Distribution of Villages by Village Government Expenditures Relative to 2000 Government Revenue*

Village Government Spending	Percentage of Villages
Equal to or less than revenue	55
1–1.5 times revenue	22
1.5–2 times revenue	8
More than 2 times revenue	15

to paying some of the back taxes owed to the township and part of which was invested in a village steel enterprise, which ultimately went bankrupt in 2000. But in 1987, in order to start a township enterprise, township officials borrowed 110,000 yuan from the village's coffers at an interest rate of 10 percent per year. The township has yet to return this money to the village coffers, so villagers and village officials feel justified in defaulting on the taxes assessed on them by the township.[73]

Bureaucratic Inflation and Corruption

The reduced accountability associated with informal institutions of public finance and extrabudgetary funds has had a negative impact on the ability of local governments to finance public goods provision, not only by allowing local officials to make poor investment decisions and waste funds that could otherwise finance public goods provision but also by enabling local officials to pocket public funds and misuse them deliberately. Although informal institutions of public finance and extrabudgetary funds also existed during the Maoist period, severe sanctions such as labor camps and public humiliation through struggle sessions deterred local officials from high levels of corruption.[74] In the reform period, unfunded mandates for public goods provision and extrabudgetary funds have increased dramatically as supervision and sanctioning of local officials have declined. In one Hebei village I visited, for example, two corrupt officials borrowed a total of 800,000 yuan between 1995 and 2000. The village Party secretary in 1996 persuaded the township government to give to him his village's contracts for the construction

[73] Interview with male village Party secretary, eastern Hebei province, May 2, 2002.

[74] See, for example, Jean Oi, "Communism and Clientelism: Rural Politics in China," *World Politics* 37, no. 2 (January 1985), 238–66.

of the township secondary school and home for the elderly because the township was building the structures on land appropriated from the village. People from both inside and outside the village were hired to do construction work but were never paid. After the completion of the projects, the village government owed 600,000 yuan to villagers for construction work, truck rental, and transportation of raw materials. Ultimately, the township removed the village Party secretary from office and made him return 85,000 yuan in embezzled funds. In 2002, according to the newly appointed Party secretary, the previous officials had embezzled more than 200,000 yuan in a village where income per capita was 2,800 yuan.[75]

Informal institutions of local finance have also allowed local governments to fund an explosive increase of government personnel. Reports surfaced as early as the mid-1980s that township governments were increasing local levies to pay for bureaucratic expansion. In 1982, the number of township personnel was at a low, having decreased to 339,000 officials from 368,000 in 1978. In 1980, there was only one township official for every thousand rural laborers. By 1985, there were 809,000 township officials, twice as many as there had been in 1982. In 1989, the number of township officials for every thousand rural laborers had more than tripled to 3.4.[76]

Administrative decentralization has also aggravated the problem. Dali Yang has noted that while new demands on local government generated by rural industrialization and increasing commercialization account for some of this increase, the timing of expansionary periods coincided with state directives attempting to rationalize the bureaucracy by separating Party and state bureaucracies in 1983 and by decentralizing more administrative responsibilities from counties to townships in 1986. In both cases, local governments used the policies to justify the creation of parallel offices and positions. Instead of simply dividing responsibilities as personnel were divided between the Party apparatus and the state bureaucracy, each side simply filled the gaps that the bifurcation created in its administrative structures by hiring more people. Similarly, the decentralization of tasks from county to township increased the number of personnel at the township level without reducing the number at the county level. "Rationalization, as intended from above, was instead transformed into duplication at the local level."[77]

75 Interview with male village head, eastern Hebei province, May 5, 2002.
76 Yang, *Calamity and Reform*, 191.
77 Ibid., 187.

Local governments also used the burdensome responsibilities for public goods provision assigned by the state's decentralization policies to justify these increases in personnel. In the name of implementing central government regulations on public goods provision, local governments can, as Justin Lin and his collaborators point out, easily "over-charge peasants to . . . expand local bureaucracy by excessive staffing, and promote personal consumption by corruption of local officials."[78] Throughout the reform period, governments at village, township, and county levels have put more and more people on their payroll and created more and more offices and affiliated enterprises to employ them.[79] Han Jun's study of three counties notes that the number of officials in one Jiangxi county jumped 33 percent from 1994 to 2000 while the number of officials in one Hubei county more than doubled. The average tax burden in all three counties of his study exceeded the state-mandated limit of 5 percent of local income per capita, ranging from 6.5 percent to 10.9 percent.[80] Kjeld Erik Brodsgaard notes that provincial governments have established, on average, fifteen more government organs than the central government allows through the *bianzhi* system. In some localities, he estimates that the number of excess people on the government payroll is as much as 50 percent of what is officially permitted.[81] Efforts by the central government to cut down on the number of officials "eating for free" (*chi xian fan*) have so far, as one village official put it, been "just for show."[82] As more township and village enterprises have gone bankrupt, local governments have been under increasing pressure to hire friends and relatives who have been laid off and who now, as Wen Tiejun has noted, all want to "squeeze into the government (*ji jin zhengfu laile*)."[83]

Wage bills for these superfluous government personnel are enormous and absorb funds that could otherwise be used for public goods and services. Table 2.5 summarizes variation among surveyed villages in terms of salaries

78 Lin et al., *The Problem of Taxing Peasants in China*, 29.

79 He Qinglian and Cheng Xiaonong note: "Even at the village level, many people are trying, through relationship manipulation, to join the privileged group to become government officials who 'bear no official title.' " He and Cheng, "Rural Economy at a Dead End," 8.

80 Han, "Public Finance Crisis in Chinese Counties and Towns," 7.

81 Kjeld Erik Brodsgaard, "Institutional Reform and the *Bianzhi* System in China," *China Quarterly*, no. 170 (June 2002), 366–9.

82 Interviews with male village head, western Fujian province, February 22, 2001, and male village official, northern Fujian province, October 15, 2001.

83 Interview with Wen Tiejun, editor of *China Reform* and agricultural economist, November 17, 2003.

Table 2.5. *Distribution of Villages by Salary Level of Village Officials in 2000*

Salary Level in 2000	Percentage of Villages
Not paid	7
Less than 1,000 yuan	25
1,000–2,000 yuan	32
2,000–3,000 yuan	15
More than 3,000 yuan	21
Level of Village Officials Relative to Village Income per Capita in 2000	
Less than village income per capita	48
1–2 times village income per capita	31
2–3 times village income per capita	10
3–4 times village income per capita	6
Over 4 times village income per capita	5

for village officials. The average village official's salary exceeded the village income per capita in more than half of the villages in the survey and was more than double the village income per capita in 21 percent of villages. On average, 23 percent of the village government revenue was spent on officials' salaries. But if we also take into account other categories of expenditures that may directly or indirectly benefit village officials, such as administrative expenses, "entertainment expenses" and other expenses unrelated to public goods provision, we can see that village officials may be consuming a large portion of village government revenues. According to the survey data, 48 percent of villages spent more than half of their revenue on expenditures unrelated to the provision of public goods and services. Eighteen percent of villages reported that these costs exceeded their total revenue in 2000.

Wen Tiejun estimates that only 30 to 40 percent of local governments have enough revenue to pay the wages of all the people on their payroll.[84] Zhao Shukai estimates that 80 percent of township governments have difficulties making wage payments on time. Zhao also notes that in all eight of the townships he studied in Shandong and Hebei, township governments were in arrears on wage payments.[85] Another report estimates that

84 Interview with Wen Tiejun, editor of *China Reform* and agricultural economist, November 17, 2003.

85 Shukai Zhao, "Township and Village Governance: Organization and Conflict (*Xiangcun Zhili: Zuzhi Yu Chongtu*)," *Strategy and Management (Zhanlue Yu Guanli)* (June 2003), 3.

70 percent or more of total local government expenditures are absorbed by personnel costs.[86] Expenditures on additional personnel include not only wages but also entertainment expenses, cell phone expenses, travel expenses, and vehicle expenses.[87] In one Shanxi prefecture, Park and others find that rural productive investment fell as a percentage of expenditure in all of the prefecture's counties. In one county the share of investment fell from 20 percent in 1980 to 2 percent in 1992. Most local governments put first priority on paying the wages of their personnel, not on providing public services.[88] For one Jiangxi county in Han Jun's study, rural productive investment accounted for 27.3 percent of total expenditures, whereas administrative costs took up 71 percent. Another county, in Henan province, had a payroll of 15,299 people who were paid 96 million yuan per year even though the county government could only generate revenues of 20 million yuan per year. Township governments in the county are even worse off. The expenditures of one township were more than twice the amount of revenue it collected. Another township's wage bill totaled 5.46 million yuan, but township revenues were only 1.8 million yuan. Township governments frequently divert funds earmarked for education, family planning, militia training, and rural road construction – as well as appropriate village government tax revenue – to pay the wages of township personnel.[89] As the Chinese economist Wen Tiejun notes, "Any subsidies from the central government turn into the expansion of government officials at local levels – funds for education, electrical grid renovation, health, everything."[90]

Government departments that provide services to the public and can thus finance themselves by charging service fees are expanding the most rapidly in terms of personnel.[91] In some places, local governments are even "reforming" these departments into quasigovernmental, "self-supporting" organizations that depend entirely on the collection of fees or fines. This strategy allows local governments to take away their budgetary funding and use it to fund surplus personnel in other offices. In this way,

[86] World Bank, *China: Provincial Expenditure Review*, 5.

[87] Saich, "The Blind Man and the Elephant," 85.

[88] Park et al., "Distributional Consequences of Reforming Local Public Finance in China," 771; Han, "Public Finance Crisis in Chinese Counties and Towns," 24.

[89] Ibid., 15.

[90] Interview with Wen Tiejun, editor of *China Reform* and agricultural economist, November 17, 2003.

[91] Ibid., 8.

local governments can claim they are "downsizing" because it reduces the number of administrative offices and personnel on the local government payroll. In actuality, villagers are double-charged for the services they receive since they continue to pay the original taxes collected to fund the departments providing services as well as new user fees charged by the newly "self-supporting" departments. As He Qinglian and Cheng Xiaonong point out, these arrangements create perverse incentives for government departments:

> For example, the justice office now thinks the more dispute cases it has in the rural areas the better; the civil administrative department wishes there were more divorce cases, because only then would they be able to "generate more income." The most absurd is that the family planning office on the one hand hunts down women for sterilization operations, and on the other hand wishes that they would be caught pregnant in violation of the family planning policy. When there is gambling in the village, the township police smile to themselves because only then would they be able to impose heavy fines on the peasants and make more money for the department.[92]

In similar fashion, grain bureaus have been renamed companies, with the pay of workers linked to profit earning.[93] Zhao Shukai makes a similar argument:

> In the administration of public security, for example, if the grassroots-level public security bureau needs to rely on fines to supplement its operating expenses or even to pay wages, in "cleaning up prostitution and punishing the illegal" it adopts the dual strategy of punishing and protecting. On one hand, it uses fines to attack them; on the other hand, it thinks up ways to make sure that these illegal activities are not eliminated so that its income from fines can continue.[94]

Numerous reforms have been proposed to halt the wasteful expansion of the local state, but it remains to be seen whether any of them would be effective. Policy makers at the Central Planning Commission's rural work conference in 2003 decided that the central government finance would pay for new public goods from now on at the county level and below. But many have doubts about the feasibility of this plan. As one Chinese economist

92 He and Cheng, "Rural Economy at a Dead End," 9, citing Jinqing Cao, *Huanghebian De Zhongguo: Yige Xuezhe Dui Xiangcun Shehui De Guancha Yu Sikao* (China by the Side of the Yellow River: A Scholar's Observation and Reflections on Rural Society) (Shanghai: Wenyi Chubanshe [Shanghai Literary and Arts Press], 2000).

93 Park et al., "Distributional Consequences of Reforming Local Public Finance in China," 775.

94 Zhao, "Township and Village Governance," 4.

points out, there are no institutionalized mechanisms for distributing state funds securely at local levels. Various provinces have attempted to merge two or more township governments into one larger township in order to cut down on bureaucratic personnel. In the localities that I visited, these attempts rarely had any impact on bureaucratic inflation. In the cases I observed, the resulting merged township government either absorbed all of the personnel from the original smaller township governments, making only a few nominal layoffs, or township governments were merged in name only to placate the provincial government but in reality continued to function in their original form.

Conclusion

The Chinese context suggests several important lessons. First, optimistic theories about the benefits of decentralization for governmental accountability and performance may only hold when democratic institutions are strong. Although it is true that local governments are likely to have better information about citizen needs, more information is useful only when citizens can hold officials accountable for responding to these needs. Second, as Jonathan Rodden and others have observed, decentralization does not necessarily result in clear division of responsibilities and greater transparency.[95] When local governments have unfunded mandates, it may not be clear whether local governments or the central government should be held responsible for poor public goods provision. Third, decentralization does not necessarily come with the hard budget constraints that are necessary for fiscal federalism and "market-preserving federalism," as we can see from the widespread accumulation of bad loans to local governments in China. Without hard budget constraints, local officials do not have strong incentives to manage public funds carefully or to provide public services in order to compete with each other for tax revenues.

The long-term consequences of fiscal and administrative decentralization in rural China may not be as bright as the short-term effects. For places with low economic growth and small revenue bases, decentralization has increased their responsibilities for funding public goods while decreasing subsidies from above. The lack of good roads, education, and basic infrastructure in these places ensures that regional inequalities will continue to grow.

[95] Rodden, *Hamilton's Paradox*.

Decentralization and Local Government Performance

Increasing local autonomy in the absence of strong institutions of bureaucratic or democratic accountability can be dangerous. The central government's decision to allow localities to develop informal institutions of local public finance in hopes of generating enough revenue to compensate for the lack of higher-level funding for public goods provision has given them free rein over how to spend public funds. Fiscal decentralization has given local officials strong incentives to use these funds for rural industrialization rather than for basic public goods provision. Although there are cases of villages with extremely successful rural enterprises where the village government has funded generous levels of public services for village residents and exemplifies what Jean Oi calls "local state corporatism," far more common are cases of village governments that have to choose between investing in rural industry and in public services. In these situations, the lion's share of funding almost always goes toward industry and other "productive" investments that can increase future revenue streams. Uncontrolled investment in rural enterprises has also decreased funding for public projects in places where these enterprises have failed and local governments have accumulated huge debts. Local governments which have lost all of their public assets are referred to as "empty shells" (*kong ke*), incapable of operating at all. Finally, informal institutions of local public finance have decreased funding for public projects by making it easier for local officials to misuse and embezzle public funds.

In short, we cannot assume that decentralization will always affect governmental performance and public goods provision in the same way that it affects economic growth and industrialization, nor should we believe that economic growth and industrialization naturally lead to better governance and public goods provision. In China, local public finance and rural tax reforms have risen to the top of policy agendas as more policy makers come to similar conclusions. Localities across the country have started experimenting with different forms of fiscal recentralization, such as pilot reforms that give townships control over village public finance or counties control over township public finance. The abolition of the agricultural tax in 2006 has increased the need for intergovernmental transfers to make up shortfalls in local government revenues and may also hasten fiscal recentralization. If transfers, however, are not sufficient to meet the expenditure needs of local governments, or if higher levels are unable to ensure responsible local spending, incentives to develop informal sources of revenue may only get stronger.

3

Local Governmental Performance

ASSESSING VILLAGE PUBLIC GOODS PROVISION

Given the multitude of problems with local public finance and governmental accountability discussed in the last chapter, it is not surprising that the provision of local public goods and services is a major problem. Reliable aggregate data are scarce, but available statistics suggest that the level of public goods provision in China is low even compared to other developing countries. The total size of China's road network in 2002, for example, as estimated by the World Bank, was 1.7 million kilometers, roughly the same as that of Brazil. In China, however, this network served a territory of 9.6 million square kilometers, an area 13 percent larger than Brazil's 8.5 million square kilometers, and a population of 1.3 billion people, more than seven times the size of Brazil's population.[1] Investment in education was comparatively low – about 2.1 percent of GDP in 2000 compared to 4.3 percent in Brazil, 4.1 percent in India, and 3.8 percent in Russia.[2] Access to water "improved" for drinking was similarly problematic: as of 2002, 23 percent of China's population lacked access to improved water, as opposed to 14 percent in India and 11 percent in Brazil.[3]

[1] World Bank, *World Development Indicators 2005* (Washington: World Bank, 2005).

[2] Data for China and Brazil from the World Bank Education Statistics Database compiled by the Education Group of the Human Development Network and the Development Data Group in the Development Economics Vice-Presidency. Investment for Brazil is for 2000. Investment for China is based on the most recent data within two years of 2000. See online at http://www1.worldbank.org/education/edstats. Data for India and Russia from UNESCO Institute for Statistics General Country Profiles. See online at http://www.uis.unesco.org/profiles/selectCountry_en.aspx. UNESCO reports investment in education to be 2.1 percent of GDP in China in 1999 and 4.2 percent of GDP in Brazil in 2001.

[3] United Nations, *Millennium Indicators Database* (New York: Department of Economic and Social Affairs, Statistics Division, April 2005).

Local Governmental Public Goods Provision

This book focuses on the provision of rural roads, schools, and water for a couple of reasons. First, these three categories of public goods have a profound impact on the quality of life everywhere and are the ones that villagers in China most often need and demand. They are critical for both day-to-day survival as well as long-term development. Yet many developing countries such as China still struggle to provide them. The second reason has to do with the focus of this study on governmental public goods provision at the village level. At the time of the fieldwork for this study (1999–2002), village roads, primary school facilities, and running water infrastructure were the most relevant, comparable, and important public goods provided by village governments scattered across a tremendously diverse country.[4] The funding and provision of these particular public goods reflected governmental performance at the village level specifically, since village governments had official responsibility for funding and organizing these goods.[5]

4 As the previous chapter noted, these arrangements may change as the central government creates new institutions in the wake of the 2006 abolition of agricultural taxes. During the time period of this study, almost all villages had their own village primary school. In 2001, however, the state began to allow localities to merge rural primary schools to make education administration more efficient as long as schools remained accessible to students. See "The Decision on the Reform and Development of Basic Education by the State Council" (*Guowuyuan guanyu jichu jiaoyu gaige yu fazhan de jueding*), issued on May 29, 2001.

5 Other rural public goods, such as electricity infrastructure and primary school teachers, are often funded in large part by higher levels of government. Health care, another important service, has largely been privatized at the village level. As we would expect given the institutional legacies outlined in the last chapter, many village governments devote little or no resources to public projects. But there are also many village governments that spend a startling amount of money funding public services. In absolute terms, the volume of investment in village public goods and services is hard to assess since official statistics record only investment provided by higher levels of government. One study of rural public goods provision in a single coastal province, Jiangsu, reported 1999 per capita village public goods investment at 38 yuan in 1985 prices (127 yuan, or about U.S.$16 in 1999 prices). See Zhang et al., "Local Governance and Public Goods Provision in Rural China," 10. (The consumer price index reported by the Asian Development Bank is used as the deflator.) Since Jiangsu is one of the wealthiest provinces in China, its village-level investment in public services is also likely to be higher than the national average. The estimate from my own survey of per capita village public goods investment in 2000, which covers four provinces in a variety of geographical regions, was 22 yuan in 1985 prices (or 74 yuan in 2000 prices, about U.S.$9). Multiplying these two estimates by a rural population of approximately 800 million gives us a range of estimated village-level public goods investment nationwide of about 59 billion yuan (U.S.$7.38 billion) to 101 billion yuan (U.S.$12.63 billion). These estimates suggest that village-level expenditures on public goods and services are quite significant in comparison to central government expenditures on public goods and services nationally. Official government statistics for central government expenditures are not broken down into categories specific to public goods and services provision, but the Asian Development Bank reported

This chapter serves several functions. For those less familiar with the particulars of rural politics and government in China, the first section of the chapter provides a historical overview of rural public goods provision since 1949 to put the current state of village governance and public goods provision in perspective. The second section of the chapter enumerates the six measures of village governmental public goods provision used in the quantitative analyses presented in the following chapters and discusses the rationale for choosing this set of measures. It also presents previously unavailable statistics on village-level provision of public goods and services in 2000. These data indicate that village governments vary widely in their provision of public goods. One obvious possibility to explain this variation is the level of economic development. Richer areas should be more likely to have better public goods than poorer areas. But surprisingly, findings from statistical analysis presented in the final section of the chapter suggest that economic development is not strongly correlated with better village governmental public goods provision across different localities. Nor has economic development necessarily led to better governmental public goods provision over time. Despite rapid economic growth, government investment in public goods has declined since the early 1980s. Figure 3.1 shows government budgetary expenditures on public goods as a percentage of total government expenditures for the four provinces in this study – Shanxi, Hebei, Jiangxi, and Fujian. We can see that all four provinces show the same downward trend. Before 1978, expenditures on public goods typically ranged between 60 and 80 percent of total provincial budgetary expenditures. By the late 1980s, expenditures on public goods had dropped to between 30 and 50 percent of total budgetary expenditures.

Rural Public Goods Provision in Historical Perspective

The first step toward understanding why economic development has not necessarily led to better governmental public goods provision is to go back into the past. Maoist-era development strategies such as the policy of local

that in 2000 total central government investment in social security and welfare, agricultural services, transportation, and communications totaled about 111 billion yuan (U.S.$34.8 billion). See Asian Development Bank, *Key Indicators of Developing Asian and Pacific Countries* (Manila: Asian Development Bank, 2002). Based on the preceding estimates, village-level public goods investment may represent from one-fifth to one-third of all the money that goes into public goods provision in China.

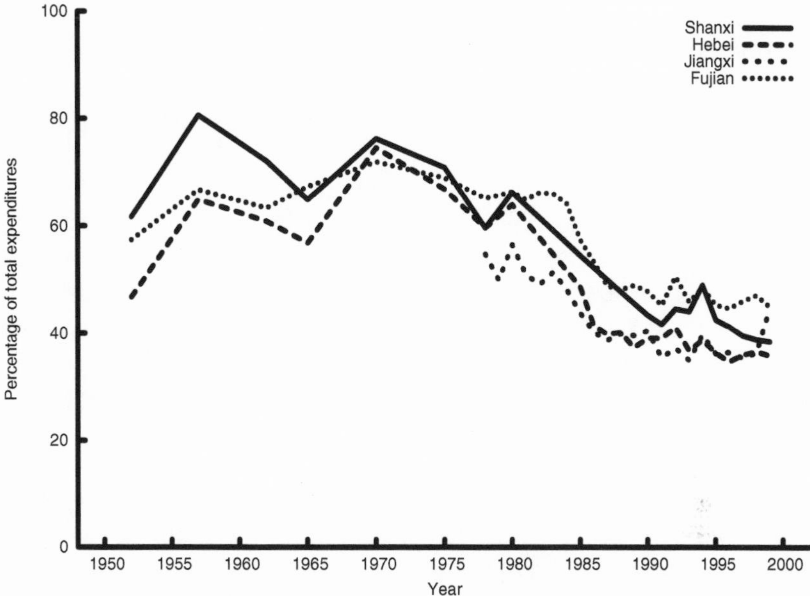

Figure 3.1. Total government expenditures on public goods by province.

self-reliance never prioritized the creation of formal systems for the delivery of rural public goods and services. During the Maoist period, socialist campaigns propelled the extension of basic public goods and services in the countryside, but formal public administration of village-level public goods and services was never established. With the start of market reforms in the late 1970s and early 1980s, the fervor of Maoist-era campaigns dwindled, but as the rest of this section explains, formal institutions to ensure the translation of increased wealth into increased public goods have continued to remain scarce.

Roads

During the Maoist period, formal budgetary funding for rural road construction extended only as far down as the county level, and even this funding was allocated in an ad hoc manner. Clear formal procedures for requesting state funding did not exist.[6] Funding for roads at levels below the

[6] See Vincent Benziger, "China's Rural Road System during the Reform Period," *China Economic Review* 4, no. 1 (1993), 7–9.

county was governed by the principle of local self-reliance, which required each level of government to take responsibility for financing the public projects within its jurisdiction. Counties were thus responsible for roads between major towns in the county. Communes – now called townships – were responsible for roads linking brigades or today's administrative villages. Each administrative unit was expected to be self-contained and largely self-financing. Since commerce and exchange between communes was supposed to be minimal, the quality of roads below the county level was of little concern to the central government.[7] Not surprisingly, rural roads in the early 1980s were not only of poor quality but many of them led nowhere.[8] The rural road system was full of dead-end roads (*duantou lu*) that would end just short of the township or county's border even when a road on the other side of the border started just a few hundred meters away.[9]

The lack of a preexisting administrative system for the rural road system combined with fiscal decentralization since the 1980s means that localities are still on their own in terms of how they organize road projects and find funding. Coordination between localities remains difficult. Because no formal system has ever been established for deciding how to distribute the cost of a road passing through multiple localities, any one locality can potentially stall or sabotage an entire road project if it is unwilling or unable to fund its share.[10] As economic liberalization progressed, funding designated for rural road construction has been reallocated to the construction of major intercity roads, and the central government has actively encouraged local governments to look beyond formal budgetary allocations to informal sources of funding. Official directives encouraged localities to "raise funds from many different channels (*duo qudao jizi*)." Such channels included but were

[7] Rural trade and commerce were virtually extinguished. See Audrey Donnithorne, "China's Cellular Economy: Some Economic Trends since the Cultural Revolution," *China Quarterly*, no. 52 (October–December 1972), 605–19.

[8] Official Chinese statistics, which do not include data on roads connecting villages, indicate that China's road density was less than half that of India. See World Bank, *China: The Transport Sector* (Washington: World Bank, 1985).

[9] A World Bank report in 1985 noted that provincial road systems were essentially separate, discrete networks with few interprovincial connections. Ibid. Vincent Benziger has estimated that in 1984 Sichuan province had 10,000 kilometers of dead-end roads at township borders and 5,000 kilometers of such roads at county borders. The same pattern existed at all levels of the road system. Benziger, "China's Rural Road System during the Reform Period," 6.

[10] Ibid., 6.

not limited to revenues from township and village enterprises, foreign funds, bank loans, and informal ad hoc subsidies from government bureaus.[11]

Implicit and explicit permission to raise funds through a variety of informal channels increased the potential resources available for rural road construction, but decreased local government accountability for actually using these resources on road construction. One example is the rise of illegal toll roads. The Roadway Law officially promulgated in 1998 directed officials to "maintain roads by relying on roads" and authorized county and provincial officials to establish toll stations and collect fees within their locality. Local officials, however, have used the law to justify the creation of informal and illegal toll stations. Numerous government offices have established tollbooths to finance expenditures completely unrelated to rural road construction, including the ministries of family planning and public health, police, forestry, taxation, industry and commerce, and urban construction, as well as numerous local governments at the county, township, and village level.[12] Before the recent rural tax and fee reforms, local governments also took advantage of central directives allowing the imposition of levies for rural road construction. In one of the most serious outbreaks of rural violence in the 1990s, villagers in Renshou county in Sichuan province rioted against repeated increases in local fees levied by county and township governments ostensibly to pay for a new road linking Renshou to the provincial capital 60 miles away. Thousands of farmers blocked traffic, burned police cars, and attacked government officials with bricks and clubs.[13]

11 Liu Zhenjiang, "Several Methods of Raising Funds for the Development of Village and Town Roads (*Duozhong xingshi jizi fazhan xiangzhen gonglu*)," *Ganglu*, no. 11, 30–2, as cited by ibid., 10.

12 Toll stations, of course, have had the same effects on interregional trade and commerce that dead-end roads did at the start of the reform period. Paving rural roads may reduce the time it takes for goods and people to travel to markets, but costs may outweigh the benefits if toll stations are needed to pay for the paving. Him Chung gives the example of a rural market located in Datang town in Deqing county of Guangdong province. Because the market was only 2 kilometers from the county border, it used to draw farmers from surrounding towns across the border in Fengkai county. Since a toll station was established at the border, Datang market has become the smallest market in the county in terms of number of visitors and turnover value. Farmers in the county across the border choose to go to markets that are two or three times as far as the Datang market because of the toll station and its tendency to charge even local bicycles for tolls. Him Chung, "Some Socio-Economic Impacts of Toll Roads in Rural China," *Journal of Transport Geography* 10, no. 2 (2002), 146. China's Roadway Law was passed during the People's Congress in July 1997 and took effect on January 1, 1998.

13 Lena H. Sun, "China's Peasants Hit Back; Rising Rural Unrest Alarms Beijing," *Washington Post*, June 20, 1993, pp. 1, 28.

Rural Education

As with rural road provision, during the Maoist period the state prioritized investment in urban areas and assigned financial responsibility for rural education to local levels of government.[14] In 1965, the state resolved to universalize primary education, but its strategy for doing so was to encourage communes and brigades to establish and fund "people-run" (*minban*) primary schools through local levies on rural residents. "People-run" schools operated outside the state's education system and budget. Communes and brigades usually appointed untrained villagers as teachers.[15] During the Cultural Revolution, the state assigned local governments increasingly onerous responsibilities for rural education.[16]

Cultural Revolution policies also made it more difficult to determine whom to hold responsible for the provision of rural education. The "Draft Program of Rural Secondary and Primary Education" published in May 1969 formally assigned responsibilities for rural education to communes and brigades (now townships and villages) but left it up to each individual commune to determine how to divide the responsibilities. The directive suggested that brigades should run primary schools and that communes should run secondary schools, but in wealthier areas, commune authorities were allowed to turn over responsibilities for secondary education to brigades. The directive also lowered education administration from the county to the commune level, giving the commune officials additional authority to decide on the institutional arrangements for funding

[14] In 1953, the State Council announced that as part of the state's industrialization strategy, state funds for new primary schools would be allocated only to urban areas. See Glen Peterson, "State Literacy Ideologies and the Transformation of Rural China," *Australian Journal of Chinese Affairs*, no. 32 (July 1994), 116, citing "Government Affairs Council Directive on Rectification and Improvement of Primary Education (*Zhengwuyuan guanwu zhengdun he gaijin xiaoxue jiaoyu de zhishi*)," November 26, 1953, in *Zhongguo jiaoyu nianjian 1949–1981* (China Education Yearbook 1949–1981) (Beijing: China Education Yearbook Editorial Board, 1984), 732–3.

[15] In one typical case, for example, a *minban* teacher in Anhui interviewed in the early 1980s reported that he had left middle school at age fifteen and worked at various jobs in his commune for six years. At twenty-one, he was appointed by the brigade to teach third-grade mathematics, although he had twice failed the entrance examination for the two-year course at Anhui Teachers' College. Peter Mauger, "Changing Policy and Practice in Chinese Rural Education," *China Quarterly*, no. 93 (March 1983), 146.

[16] Dwight Perkins and Shahid Yusuf note that the education strategy from 1966 to 1976 transferred almost all financial and administrative responsibility for rural primary schools to brigade authorities. Dwight Perkins and Shahid Yusuf, *Rural Development in China* (Baltimore: Johns Hopkins University Press, 1984), 176.

and providing education in their locality. Not surprisingly, commune officials often exercised this authority by pushing expenditure responsibilities down to the brigade and team levels. Even in areas that were not particularly wealthy, brigade primary schools often had responsibility for providing two years of secondary education, a practice that continued to spread throughout the 1970s.[17]

It became increasingly difficult to monitor the use of education funds as more and more funds were given to localities without distinct guidelines for their use. Prior to the Cultural Revolution, education funds had been earmarked for very specific purposes. Many of these formal regulations, however, broke down during the Cultural Revolution, making it easy for local officials to divert funds away from primary education toward other purposes. Because of poor monitoring of officials in the wake of the Cultural Revolution, increases in the state education budget did little to help localities meet regular, recurrent costs of education provision such as school facilities maintenance, classroom supplies, and heating and electricity bills. Instead, budgetary increases intended for these purposes were often absorbed by overdue promotions and salary raises owed to teachers, staff, and workers; back pay for intellectuals who had been rehabilitated; elite education; and wages for *minban* teachers put on the state payroll during the Cultural Revolution.[18]

These problems continued even after the start of rural reforms in the late 1970s.[19] In May 1983, a circular jointly promulgated by the State Council and the Chinese Communist Party (CCP) Central Committee reiterated the Maoist policy that primary education could be achieved only by "walking on two legs" and that localities could not rely on increased state funding to raise educational standards. Regulations formulated by various provincial governments again declared that state money would stop at the county level.[20] To compensate for the drop in funding from the central government, policy makers urged localities to allocate more resources and citizens to

[17] Pak-Tao Ng, "Open-Door Education in Chinese Communes: Rationale, Problems, and Recent Changes," *Modern China* 6, no. 3 (July 1980), 331–2. See also Mauger, "Changing Policy and Practice in Chinese Rural Education," 138.

[18] Stanley Rosen, "Recentralization, Decentralization, and Rationalization: Deng Xiaoping's Bifurcated Education Policy," *Modern China* 11, no. 3 (July 1985), 331–4.

[19] As of the early 1980s, primary and secondary school funding per student had yet to return to its pre–Cultural Revolution levels. See ibid.

[20] Deborah Davis, "Chinese Social Welfare: Policies and Outcomes," *China Quarterly*, no. 119 (September 1989), 577–97.

donate money to help local governments establish and run schools.[21] Not surprisingly, reliance on voluntary donations and local funding resulted in poor educational outcomes and deteriorating school buildings.[22]

Formal laws and regulations on rural education passed in the reform period only reinforced the Maoist-era institutional arrangements that had blurred accountability for education provision and burdened local governments with unfunded mandates. The CCP Central Committee's "Decision on the Reform of the Educational Structure" echoed the Draft Program of 1969. The new policy reiterated that counties and townships were responsible for primary and junior secondary education and allowed the local governments to decide how to divide the responsibilities among themselves. This policy officially decentralized education administration and financing. It required local governments to "diversify" their sources of funding for education but failed to specify what these sources might be. The subsequent "Compulsory Education Law" promulgated by the National People's Congress mandated six years of primary education and three years of junior secondary education as compulsory for all children, but also neglected to guarantee fiscal resources that would enable all localities to implement the policy.[23]

Decentralizing the responsibility for funding rural education allowed the state to avoid establishing a system of interregional transfers through which poorer areas would be subsidized by wealthier areas. Instead, subsidies from the central and provincial governments were given on an ad hoc basis and negotiated with specific localities year to year. These subsidies were often

[21] Rosen, "Recentralization, Decentralization, and Rationalization," 325.

[22] In a 1984 World Bank study, Perkins and Yusuf noted that "most rural elementary schools [were] housed in ramshackle, poorly lit, and unheated buildings with very rudimentary furniture." See Perkins and Yusuf, *Rural Development in China*, 182. In 1981, only 61 percent of students in Guangdong province completed primary school. See Mauger, "Changing Policy and Practice in Chinese Rural Education," 139. Even optimistic official statistics estimated that only 67 percent of primary school graduates from 1978 to 1983 went on to attend secondary school. See Rosen, "Recentralization, Decentralization, and Rationalization," 301–46.

[23] Mun C. Tsang, "Intergovernmental Grants and the Financing of Compulsory Education in China," *Harvard China Review* 3, no. 2 (2002), 11; Breton, *Competitive Governments*; Emily Hannum and Albert Park, *Children's Educational Engagement in Rural China* (unpublished manuscript, 2002), citing People's Republic of China Law on Compulsory Education, Ministry of Education (electronic document posted to http://www.moe.edu.cn/); Keith Lewin, Angela Little, and Jiwei Zheng, *Educational Innovation in China: Tracing the Impact of the 1985 Reforms* (Essex: Long Group Limited, 1994), 20.

project-based categorical grants designated for specific one-time expenses and did not help localities meet recurrent costs.

In short, current formal state institutions not only fail to provide enough money for rural education provision to match the standards that they mandate, but they also fail to hold state officials accountable for education provision.[24] Efforts to raise the quality of education have centered on improving teacher training and admission examinations rather than on reforming the education bureaucracy and improving the accountability of officials.[25] The "diversification" of funding sources encouraged by the central government has also decreased accountability, as local officials have used their formal responsibilities for education provision to justify the creation of a multitude of informal institutions not explicitly sanctioned by the state, including local education taxes levied on farmers and rural enterprises, enterprises run by rural schools themselves, and tuition fees charged to parents.[26] Not only are many of these informal, nonbudgetary revenues technically illegal, but both government and newspaper reports detail many cases of local officials diverting these kinds of funds toward noneducation expenditures and private gain. One researcher estimated that farmers in 1989 living in areas with average incomes and no village enterprises may have spent as much as 50 percent of their disposable cash income on educational fees.[27] Local, nonbudgetary sources of funding increased rapidly in the 1980s and 1990s. Between 1982 and 1984, 80 percent of the funds used to build and repair rural schools were being raised locally.[28] Between 1986 and 1992, the share of funding for primary and secondary education from nonbudgetary sources had increased from 21 percent to 39 percent.[29] By 1997, nonbudgetary funding accounted for 46 percent of the total funding for primary and secondary education.

24 As of the late 1990s, funding budgeted by the state covered only teachers' wages. Emily Hannum, "Families, Teachers, and Children's Educational Engagement in Rural Gansu, China," paper presented at the Annual Meetings of the Population Association of America, Atlanta, March 2002, 4.

25 Mauger, "Changing Policy and Practice in Chinese Rural Education," 138.

26 Tsang, "Intergovernmental Grants and the Financing of Compulsory Education in China," 3.

27 Davis, "Chinese Social Welfare," 583.

28 Rosen, "Recentralization, Decentralization, and Rationalization," 336, quoting *Jiaoyu Wenzhai* (documents from the Ministry of Education), 1984.

29 Tsang, "Intergovernmental Grants and the Financing of Compulsory Education in China," 4.

It remains to be seen whether recent reforms will improve the provision of rural education significantly. State funding of rural and primary education is increasing.[30] Perhaps more importantly, recent reforms are attempting to clarify the responsibilities of each office in the education administrative system. In 2003, the state simplified the financing and administration of education from four levels of government to three: central, provincial, and county. Township governments, widely considered the level most susceptible to financial mismanagement, no longer have formal authority to allocate educational funding. By May 2003, more than 98 percent of county governments had reportedly taken back the management of teachers' payrolls from township governments and 94 percent had taken back the management of school personnel. Attempts have also been made to standardize tuition fees in primary and secondary schools.[31]

Rural Water Provision

Infrastructure for running water was virtually nonexistent during most of the Maoist period. At most, the state merely publicized the importance of drinking water sources through movements such as the Patriotic Sanitation Movement (*Aiguo weisheng yundong*). The Patriotic Sanitation Movement, which was initiated in the early 1950s and expanded in the 1960s, mobilized villagers to prevent disease through the proper maintenance of manure pits and the elimination of unclean ditches and ponds. Historically, villagers had drawn water from streams, ponds, and deep wells. Slightly more elaborate systems consisted of artesian wells or reservoirs connected to individual houses using bamboo "pipes" or, in later times, plastic hoses.[32] When there was a shortage of water, local authorities might have mobilized people to dig water pits, water-retention wells, and household water tanks, but only on a very small scale.[33] Such efforts varied widely from locality to locality.

[30] In 2002, state budgetary investment in compulsory education increased by 20.4 billion yuan (about U.S.$2.4 billion). "China's Rural Education Achieves Great Development," *People's Daily Online*, July 30, 2003. According to another official report, total budgetary investment in rural compulsory education rose from 43 billion yuan (U.S.$5.2 billion) in 1997 to 99 billion yuan (U.S.$11.97 billion) in 2002. "Three Goals Set for China's Rural Education Reform," *People's Daily Online*, September 16, 2003.

[31] "China's Rural Education Achieves Great Development."

[32] Ronald G. Knapp, "Rural Housing and Village Transformation in Taiwan and Fujian," *China Quarterly*, no. 147 (September 1996), 779–94.

[33] Asian Development Bank, *A Study on Ways to Support Rural Poverty Reduction Projects* (Manila: Asian Development Bank, 2000), 3.

While model villages had capped wells, covered latrines, and animal pens separated from residential spaces, in general these movements produced little change in most villages.[34]

Not until the early 1970s did a drought in northern China lasting several years impel the state to allocate special funds for irrigation development and drinking water projects. Motor-pumped wells started becoming more commonplace in 1973, but as of 1979, 80.1 million people still suffered a shortage of drinking water. Modest state investment in drinking water facilities continued in the 1980s. Population growth, however, not only absorbed all of this investment but exacerbated existing shortages. By the end of 1984, 76 million more people had access to drinking water, but because of population growth, by the end of 1985, 159.8 million people were in urgent need of a clean water supply.[35]

As with rural road and education provision, rural water provision follows the official state policy of "build, own, and manage" locally.[36] Even when higher levels fund the construction of rural infrastructure for water delivery or roads, operation and maintenance of the infrastructure are left to the villagers themselves. Localities are supposed to rely on locally donated labor and voluntary donations from villagers, with minimal dependence on state subsidies. Building the infrastructure and getting the initial capital investment are often the easiest parts of water service provision. Researchers have pointed out that meeting the recurrent costs and sustaining the system have been much more difficult.[37] Funds for operation and maintenance generally have to come from user charges, but effective institutions for setting and collecting charges are often missing. When community investment builds running water facilities, property rights can be unclear. Since waterworks typically lose money, village governments shy away from running them and instead appoint or contract a person to be responsible for the management and maintenance. Due to unclear ownership,

34 Knapp, "Rural Housing and Village Transformation in Taiwan and Fujian," 780–1.

35 Asian Development Bank, *A Study on Ways to Support Rural Poverty Reduction Projects*, 3. Another report estimates that by the end of 1988, only 8.5 percent of villages had access to tap water. Vikram Bhatt, *Village Upgrading*, Vol. 2 of *Housing a Billion*, Research Paper No. 15 in the Minimum Cost Housing Group Publication Series (Montreal: McGill University, 1993).

36 Asian Development Bank, *A Study on Ways to Support Rural Poverty Reduction Projects*, 7.

37 WHO and UNICEF, *Global Water Supply and Sanitation Assessment 2000 Report* (New York: World Health Organization and UNICEF Joint Monitoring Program for Water Supply and Sanitation, 2000).

however, no one is held accountable for properly maintaining the infrastructure.[38]

Problems with accountability for rural water provision also exist at higher levels of the state. Unlike with the provision of roads or education, no one ministry or department is specifically in charge of providing water for rural household use. Water resource management is separated among development, pollution, control, and public health agencies at the national and local levels. The Ministry of Water Resources takes nominal responsibility for rural water supply in general, but other than its Bureau of Rural Water Conservancy, which focuses on irrigation, there are few formal institutions for the provision of running water infrastructure at the village level. The State Environmental Protection Administration (SEPA) is responsible for protecting water quality and enforcing water quality standards, but SEPA must rely on local environment protection bureaus, which may have different interests since they report to the local government. The Ministry of Health is responsible for actually monitoring water quality, but there is no formalized coordination between the Ministry of Health and the local environment protection bureaus. As of 1999, there were no formal working groups or commissions to coordinate specific areas of overlapping responsibilities.[39]

Despite weak formal administrative institutions for rural water provision, there has been considerable state funding in recent years, and rural access to tap water has increased substantially.[40] Provincial governments have also devised their own ad hoc arrangements. In Jiangsu province, for example, the provincial government allocated 25 million yuan of "special funds" to improve drinking water infrastructure in the less-developed northern part of the province. At the same time, the provincial government

[38] Asian Development Bank, *A Study on Ways to Support Rural Poverty Reduction Projects*, 9.

[39] Changhua Wu et al., "Water Pollution and Human Health in China," *Environmental Health Perspectives* 107, no. 4 (April 1999), 251–6.

[40] From 1991 to 1995, the government spent 14.45 billion yuan (U.S.$1.35 billion) to improve the drinking water supply in rural areas. World Resources Institute, "China's Health and Environment: Water Scarcity, Water Pollution, and Health," in *World Resources 1998–1999* (Washington: World Resources Institute, 1998–9). Domestic and international loans have also funded drinking water projects. Asian Development Bank, *A Study on Ways to Support Rural Poverty Reduction Projects*, 3. The rural population with access to tap water more than doubled between 1987 and 1995. World Resources Institute, *China's Health and Environment*. According to estimates by the Asian Development Bank, the percentage of rural households with tap water increased from 17 percent in 1992 to 43 percent in the central and western regions and 64 percent in the eastern regions in 2000. Asian Development Bank, *A Study on Ways to Support Rural Poverty Reduction Projects*, 4.

asked thirteen wealthier counties and municipalities to supply 1 million yuan per year to support these water projects.[41] Nevertheless, rural water supply continues to be increasingly problematic in terms of both economic development and health concerns.[42] For the past two decades, diarrheal diseases and viral hepatitis, which are both associated with fecal pollution, have been the two leading types of infectious diseases in China. Between 1991 and 1995, the incidence of hepatitis rose 46 percent.[43] Despite state efforts, poor provision of running water continues to limit rural consumption and development in many areas. Rural water provision problems may in fact be more problematic in more-developed areas than in less-developed areas. The massive rural industrialization of the 1980s and 1990s fueled rural economic development, but as a result the provision of safe drinking water has become a matter of intense concern. Not only has rural industry increased the demand for water, but higher industrial water usage has exacerbated the problems of drinking water provision, as waste water often drains untreated into rivers and ground water. Since 1970, deaths from liver cancer – a disease associated with high levels of inorganic substances in surface water – have doubled, and China now has the highest liver cancer death rate in the world.[44] Pollution has become such a critical social problem that protests have erupted, some of which have been organized by local officials.[45]

41 The state has continued to prioritize county-level roads over township and village roads. Gang Gao, "More Rural Residents Ensured Better Quality Potable Water," *Beijing Review* (October 30 1997).

42 Justin Lin, a Chinese economist, has argued that without running water and electricity, villagers will not buy consumer goods such as washing machines and refrigerators, which would not only improve living conditions but also relieve the problem of glut in the manufacturing sector. Justin Yifu Lin, "China's Economy: Boom or Bust?" (unpublished manuscript, January 30, 2004).

43 World Resources Institute, *China's Health and Environment*. See also WHO and UNICEF, *Global Water Supply and Sanitation Assessment 2000 Report*. The simple act of washing hands with soap and water reduces diarrheal disease transmission by one-third, but water use drops significantly when water must be carried from a source more than a few minutes away. United Nations Population Fund, *The State of World Population 2001* (New York: United Nations Population Fund, 2001), chapter 2.

44 World Resources Institute, *China's Health and Environment*, 120–2. The impact of water pollution on human health in China has been valued at 41.73 billion yuan per year (U.S.$3.9 billion), almost certainly an underestimate. A 1999 government report estimated the total health costs of air and water pollution in China to be more than U.S.$46 billion annually, or nearly 7 percent of GDP. Ibid.

45 In 2001, a village in Shaanxi province attracted national attention when the elected village head organized the thirty families in the village to draft a petition demanding an investigation of the unnaturally high mortality rate in the village and its connection to

Measuring Village Governmental Provision of Public Goods

This book aims to assess village governmental provision of basic public goods in China. In choosing measures for the survey, I had several concerns. I wanted to be able to assess village governmental public goods provision across a wide variety of places. I wanted measures that were not only broadly comparable in different parts of China but also ones that were central and relevant to local governance everywhere. But I also needed indicators that would capture variation in village governmental public goods provision – provision by *village*-level governments in particular. Finally, I wanted to evaluate the actual public goods provided as well as public investment in public goods. The amount invested by the government does not matter much if the investment does not translate into the production of tangible goods. Measures of tangible public goods are also more reliable and easily confirmed by survey administrators who can simply go and look at them.

The quantitative analyses in this book thus use the following six indicators of village public goods provision in 2000: per capita government investment, the existence of paved village roads; the existence of paved village footpaths, the percentage of classrooms usable during rainy weather, the newness of the school building (in terms of years since construction or last major renovation), and the existence of running water (see Table 3.1). Together, this set of six indicators satisfies the previously identified criteria. We look at both government investment and actual public goods. Different localities require different things from their governments. Per capita government investment in public projects can be a broadly comparable measure if we can control for factors such as local prices and location, which may make the cost of the same public good different in different places. In interviews, villagers repeatedly listed village-level roads, primary school buildings, and running water infrastructure as the public goods that they most often needed and demanded. These indicators also reflect the performance of village governments – and *only* village governments. In contrast to other public goods and services such as telephone service, television service,

three TVEs located next to the village – a fertilizer plant, a steel mill, and a radio plant. Since 1974, 59 out of 154 people have died, and more than 60 percent died of cancer. By comparison, in a neighboring village only two people have died of cancer in the past three decades, and nationwide, cancer accounts for 15 to 19 percent of deaths in rural China. Philip P. Pan, "Cancer-Stricken Chinese Village Tries to Pierce a Wall of Silence," *Washington Post*, November 5, 2001.

Table 3.1. *Measures of the Dependent Variable: Village Provision of Public Goods*

Variable	Mean	Standard Deviation	Number of Observations
2000 total village government expenditure on public projects per capita (yuan)	66.76	192.42	312
Existence of paved roads (1 = yes, 0 = no)	0.5	0.5	316
Existence of paved paths (1 = yes, 0 = no)	0.13	0.33	312
Percentage of classrooms unusable in rain	0.11	0.29	310
Average age of school building (years)	27.26	18.26	309
Existence of running water (1 = yes, 0 = no)	0.47	0.5	316

and electricity grids, which are subsidized by higher levels, village roads, primary school buildings, and running water infrastructure are supposed to be the sole responsibility of the village.

Looking at indicators of *multiple* public goods also allows for the possibility that different places prioritize different goods. Using multiple measures of village public goods provision is crucial because in an environment of scarce resources, citizens and officials have to make difficult choices about how to spend public funds. Few villages are able to fund roads *and* schools *and* running water. If we looked at only one of these indicators, we would not be able to compare the performance of different village governments. If, for example, we looked only at the quality of primary school facilities as our sole indicator of village governmental public goods provision, we would wrongly characterize a village government that had invested heavily in the provision of running water as performing poorly. Using multiple indicators of governmental public goods provision acknowledges that localities have to make trade-offs between different public goods.[46]

46 Because villages have to make these trade-offs between different public services, the provision of one public service may not be strongly correlated with the provision of another public service. The survey data indicate that the intercorrelations between the six different measures of village governmental provision of public goods are fairly weak, which is also consistent with evidence from village case studies. See Table A3.1. As we would expect, more government investment is weakly associated with better provision of all specific public services, whereas more funding is generally correlated with better roads, schools, and water infrastructure. Villages that are good at providing one public service, however, are not necessarily good at providing others. Villages with paved roads are somewhat less likely to have good school buildings. Villages with better school buildings are somewhat less likely to have running water or paved roads. Villages with schools that are better maintained in terms of having more classrooms usable in rainy weather are, interestingly, less likely to have recently rebuilt or completely renovated the school building. The negative

Variation in Village Governmental Provision of Public Goods

Village governmental provision of public goods in 2000 as measured by our set of six indicators – 2000 per capita government investment in public projects, the existence of paved roads, the existence of paved paths, the percentage of classrooms usable during rain, the newness of the school building, and the existence of running water – varied widely (see Table 3.1). Half of the villages in the survey reported paved roads in their village, and half did not. Villages were similarly split in terms of running water infrastructure. Paved paths were less common. Villages varied widely in per capita investment in public projects. As we can see from the standard deviation, which tells us that approximately two-thirds of the villages in the survey had a per capita investment between 0 yuan (the mean investment minus 192 yuan, or in this case 0 since a negative figure is impossible) and 259 yuan (the mean plus 192 yuan), the distribution of villages was widely spread out in terms of per capita investment. Variation in the state of primary school facilities was similarly high.

correlation between these two measures is consistent with case study evidence that villages either wait until the school building is in serious disrepair and then rebuild it entirely *or* keep up repairs on the school building and maintain its condition to avoid a major reconstruction project. The existence of paved village paths has a weak positive correlation with all the other public goods provision indicators, perhaps because it is both less costly and less necessary than the others. Villages with a little money left over from another project may choose to pave their village paths if there is sufficient provision of the more critical public services. Paved paths are particularly likely in villages with paved roads, perhaps because leftover materials from road projects can be used on paths and minimal additional labor is required. Multiple indicators of village governmental public goods provision are also an advantage during statistical analysis because they enable us to use a powerful strategy for estimating the impact that an explanatory variable has on village public goods provision by polling the data across outcomes. Because intercorrelations among the six measures of village governmental public goods provision are weak, combining the six measures into a single scale is inappropriate. Following Edward Miguel (2004) in his analysis of public goods provision in Kenya and Tanzania, we can use seemingly unrelated regression (SUR), which allows disturbance terms across outcome measures to be correlated during hypothesis testing. Edward Miguel, "Tribe or Nation? Nation Building and Public Goods in Kenya versus Tanzania," *World Politics* 56 (April 2004), 327–62.When different public goods provision outcomes are only imperfectly correlated due to idiosyncratic factors such as personal preferences for particular services or the competence of a particular official, the confidence interval around the estimated impact of an explanatory variable is considerably narrower than the confidence interval for any single outcome. This strategy allows us to be more certain that the estimated impact is accurate. See Edward Miguel and Mary Kay Gugerty, "Ethnic Diversity, Social Sanctions, and Public Goods in Kenya," *Journal of Public Economics* 89, nos.11–12 (2005), 2325–68; Jeffrey Wooldridge, *Econometric Analysis of Cross Section and Panel Data* (Cambridge: MIT Press, 2002).

Table 3.2. *Variation in Government Investment (in Yuan)*

Province	Mean	Standard Deviation	Minimum	Maximum	Number of Villages
Total sample	*67*	*192*	*0*	*1812*	*312*
Fujian	130	356	0	1812	78
Hebei	85	94	0	494	79
Shanxi	37	70	0	486	79
Jiangxi	14	30	0	201	76

Village Government Investment in Public Projects

Looking specifically at investment, villages varied from a low of no investment at all to a high of 1,812 yuan of investment per person. On average, village governments spent 67 yuan per person (4.4 percent of the village income per capita) on investment in village public projects (see Table 3.2). Out of the 316 villages in the sample, 26 villages failed to spend anything on public projects. Village governments in Fujian invested the most, averaging 130 yuan per person. Jiangxi villages were at the bottom of the list, averaging only 14 yuan per person.

Roads and Paths

As of 2000, almost all the villages in the survey had some sort of road that connected them to the rural road system. One to three percent of the villages sampled in each province lacked roads of any kind that could be used by a motor vehicle.

The percentage of villages with paved roads was about the same – around 60 percent – in Fujian, Hebei, and Shanxi (see Table 3.3). Jiangxi again lagged behind with only 14 percent of villages reporting paved roads. In terms of paved paths, Fujian had by far the highest percentage of villages with paved paths – 33 percent (see Table 3.4). In all three other provinces, less than 10 percent of villages had paved paths.

Village School Facilities

Out of the 316 villages in the survey, 28 villages reported that none of their classrooms could be used during rainy weather. The mean percentage of unusable classrooms was 11 percent for the whole sample (see Table 3.5),

Table 3.3. *Variation in Paved Roads*

Province	Mean	Standard Deviation	Number of Villages
Total sample	50%	50%	*316*
Fujian	59%	50%	80
Hebei	60%	49%	80
Shanxi	65%	48%	80
Jiangxi	14%	35%	76

Table 3.4. *Variation in Paved Paths*

Province	Mean	Standard Deviation	Number of Villages
Total sample	13%	33%	312
Fujian	33%	47%	79
Hebei	6%	25%	78
Shanxi	8%	27%	79
Jiangxi	4%	20%	76

Table 3.5. *Variation in Classrooms Unusable During Rainy Weather*

Province	Mean	Standard Deviation	Minimum	Maximum	Number of Villages
Total sample	*11%*	*29%*	*0%*	*100%*	*310*
Fujian	16%	35%	0%	100%	78
Hebei	7%	22%	0%	100%	79
Shanxi	12%	29%	0%	100%	80
Jiangxi	11%	30%	0%	100%	73

but among those villages that reported one or more unusable classrooms, the average percentage of unusable classrooms was about one-third. The average village school building in the sample had gone twenty-eight years without reconstruction or a major renovation (see Table 3.6). More than half of the villages in the survey reported that their village school building had not been rebuilt or given a major overhaul since 1978. More than 20 percent of the surveyed villages reported that the last major rebuilding or renovation had occurred before 1949.

The average village school building in Fujian was newer than village schools in the other three provinces. Fujian, however, also had the highest

Table 3.6. *Variation in Years since the Construction or Last Major Renovation of the Village School Building*

Province	Mean	Standard Deviation	Minimum	Maximum	Number of Villages
Total sample	*28*	*18*	*0*	*88*	*309*
Fujian	17	12	2	53	77
Hebei	25	20	1	88	79
Shanxi	37	16	1	53	80
Jiangxi	30	19	0	81	73

Table 3.7. *Variation in Probability of Running Water*

Province	Mean	Standard Deviation	Number of Villages
Total sample	*42%*	*47%*	*313*
Fujian	57%	45%	78
Hebei	18%	36%	79
Shanxi	90%	28%	80
Jiangxi	2%	12%	76

average percentage of unusable classrooms, suggesting that villages may be choosing from one of two strategies: waiting until the village school is extremely rundown and then making a large one-time investment in rebuilding the school, or scraping up enough money to keep the classrooms usable from year to year and getting by without planning a major reconstruction project.

Village Water Delivery

Out of the 316 villages in the sample, 42 percent had running water infrastructure, either in the form of household taps or shared public taps (see Table 3.7). There was, however, a great deal of variation among provinces. Shanxi province had the highest percentage of villages with running water – 90 percent – while Jiangxi again came in last with only 2 percent of villages reporting running water. A substantial percentage of villages in Fujian had running water (57 percent), but only 18 percent of villages in Hebei, the other coastal province, reported running water.

The high percentage of villages with running water in Shanxi province, however, may reflect not unusually good governmental provision of water but the severe water shortage in much of the province. Often, getting any water at all requires boring wells as deep as 280 meters and using electric pumps to pump the water out. Most villages therefore have running water, but in many places the pump is operated only for several hours each morning since the cost of electricity is so high. Wells, moreover, drilled in the late 1970s or early 1980s to only 130 or 150 meters deep have started to run dry.[47] The book's statistical analyses thus take this factor into account by controlling for the county and province in which the village is located.

Public Goods Provision and Economic Development

So what explains all the variation we see in village governmental public goods provision? Some village governments pave roads, provide running water, and maintain good school facilities. Others do little or nothing. One obvious possibility is wealth – richer areas should be more likely to have better public goods than poorer areas. In places with higher levels of economic development, citizens have more resources to fund the provision of public goods, and local governments can generate more revenue. More industrialized areas may also have higher demand for public goods provision.

Findings from the Survey

Contrary to these expectations, village governmental public goods provision was not strongly correlated with economic development in the survey data. I evaluated the impact of five different economic factors: income per capita in 1997, government assets in 1997, tax revenue per capita in 1997, the existence of village government enterprises in 1995, and the existence of

[47] One Shanxi villager described the trickle of water from the well in his village as "just like a child peeing (*sa niao*)." He noted that another well 260 meters deep had been drilled in 1996 for a cost of 220,000 yuan, much of which was subsidized by the state. Villagers, however, have yet to use the well because they lack sufficient funds both for a transformer for the well's electric pump and for the electricity itself. Wells in the county town are able to pump 80 metric tons of water per hour. If this new well were operational, it would be able to pump only 25 metric tons of water per hour for the same amount of electricity. Interview with male villager, southwestern Shanxi province, April 19, 2001.

private enterprises in 1995.[48] By looking at measures of economic development in years previous to 2000 (the year for the data on village governmental public goods provision), we can be sure that any correlations we observed were not due to good public goods provision causing the level of economic development in that year.

There were, however, no strong indications that economic factors had a statistically significant or substantively important positive effect on village governmental provision of public goods after controlling for geographic, demographic, and institutional factors, although there were some indications that the existence of private enterprises had a positive effect on the provision of paved roads and paths.[49] For the average village, an increase, for example, in 2000 income per capita from the 25th percentile to the 75th

[48] Following Miguel, "Tribe or Nation?" I use seemingly unrelated regression (SUR), which estimates a system of six equations, one for each of the six public goods provision outcomes, and allows the errors in the different equations to be correlated. Because each measure of public goods provision is regressed on the same set of explanatory variables, the coefficients and standard errors produced by SUR are identical to those produced by ordinary least squares regression (OLS). The advantage to using an SUR software routine in this case is that it automatically produces the covariances between estimators from different equations, which allows us to test joint hypotheses involving parameters in different equations. See ibid.

[49] The full model results are presented in Appendix Table A3.2. All five economic indicators are estimated in the same model. Missing data are multiply imputed using the EMis algorithm developed by Gary King, James Honaker, Anne Joseph, and Kenneth Scheve, "Analyzing Incomplete Political Science Data: An Alternative Algorithm for Multiple Imputation," *American Political Science Review* 95, no. 1 (March 2001), 49–69. In this model, robust standard errors are not reported because the existing software program for combining multiply imputed datasets for analysis does not support seemingly unrelated regression with robust standard errors. See Michael Tomz, Jason Wittenberg, and Gary King, CLARIFY: Software for Interpreting and Presenting Statistical Results, Version 2.0 (Cambridge: Harvard University, 2001). Controls include distance from county town, number of natural villages, village population, village terrain, Party membership of village head, percentage of village officials in Party, the existence of bureaucratic targets for public projects, implementation of village democratic reforms, county dummies, the existence of a temple manager, the existence of an active village pastor, and the existence of single and multiple lineage halls. The estimated relationship between village public goods provision and 1997 income per capita was positive for five outcomes (investment, roads, paths, classrooms, and newness of school) and statistically significant for roads. The magnitude of the effect, however, was relatively small for investment and roads and very small for paths, classrooms, newness of school, and water. Results were similar regardless of which control variables are included or excluded, whether missing data are multiply imputed or deleted listwise, or whether models are estimated by logit, and are available online at http://www.cambridge.org/9780521871976.

percentile was associated with only a 4 yuan increase in investment, a 3 percent increase in the probability of paved roads, and a 2 percent increase in the probability of paved paths. The size of government assets and per capita tax revenue in 1997 had little effect of any sort on any of the public goods provision outcomes.[50] Nor did the existence of village government enterprises in 1995 have any statistically significant effect on any of the six public goods provision outcomes. The existence of private enterprises in 1995 did have a statistically and substantively significant positive effect on two of the provision outcomes: the probability of paved roads and paths in the village.[51] But this positive effect on roads and paths was *not* accompanied by a significant positive effect on village government investment in public projects. Although private enterprises may be associated with better provision of village public goods, it is not entirely clear that they are associated with better *governmental* provision.

Provincial-Level Variation

Village public goods provision is uncorrelated with economic development at the provincial level as well. Figure 3.2 compares provincial variation in average income per capita to variation in public goods provision. As we can see, Jiangxi has the lowest income per capita, at 1,273 yuan. Shanxi is slightly wealthier with an income per capita of 1,428 yuan, with Fujian following closely at 1,495 yuan. Hebei province is considerably wealthier than the other three with an income per capita of 1,927 yuan. Per capita government investment also follows the same pattern: from lowest to highest, Jiangxi, Shanxi, Fujian, and Hebei.

In terms of the provision of actual public goods, however, the provinces are ranked differently. Hebei is clearly first in terms of income per capita but not in terms of its village roads, schools, or water provision. Fujian has the most villages with paved paths and newer village school facilities

[50] The estimated effect of 1997 government assets on village provision of public goods was statistically insignificant and of a very small magnitude for all six of the outcomes. The estimated effect of 1997 per capita tax revenue on village provision of public goods was negative for four outcomes (investment, paths, classrooms, and newness of school) and statistically significant only for paths. See Appendix Table A3.2.

[51] The estimated effect of village government enterprises in 1995 on village provision of public goods was statistically insignificant and of small magnitude for all six outcomes. The estimated effect of private enterprises in the village in 1995 on village provision of public goods was positive for five out of six outcomes (excepting newness of school) and statistically significant for two (roads and paths). See Appendix Table A3.2.

Village income per capita (yuan)

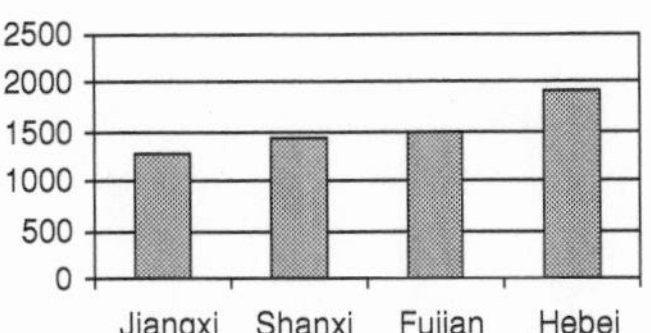

Per capita investment (yuan)

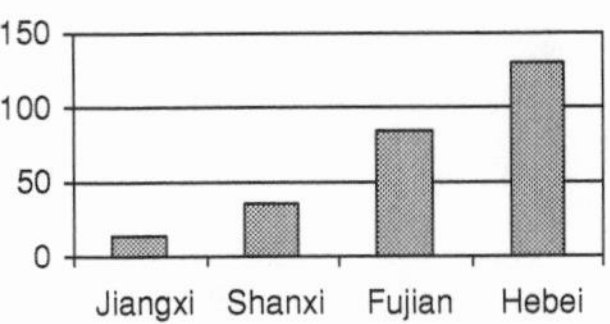

Percentage of villages with paved roads

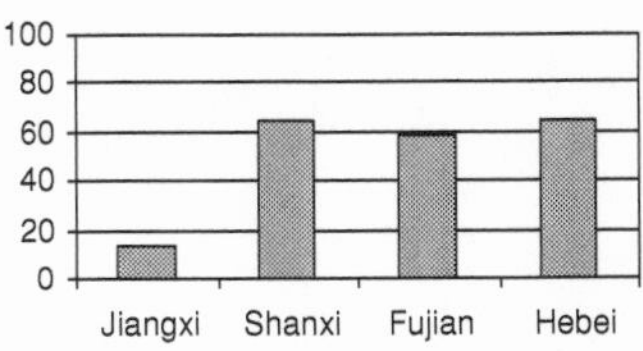

Percentage of villages with paved paths

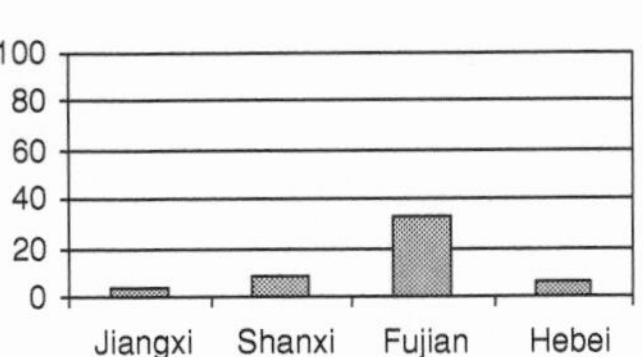

Mean percentage of usable classrooms

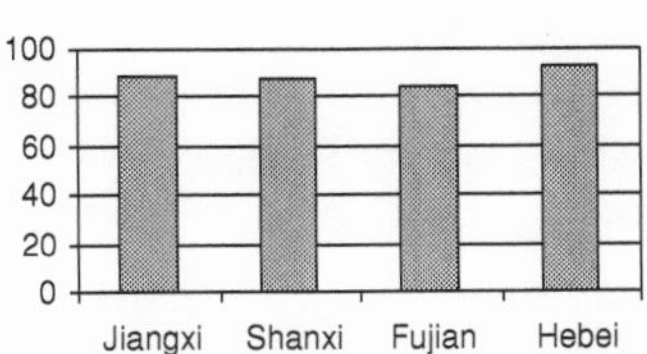

Mean age of village school building (years)

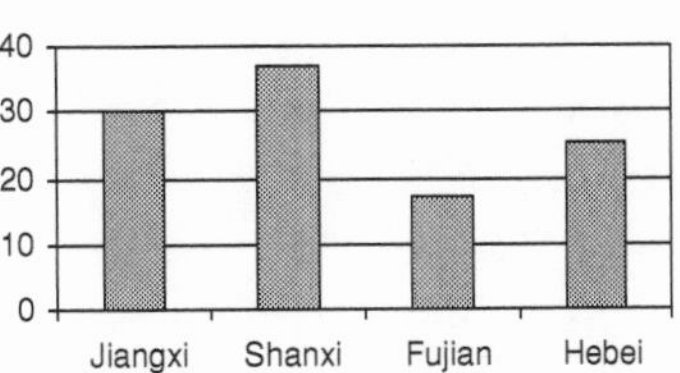

Percentage of villages with running water

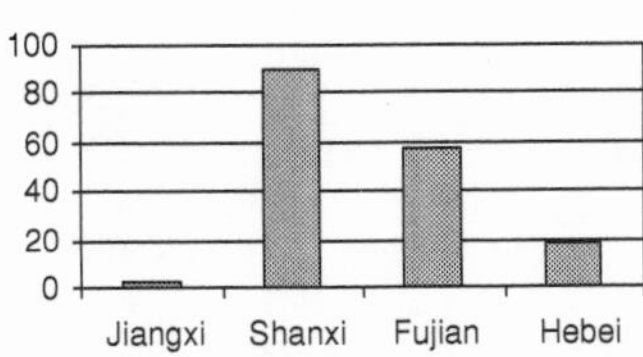

Figure 3.2. Provincial variation in village income per capita and public goods provision outcomes.

on average, while Shanxi has the most villages with running water. Nor does Hebei do markedly better than other provinces in terms of villages with paved roads and the percentage of classrooms usable during rainfall.

Understanding Local Governmental Public Goods Provision in Rural China

The provision of rural roads, schools, and water infrastructure is critical for the quality of people's lives and for long-term development. The quality of local roads affects how quickly villagers can get their goods to market, how easily their children can get to school, how easily they can transport materials for building new houses, and how costly it is to migrate to other areas for better jobs. Rural education remains a primary channel for economic and social mobility. The availability of water has an enormous impact on health, on sanitation, and – because the burden of obtaining water for household use falls disproportionately on women and girls – on the quality of women's lives in particular.[52]

As we can see from the survey data, improving village governmental public goods provision is not simply a matter of promoting economic development. More money does not necessarily translate into better roads, schools, and water. Village governments that lack sufficient funds get little help from higher levels. As a village Party secretary in Fujian noted, "The things that the people care about most, like repairing roads, building schools, the township doesn't care about because there are no benefits (*xiaoyi*), no returns (*huibao*)."[53] Village officials who have sufficient funds do not necessarily have an incentive to invest them in public goods provision. Formal institutions of public administration for ensuring that local officials spend the resources they have on public goods investment are weak. The Maoist legacy of local self-reliance has not only allowed the central government to put off the formalization of a system for rural public goods provision but has also enabled local governments to justify the development of informal institutions for raising revenue. As the previous chapter argued, it is extremely difficult for higher levels to ensure that local government revenue generated

[52] Families who rely on a public standpipe more than a kilometer away typically use less than 10 liters a day, an amount far below the 50 liters per capita per day that the UN has defined as a basic daily water requirement for drinking, sanitation, bathing, cooking, and kitchen needs. United Nations Population Fund, *The State of World Population 2001*, chapter 2. It estimates that sixty-one countries with combined populations of 2.1 billion people in 2000 were using less water than the basic water requirement. The provision of running water has a particularly large impact on women. Women spend almost five times as much time collecting water for family use as men do. Ibid., chapter 2. Improved water supply has been shown to increase the school entrance rates of female children. Asian Development Bank, *A Study on Ways to Support Rural Poverty Reduction Projects*, 5.

[53] Interview with male village Party secretary, western Fujian province, February 22, 2001.

through informal channels is in fact invested in public goods provision. One county official in Shanxi noted: "Villagers want to pay for public projects. The agricultural special products tax or the township levy they might not be willing to pay, but for public projects villagers are willing to shell out this money (*tao zhe ge qian*). They are just afraid that village cadres won't get the projects done or can't do them well or will eat and drink up all the money."[54]

In sum, village officials not only receive little help from higher levels for village public goods provision but also little supervision. Because of these unfunded mandates, higher levels have allowed local officials to extract locally determined fees and levies from villagers but often do not check to see how these revenues are actually used. Given these conditions, why would any local officials in China provide more than the minimal level of public goods needed to avoid outright rebellion? Why is it that some villages actually have relatively good public goods provision? To explain the immense amount of regional variation in village governmental provision of public goods, we have to turn to local factors.

[54] Interview with male county civil affairs bureau official, southern Shanxi province, April 19, 2001.

4

Informal Accountability and the Structure of Solidary Groups

Imagine the mayor of a small town in the United States with only one church. Church suppers and picnics are a major part of the town's social life, and the church hall might be the only place that people can rent or borrow for social gatherings. Even if not everyone goes to church regularly, everyone sees the church as representative of the town community. If the mayor does something exemplary such as bringing down the crime rate by strengthening the police force, the minister might very well mention his good work in front of the congregation during his Sunday sermon. Getting commended by the minister during services can give the mayor a measure of moral standing in addition to whatever status he might already possess as a public official or member of the social elite. The mayor benefits personally from this increased standing. People stop him on the street to praise his work, storekeepers treat him with more deference, the bank is more willing to give him a bigger mortgage, and his children receive more attention at school. Increased moral standing may also make his mayoral tasks easier to carry out. When he tries to implement a difficult state policy – a new requirement, for example, that students of a different ethnic group be bused into the town school – additional standing can help him elicit compliance from his constituents. Moral standing helps the local official by strengthening the belief of citizens in his good intentions. It can make citizens more likely to trust that the mayor is right and defer to his judgment on whether the policy should be implemented. A local official with sufficient moral standing is also more likely to be able to persuade leaders of the community group for help in implementing the difficult state policy. The mayor in our hypothetical town might, for example, ask the minister to talk to particularly stubborn opponents of the policy and draw on his moral authority to convince them to comply.[1]

[1] See Lily L. Tsai, "Solidary Groups, Informal Accountability, and Local Public Goods Provision in Rural China," *American Political Science Review* vol. 101, no. 2 (2007), 355–72.

Informal Accountability and Solidary Groups

Change the town to a village in rural China, and the church to a temple, and we have the real-life example of West Gate village in Fujian province, one of the four villages described in the introduction of the book. West Gate's temple community council organizes a wide variety of religious and community activities for the village. As with temple groups in many other villages, West Gate's temple council evolved out of an informal group of villagers who decided after the start of liberalization in the late 1970s to start rebuilding village temples that were destroyed during the Cultural Revolution. Unlike larger, official Buddhist temples, these small village temples are a part of Chinese folk religion; they house deities that people consider the guardians of their specific village. During festival holidays, temples organize parades, opera performances, and other ritual festivities to pay tribute to the village's guardian deities. Village residents are expected to make donations to the temple to fund these activities. Names of donors and the amount they donated are posted publicly on the temple wall. West Gate's twelve village officials – who, like almost all village officials in China, come from within the village – are not members of the temple leadership but participate in and support the temple's activities as ordinary members. Party secretary Sun, for example, was one of the two top donors, having contributed 2,000 yuan to a recent construction project, about the same as the national average per capita rural income. West Gate's officials are also very responsive to citizen demands for public goods and services. Villagers observed that when the temple council asked village officials to repair the village school or pave one of the village's roads, officials were quick to respond. In exchange, the temple council head noted, the temple gives the village government a good name and "half of the spotlight." The council also helps officials elicit compliance from villagers. Council members have helped mobilize villagers to attend meetings convened by the village government, policed the ban on firecrackers during the New Year holiday, and persuaded villagers to give the village government right of way through their fields for the building of a public drainage channel.

Why do the officials in West Gate or the mayor in our hypothetical American small town work so hard to construct better roads or build up the police force? Why don't they just do the minimum they need to get by and perform just slightly better than the next most likely candidate for office would? One possible answer is that the state holds local officials accountable for performing their duties. But what happens when state institutions are weak and fail to do so? We might still expect the local officials in these two examples to provide public goods because they are upstanding members of their temple or church. If they just did the minimum they needed to get by, they might not get voted out of office, but fellow residents would not look up to them in the same way anymore, and the temple or church leadership would probably be much less inclined to support them in trying to implement difficult state policies.

This chapter is concerned with answering the following question: how can citizens make government officials organize and fund public goods and services when formal institutions of accountability are weak? Public goods provision in general always has a collective action problem with it. Everyone has an incentive to free-ride on the efforts of everyone else. But *governmental* public goods provision has the additional problem of *accountability*. To some extent, this chapter addresses both the collective action problem and the accountability problem, but its main focus is on governmental accountability. In places where democratic institutions are weak, once public funds are in the hands of government officials, how can citizens make sure that officials use these funds to pave roads, build schools, and invest in local public projects?

I propose a model of *informal* accountability. Even when formal accountability is weak, officials may still have a strong incentive to provide public goods when they are subject to obligations and institutions set by social groups. Citizens award officials moral standing when they comply with these informal institutions and take away moral standing when they fail to do so. Moral standing can be a powerful incentive. It not only makes people feel good about themselves, but it can translate into increased economic and social opportunities. Government officials with high moral standing find it easier to elicit citizen compliance with state policies. Regardless of what combination of motivations an official might have, moral standing can be a useful resource.

This chapter has two objectives. The first is to theorize about the model of informal accountability and the conditions that make citizens more likely to reward officials with moral standing for providing public goods. The second is to illustrate how the mechanisms of a model of informal accountability might work empirically by drawing on real-life examples from the context of rural China.

The Benefits of Moral Standing

Moral standing is a type of prestige. Prestige is defined as "the esteem, respect, or approval that is granted by an individual or a collectivity for performances or qualities they consider above the average."[2] Prestige, as William Goode notes, may be granted according to many different types of standards – qualities such as noble birth, musical genius, or membership in a caste, and above-average performance in areas highly valued by a group, such as scoring the most points in a basketball game, founding a successful Internet startup, or finding a cure for cancer. Not all of these standards define who should be considered morally good. Moral standing can be defined as the esteem or respect that is granted for above-average performance of actions that are considered to be morally good. What those specific standards and actions are vary.

Why do people want moral standing? Moral standing can be desirable as both an end and a means. Internally, we want to think of ourselves and for others to think of us as good, not wicked – even if being thought good does not help us to achieve any other purposes. Feeling good about ourselves is an end in itself as psychologists, anthropologists, and sociologists have long studied, and one that economists now refer to as the "warm glow" benefit.[3]

But it can also be very useful to be thought a good person by others. Moral standing can help individuals pursue their own interests. A typical example is provided by Robert Bellah and his colleagues in their description of a local businessman in the United States: "His business success depends on the support of his community. But this support has not been gratuitously given. He has earned it by providing charity to its members. He and other local businessmen do this mainly through 'service clubs' such as the town Rotary Club."[4] Timur Kuran compares the establishment of *waqfs*, or Islamic charitable trusts, by prominent elites to philanthropic donations to universities: "Just as a gift to a modern university affirms its donor's social prominence and civic mindedness, forming a waqf served as a vehicle for achieving status and authority."[5]

Moral standing can also help government officials implement state policies and elicit citizen compliance. In places such as China, where citizen distrust of the state is high and officials either cannot or do not want to use

2 William J. Goode, *The Celebration of Heroes: Prestige as a Control System* (Berkeley: University of California Press, 1979), 7.

3 See James Andreoni, "Giving with Impure Altruism: Applications to Charity and Ricardian Equivalence," *Journal of Political Economy* 97, no. 6 (December 1989), 1447–58.

4 Bellah et al., *Habits of the Heart*, 173.

5 Tim Kuran, "The Provision of Public Goods under Islamic Law," *Law and Society Review* 35, no. 4 (2001), 853.

coercion, this moral standing can be an invaluable political resource that helps them to implement difficult state policies such as tax collection and birth control. "The strongest man," Jean-Jacques Rousseau noted, "is never strong enough to be master all the time, unless he transforms force into right and obedience into duty."[6] High prestige and status in general may also help to some extent in eliciting deference and achieving these objectives, but their utility is limited unless officials can transform their high status into high moral standing. A movie star or successful Internet entrepreneur who becomes a government official may be better able to garner popular support for her policies initially. She may also have an advantage in mobilizing support for policies on which citizens lack a strong opinion. But unless citizens come to respect her as a good government official, they are still likely to put up considerable resistance to a policy that seems to hurt their interests. If she turns out to be corrupt, we are unlikely to comply with policies that do not benefit us no matter how much prestige she has. High status and the deference it elicits can also be domain-specific. We might be willing to defer to the movie star if we are casting a movie but not so willing to comply with her policies on stem cell research. Moral character is less likely to be viewed as domain-specific. We generally assume that the movie star who is a known philanthropist will still be philanthropically minded if she becomes a government official.

Officials who can achieve moral standing and persuade citizens they are motivated by benevolent intentions have a huge advantage in eliciting citizen compliance with state demands. Margaret Levi argues that rulers who "live up to the prevailing norms of fairness" and demonstrate that they are willing "to act for principle and against self-interest" can elicit compliance with taxation and military service more cheaply and effectively than rulers who do not.[7] John Kane elaborates:

> Political agents and institutions must be seen to serve and to stand for *something* apart from themselves, to achieve *something* beyond merely private ends. They must, in other words, establish a moral grounding. This they do by avowing

[6] Jean-Jacques Rousseau, *The Social Contract*, Book 1 Chapter 3 (New York: Penguin Press, 1968), 15.

[7] Margaret Levi, *Of Rule and Revenue* (Berkeley: University of California Press, 1988), 50–3. See also Margaret Levi, *Consent, Dissent, and Patriotism* (New York: Cambridge University Press, 1997). Like Levi, I do not attempt to explain the sources or content of a solidary group's moral norms and ethical standards, but whereas Levi focuses on how normative and ideological convictions affect citizen compliance with state demands, my interest is in how norms and standards can affect governmental accountability and performance.

their service to some set of fundamental values, principles, and goals that find a resonant response in significant numbers of people. When such people judge the agent or institutions to be both faithful and effective in serving those values and goals, they are likely to bestow some quantum of respect and approval that is of great political benefit to the receiver. This quantum is the agent's moral capital.[8]

Empirical studies have also demonstrated the importance of moral standing in eliciting compliance. Survey research carried out by Tom Tyler and Peter Degoey has found that people are more likely to accept the decisions of authorities when they believe that the authorities have benevolent intentions. In fact, confidence in the moral character of authorities seemed to have a more sizable and statistically significant impact on compliance than confidence in their abilities and competence.[9] Martin Daunton has argued that the British state was able to extract higher taxes from citizens than any other European state because politicians successfully persuaded the public that they were "disinterested" and motivated by a sincere interest in the public good.[10]

It is important, however, to note that there is always a fine line between using moral standing that one has already acquired as a political resource and losing moral standing by giving the impression that one is acquiring it *in order to use it as a political resource*. Robert Wuthnow, for example, has noted that lobbying for political measures weakens the spiritual position of churches in the United States.[11]

[8] John Kane, *The Politics of Moral Capital* (Cambridge: Cambridge University Press, 2001), 10.

[9] Tom Tyler, "Trust and Democratic Governance" in *Trust and Governance*, 285.

[10] Martin Daunton, "Trusting Leviathan: British Fiscal Administration from the Napoleonic Wars to the Second World War," in *Trust and Governance*.

[11] R. Wuthnow, *The Restructuring of American Religion* (Princeton: Princeton University Press, 1988), 65. Robert Roy Reed's study of democratization in a Portuguese village shows how civic group leaders lost their moral standing once they became election candidates. Under an authoritarian regime, there was no way for highly respected civic group leaders to translate their moral standing into political power, but with the implementation of democratic reforms in the early 1980s, civic group leaders became the most popular candidates in village elections. Their political successes, however, eroded the ability of community solidary institutions to confer moral standing: "Villagers soon noted the connection between civic and political involvement.... Soon, villagers were saying that the seemingly selfless acts of some volunteers were actually postures calculated for maximum political advantage." Robert Roy Reed, "From Utopian Hopes to Practical Politics: A National Revolution in a Rural Village," *Comparative Studies in Society and History* 37, no. 4 (October 1995), 670–91.

The Awarding of Moral Standing

So when are people more likely to reward officials with moral standing for providing public goods? First, citizens and officials have to share some set of criteria for awarding or withdrawing moral standing. At minimum, these criteria include the standard that contributing to the good of the group deserves moral approval. The larger this shared set of standards for ethically good behavior and the more strongly held these standards are, the more able a group is to award moral standing. Moral standing, like money, is a "shared convention."[12] Standards help to define both acceptable behavior and exemplary behavior.[13] Second, the more we believe that officials share this set of ethical standards and the more we know about whether or not they behave according to these standards, the more likely we are to award them moral standing. Like all forms of prestige, moral standing is dependent on the "verbal information disseminated in the community relating news and approval of an individual's activities."[14]

When are communities most likely to have these conditions? Theories of civil society and social capital highlight the importance of civic participation and associational activity in promoting norms of "civic virtue" or public-spiritedness. When people participate in birdwatching clubs, choral societies, and numerous diverse associations, as Robert Putnam suggests, they get to know a variety of people and learn to cooperate with them.[15] The heart is thus enlarged, as Alexis de Tocqueville noted, and people come to care more and more about the public good.[16] Theories of civil society and social capital do not generally focus on the importance of moral standing as a possible motivation for good governmental performance. Instead,

[12] See Friedrich Kratchowil, "Is the Ship of Culture at Sea or Returning?" in *The Return of Identity and Culture in IR Theory*, ed. Yosef Lapid and Friedrich Kratchowil (Boulder: Lynne Rienner, 1996), 212. See also Rodney Bruce Hall, "Moral Authority as a Power Resource," *International Organization* 51, no. 4 (Autumn 1997), 597. In the words of Philip Pettit, "if there are standards and models in a society that establish what it is to be honorable . . . then even those who are not possessed of such virtue will desire to be thought to have it; they will desire to be regarded as honorable." Philip Pettit, "Republican Theory and Political Trust," in *Trust and Governance*, 306.

[13] Goode uses the term "working ideal" to refer to the standard of performance required for an individual to earn an average amount of prestige and continue to be acceptable in a certain group, and the term "ideal ideal" for a level of performance far above the working ideal. Goode, *The Celebration of Heroes*, 12.

[14] David Riches, "Hunting, Herding, and Potlatching: Towards a Sociological Account of Prestige," *Man* 19, no. 2 (June 1984), 235.

[15] Putnam, *Making Democracy Work*, 90.

[16] Alexis de Tocqueville, *Democracy in America* (New York: Penguin Classics, 2003), 515.

their general line of argument connecting civic virtue to good governance posits that civic participation and civic virtue help people overcome collective action problems and organize into groups that improve their ability to voice their demands in a democratic system. We can, however, reinterpret the importance of civil society and social capital through the model of informal accountability. In societies rich in associational life and social capital, people are likely to share a set of ethical standards that reward generalized reciprocity and contribution to the public good. As fellow members of this community, local officials are likely to share these standards. Since everyone is connected by wide-ranging social networks produced by crosscutting associations, information about the behavior of officials is easily obtainable. Under these circumstances, local officials have more incentive to provide public services than they would otherwise because the community is more likely to award them increased moral standing.

So a vibrant civil society might be one pathway to informal accountability, but what about places without a historical tradition of voluntary associations where the state might discourage or even repress the formation of such associations? I argue that another pathway is also possible. I argue that instead of having many diverse kinds of crosscutting associations, having social groups that are *encompassing*, *embedding*, and *solidary* can also make citizens more likely and able to use moral standing to reward officials for providing public goods.

Encompassing and Embedding Solidary Groups

What do I mean by each of these terms? For the sake of simplicity, I will define encompassing and embedding solidary groups in terms of what Max Weber called "ideal types." In actuality, each of these characteristics varies along a continuum – groups can vary in how solidary they are, how embedding they are, how encompassing they are, and how much of a group they are.

Groups can be defined as collections of individuals that have two characteristics: they are engaged in a mutually oriented activity or set of interconnected activities, and they are required to meet one or more membership criteria in order to enter into group activity. Groups are thus different from crowds, which have no membership criteria though they may be engaging in the same activity; from social categories, which define membership criteria for people who are not necessarily participating together in any activity; from networks, which have no membership criteria and are not necessarily engaged in a mutually oriented activity, although individual members of the network engage in activities with each other; and from corporations, which are defined by collectively owned property rather than joint participation.[17]

Groups are solidary to the extent that membership is based on shared moral obligations and ethical standards.[18] Clans, ethnic groups, philanthropic groups, and fraternal organizations can thus be highly solidary. Religious groups are also highly solidary. As Wuthnow notes, "religions become embodied as moral communities – as networks of deeply felt obligation to one another and to collective rituals and beliefs.... The very beliefs and ideas of which any religion is comprised reflect and dramatize these moral obligations."[19] In solidary groups, members are obligated to

[17] Michel Verdon, "Kinship, Marriage, and the Family: An Operational Approach," *American Journal of Sociology* 86, no. 4 (1981), 796–818.

[18] The term "solidary" has been used in many different ways. The definition used here is perhaps closest to how Theda Skocpol (who brought this term to my attention) uses it to describe fraternal groups in the United States: "Americans were avid participants in 'fellowship associations' – groups emphasizing and expressing solidarity among citizens or among 'brothers' and 'sisters' who see themselves as joined in shared moral understandings." Theda Skocpol, "Voice and Inequality: The Transformation of American Civic Democracy," *Perspective on Politics* 2, no. 1 (2004), 3–20. The definition I use is related to but different from the use of the term "solidary group" to indicate a group that is "tight-knit" or more cohesive (see, for example, Christine Horne, "The Enforcement of Norms: Group Cohesion and Meta-Norms," *Social Psychology Quarterly* 64, no. 3 [2001], 253). Talcott Parsons suggests that solidarity is a matter of how strongly members identify with the group in terms of having a "'deep' motivational 'commitment.'" See Talcott Parsons, "Equality and Inequality in Modern Society," in Edward Laumann, *Social Stratification: Research and Theory for the 1970s* (Indianapolis: Bobbs-Merrill, 1970), 48. These usages conceptualize "solidary groups" as groups with a high degree of "solidarity." Michael Hechter notes that group solidarity is a function of two independent factors: the extensiveness of the group's corporate obligations, and the degree to which individual members actually comply with these obligations. In his words, "solidarity = $f(ab)$, where a = the extensiveness of a group's obligations and b = the rate of members' compliance to them. Groups attain high levels of solidarity when the values of both a and b are relatively high." See Michael Hechter, *Principles of Group Solidarity* (Berkeley: University of California Press, 1987), 18. If we define "solidary groups" as groups with shared moral obligations and ethical standards, it seems reasonable to expect that solidary groups are likely to have a higher level of "solidarity" in this sense than other groups since moral obligations are likely to be more demanding on members as well as more rigorously enforced than other types of obligations. Finally, the definition of "solidary group" that I use also differs from Karl Deutsch's "solidarity-oriented groups," which are distinguished by their primary emphasis on conviviality and enjoyable social relations. See Karl Deutsch, "Equity, Equality, and Need," *Journal of Social Issues* 31, no. 3 (1975), 146–8.

[19] Wuthnow, *The Restructuring of American Religion*, 308.

behave and judged according to the group's standards of what constitutes a good person and a good member – "good" meaning not just what is good for the group but the goodness (versus badness) of human action and character. Members of church congregations feel obligated to contribute something when a donation basket is passed around during services because that is what good congregants are expected to do. Members of clans are expected to and commended for siding with fellow clan members in disputes with outsiders.

Other groups are considerably less solidary. The set of ethical standards shared by groups such as industry associations, which are based primarily on shared economic interests, or groups based on recreation and conviviality such as book clubs and choral societies may be very small and not very strongly held. Members of industry associations and book clubs may have professional or social obligations – they may be expected to show up to meetings on time, practice before rehearsal, and so forth – but the sanctions for failing to meet these obligations are more likely to be minor. These kinds of groups may look favorably upon members who do more than their fair share – a company in a trade association who volunteers to do extra research on a subject or a book club member that always brings cookies for everyone – but the moral approval that these members earn is also likely to be minor.

Note also that a group whose membership is based on the acceptance and observance of shared ethical standards is different from a category or network of people who happen to share ethical standards. People who share a set of ethical standards can of course confer moral standing on whomever they observe to be meeting or exceeding those standards. But the conferral of moral standing within a solidary *group* is more likely and more effective. Solidary group members are likely to care more about their shared ethical standards since they deliberately made a decision to join a group based on these standards.

Not only do solidary groups set ethical standards for awarding moral obligation, but group activities provide opportunities for individual members to show that they accept and observe these standards. In rural China, representatives from every household are expected to attend group rituals of respect for shared ancestors. Members of philanthropic groups are expected to organize and work at fundraisers. Churches hold services. Group activities make it easier to publicize exemplary behavior widely and obtain moral approval broadly. Compare, for example, members in an environmental conservation group to people who care about environmental conservation but do not belong to a group. Members in the group who write letters to their congressional representatives on conservation are more likely to obtain moral approval than individuals who are not in a group and do the same. Members in the group are more likely to meet regularly and tell each other about their activities. Individuals who care about conservation but do not belong to a group may also express approval of someone who has written a similar letter. But people are simply less likely to know about the action and less likely to prioritize such behavior. For moral standing to be conferred on an individual, both the individual's actions and acceptance of shared standards have to be, as Michael Chwe puts it, "common knowledge."[20] People have to know not only that the individual performed activities that merit approval but that he performed these activities because of shared ethical standards, not for some ulterior motive or by coincidence.

So far we have discussed how solidary groups enable people to acquire moral standing and how moral standing can be a valuable resource. But not all solidary groups enable citizens to use moral standing as an incentive specifically for public goods provision. The more that a solidary group *encompasses* all the citizens in a particular local governmental jurisdiction and the more that a solidary group *embeds* local officials in its activities, the more effective it is at enabling citizens to hold local officials accountable for public goods provision. When the boundaries of a solidary group overlap with local administrative boundaries, embedded officials have a strong *social* obligation to contribute to the good of the group. But because the group and the public are the same in this case, officials have an extra incentive to provide public goods. People in localities with encompassing and embedding solidary groups are likely to value public goods provision more highly than people in localities without these groups. Officials in localities with encompassing and embedding solidary groups are thus likely to earn more moral standing for providing public goods (and to suffer more severe social sanctions for not doing so) than officials in localities without these groups. Examples of such groups might include parish churches in

[20] In game theoretic terms, getting people to participate in the awarding of moral standing is a coordination problem since people want to participate in the awarding of moral standing only if everyone else does too. See Michael Chwe, *Rational Ritual: Culture, Coordination, and Common Knowledge* (Princeton: Princeton University Press, 2003).

nineteenth-century England,[21] local fiesta organizations in Latin America,[22] and chieftaincies that overlap with district and regional boundaries in Africa.[23]

What happens when solidary groups are less than perfectly encompassing or embedding? As solidary groups move further away from perfectly overlapping with local administrative boundaries and encompassing all the citizens in a local jurisdiction, embedded local officials are still likely to provide collective goods for the group to which they belong. When the group encompasses most of the citizens in a jurisdiction, the collective goods that officials provide are still likely to be public goods. Groups that have members who are geographically scattered across the area of the jurisdiction may also encourage embedded officials to provide public goods. But if group boundaries clearly encapsulate only a subset of the locality's population, collective goods provided by officials for the group are much less likely to be public goods for all of their constituents. In villages with multiple lineage groups, for example, an official is more likely to pave the section of road or construct running water infrastructure where his fellow lineage members reside but less likely to do so for the entire village, all other things being equal.

Conversely, as solidary groups move further away from completely embedding local officials as full members of the group, citizens are likely to be less confident that officials actually share the group's ethical standards and less likely to award them moral standing. The less often the small town mayor goes to church, participates in church activities, and identifies himself as a staunch member of the church, the less likely he is to be commended by the pastor and the less incentive he will have, all other things being equal, to provide public services. Even if a non-churchgoing mayor does organize a new road-paving project, citizens are more likely to wonder if he has ulterior motives for doing so, such as kickbacks from construction contracts or promotion to a higher position. Under these conditions, the town church is not embedding but still encompassing. Encompassing solidary groups that are not embedding may still be quite good at organizing

[21] Robert Morris, "Structure, Culture, and Society in British Towns," in *The Cambridge Urban History of Britain*, ed. Martin Daunton (Cambridge: Cambridge University Press, 2000).

[22] Jennifer Burrell, "Migration and Transnationalization of Fiesta Customs in Todos Santos Cuchumatan, Guatemala," *Latin American Perspectives* 32, no. 44: 5, 12–32.

[23] Pierre Engelbert, "Born again Buganda or the Limits of Traditional Re-Surgence in Africa," *Journal of Modern African Studies* 40, no. 3 (2002), 345–68.

members to fund and organize public projects independently of the town government. In a democratic system, such groups might also be good at mobilizing members to vote a poorly performing official out of office. In places where democratic institutions are weak, however, they may have much less impact on *governmental* public goods provision.

Moral Standing as Political Leverage

So far we have talked mostly about conferring moral standing on local officials as an incentive for providing public goods and services. But when people share a set of ethical standards and moral obligations that they hold strongly, as they do in solidary groups, ordinary citizens can also earn moral standing that gives them leverage over government officials. Individuals who earn moral standing can exert leverage over officials in several ways. First, individuals and social groups with high moral standing can help government officials elicit compliance by vouching for their credibility and good intentions.[24] Second, social actors can use their moral standing to mobilize other citizens to comply with state tasks, which again provides a positive inducement for officials to respond to citizen demands for public goods provision. Third, social actors can also use their moral standing to mobilize others for concerted noncompliance as a negative sanction, thereby giving political force to what James Scott calls the "weapons of the weak" – tactics such as foot dragging, dissimulation, false compliance, slander, sabotage, and so forth.[25] Noncompliance, as Levi also notes, "is a power resource in the political struggle between the relatively weak and those who exercise authority over them." [26]

[24] Actors with high moral standing can also lose their standing by vouching for government officials who are perceived to be immoral. David Corbin discusses the example of Appalachian miners in the early twentieth century seeking to unionize. When preachers and clergy from company-controlled churches sided with the mining companies, miners disrupted services in company churches and discredited company ministers. In the words of one miner, "We are beginning to see the light for ourselves and realize that the company preachers are selling us out to the bosses for a mere mess of the porage [sic]." David Corbin, *Life, Work, and Rebellion in the Coal Fields: The Southern West Virginia Miners, 1880–1922* (Champaign: University of Illinois Press, 1981), cited in Dwight B. Billings, "Religion as Opposition: A Gramscian Analysis," *American Journal of Sociology* 96, no. 1 (July 1990), 17.

[25] James C. Scott, *Weapons of the Weak: Everyday Forms of Peasant Resistance* (New Haven: Yale University Press, 1985), xvi.

[26] Levi, *Consent, Dissent, and Patriotism*, 215.

Solidary Groups in Rural China

This chapter has thus far focused on providing a purely theoretical account of the model of informal accountability. The model has identified mechanisms that make moral standing an important incentive and resource and discussed the kinds of social groups and institutions that can provide a system of informal governmental accountability.

In this section, we turn to the chapter's second objective and use empirical examples from the context of rural China to illustrate how the model's causal mechanisms work in practice. This section also provides some historical background for the following two chapters, which use qualitative and quantitative analysis to evaluate hypotheses derived from the model.

Solidary Groups in the Early Twentieth Century

Rural China has a long history of vibrant solidary groups. For centuries before the Communist period, ordinary villagers had participated in lineages, secret societies, fraternal and sororal groups, rotating credit associations, temples to local guardian deities as well as officially sanctioned religion, Christian churches, and all manner of combinations thereof.[27] In many places, temples for local guardian deities specific to each village were the focus of community life.[28] In contrast to official Buddhist and Taoist temples, these village folk temples lacked priests or clergy and were instead run by community councils of local elites who typically had political and fiscal authority to collect funds from villagers, manage the temple's assets and land, and, sometimes, organize local defense. Villagers congregated on holidays for festivals and rituals designed to pay tribute to the patron deities specific to their village: "Patterns of reciprocal feasting at every

27 See, for example, the classic anthropological studies of Arthur H. Smith, *Village Life in China* (New York: Kegan Paul, 2002), 136–45; Morton Fried, *The Fabric of Chinese Society* (New York: Praeger, 1953); Francis Hsu, *Clan, Caste, Club* (Princeton: Van Nostrand, 1963); Martin Yan, *A Chinese Village* (London: K. Paul, Trench, Trubner, 1948); C. K. Yang, *Religion in Chinese Society: A Study of Contemporary Social Functions of Religion and Some of Their Historical Factors* (Berkeley: University of California Press, 1961); Xiaotong Fei, *Chinese Village Close-Up (Sanfang Jiangcun)* (Beijing: New World Press (*Xinshijie chubanshe*), 1983).

28 On popular religion in China, see P. Steven Sangren, *History and Magical Power in a Chinese Community* (Stanford: Stanford University Press, 1987); R. P. Weller, *Unities and Diversities in Chinese Religion* (Seattle: University of Washington Press, 1987); Duara, *Culture, Power, and the State*.

important ritual further brought people together."[29] Lineages were also central in many places, organizing religious rites to honor shared ancestors and reinforce kinship-based obligations.[30] Some but not all lineages had collective land holdings.[31] In many places, lineages rather than village temples provided the basic framework structuring local social and political interaction.[32] Lineages could bring together thousands of people, and when they did, "they formed a kind of tie that went far beyond family, even though it remained rooted in kinship."[33] Secret societies and fraternal groups organized by groups of friends who felt particularly close drew on the supernatural powers of deities to sanctify their bonds as sworn brothers or sisters and to provide punishment for those who violated these bonds of loyalty. Throughout the imperial period, the state struggled to control these local solidary groups, but complete control always eluded it. Particular groups varied over time, with new ones emerging and others disappearing completely: "Sacrifices were offered in decreasing regularity and communal interest in maintenance of the temple waned after several generations, until the cult finally disappeared, and its role was replaced by a new cult."[34]

In all of these solidary groups, members shared a set of ethical standards and a strong moral obligation to contribute to the good of the group. The content of their ideologies as well as the structure of their group, however, varied widely. Some groups embedded local officials. Others did not. In village temples deifying local heroes, "formal worship was undertaken at the spring and autumn sacrifices, at which local government officials or

[29] See Robert P. Weller, *Alternate Civilities: Democracy and Culture in China and Taiwan* (Nashville: Westview Press, 2001), 31.

[30] See Fried, *The Fabric of Chinese Society*, 93–4. See also Myron Cohen, "Lineage Organization in North China," *Journal of Asian Studies* 49, no. 3 (August 1990), 509–34; P. Steven Sangren, "Traditional Chinese Corporations: Beyond Kinship," *Journal of Asian Studies* 43, no. 3 (May 1984), 391–415; Morton Fried, "The Classification of Corporate Unilineal Descent Groups," *Journal of the Royal Anthropological Institute of Great Britain and Ireland* 87, no. 1 (1957), 1–29.

[31] See James Watson, *Emigration and the Chinese Lineage* (Berkeley: University of California Press, 1975); James Watson, "Chinese Kinship Reconsidered: Anthropological Perspectives on Historical Research," *China Quarterly*, no. 92 (December 1982), 589–622.

[32] Duara identifies two ideal types of villages in the early twentieth century: the lineage-community type and the religious-community type. He notes, however, that in practice elements of one can be found in examples of the other. See Duara, *Culture, Power, and the State*.

[33] See Weller, *Alternate Civilities*, 32.

[34] See Yang, *Religion in Chinese Society*, 172–3.

community leaders or both would officiate and the local population would participate as spectators."[35] In other cases, when the deities were not officially sanctioned by the state, local officials tried to avoid embeddedness, although they were not always successful: "The official was forbidden by law to worship any deity not on the official lists, but he risked widespread popular disapproval and disturbance if he refused."[36] The prevalence of embedded solidary groups varied over time as well. As the state weakened in the late Qing and Republican periods, political leadership in villages became increasingly less embedded and more dominated by what Prasenjit Duara calls "entrepreneurial state brokers" who simply saw political office as a means of entrepreneurial gain and were not embedded in community solidary institutions.[37] In places where solidary institutions continued to be strong, these institutions substituted for the state and "avert[ed] the collapse of the moral order at a time when there was a high degree of instability in government and law."[38]

Solidary groups in the pre-Communist period also varied in whether they were encompassing. Lineages and village folk temples were based in particular localities and communal identities, but not all of these groups were encompassing in the sense of having boundaries that overlapped with the political boundaries of the local administrative unit set by the state. Duara distinguishes between four categories of rural religious organizations in the early twentieth century: ones involving only a segment of the village population ("village-bound"); ones involving members of the village as well as people outside the village ("supra-village"); ones including everyone who could be defined as a village member or what we would call encompassing ("ascriptive village associations"); and ones uniting several "ascriptive" village associations into, for example, federated community self-defense associations ("supra-village ascriptive associations").[39] Still other groups were not necessarily locally rooted at all. Secret societies and fraternal groups traveled along rivers and later railroads looking for new

[35] See ibid., 167. "Involvement in religious activities, such as worshiping the gods or engaging in temple building and repair, was a legitimate area of elite responsibility in Confucian China," Duara notes, and the "practice of officials' revering the gods as part of their duties" was common. Duara, *Culture, Power, and the State*, 132.

[36] Emily Ahern, *Chinese Ritual and Politics* (New York: Cambridge University Press, 1981), 84.

[37] Duara, *Culture, Power, and the State.*

[38] Yang, *Religion in Chinese Society*, 375.

[39] Duara, *Culture, Power, and the State*, 120–32.

members and disciples or sometimes for smuggling and banditry opportunities.[40] In places such as the southern coast, migration to cities and even other countries expanded lineage ties into common surname associations.[41]

Solidary Groups in the Maoist Period

Even before the Communist Party came to power, the state had already started trying to suppress popular folk religion as part of its modernization efforts. The late imperial state embarked on campaigns to convert temples into schools. The Nationalists passed a directive in 1928 banning village temples. This order was never enforced successfully, but the Nationalist-controlled government was effective in confiscating the assets of numerous temples to supplement its revenue.[42]

When the Communist Party took over in 1949, its goal was to reinvent and revolutionize all aspects of society. All assets were to be collectively owned by the people, and everyone was to take active part in the building of the new society. Communist ideology demanded from the individual "unconditional surrender of all his personal concerns," which naturally implied the destruction of existing communal obligations.[43] Personal loyalties were to be replaced with a politicized and generic "comradeship," and community solidary groups were to be replaced with the exclusive solidary group of "the people" in which individuals were identical and undifferentiated.[44]

At first, the new state tried to discourage popular religion by using anti-superstition propaganda campaigns and taxes on "superstitious commodities" such as incense sticks and candles. Villagers were encouraged to make claims on lands held in ancestral trusts to help dismantle lineage organizations.[45] Temple property was appropriated to fund the new peasant associations organized by the Party, and temple buildings were taken over as

40 See Elizabeth J. Perry, *Rebels and Revolutionaries in North China, 1845–1945* (Stanford: Stanford University Press, 1980). See also Weller, *Alternate Civilities*, 21–31.

41 Ibid., 32.

42 Yang, *Religion in Chinese Society*, 375.

43 Ibid., 384.

44 Richard Madsen, *Morality and Power in a Chinese Village* (Berkeley: University of California Press, 1984), 181–7. See also Weller, *Alternate Civilities*, 54–5.

45 Helen Siu, *Agents and Victims in South China: Accomplices in Rural Revolution* (New Haven: Yale University Press, 1989), 128–30.

their offices. As the state consolidated its power, its strategies became more coercive.[46] Land reform campaigns between 1950 and 1952 closed all rural churches.[47] Youths in particular were encouraged to smash local religious shrines and statues. During the radical periods of the Great Leap Forward and the Cultural Revolution, antireligious riots and other violent measures became more common. Ancestral tablets and figures of local deities were destroyed. Temples and lineage halls were turned into schools, granaries, or even barns and pigsties.[48]

The Communist state's control over rural society far exceeded the Republican and imperial states. Its reach was not always uniformly distributed, but in most places the state succeeded in eliminating public activities by unsanctioned groups, and solidary groups such as lineages and village temple groups faded from the associational landscape. Any local religious and social institutions that continued to operate in more peripheral areas went underground, eschewing political involvement and often disassembling into individual and household-based activities. Interestingly, some of the ritual forms used by traditional solidary groups remained but became filled with different ideological content. Villagers, for example, continued to maintain household shrines but replaced their ancestral tablets and pictures of deities with pictures of Mao and other top leaders.[49] Some of the social connections and networks created by the solidary groups of the pre-Communist period may have survived informally, but more research is needed in this area. What is clear is that informal ties and personal networks continued to be important. In the countryside, scarce resources in the planned economy encouraged the development of informal clientelist

46 Donald MacInnis, *Religious Policy and Practice in Communist China* (New York: Macmillan, 1972); Yang, *Religion in Chinese Society*, 389, 391–2; Jasper Becker, *Hungry Ghosts: Mao's Secret Famine* (New York: Henry Holt, 1998), 51. See also Anita Chan, Richard Madsen, and Jonathan Unger, *Chen Village under Mao and Deng* (Berkeley: University of California Press, 1992), 88–90.

47 M. Searle Bates, "Churches and Christians in China, 1950–1967: Fragments of Understanding," *Pacific Affairs* 41, no. 2 (Summer 1968), 200. On the Chinese Communist Party's cooptation of the Chinese Catholic Church, see Richard Madsen, *China's Catholics: Tragedy and Hope in an Emerging Civil Society* (Berkeley: University of California Press, 1998), 34–9. Suppression campaigns against sects and secret societies were also carried out, although not without sometimes violent resistance. See Elizabeth Perry, "Rural Violence in Socialist China," *China Quarterly*, no. 103 (1985), 416–17.

48 See, for example, G. Ruf, *Cadres and Kin: Making a Socialist Village in West China, 1921–1991* (Stanford: Stanford University Press, 1998), 84–6.

49 See Ahern, *Chinese Ritual and Politics*, 107–8.

ties between farmers and local officials as well as more generalized networks of horizontal reciprocity.[50]

Solidary Groups and Rural Governance in the Reform Period

In the late 1970s, economic and political liberalization triggered a groundswell in the reopening of local festivals and the reconstruction of village solidary groups such as lineages, temples, and churches.[51] Both the case study and survey data from my research suggest that these kinds of community solidary groups were more likely to appear in villages that had a legacy of such groups from before 1949, but by no means did solidary groups reappear in every village that had had a solidary group in the pre-Communist period. Moreover, solidary groups sometimes also emerged in villages that had not had them in the pre-Communist period.

Interviews with villagers suggest that the revival of solidary groups was to a large extent contingent on whether social entrepreneurs happened to emerge in the village – people who were interested in reviving the group and skilled and respected enough to mobilize an initial project. In the survey, villages in Jiangxi and Fujian provinces were more likely than villages in Shanxi and Hebei to have village temple and lineage groups in the reform period, but otherwise the creation or re-creation of these groups seemed to be random. Data from the 2001 survey do not show any correlation between the existence of one of these groups in the reform period and the level of economic development as measured by village income per capita, the distance of the village from the county town, the number of natural villages, or whether the village was located in a mountainous or flat area. The probability of a solidary group was higher – but only minutely so – in villages with more people.

The solidary groups that have been organized after the start of reforms have much in common with solidary groups from the pre-Communist period. Village temple and lineage groups again organize many of the same social, religious, and welfare provision activities, and they are still rooted in particular localities and communal identities. Fairs and festivals take place again on important holidays. Villagers gather for collective rituals and banquets. Groups collect donations from members for temple and

[50] Oi, *State and Peasant in Contemporary China*; Mayfair Mei-hui Yang, *Gifts, Favors, and Banquets: The Art of Social Relationships in China* (Ithaca: Cornell University Press, 1994).

[51] See, for example, Chan et al., *Chen Village under Mao and Deng*, 323–7.

lineage hall reconstruction as well as other projects ranging from ritual opera performances and basketball tournaments to road paving and educational scholarships for members. As in the pre-Communist period, groups garner widespread participation and support from villagers, including village officials.

One significant difference between solidary groups now and solidary groups in the pre-Communist period lies in their relationship to the state. In the pre-Communist period, the state actively sought to integrate local community solidary institutions into part of their ruling apparatus and system of legitimation. Although tension always existed between the official state religion and popular folk religion, the two could also be complementary. Many local deities were considered deified celestial officials integrated with living government officials into a single cosmic bureaucracy. In the contemporary period, the state still officially frowns upon folk religion and lineage activity as "feudal superstition." Its current approach is to tolerate the existence of these groups as long as they confine their activities within the boundaries of the village.

This approach has had several effects on contemporary rural solidary groups. Rural solidary groups are now almost all either villagewide groups or subvillage groups. Supravillage groups drawing on members from multiple villages are very rare unless they are officially registered and sponsored.[52] Another consequence of state disapproval is that village officials are more likely to participate in contemporary solidary groups as ordinary members rather than as group leaders, especially for temple groups. For village churches, state disapproval is even stronger. While churches are often encompassing, they are almost never embedding since the state expressly forbids Party officials from participating. Underground "household churches," which are not sanctioned by the state, also operate in many areas, but data on these groups are extremely difficult to obtain. Underground churches are also less relevant to this study because they are rarely encompassing and embedding.[53]

[52] Of course, supravillage *networks* based on lineage and religion still exist and constitute foundations for the mobilization of social protest. See Perry, "Rural Violence in Socialist China," 414–40. These networks, however, rarely constitute groups in the sense of organizing regular activities.

[53] As with village temples, liberalization provided an opening for the re-establishment of church institutions, but the state expends enormous effort to regulate their activities. Government figures report that the number of Christians participating in state-regulated churches grew from 3 million in 1982 to 7 or 8 million in 1994. Unofficial and illicit

Contemporary village solidary groups also differ from their predecessors in that few own any collective land or assets other than their hall of worship.[54] The link between the leadership of solidary groups and a landed gentry class has also been broken. Group leaders in the places I visited included people with a variety of backgrounds – mostly men but sometimes women, farmers and entrepreneurs, wealthy as well as more ordinary individuals. Temple groups rarely had village officials among their leadership since the state continues to discourage active promotion of "feudal superstitious activities," although village officials almost always participated in the group's activities as ordinary members. Lineage groups were more likely to have village officials as leaders since lineage activity is not considered religious. Most solidary group leaders were, however, somewhat older, at least in their forties, no doubt because younger people rarely achieve the high degree of respect and deference needed to mobilize the community for collective endeavors.

De-collectivization and liberalization in the late 1970s and early 1980s also led to dramatic changes in rural governance. Officials in villages with profitable collective industrial sectors – rural enterprises owned and operated by the village government – retained control over valuable resources such as jobs, access to investment, and information about markets. But in villages without collective industry – that is, in most of China's villages – there was now little reason for people to construct and maintain good relations with village officials. The resources and life opportunities that local officials had once controlled gradually became available through other channels such as the market. Both villagers and rural officials, as Richard Latham has reported, saw de-collectivization and the implementation of the household responsibility system as eliminating the need for village officials and village government. Many positions were eliminated. Village officials lost much of their prestige and political advantage.[55] Fiscal and administrative

underground "house churches" have also mushroomed, and one 1994 report estimated the total number of Christians at around 50 million. Yang, *Calamity and Reform*, 200.

[54] On lineages as corporate landholding groups, see Maurice Freedman, *Lineage Organization in Southeastern China* (Oxfordshire: Berg, 2004); David Faure, *Structure of Chinese Rural Society* (New York: Oxford University Press, 1986); Patricia Ebrey and James Watson, *Kinship Organization in Late Imperial China* (Berkeley: University of California Press, 1986); Watson, "Chinese Kinship Reconsidered," 589–622. On the relationship between lineages and land, see David Faure and Helen Siu, eds., *Down to Earth: The Territorial Bond in South China* (Stanford: Stanford University Press, 1995).

[55] See Richard Latham, "Rural Reforms and Grassroots Cadres," in *The Political Economy of Reform in Post-Mao China*, ed. Elizabeth Perry and Christine Wong (Cambridge: Harvard

decentralization (see Chapters 2 and 3) deprived these officials of resources from above but made them almost solely responsible for implementing state directives such as birth control and state tax collection and for funding and organizing village public projects. Even when officials in these villages wanted to organize public projects, such as road building, they often lacked the necessary resources and cooperation from villagers, many of whom had come to look upon them as parasitic.[56]

Moral Standing as a Political Resource for Local Officials

Under these conditions, the moral standing conferred by solidary groups can be an important resource for officials who have lost many of their other political and economic resources. China has a long history of government officials using moral standing to elicit compliance with their decisions and state policies: "The state was the central power in Chinese society from the start, and exemplary behavior, rites, morality, and indoctrinations have always been considered in China as a means of government."[57] Opportunities to earn moral authority became all the more valuable when villagers began to question the legitimacy of village government officials. The main challenge facing local officials was to identify a way of reestablishing a sense of obligation toward the state, or at least toward agents of the state.

Those who are able to accomplish this arduous task often rely on tactics of moral exemplarity and participation in solidary activities in order to regain the confidence of villagers and to signal their own commitment to community norms and obligations. In one Shanxi village, for example, when 80 percent of households refused to pay village taxes due to missing account books and mismanagement of public funds by officials previously in power, the new Party secretary and accountant were able to recover some authority by paying the back wages owed to village teachers out of their own pockets.[58] In another village, officials gave up their own wages

University Press, 1985), 160; John P. Burns, *Political Participation in Rural China* (Berkeley: University of California Press, 1988). See also Minxin Pei, *From Reform to Revolution: The Demise of Communism in China and the Soviet Union* (Cambridge: Harvard University Press, 1994), 135.

56 Kevin O'Brien, "Implementing Political Reform in China's Villages," *Australian Journal of Chinese Affairs*, no. 32 (July 1994), 39.

57 Stuart Schram, *The Scope of State Power* (London: School of Oriental and African Studies, 1985).

58 Interviews with village accountant and village Party secretary, southwestern Shanxi, July 26, 2001.

in order to fund village projects. Another common tactic was for village officials to use their own personal connections and risk their own reputations in order to secure funding for public projects from higher levels of government.[59]

The Case of Chestnut Village Officials who participate in solidary groups are better able to maintain villager confidence in government and obtain compliance with government regulations. Chestnut Village in Hebei province is an interesting success story in this respect. Chestnut Village's Party secretary Sun, one of only four female Party secretaries in the county, is an active member of the village's fan dance group, which along with several other performance groups make up the sixty members of the village's performance association, which is run by three managers. Practically all of the village's households make an annual donation to the council, which is typically between 2 and 100 yuan. Sun does not join the fan dance group in their performances at regional temple fairs since the Party officially discourages these activities, but she frequently rehearses with them and helps them raise funds. She takes obvious pleasure in dancing with the village group, acknowledging modestly that she has a terrible singing voice but can hold up her role in fan dances. When the performance association was reestablished around 1990, it focused mostly on a traditional form of performance involving stilts (*cai gaojiao*). In recent years, however, Sun has encouraged the group to change its focus to dancing, which is easier, to maximize participation and include village children who want to participate but are too young for stilts.

Party Secretary Sun's participation allows her to signal solidarity with ordinary villagers and acceptance of the village's moral standards. She comments, "In order to be a cadre, it's necessary to be the same as all the other households (*zuoganbu bixu gen jiaohu yiqi yang de*)."[60] Her participation gives her standing that she can use in negotiating with villagers and enforcing government decisions. During the last land reallocation, for example, Sun was responsible for persuading villagers to return all their land back to the village government and negotiating a fair plan for redistributing the land. Households that had become larger through marriage or births would receive more than they had previously, whereas households that had become smaller would receive less.

[59] Interview with female villager, southern Jiangxi province, February 7, 2001.
[60] Interview with female village Party secretary, eastern Hebei province, May 1, 2002.

Needless to say, land reallocations are some of the most contentious, complex tasks for which village governments take responsibility. Villagers with higher-quality land or who had invested in planting chestnut trees on their land were naturally unwilling to return their land for redistribution. The township had in fact removed the previous Party secretary from office for putting off the village's land distribution repeatedly. As one of the villagers with better land, the previous Party secretary himself had been unwilling to give up his current holdings. To jump-start the land redistribution, Party Secretary Sun decided to set an example for villagers to follow by being the first to return the land assigned to her daughter who, it could be argued, was no longer entitled to it as she had moved to the county town. At first her daughter and husband tried to convince her not to give the land back, as the daughter's move might very well turn out to be temporary. Interestingly, Sun then recruited friends to pressure her daughter and husband to agree, which they eventually did. Her moral standing in the village and her reputation as a well-intentioned and responsible member of the community shamed everyone else into complying. Sun commented, "Leading the way placated all the villagers below me (*Wo xian daitou rang xiamian de xing dou ping xia*)." (Literally translated, the Party secretary "took the lead, which calmed down the emotions of all the villagers below," who, it is implied, were primed to defend their interests and battle anyone threatening these interests.) By demonstrating her commitment to the community's solidary norms and moral obligations, and going above and beyond her expected contribution to the good of the community, the Party secretary earned a large amount of moral standing with villagers, which she was able to parlay into tactics of moral exemplarity that shamed or obligated villagers to follow suit.

The Case of Tang Gully Village Tang Gully village provides another example where the village's encompassing and embedding solidary group enables village officials to earn moral standing, which then allows them to elicit deference and compliance from villagers with state tasks. Villager Li, a confident and funny woman of about forty, has participated in the village's festival performance group since she was a child. Li's family has been prominent in both the village's solidary group and in village government. Her father was a brigade official during the Maoist period, and her grandmother was a core member of the village opera troupe in the 1930s and 1940s. A box of the hand-embroidered costumes that her grandmother made over fifty years ago is still carefully stored along with newer costumes in the village government building for the current troupe's members to use.

In 1994 Li became chair of the village's state-mandated women's association. In most places, women's association chairs are not formally members of the village government, but the status of this position varies from place to place, and in Tang Gully, Li is one of the village's four government officials who draw a full salary and make village policy. Her responsibilities extend beyond birth control. In one recent village government project, she supervised the terracing of unused village land on the hillside and its conversion into lucrative groves of chestnut trees.

Under Li's direction, Tang Gully has acquired a countywide reputation for its outstanding enforcement of birth control policy and implementation of women's health education. Li modestly claims that this success cannot be attributed to her and belongs more to the eight or nine women from the village's performance group whom she recruited into the women's association. They explained that when Li asked them to join, they felt obligated to accept. Turning Li down, they felt, would have been considered disrespectful, not only by her but by the rest of the village since Li was so highly regarded. In the words of one woman, "we were too embarrassed (*bu hao yisi*) not to do it."[61] After joining, these villagers drew on their own moral standing in the village to elicit compliance with birth control and to mobilize women to attend meetings that disseminated information about women's health. Interestingly, the villagers have also imported activities from the village performance group into the women's association. The day I arrived in the village, for example, Li and the women's association members were rehearsing, with a great deal of mirth and camaraderie, a type of comedy skit (*xiaopin*) traditionally performed at temple fairs that they had converted into a skit encouraging villagers to follow the birth control policy. Similar skits were also performed in Chestnut Village, where the birth control workers reported that they performed skits to make fun of "out-of-quota birthing guerrillas" (*chaosheng youji dui*), villagers who go into hiding in order to give illegal out-of-quota births.

Participation in solidary group activities allows village officials to signal that they are willing to abide by the same social norms and moral standards as other villagers and to develop strong relationships with villagers that are

[61] Interview with female villager, eastern Hebei province, May 2, 2002.

overlaid with personal feeling. When these relationships are successfully developed, it is much more likely that a villager will acquiesce when an official frames a request for compliance with tax collection or birth control.

Moral Standing as a Political Resource for Citizens

The moral standing provided by solidary groups can also improve village government accountability by being an important source of soft power for ordinary villagers as well as village officials. Leaders of solidary groups are often called on to mediate disputes and solve village problems. In one Fujian village, for example, teenagers were vandalizing a factory owned by outsiders, so the factory manager went to the village community temple council for help. The council head recruited fellow council members as well as a number of other villagers with high moral standing to visit the house of each teenager and "pat them on the shoulder" *(paipai jianbang)*, or use their authority to elicit obedience and better behavior. The council head explained, "I used *guanxi* to solve the problem (*guanxi* is sometimes translated as "personal connections," but in this case refers to the ethics of personal relationships). They listened to us because they didn't dare embarrass us (*diu women de mianzi*, literally "lose our face") or offend me *(bugan dezui wo)*." [62] By connecting their bad behavior to the reputation of the council members and the village community as a whole, the teenagers were shamed and pressured into behaving. By agreeing to mediate, the council head in a sense loaned his moral standing to the factory manager, who had no authority over the teenagers. Any subsequent vandalism or bad behavior would publicly embarrass both the council head personally and the village community collectively. By risking their personal reputations or "face" to preserve good relations with local businesses for the good of the community, the mediators acquired even greater moral standing in the community.

The Case of West Gate Village When leaders of solidary groups or villagers with high moral standing approve of and respect the village officials, they may also choose to lend officials their moral standing or

[62] Interview with village community council head, eastern Fujian province, June 7, 2001. On *guanxi* ethics, see Yang, *Gifts, Favors, and Banquets*.

vouch for village officials in front of villagers to help the village government enforce state policies and regulations. West Gate again provides a good example. When West Gate's village government tried to dig a new drainage channel through the fields of some households for wastewater from local factories, villagers refused to agree to the loss of their land until council members joined village officials in visiting each household to persuade them to acquiesce. Village officials noted that it was easier to persuade villagers (*bijiao rongyi shuofu cunmin*) when they drew on the council's moral authority than when villagers perceived them as "the government" (*ganjue shi zhengfu*) trying to elicit compliance by invoking the authority of the state.

As long as village officials in West Gate fulfill their communal obligations, the members of the community council feel they have a duty to assist the village government and help improve its performance.[63] On religious holidays, the council supplements religious rituals with opera performances, basketball tournaments, and performances by the village singing troupe. According to one of the council members, "when we organize these activities, we're helping the village government to secure face. When people outside the village talk about the tournament, they don't say that the West Gate temple council is sponsoring a tournament, they say that the West Gate village government is sponsoring a tournament." The village government is expected to behave accordingly and provide funding for the council's activities:

> The village government gets half of the glory, so they should provide some of the funding. It's the same with the village singing troupe. When they go out to perform in regional singing festivals, the village government hangs its own sign over the group. I tell them if you want to take credit, then you have to take responsibility for funding their transportation and costumes.[64]

In West Gate, villagers with high moral standing in the community lend their moral standing to village officials who observe community norms and contribute to the good of the community by providing public goods and services. Moreover, because they can use their moral standing to mobilize villagers to punish violators of community norms, they can also implicitly threaten village officials who fail to provide public goods.

63 There is a long history of this approach by temple organizations.

64 Interview with village community council member, eastern Fujian province, November 6, 2000.

The Awarding of Moral Authority

The model of informal accountability posits that solidary groups make the awarding of moral standing possible, first, by establishing a set of shared moral and ethical standards, and, second, by providing opportunities for members to demonstrate their adherence to these standards publicly.

Shared Moral Obligations and Ethical Standards

Solidary groups make the village community more valuable to villagers. The more value that individuals derive from membership, the greater their debt and the stronger their moral obligation to contribute to and repay the group for the benefits it provides.[65] In rural China, solidary groups such as temple groups, temple festival associations, and villagewide lineages increase the value of the village community to its members in several ways. Village community solidary activities increase the "face" (*mianzi*) of the village. More face means more prestige and self-respect. One accumulates face by "showing oneself capable, wealthy, generous, and possessed of a wide network of social relationships."[66] In rural China, where restrictions on migration from the Maoist period have lifted only gradually, the "face" of the village – its physical appearance, outward signs of prosperity, and its local reputation – is still considered a strong reflection of the individuals living in the village. As a county official in Shanxi remarked: "All villagers want their villages to have good roads. No girl wants to marry into a shabby, ragtag (*popo lanlan de*) village. Boys in villages with good roads all have an easier time finding wives than others."[67] Visible signs of solidary activities – festival celebrations, religious rituals, even the design of the village's temple building or lineage hall – can all increase the village's face. "A beautifully built temple," as Adam Chau notes, "and a well attended temple festival attest.... to the organizational ability of the temple association and the community."[68] When asked about donating to temple reconstruction, few villagers mentioned religious beliefs as motivations. Although some villagers said they

65 Studies done by Tom Tyler show that citizens who have higher levels of pride about their group are more likely to conform to group rules and comply with local political authority. See Tyler, "Trust and Democratic Governance," 282.

66 Yang, *Gifts, Favors, and Banquets*, 140.

67 Interview with head of county civil affairs bureau, southwestern Shanxi province, April 17, 2001.

68 Adam Chau, "The Politics of Legitimation and the Revival of Popular Religion," *Modern China* 31, no. 2 (2005), 236–78.

made donations to gain favor with the gods, most reported that they wanted to contribute as much as possible because larger and more ornate temples impress outside villagers and give the village a better reputation and more face. Villagers in communities with encompassing solidary groups also felt a sense of deep gratitude and indebtedness toward the village. The wife of one community council head explained the extremely high levels of participation in temple reconstruction projects this way: "[Villagers] have deep emotional attachment *(ganqing)* toward this village – this village gave them land when they moved here, this is where they were born, this land has given them food to eat."[69] The feeling that people should "do a little something for the village" (*gei cunzi zuo yidian shi*) was also a common sentiment voiced by solidary group members.

The Cases of Yang Hamlet and Wen Hamlet In areas where many villages organize temple and festival activities, villagers as well as local officials see villages that lack these activities as inferior. Yang Hamlet and Wen Hamlet, for example, are two neighboring villages in an area of northeastern Hebei province famous for a number of very large regional temple fairs. People from all over the countryside and even the cities come to enjoy the festivities, treat themselves to snacks from street peddlers, and watch performance groups from different villages vie for recognition. Villagers in Yang Hamlet proudly report that their village's folk dancing group (*hua hui*) is "rather well known" in the area.[70] Forty to fifty people ranging in age from eight to seventy years participate in the group's performances at temple fairs as well as impromptu gatherings during summer evenings for recreation and the entertainment of fellow villagers.

Village performance groups are more than just recreational groups, though – they are also an important reflection of a village's identity and individuality. Since Yang Hamlet's performance group was revived in the 1990s (after being banned by the government in 1960), villagers from Wen Hamlet, its neighboring village, have participated as lesser members. For a few years, both villages found this arrangement quite efficient. Both villages are very small and their houses are clustered together in one settlement, so a single group can draw effectively on participants and resources from both

[69] Interview with female villager, eastern Fujian province, May 26, 2001. On the concept of *ganqing*, see Yang, *Gifts, Favors, and Banquets*.

[70] Interview with male villager, northeastern Hebei province, May 1, 2002.

communities. Yet Yang Hamlet villagers always dominated the organization. People at temple fairs saw the group as representing Yang Hamlet, not Wen Hamlet, and all of the group's organizers were Yang Hamlet villagers. In 2000, Wen Hamlet villagers decided to start their own performance group, reasoning that "we are different villages, therefore we should have our own group." Participating under the aegis of Yang Hamlet signified to Wen Hamlet villagers as well as to outsiders that Yang Hamlet village was the better organized and more prosperous of the two.

The Cases of Su Mountain Grove and Yuan Dwelling Differences in village rituals and solidary activities help generate each village's distinct identity and history. The particulars of each village's gods, rituals, and beliefs vary from village to village, although the general outlines may be the same. Both Su Mountain Grove and Yuan Dwelling, neighboring villages in Fujian province, worship a tutelary deity who, historically, was a regional lord with an office in the imperial bureaucracy. According to local legend, this lord would tour the countryside every few years, inspecting his lands and addressing villager petitions. Eventually, the historical figure evolved into a guardian deity offering protection to villages in the region. Unlike more universally worshipped gods such as Mazu and the Earth God (*Tudigong*), who have established birthdays on which people everywhere celebrate, each village in this region commemorates a different day on which the official and his entourage visited their specific village. On the anniversaries of these visits, the lord, now an official in the celestial bureaucracy, again visits the village that holds a festival to honor him. During the festival, the deity is particularly receptive to villagers' prayers and petitions during the festival. Yuan Dwelling's festival takes place on the sixteenth day of the tenth lunar month before the one in Su Mountain Grove and lasts for three days. On the third day, Yuan Dwelling's villagers ritually send the lord on his way by pushing a giant papier-maché boat with papier-maché figures in it out to sea while burning miniature sticks of wood, tiny baskets of rice and sugar, as well as ritual money in order to symbolize provisions that the village has supplied to the entourage. The lord then makes his way, in the mythical sequence of his tour, to Su Mountain Grove, which organizes a smaller two-day festival starting on the eighteenth day of the tenth lunar month.

The two villages are distinguished not only by the different days on which they hold festivals but also by differences in their ritual practices and legends. In Su Mountain Grove, villagers worship the deified official in the same temple as the one for the goddesses of birth and death. Villagers in Yuan Dwelling, however, claim that the official was actually an ancestor of theirs, also surnamed Yuan. Yuan Dwelling's villagers therefore worship the official in the village lineage hall, which also doubles as a temple incorporating Buddhist and Taoist deities. This fusing of lineage and village deity institutions together doubly reinforces community solidarity. Yuan Dwelling is known throughout the region as the village with the most lively (*renao*) festivals and the highest degree of community unity.

Public Fulfillment of Obligations and Conferral of Moral Standing

Village solidary groups thus assert the value of a village's particular history and identity. Donating time and money is not only a way of gaining favor with gods and spirits but is also an important way of gaining and maintaining face within the village. Those who fulfill the standard of doing one's fair share protect their standing. Those who go beyond the minimum standard can increase their moral authority. Refusing to contribute to solidary groups, or even failing to make sure one's family members and relatives contribute, can result in a serious loss of face and respect from other villagers.

The case of West Hu Hamlet. Take the example of West Hu Hamlet. Village officials in West Hu Hamlet enjoy the luxury of overflowing village coffers and the power that goes along with it, thanks to the village's plum location next to a Coca-Cola plant in the suburbs of the Xiamen Special Economic Zone. Yet even they think twice about shirking their responsibilities to contribute to the village temple organization. In 2000, after a typhoon decimated the old village temple, villagers decided to establish a temple rebuilding committee. Representatives from each household convened in front of the wreckage, nominated four people to oversee the construction, and agreed on a budget of 210,000 yuan (about U.S.$26,000) based on an expected contribution of 600 yuan per person (roughly a month's income for the average villager). Only two households refused to contribute. To the horror of the village's Party secretary, his own son and daughter-in-law's family was one of them. Their excuse was that unlike most villagers, they had not received compensation for the state's recent appropriation of village land, but the Party secretary told them that was ridiculous because they both worked in factories paying over 1,000 yuan per month. "I asked them, do you want money or do you want face (*yao qian haishi yao lian*)? Our descendants are going to wonder, why is *our* family name not carved on the temple's memorial tablet of donors!"[71]

The widespread practice of publicizing the names of donors and their donations is (not surprisingly) a highly effective way of motivating villagers to fulfill their obligation to contribute resources to the solidary group. Posting the names of all the donors and the amount of their donations on a poster in the village center not only allows everyone to monitor the solidary organization's finances, but it also allows everyone to evaluate the donations of everyone else and judge whether the size of a person's donation was appropriate or particularly large or small given the household's economic circumstances.

Temple and lineage hall reconstruction projects impose particularly serious sanctions. Names of donors and the amount of their donations are typically engraved on a marble or stone stele placed at the entrance of the new temple or set directly into one of the temple's walls. In contrast to posters that are public but ultimately temporary as they peel and fade from exposure to rain and sun, temple steles make sure that each household's contribution and, by extension, its standing in the village community are literally carved in stone. Names are always organized in a hierarchy from largest to smallest donation. In some places, the most generous donors' names are carved in larger characters or painted in gold or red to set them above the rest of the donors more clearly. When West Gate's community council decided to rebuild the village's Guandi temple for an estimated cost of 260,000 yuan, they simply spread the word that anybody who donated by a certain date would get their family's name carved on the temple wall. Eighty percent of households turned in their donations a month before the deadline. Although the council did not approach households in economic straits, one council member noted, "People from these households came to us with donations anyway, saying, 'Do you look down on me or something?'"[72] He gave one example of a household of four that wasn't able to make a contribution at the time because the mother was ill and the family owed the two children's school fees. It wasn't until three years later that the head of the household finally came to the council with their contribution. At that point, the council chair said, "forget about it, we knew you had economic difficulties," but the man insisted they accept the donation, and

[71] Interview with male village Party secretary, eastern Fujian province, December 3, 2000.

[72] Interview with village community council deputy head, eastern Fujian province, November 12, 2000.

the council consequently made arrangements for his name to be added to the stele of donors.

Specific standards of fairness naturally vary depending on the locality and the group member's capabilities. In Jinglong, a village in Hebei province, the norm for financing the organization of activities for New Year's – the most important holiday of the year – is to expect contributions only from households lucky enough to own land where lucrative coal deposits have been discovered. Jinglong's Party secretary is one of the village's prominent donors, contributing 50 out of the 400 yuan that the festival organization collected in 2001. Ordinary households are not expected to contribute, although when they do, others speak highly of them. In other places, every household is expected to participate or donate to the village's solidary group. In Yang Hamlet, performance association members visit each house repeatedly to solicit donations if no one is at home. After each collection, they paint each donor's name and the amount of their donation on red poster paper and paste it to the wall of a house in the village center. In Yuan Dwelling, village households draw straws for the honor of financing the village's locally renowned festival celebrating the visit of the deified lord. Putting on the festival can cost up to 100,000 yuan – about fifty times the rural income per capita. The more elaborate the festival – beautifully prepared banquet dishes, ritual opera and dance performances, firecrackers and fireworks displays, chants by Taoist monks, an elaborate parade to send the lord off on the rest of his journey – the more the village considers the family devout and devoted to the collective good.[73]

Conclusion

These examples from the Chinese context help to illustrate the causal processes posited by the theoretical model of informal accountability. The model suggests that citizens in localities with encompassing and embedding solidary groups are more likely to share a set of common ethical standards and moral obligations and to participate in common activities that facilitate widespread knowledge of whether people are living up to these standards and obligations than citizens in localities without these groups.

[73] David K. Jordan describes relationships of reciprocity between the supernatural and families and villages in 1960s Taiwan. See David K. Jordan, *Gods, Ghosts and Ancestors* (Berkeley: University of California Press, 1972).

Note that this model does not propose that the ethical standards and moral obligations of solidary groups are in some way transferable or "spill over" to compliance with state policies. Obligations to contribute to the solidary group do not somehow convert into obligations to comply with state tasks. Instead, these obligations enable the generation of moral standing that can be used by whomever earns it to elicit deference in diverse potential situations for diverse purposes. For officials, these purposes include the implementation of state policies.

Nor does the importance of shared moral obligations and ethical standards in this model mean that people do not pursue individual interests. Instead, the model suggests that in communities with solidary groups that are structured in certain ways so that they fit with the formal political administrative structure, "ethical standards and egoistic interest are in fact both compatible and mutually reinforcing."[74] Solidary obligations of doing one's fair share and repaying the community simply mean that self-interested behavior should be "expressed and satisfied *through* various social bonds of affect, obligation, and propriety."[75] In the next two chapters, we turn to a more systematic assessment of this model's plausibility and generalizability.

74 Levi, *Consent, Dissent, and Patriotism*, 213.

75 Yang, *Gifts, Favors, and Banquets*, 140. Emphasis in the original.

5

Temples and Churches in Rural China

The model of informal accountability hypothesizes that in political systems with weak formal institutions of accountability, localities with encompassing and embedding solidary groups are likely to have better local governmental provision of public goods than localities without these groups, all other things being equal. To evaluate the plausibility of this hypothesis, this chapter derives its observable implications for two types of solidary groups common in rural China: village temples and village churches. If the hypothesis is correct, we should expect that village temples, which are usually encompassing *and* embedding, will be more likely to have a positive effect on village governmental provision of public goods. Village churches, on the other hand, are encompassing but not embedding, so they should be less likely to have a positive effect on village governmental provision of public goods.

The Structure of Temples and Churches in Rural China

As with most rural solidary groups, the state tolerates the existence of village temples and village churches as long as they limit their activities to the boundaries of the village. Within the village, temples and churches are typically open to everyone, temples because they have a strong historical association as symbols of the village community as a whole and churches because the forms of Christianity that are practiced in rural China are generally inclusive of and welcoming to new adherents. Thus, village temples and village churches are both generally encompassing solidary groups.

The historical link between village temples and the definition of the village polity continues to make temples powerful symbols of village identity. Village temples may sometimes have pilgrimage networks that extend into other townships and counties, but pilgrims from other places are usually occasional or one-time visitors rather than regular participants in the organizational activities of the temple and do not have the same moral obligations to contribute to the group in the same way that members of the village community do.[1] Village temples in places like Fujian and Guangdong often have extensive overseas networks, but these networks are still based on loyalties to the native village.

Village temples and churches differ dramatically, however, in terms of their relationships with the state and their ability to embed village officials in their institutions and activities. In imperial times, village temples often helped to reinforce state power. The authority of each village's temple stemmed from its access to the divine power of guardian deities in control of the village's welfare. These guardian deities were considered deified celestial officials and integrated with living government officials into a single cosmic bureaucracy by state-sanctioned popular religion. Just as government officials were assigned responsibility for administering a certain area, officials in the celestial bureaucracy also took responsibility for a particular village or district.[2] Villagers acquired political and moral authority by serving as temple councilors, positions they were granted for contributing more money than others to religious ceremonies and temple repair. Because the temple community was coterminous with the village, authority over temple institutions translated into further governance responsibilities over village issues and village finance.[3] Contemporary village temple groups continue to

[1] Although some village temples are visited by pilgrims from neighboring localities and earn a significant income from the donations of visiting pilgrims, their religious and nonreligious activities focus on the village community. Villagers are usually the most frequent participants, and they typically consider their village temple to be hosting visitors rather than seeing visiting pilgrims as fellow members of the temple. In one Fujian village, residents were extremely pleased with the success of their newly reconstructed village temple. Because their village temple happens to host guardian deities who are well known outside the village, it enjoys a steady stream of visitors from surrounding areas. The temple brings in 400,000 yuan (about U.S.$50,000) a year in donations, many of which are from visitors. This amount far outstrips the village government's yearly revenue of 100,000 yuan. One villager noted that villager efforts to rebuild the temple have been rewarded: "Villagers supported the temple, now the temple has started to support the villagers (*ben di ren yang le miao, miao kaishi yang ben di ren le*)." Interview with male villager, eastern Fujian province, December 9, 2000

[2] Arthur Wolf, *Religion and Ritual in Chinese Society* (Stanford: Stanford University Press, 1974), 133–5.

[3] In his research on rural marketing networks, G. William Skinner identifies a type of community in Sichuan he calls a "dispersed village": a group of farmhouse clusters whose members frequent the same small cluster of shops and "form themselves into natural groupings, each

promote norms of contributing to the good of the community, and although many groups are more secular than religious, lingering connections with the sacred help to reinforce the moral authority of these norms.

Village churches, in contrast, have a very different legacy. Christian proselytizing has historically been linked to Western imperialism. Joseph Esherick notes, for example, that "[t]he missionaries supported the opium wars because they were convinced that as China was opened to trade, so would she be opened to Christ." A series of treaties in the 1800s supplied a wealth of concessions to Catholic missionaries under French protection.[4] Foreign priests were given special legal privileges and powers.[5] Even in nonreligious disputes, Christian villagers often had the advantage of support from foreign missionaries and priests who could inject the charge of religious persecution into the legal proceedings.[6] Church institutions also indirectly undermined the state's control over its local officials. In lawsuits involving Chinese Christians, a mere visit from a foreign missionary to the Chinese official in charge often resulted in a favorable ruling as the involvement of foreign consuls, ministers, and the official's superiors constituted an unappealing alternative.[7] In his study of the Chinese Catholic Church, Richard Madsen notes: "To be a Catholic was to enjoy a special relationship not only with God or with the pope but also with the foreign powers that were attempting to dominate China."[8]

As foreign-connected church institutions eroded the power of the imperial state, at the grassroots level village churches could sometimes reinforce the power of village elites over ordinary villagers. William Hinton's study of

focused on a single *t'u ti miao* (earth-god shrine)." He continues: "[B]oth the dispersed village of Szechwan and the nucleated village more commonly found elsewhere in China may be considered 'village communities.'" G. William Skinner, "Marketing and Social Structure in Rural China: Part I," *Journal of Asian Studies* 24, no. 1 (November 1964), 6.

4 Joseph Esherick, *The Origins of the Boxer Uprising* (Berkeley: University of California Press, 1987), 74.

5 See Madsen, *China's Catholics*; Esherick, *The Origins of the Boxer Uprising*. The imperial government issued a directive in 1899 granting foreign Catholic bishops the same powers as provincial governors, and foreign priests the same powers as provincial judges and county magistrates, thereby formalizing what had been in practice since 1860. William Hinton, *Fanshen: A Documentary of Revolution in a Chinese Village* (New York: Random House, 1968, c1966), 60.

6 A recent study of Christianity in rural, pre-Communist Jiangxi finds that conflicts typically occurred over secular, nonreligious issues such as property disputes and usually involved ordinary villagers rather than local gentry.

7 Kenneth Scott Latourette, *A History of Christian Missions in China* (New York: Macmillan, 1929), 29. See also Esherick, *The Origins of the Boxer Uprising*, 84.

8 Madsen, *China's Catholics*, 32.

a Shanxi village describes how the village head appointed by the provincial governor together with other village gentry operated the village church's charitable society, initially founded through donations by village Catholics to support the local orphanage, as a usury business that eventually made the church the village's largest landholder. By drawing on foreign legal protection, village elites were able to convince county officials to turn a deaf ear to protests from ordinary villagers.[9]

Village churches were often in direct conflict with village temple organizations reinforcing the authority and legitimacy of the state, as they controversially encouraged Christian villagers to stop contributing fees for local festivals or for the upkeep of village temples.[10] Missionaries also contributed to the weakening of village identity and community by mobilizing families from established Catholic communities to migrate to villages where they had set up new churches.[11] Within existing communities, they encouraged villagers to abolish rituals reinforcing community identity and solidarity, such as traditional funeral practices.[12]

In sum, village temples are associated with reinforcing state authority and legitimacy whereas village church institutions are associated with dangerous connections to foreign actors and the undermining of state authority.[13] These legacies have a major impact on the relationship that these social organizations have with the state today. Village temples are also less threatening to the state because of the inherent cellularization of most

[9] In one incident, Hinton reports that nine hundred villagers walked to the county seat in protest only to be turned away by soldiers authorized by the county magistrate, who was fearful of repercussions from angry foreigners. Hinton, *Fanshen*, 62; Lianjiang Li, "The Politics of Introducing Direct Township Elections in China," *China Quarterly*, no. 171 (September 2002), 704–23.

[10] Alan Richard Sweeten, *Christianity in Rural China: Conflict and Accommodation in Jiangxi Province, 1860–1900*, vol. 91. Michigan Monographs in Chinese Studies. (Ann Arbor: Center for Chinese Studies, University of Michigan Press, 2001).

[11] Hinton, *Fanshen*, 61.

[12] Madsen, *China's Catholics*, 43.

[13] The Qing imperial state prohibited religious groups such as White Lotus Societies that the state deemed sects and heterodox. As a result, these kinds of groups rarely constructed public places of worship such as temples, and should not be thought of as village *temple* organizations. Susan Naquin says of the White Lotus Societies: "In consequence, its ideas and practices were transmitted in simple fashion on an individual basis with little reliance on public institutions such as temples or clergy." These types of religious groups, unlike conventional village temple organizations, were a major threat to the state and viewed with suspicion. See Susan Naquin, *Millenarian Rebellion in China: The Eight Trigrams Uprising of 1813* (New Haven: Yale University Press, 1976), 7; Lewin et al., *Educational Innovation in China*.

groups. Because their moral authority derives from their reinforcement of *village* identity, the basis for solidarity and collective action is geographically limited. The Chinese party-state thus takes a more benign view toward village temples, making village officials more likely not only to permit or support the establishment of temple institutions but also to participate in them personally. Village churches, however, lack the same kind of self-limiting quality. The state sees churches as organizations with high subversive potential and therefore regulates them closely and bans local officials from participating in them.

Findings from the Survey Data

Statistical analysis of the 2000 village survey data indicates that villages with temple groups are more likely to have better village governmental provision of public goods than villages without such groups, all other things being equal.

Measuring the Dependent Variable

I use six measures of village governmental public goods provision as discussed in Chapter 3: per capita village government expenditure on public projects in 2000; the existence of paved village roads; the existence of paved village footpaths; the percentage of village classrooms usable in rainy weather; the newness of the village school building in terms of years since construction or the last major renovation; and the existence of running water.

Measuring the Explanatory Variable

To measure village temple groups, I look at two indicators: the existence of a formal temple manager (a dichotomous variable); and the percentage of households that have participated in village temple reconstruction projects by donating money, labor, or materials since the beginning of the reform period in the late 1970s. Village temple groups vary in the degree of organization, although they engage in similar activities: mobilizing donations from villagers, organizing religious rituals and nonreligious community activities, and overseeing and publicizing the temple's accounts. In some villages, a temple manager, sometimes overseeing a temple council, organizes these activities.[14] But in many other cases, temple activities are more impromptu affairs that are organized informally by an ad hoc group of villagers. Since temple reconstruction is one of the most common temple activities, the percentage of households that can be mobilized to participate in these projects is a good measure of temple groups, regardless of how formal they are. Fourteen percent of villages reported that they had a temple manager. The average proportion of households participating in temple reconstruction across all villages in the sample (including the ones that did not have temples or engage in temple reconstruction) was 9 percent, but among the fifty-eight villages reporting temple reconstruction projects, the average percentage of households participating was 58 percent.

Two similar measures are used for village church groups: the existence of a state-approved Protestant minister or Catholic priest who organizes church services and activities; and the existence of a church that has been renovated or rebuilt in the reform period. As with the measures of temple groups, the first indicator captures whether a village church organization with a minimal level of formalization exists, whereas the second indicator looks more at the church group's capacity to organize a large-scale project. Seven percent of villages reported that they had a church with a minister or priest organizing services and activities, and 4 percent reported that the church had organized a reconstruction project since the start of the reform period.[15]

Control Variables

To identify the effects that solidary groups have on village governmental performance and public goods provision, we have to be able to distinguish

[14] Procedures for selecting temple managers vary from village to village. In some places, male villagers draw lots and take turns rotating through the temple council and its different positions. In other places, the temple manager is simply a civics-minded villager with leadership skills who decided to organize everyone for an initial temple activity, such as the rebuilding of the village's temple. Villagers sometimes also convene an assembly of household representatives who select a temple manager through discussion. Temple managers tend to be older men in their fifties and sixties who are highly respected for their integrity and their good judgment. Often, temple managers are successful entrepreneurs, or farmers who have managed their agricultural production and household affairs well. Occasionally, temple managers are women who are respected in the village for their good judgment and organizational skills.

[15] I do not use the percentage of households participating through donation in church reconstruction as I do for temple reconstruction because many church reconstruction projects are funded by grants from the state Religious Affairs Bureau and thus do not solicit household donations.

their effects from those of other factors that may also have an impact on governmental provision of public goods.[16] Regression analysis allows us to control for these other factors.[17]

Geographic and Demographic Controls The first set consists of geographic and demographic factors. Distance from the county seat, village terrain (flat or not flat), the number of natural villages (a proxy for the spatial dispersion of village residents), and village population in 2000 were included to control for variation in demand for specific public goods as well as variation in costs for the same goods in different places.[18]

Economic Controls The analyses also control for the level of economic development, local resources, and industrialization by including the following measures: 1997 village income per capita, 1997 village government assets, 1997 village government tax revenue per capita, the existence of village government enterprises (*cunban qiye*) in 1995, and the existence of private enterprises (*siying qiye*) in 1995.[19] Economic data from 1995 and 1997 are used instead of data from 2000 in order to reduce problems with identifying the direction of causality.[20]

Democratic and Bureaucratic Institutions The analyses also control for a third set of factors – formal institutions of accountability – that existing theories identify as central to governmental performance. To control for top-down institutions that enable higher-level officials to supervise lower-level officials, the analyses include measures of Party and bureaucratic institutional strength: the Party membership of the village head (a dichotomous variable); the percentage of village officials who are Party members; and the existence of performance contracts with public project targets that village officials must sign with higher-level officials.

16 These same control variables are used in all of the book's statistical analyses (specifically in Chapters 5, 6, 7, and 8).

17 Descriptive statistics are presented in Appendix Table A5.1.

18 Dummy variables for the eight counties from which the villages were randomly sampled were also included.

19 The effects of these factors are estimated in Chapter 3. Following the original official definition used in China, private enterprises are enterprises with eight or more people.

20 If we were, for example, to find a correlation between investment in public projects in 2000 and income per capita in 2000, it would be difficult to determine whether higher incomes were leading to more investment in public projects or whether more investment were leading to higher outcomes.

In addition to formal top-down institutions of accountability, the analyses also control for the effects of bottom-up democratic institutions – specifically, direct elections for village officials and deliberative villagers' representative assemblies, which have been in the process of implementation since the late 1980s.[21]

Analysis and Findings

Village Temple Groups I first investigated the effects of village temple groups. Statistical analysis indicated that villages with temple groups were more likely to have better village governmental public goods provision than villages without such groups, all other things being equal.[22] The estimated relationship between village public goods provision and village temple groups as measured by the existence of a temple manager was positive for all six public goods outcomes, and we can conclude that village temple groups have a definite effect on village governmental provision of public goods with a high level of confidence.[23] Similar results are obtained regardless of what control variables are included or excluded, whether measures of other kinds of solidary groups such as churches and lineages are included or excluded, and whether villages with missing data are simply deleted from the dataset or whether missing data are multiply imputed using existing information in the dataset.[24] These findings are reinforced when we look

[21] The construction of this measure is discussed in greater detail in Chapter 7, which focuses on the relationship between village democratic institutions and village governmental performance. But the findings here remain the same even when the implementation of democratic reforms is measured in different ways, such as a simple additive index.

[22] As with previous analyses in Chapter 3, I used seemingly unrelated regression (SUR). See appendix for a more detailed discussion of the SUR method.

[23] Using SUR, we can reject the null hypothesis that the coefficient estimate on a village temple manager is jointly equal to zero across all six outcomes at a 99 percent confidence level (p-value = 0.0058). The full model results are presented in Appendix Table A5.2. The estimated relationship between village provision of public goods and village temple groups as measured by a village temple manager was positive for all six outcomes and statistically significantly different from zero for three outcomes (paths, classrooms, and water). Missing data were deleted listwise, and Huber heteroskedasticity-robust standard errors are reported.

[24] The full model results when missing data are multiply imputed are presented in Appendix Table A5.3. The estimated relationship between village governmental provision of public goods and village temple manager is again positive for all six outcomes and statistically significant for classrooms. We can reject the null hypothesis that a village temple manager has no effect on village governmental provision of public goods jointly across public goods provision outcomes at a 90 percent confidence level (p-value = 0.099). In general, both

at the estimated relationship between village governmental provision of public goods and village temple groups as measured by the percentage of households participating in temple reconstruction. Again, we can conclude that village temple groups have a definite effect on village governmental provision of public goods with a high level of confidence.[25] The estimated effect of village temple groups as measured by temple reconstruction is positive for four of the public goods provision outcomes (investment, roads, classrooms, and water). For two outcomes (paths and newness of school), the estimated effect is negative but also highly uncertain and small in magnitude. Again, similar results were obtained regardless of what control variables were included or excluded or how missing data were treated.[26]

In sum, results from statistical analysis are consistent with the hypothesis that encompassing and embedding village temple groups have a positive impact on village governmental provision of public goods. Both measures

the coefficient estimates and the standard errors are somewhat smaller than the estimates produced when listwise deletion is used. Missing data are multiply imputed using the EMis algorithm developed by King et al., "Analyzing Incomplete Political Science Data." In this model, robust standard errors are not reported because the existing software program for combining multiply imputed datasets for analysis does not support seemingly unrelated regression with robust standard errors. See Tomz et al., CLARIFY. For additional information, see Gary King, Michael Tomz, and Jason Wittenberg, "Making the Most of Statistical Analyses: Improving Interpretation and Presentation," *American Journal of Political Science* 44, no. 2 (April 2000), 347–61. Results for models using different sets of control variables are similar to the results presented here and are available online at http://www.cambridge.org/9780521871976.

25 Using SUR, we can reject the null hypothesis that the coefficient estimate on participation in temple reconstruction is jointly equal to zero across all six outcomes at a 95 percent confidence level (p-value = 0.012). The full model results are presented in Appendix Table A5.4. The estimated relationship between village public goods provision and village temple groups as measured by the percentage of households participating in temple reconstruction was positive for four outcomes and statistically significant or close to significant for two outcomes (classrooms and water). Missing data were deleted listwise, and Huber heteroskedasticity-robust standard errors are reported.

26 The full model results when missing data are multiply imputed are available online at http://www.cambridge.org/9780521871976. The estimated relationship between village governmental provision of public goods and participation in temple reconstruction is again positive for four outcomes and statistically significant or close to statistically significant for two outcomes (classrooms and water). The estimated effect of participation in temple reconstruction jointly across outcomes is statistically significant at a 95 percent confidence level (p-value = 0.05). When multiple imputation is used instead of listwise deletion, the coefficient estimates tend to be larger, whereas the standard errors are larger for some estimates and smaller for others. Again, missing data are multiply imputed using the EMis algorithm developed by ibid. Results for models using different sets of control variables are similar to the results presented here and are available online at http://www.cambridge.org/9780521871976.

of temple groups had a clear positive effect on government investment in public projects as well as the provision of actual public goods.[27]

But what if the existence of these groups is an effect of good public goods provision rather than a cause? To examine this possibility, we can use instrumental variables (IV) estimation, a statistical technique that enables us to isolate and estimate the effect of village temple groups on village governmental provision of public goods even when temple groups are endogenous.[28] To use this technique, we need an instrument, a variable that is correlated with village temple groups (the endogenous explanatory variable) and that affects village governmental provision of public goods only through its effect on village temple groups.[29] In this analysis, we can use the existence of temple activity before 1949 as an instrument for the current existence of village temple groups as measured by the existence of a village temple manager.[30] Because of the nearly complete eradication of community temples and collective temple activities and the radical social upheaval during the Maoist period, it is unlikely that a history of pre-Communist temple activity has influenced the current performance of village governments in any way except by making the current existence of temple groups more likely by providing a familiar template for villagers interested in building social groups and community.

Results from IV estimation also indicated that the estimated effect of village temple groups as measured by a village temple manager was positive.[31] In fact, the estimates produced by IV estimation were generally even

[27] Findings from bivariate SUR regression for the six public goods provision measures as well as logit models for the three dichotomous measures of public goods provision (existence of paved roads, existence of paved paths, and existence of running water infrastructure) were similar to the multivariate SUR estimates and generally provided even stronger support for this hypothesis. These results can be viewed online at http://www.cambridge.org/9780521871976.

[28] IV estimation gives us estimates of the effects of endogenous explanatory variables that are consistent. These estimates converge in probability to the actual effect as the sample size grows without bound.

[29] In other words, the variable being used as an instrument must be partially correlated with the endogenous explanatory variable as well as uncorrelated with the error term of the structural equation. See Wooldridge, *Econometric Analysis of Cross Section and Panel Data*, 484–514.

[30] This instrumental variable was set to one for villages with a pre-Communist legacy of temple activity and zero for villages without this legacy.

[31] The bivariate IV model results are available online at http://www.cambridge.org/9780521871976. The estimated relationship between village governmental provision of public goods and the existence of a temple manager was positive for five outcomes (investment, roads, paths, newness of school, and water) and statistically significant for water. For

larger in magnitude. Statistical tests indicated, moreover, that this technique was not necessarily warranted since the differences between these estimates and estimates produced without using an instrument were not significant enough to suggest that village temple groups were endogenous.

So, as we can see, even when we control for level of economic development and industrialization, variation in bureaucratic and democratic institutions, and differences in the demand for particular goods or the cost of particular goods due to variation in location, geography, and size, village temple groups have a significant positive effect on village governmental provision of public goods. (These findings also remain the same when we control for the effects of other types of solidary groups such as churches and lineages.[32])

To give us a more concrete idea of how big this effect is, Figure 5.1 compares the mean level or likelihood of different public goods in an average village with a temple manager to an average village without a temple manager (average in the sense that all the control variables are set at their means).[33] The mean per capita investment for an average village with a village temple group is 109 yuan (about U.S.$14), which is much higher than 60 yuan (about U.S.$7), the mean investment for an average village without a temple group. The average village with a temple group has a 59 percent probability of having a paved road, compared to a village without a temple group, which has a 48 percent probability. Villages with temple groups are likely to have better public goods provision than villages without temple groups in every case except for the age of the school building. The uncertainty around some of these estimates (indicated by the gray lines showing 95 percent confidence intervals) is somewhat high, but the fact that we see the same pattern regardless of how public goods are measured makes us more confident that village temple groups really do have a strong positive effect on village governmental provision of public goods.

these five outcomes, Hausman tests indicated that the differences between IV estimates and OLS estimates (which in this case are the same as the SUR estimates discussed previously) were not different enough to suggest that OLS or SUR estimates were inconsistent and that village temple groups were endogenous. For classrooms, a Hausman test indicated that the difference between IV estimates and OLS estimates was statistically significant and that OLS estimates could be inconsistent.

32 Full model results when measures of village churches, villagewide lineages, and subvillage lineages are estimated in the same model as village temple manager are presented in Appendix Tables A5.5 (in which missing data are deleted listwise) and A5.6 (where missing data are multiply imputed).

33 These fitted values are calculated using the model results presented in Appendix Table A5.3.

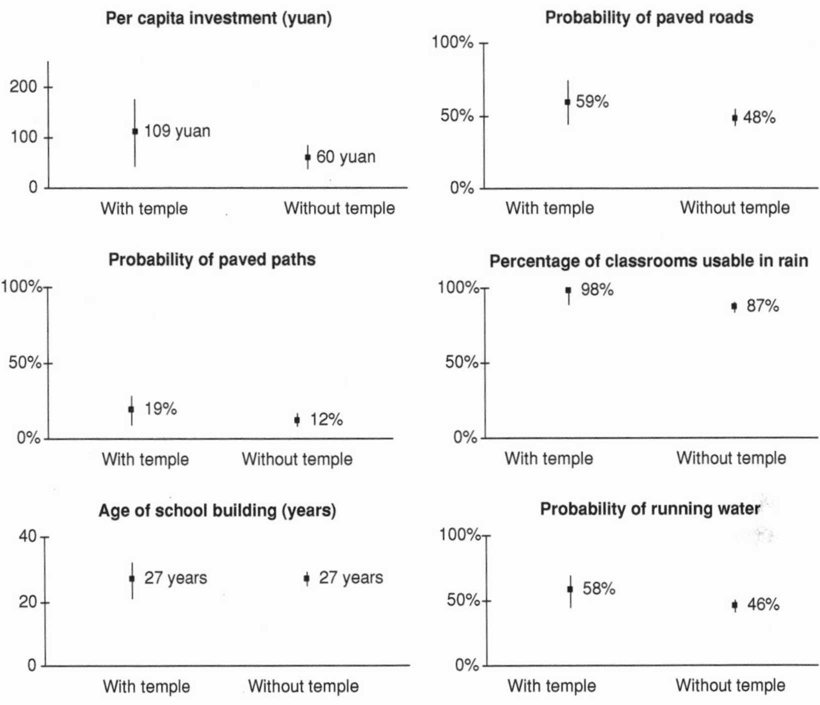

Figure 5.1. Provision of public goods in villages with and without temples.

We also see a similar pattern when village temple groups are measured by the percentage of households participating in temple reconstruction. Increasing the participation rate from zero to the mean participation rate of 58 percent was associated with an average increase of 29 yuan in investment, 4 percent in the probability of paved roads, 13 percent in the percentage of classrooms usable in rain, and 9 percent in the probability of running water.[34]

Village Churches Next I examined the effect of village churches on village governmental provision of public goods. Unlike village temple groups, village churches do not have a clear positive effect on village governmental provision of public goods. The estimated effect of village churches as measured by an active village pastor was negative for four measures (investment,

[34] These fitted values are calculated based on SUR model results with all controls and missing data multiply imputed. Full model results are available online at http://www.cambridge.org/9780521871976.

paths, classrooms, and water) and positive for two measures (roads and newness of school building) when all control variables were included and when villages with missing data were dropped from the analysis.[35] The uncertainty, however, around the estimated effects on three of these outcomes (paths, newness of school, and water) was very high. These results were not robust when different control variables are included or excluded or when missing data are treated differently. If we obtained the same estimates using different methods, we could be relatively more certain that the estimates are accurate than if the estimates changed when different methods were used. But when control variables were not included, the estimated effect on the probability of paved paths and the probability of running water changed from negative to positive.[36] When data were multiply imputed instead of deleted listwise, the estimated effect of churches on the probability of running water changed from negative to positive.[37]

For the other three public goods provision outcomes (investment, roads, and classrooms), the uncertainty around the estimated effect of church groups was lower. The existence of a village church as measured by an active village pastor had a consistently negative effect on investment and classrooms and a consistently positive effect on paved roads. Figure 5.2 gives

[35] Again, I use SUR to estimate these effects. See appendix for a more detailed discussion of the SUR method. The full model results are presented in Appendix Table A5.7. The estimated relationship between village churches as measured by the existence of an active village pastor who organizes church services or activities is negative for four outcomes (investment, paths, classrooms, and water) and statistically significant for investment and classrooms. The estimated relationship is positive for two outcomes (roads and newness of school building) and statistically significant for roads. Missing data were deleted listwise, and Huber heteroskedasticity-robust standard errors are calculated.

[36] Findings from bivariate SUR regression for the six public goods provision measures as well as results from models using different sets of control variables and results from logit models for the three dichotomous measures of public goods provision (existence of paved roads, existence of paved paths, and existence of running water infrastructure) can be viewed online at http://www.cambridge.org/9780521871976 and are similarly mixed.

[37] The full model results when missing data are multiply imputed are presented in Appendix Table A5.8. The estimated relationship between village governmental provision of public goods and an active village pastor is negative for three outcomes (investment, paths, and classrooms) and statistically significant or almost significant for investment and classrooms. The estimated relationship is positive but statistically insignificant for three outcomes (roads, newness of school, and water). In general, multiple imputation of missing data resulted in smaller estimated effects (and slightly smaller standard errors) than listwise deletion. Missing data are multiply imputed using the EMis algorithm developed by King et al., "Analyzing Incomplete Political Science Data." When the existence of temples and lineage groups is also controlled for in the analysis (see Appendix Table A5.6), the estimated effect on water flips back to negative.

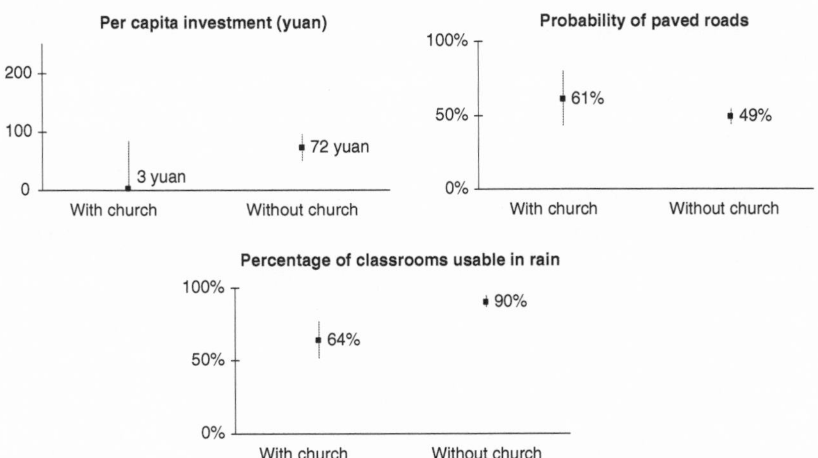

Figure 5.2. Provision of public goods in villages with and without churches.

a sense of how big these effects are.[38] The mean per capita investment in the average village with an active church pastor – 3 yuan – is much lower than the mean investment in an average village without a pastor – 72 yuan – but the probability of paved roads in the average village with a pastor – 61 percent – is much higher than the probability in a village without a pastor – 49 percent. The percentage of usable classrooms, however, was like investment – much lower in villages with churches.

These findings suggest that any positive effect that village churches have on roads is not taking place through a positive effect on village government or village governmental investment in public projects. One explanation for this finding, which we discuss at greater length in the next section's case studies of actual villages with temple and church groups, is that village church groups can *substitute* for village government provision of public services. As solidary groups that encompass the entire village, village churches have the capacity to mobilize resources from the entire village and organize public services themselves. But because village churches are not embedding and do not incorporate the participation of village officials, they cannot hold officials responsible for *governmental* provision of public services.

Similarly mixed findings for the effects of village church groups result when village churches are measured by the existence of a church reconstruction project since the beginning of political and economic

[38] These fitted values are calculated using the model results presented in Appendix Table A5.8.

liberalization in the late 1970s. The estimated relationship between village public goods provision and this measure of churches is negative for three outcomes (investment, paths, and classrooms) and positive for three outcomes (roads, newness of school, and running water). As with the previous analysis, the positive estimated effect on roads and the negative estimated effect on investment have relatively low uncertainty.[39] Per capita village government investment in public projects was, on average, 71 yuan lower in the average village that had undertaken church reconstruction projects, but paved roads were, on average, 32 percent more likely.[40]

Villages with Both Temples and Churches

Only six out of the 316 villages in the survey had both a village temple and a village church.[41] Statistical analysis suggested that villages with both temples and churches have worse village governmental provision of public goods than villages that have only a temple or only a church, but it is important to note that with such small numbers, we cannot generalize very confidently about what happens when these groups coexist in the same place. With that caveat in mind, villages with both temples and churches were likely to have lower village government investment in public projects, a lower likelihood of paved roads, a lower likelihood of paved paths, a higher percentage of classrooms usable in rain but in slightly older school buildings, and a lower likelihood of running water than villages with just a temple group or villages with just a church group.[42]

[39] Coefficient estimates and standard errors are similar regardless of whether missing data are deleted listwise or multiply imputed. Full model results using listwise deletion and robust standard errors are available online at http://www.cambridge.org/9780521871976. Full model results using multiple imputation are presented in Appendix Table A5.9. When listwise deletion is used, the estimated relationship between church reconstruction and village governmental provision of public goods is statistically significant for investment and roads. When multiple imputation is used, the estimated relationship is statistically significant for investment. Findings from bivariate SUR regression for the six public goods provision measures as well as logit models for the three dichotomous measures of public goods provision (existence of paved roads, existence of paved paths, and existence of running water infrastructure) were similar to the multivariate SUR estimates. These results can be viewed online at http://www.cambridge.org/9780521871976.

[40] These fitted values are calculated using the model results presented in Appendix Table A5.9.

[41] Four of these villages had a temple and church but no lineage group; two of these villages also had a lineage group.

[42] When a multiplicative interaction variable for village temples as measured by a village temple manager and village churches as measured by an active village pastor was included in

Unfortunately without case study data from the villages that have both types of solidary groups, we cannot know how the groups really interact. One hypothesis for further examination might be that in these cases temples and churches are no longer encompassing solidary groups that incorporate the membership of the entire village. Instead, they may compete with each other for the allegiance of people in the village, thus fragmenting the village into separate subvillage solidary groups. In theory, people can create belief systems that enable them to engage in both temple and church activities, but these very preliminary findings are more consistent with the hypothesis that these two kinds of religious groups are likely to conflict with each other.

To summarize, statistical analysis of the survey data indicates that villages with temple groups, which are encompassing *and* embedding, are likely to have higher government investment and better public goods provision than villages without temple groups, all other things being equal. In contrast, villages with churches, which are encompassing *but not* embedding, did not have a clear positive impact on village governmental provision of public goods, and in fact, seemed to have a negative impact on investment and village classrooms. Villages with churches did seem more likely to have paved roads, but since government investment in public projects was lower in these villages, it is likely that these roads were provided through church-organized public projects that bypass village officials rather than the village government.

But do we know *why* solidary groups that are both encompassing and embedding have a positive effect on village governmental public goods provision? The village case studies presented in the next section provide concrete examples to illustrate the differences between village temple groups and village churches. Moral and social standing provided by village temple and solidary institutions motivates officials to provide public goods, allows villagers to hold officials accountable, and helps officials to secure

the SUR analysis, the interaction effect was negative for five out of six outcomes (investment, roads, paths, newness of school, and water) and statistically significant for paths and classrooms. The magnitude of this negative effect ranged from modest to very large. The interaction effect on classrooms was positive and statistically significant. The estimated effects for both temple groups and church groups remained similar to the estimates produced when an interaction effect was not included. Village temple groups still had a clear positive effect on village governmental provision of public goods. Village church groups still had a negative effect on investment and classrooms and a positive effect on roads. Full model results are presented in Appendix Table A5.10. Missing data are deleted listwise, and robust standard errors are calculated.

compliance with policy decisions. In contrast, the inability of village officials to participate in village churches prevents them from accessing the moral standing that church institutions can confer.[43]

Village Case Studies

This section presents case studies of three villages: West Gate, which is in the southern province of Fujian, and Yang Hamlet and South Bend, which are both in the northern province of Hebei.[44] In some ways, these villages look very similar. Top-down institutions of supervision are relatively strong, and all of the villages adhere closely to national-level and provincial-level regulations for village elections. The county and township officials overseeing South Bend are so scrupulous about election reforms that in 1999, when the provincial government passed revisions to the election law in the middle of South Bend's election process, they decided to start elections in South Bend all over again from the beginning to make sure all of their actions conformed to the provincial law. In Yang Hamlet, which is in the same county and township as South Bend, village officials reported that Party and township officials refrained from interfering in any part of the nomination and election process. Secret ballots and fixed ballot boxes were used during the election, and afterward votes were counted publicly in front of the village. Absentee voting was allowed, but only with the proper documents of certification. Elections in West Gate, the third case study, have been implemented equally conscientiously. I observed the 2000 elections and postelection period in West Gate for five months and observed them using popular nominations of candidates by any villager, primary elections, campaign speeches as well as written copies of speeches at each polling station, in addition to secret voting booths and public vote tabulations.

43 This book looks only at officially registered village churches. Survey data on illicit house churches and congregations are impossible to obtain. Since 1994, all legal religious groups have been required to register with the State Council's Religious Affairs Bureau. According to one report, the government officially recognizes 2,600 Catholic priests. "China Tightening Its Grip on Catholics: Three Documents Stress a 'Democratic' Church Separated from Rome," Zenit.org, Rome, May 28, 2003. Officially registered churches experienced a seventeen-fold increase between 1979 and 1996, according to official government figures. See Center for Religious Freedom, Freedom House, http://freedomhouse.org/religion/country/china/china˙persecution.htm.

44 The case of West Gate village is also discussed at some length in Chapters 1 and 4, and the case of South Bend village in Chapter 4.

Neither top-down bureaucratic institutions nor democratic reforms, then, can account for variation in public goods provision among these three villages. Village officials in the first two cases, West Gate and Yang Hamlet, regularly fund and organize village public projects. In the third case, South Bend, the village government fails to organize any public projects at all.

Table 5.1 shows, however, that these three cases differ along a number of other significant dimensions, enabling us to engage in structured comparative analysis. Taken together, the first and second cases – West Gate and Yang Hamlet – constitute a comparison between "most different" cases. In most ways, the two villages are polar opposites. West Gate is located in the suburbs of a special economic zone in Fujian, a coastal province in southern China, whereas Yang Hamlet is located in a primarily agricultural and somewhat mountainous region of Hebei province in northern China. West Gate is a very large and very wealthy village of almost four thousand people, whereas Yang Hamlet is a tiny community about one-tenth the size of West Gate with an income per capita below the national average. Both villages are, however, remarkably similar in that they both have prominent temple or temple festival institutions actively supported by village officials and that they both enjoy relatively responsible government provision of public goods and responsive government. In other words, all other potentially explanatory variables vary except for the existence of village temple institutions, which supports the argument that village temple institutions are associated with better governance and public goods provision.

The second and third cases – Yang Hamlet and South Bend – constitute a comparison between "most similar" cases. Yang Hamlet and South Bend are located in the same township of rural Hebei. Both are small, poor, and completely agricultural. Yet, public goods provision is very different in the two villages. Public goods investment in Yang Hamlet is modest but consistent. Its officials are conscientious about investing money every year to maintain village roads. In contrast, village officials in South Bend do not invest any money in public goods provision. The two villages also differ in another critical dimension. Yang Hamlet has a vibrant temple festival association that reinforces village loyalties and exerts moral authority over villagers and village officials. South Bend has a thriving church attended devoutly by everyone in the village except for the village Party secretary, who says that he is Christian but, as a Party member, cannot be seen to encourage religious activity. In short, all potential explanatory variables in the second and third cases are held constant whereas the type of village social group varies. The fact that public goods provision also varies between these

Table 5.1. *Comparing Temple-Dominated Villages and Church-Dominated Villages*

	West Gate	Yang Hamlet	South Bend
Income per capita	6,712 yuan	1,500 yuan	1,300 yuan
Public funds	Very wealthy	Poor	Average
Implementation of democratic reforms	Good	Good	Good
Distance from county seat	Close	Distant	Distant
Settlement pattern	Multiple clusters of settlements	Single-cluster settlement	Single-cluster settlement
Village population	3,900 people	367 people	352 people
Geographical location	Coastal Fujian province in south China	Hebei province in north China	Hebei province in north China
Village social institutions			
Encompassing and embedding solidary group?	Yes: community temple councils	Yes: temple festival association	No: Catholic church
Embeddedness: participation by village officials	High	High	Low
Public goods outcomes			
Quality of village public goods and services	Good	Good	Mixed: Poor school facilities, good roads
Government investment in public goods and services	High	Modest but regular	None
	Most different cases: different in almost every way but similar social institutions and similar public goods outcomes (West Gate and Yang Hamlet)	**Most similar cases:** Similar in almost every way but different social institutions and different public goods outcomes (Yang Hamlet and South Bend)	

two cases is further evidence that differences in village social organization have an effect on village governmental performance.

Case 1: West Gate Village – Temple Councils and Moral Authority

Walking into West Gate from the west, the importance of community religious institutions is immediately apparent. On the edge of the village, a beautifully poured concrete pool holding water for irrigation has stamped into it a large eight-trigrams symbol traditionally used for divination. Just after the pool is a small public square bordered by one of the village's smaller temples (which doubles as a polling station during village elections), a basketball court, and, under construction, a theater stage for opera performances during temple festivals.

West Gate is a wealthy village located in the suburbs of the Xiamen Special Economic Zone in Fujian province. In 2000, village income per capita was almost 7,000 yuan, more than three times that of the national average, and West Gate's village government enjoys an annual revenue of around 1 million yuan. The village is relatively large, with 3,900 people.

West Gate has a temple community council that plays a significant role in village affairs and governance. The council has twenty-three members, most in their fifties and sixties, who meet five times a year and in subgroups more frequently. The temple council actively asserts the value of the village's history and identity. When the temple was rebuilt, for example, the council made sure to create for one of the walls a marble tablet with the history of the village community and its temple institutions. The tablet goes back five hundred years, but it becomes particularly detailed starting in 1856, when it describes a village project to renovate the temple. Even now, villagers consider rebuilding village temples an important duty and central to maintaining the village's local reputation. In interviews, villagers complained repeatedly that the temple council should start thinking about renovating the village Mazu temple because when visitors come, they will see that it is old and rundown.

What is remarkable about West Gate is the strong sense of village identity and loyalty promoted by the village temple council. The moral obligation to contribute one's fair share and give back to the village community is very strong. When the council decided to rebuild the village's Wu ancestral temple in 1996, even households of other surnames contributed to the project without solicitation. Ultimately 99 percent of the village's households – including those of the village's officials – contributed to the project. According to one council member, even families with other surnames contributed because they felt deeply grateful and indebted to the Wus for allowing them to acquire land and a livelihood when they moved to the village generations ago and have adopted the Wu ancestors as local guardians for the community as a whole.[45]

In addition to protecting the village's reputation and "face," the temple community council also acquires moral authority by setting an example for the village government through its governance institutions and financial transparency practices. Since the early 1990s, the state has frequently exhorted local officials to promote transparency in village public finance as part of grassroots democratic reforms. Although these efforts have had some success, in many places the publicized figures literally do not add up, and villagers assume that officials have doctored them. In contrast, West Gate's temple council makes the council's accounts and receipts freely available at any time to public scrutiny. The council also documents and posts the amount of each donation and the name of the donor. The council oversees about 40,000 yuan of donations every year to the hamlet's various temples, and also solicits additional contributions from households when planning large-scale projects, but the significance of these institutions is far greater than the amount of revenue that they oversee would suggest. Such meticulous financial management sets an ideal to which villagers naturally compare the performance of village officials.

It would be totally inaccurate, however, to characterize the temple council as subverting the village government's authority. Village officials are deeply embedded in the temple's institutions and support its activities. Both village officials and council members see their interests as complementary, so much so that in 1996, when the district government directed all its villages to set up senior citizens' associations, village officials and council members agreed to make the temple council (which had already been operating since the 1980s) the village senior citizens' association. By giving the council this official title, the council head explained, village officials would be able to attend and participate in the council's activities, which before they had avoided in accordance with the state's ban on "feudal superstition," and the council would be camouflaged from state censure. In addition to the title of senior citizens' association, two glass-framed certificates in the village temple also identify the temple as a branch of the village's family planning

[45] Interview with village community council deputy head, eastern Fujian province, November 12, 2000.

committee. Both villagers and officials refer to these certificates as "just propaganda" – in other words, propaganda created jointly by villagers and local state agents to deceive (or at least give a certain impression to) higher levels of the state.

The temple council exerts a significant amount of leverage over village officials. Council members report that they regularly seek out the village Party secretary and village head "to tell them the good and bad things they are doing."[46] In comparison to neighboring villages (without villagewide temple groups), West Gate's officials organize an impressive variety of public services, ranging from dumpsters and sanitation workers to paved village roads bordered with rudimentary gutters. According to West Gate's villagers, the village's temple groups take the lead in collecting donations to repair a local road or build a drainage system and then push the village government to fund the rest of the project. In the words of the temple council's chair:

For the construction and repair of roads, the community council has to lead the way. A few years ago, this village was kind of backward, especially in sanitation. There used to be a lot of flies, and the roads were pitted with potholes. Now things are better due to our own efforts. Since villagers give money to the temples, asking the gods to protect us all, the money should be used for public facilities and welfare, such as paving roads and constructing drainage gutters. Frankly, these are things that the village committee should be taking care of, tasks within the scope of their responsibilities.[47]

By upholding the moral standards of the temple council and fulfilling their obligations to contribute to the good of the group, village officials have earned substantial moral authority in the village. As the council head observed, "we help the village cadres 'obtain face' (*zheng mianzi*)."[48] Village officials recognize that cooperating with the council allows them to leverage the council's moral authority to achieve state objectives in the village. The temple council helps mobilize villagers to attend meetings convened by the village government. Village officials and council members have successfully worked together to keep villagers from violating the state firecracker ban and (as discussed in Chapter 4) to persuade villagers to give rights of way for the construction of a public drainage channel. Providing help to the village

[46] Interview with male village community council member, eastern Fujian province, June 7, 2001.

[47] Interview with village community council head, eastern Fujian province, November 6, 2000.

[48] Ibid.

government allows the temple council to propose needed public projects and to pressure the village government to organize them.

The temple council's power to give input about village policies and to hold officials accountable for public goods provision has been institutionalized. Even when the specific people holding positions in the village government change, village government officials, regardless of who they are, make it a point to ask temple council members for advice in dealing with village issues. Temple council members, for their part, also make suggestions and give criticisms even when unsolicited. In West Gate, for example, the council head is on good terms with both the current village head and the previous village head. During the 2000 elections, both came to chat with the temple head, who told the current village head that he needed to make a public commitment to improving the village economy in order to get elected and advised the previous village head to address rampant gossip among villagers about corruption during his previous term in the bidding for village government construction projects. In short, the temple council in West Gate provides informal institutions of accountability by mobilizing villagers to sanction village officials for poor performance and rewarding officials for providing public goods by helping them mobilize compliance with state tasks.

Case 2: Yang Hamlet – Temple Festival Associations and Moral Authority

In most ways, Yang Hamlet, a cluster of adobe houses shaded by poplar trees four hours northeast of Beijing in Hebei province, is the polar opposite of West Gate. Village government revenue is only about 10,000 yuan per year, and almost 70 percent goes toward paying various fees levied by the township government. Government coffers are empty. In 2000, income per capita was around 1,500 yuan, significantly below the official figure given by the state as well as the average in the survey sample. In addition to the corn everyone grows, half of the village contracts additional land from the village government on which to grow apple trees with beans and peanuts below them. With just over a hundred households, the fifty villagers with manual labor jobs in the county town also contribute a substantial proportion of household income.

But as in West Gate, the solidary institutions in Yang Hamlet make the conferral of moral standing possible and an important political resource for village officials. This region of Hebei province is renowned for a number of very large temple fairs, although these events are far more secular than their counterparts in Fujian province and elsewhere in southern China. Dating back to imperial times, troupes and festival associations have been institutions that assert the value of a particular community's history and identity and give a community a good reputation. Villagers thus accord association organizers higher moral and social standing for their leadership and contributions.

Yang Hamlet's folk dancing group, or "flower association" (*hua hui*), performs every year on the nineteenth day of the second lunar month at Xinji, the biggest temple fair east of Beijing. Although disbanded in 1960, it was reorganized in the early 1990s by two villagers, now fifty and sixty years old, who enjoy a high level of respect and prestige (*weiwang*) and are old enough to remember the association's activities from their childhoods. The group now numbers forty to fifty participants who range in age from eight to seventy years old. In addition to performing at various regional temple fairs, the group congregates to perform for their own recreation and the village's entertainment. Families that do not perform in the group still feel obligated to show their support by making donations to the association. In 2002, 70 percent of households, including those of village officials, made donations of between 5 and 50 yuan. The association's annual revenue is not huge – about 2,000 yuan in 2002 – but compared to the 3,000 yuan the village government retains after paying various township fees, it is a nontrivial amount.

In addition to reinforcing a sense of obligation to the village community among residents, the association's financial transparency institutions set and legitimize performance standards for village governance. The amount of each donation and the name of the contributor are meticulously recorded and written on a poster that is pasted to the outside wall of a house in the village center that acts as a bulletin board. Mimicking the format of the village government's account sheets, the association itemizes and posts its income and expenditures every three months. When I visited in May 2002, remnants of posters from April and February as well as from November 2001 were still visible. In contrast, the village government publicizes its accounts once at the end of the year. The festival association's practices not only uphold the virtues of financial transparency, but they constitute a constant and highly visible moral exemplar for the village government to follow.

Village officials in Yang Hamlet strive to meet the temple festival's association's ethical standards and ideals of public service. For the last two years, none of the village officials have taken their officially mandated salaries of

2,000 to 3,000 yuan per year. As compensation for their work, they instead take exemptions for the land they rent from the village collective, which amounts to no more than a few hundred yuan for each official. In this way, they conserve village funds for the maintenance of roads and the bridge in the village, which they carry out conscientiously every year. Large-scale public projects are beyond their means, but as with many communities that instill a strong sense of affection mixed with obligation (*ganqing*) in their members, Yang Hamlet's officials seek influence from members and former members of the community to obtain small-scale public works. For example, in 1999, they contacted a former villager working in the county electricity bureau who recommended Yang Hamlet for a state-subsidized experimental project for laying underground electricity lines. By invoking native-place loyalties and obligations, village officials obtained 250,000 yuan – an extraordinary sum – for grid renovation in the village.

By living up to the expectations of villagers and the standards set by village solidary institutions, officials have acquired a certain amount of legitimacy and moral authority. This authority allowed them to collect 95 percent of township taxes assigned for 2001, a compliance rate significantly higher than 80 percent, the average for the sample surveyed in 2000, or 76 percent, the average for Hebei villages in the sample. Although the township government offers to provide them with extra personnel to extract taxes from the villagers, village officials refuse their help, for two reasons. First, village officials believe that drawing on township coercive resources will damage their legitimacy with the villagers. One official commented, "Having township officials here would just create trouble (*zaocheng maodun*) with the villagers." Second, village officials do not consider calling in people from the township because they do not view noncompliance as inherently wrong. When I asked why villagers would not want to pay taxes, the same official retorted, "Why would they? (*tamen zhenme hui yao jiao?*)" [49]

Case 3: South Bend Village – Church Institutions Substituting for Village Government

Located in the same township as Yang Hamlet, South Bend is very similar in geographical and socioeconomic terms, but one difference is immediately apparent. The church in South Bend, a nominally Catholic one, is easily the grandest building for miles. When the priest approved by the state

[49] Interview with male village Party branch member, eastern Hebei province, May 1, 2002.

Religious Affairs Bureau is in town, mass is held every day. When he is traveling around the county serving the congregations of the eight other state-registered house churches, mass is held weekly. At any given service, about one-third of the village is in attendance, and just about everyone in the village identifies himself or herself as Christian.

Otherwise, both villages are equally small in terms of population. Both villages consist almost entirely of mud brick houses, although the income per capita in South Bend is somewhat lower than that in Yang Hamlet – slightly above 1,000 yuan. South Bend's village government has more resources at its disposal, with 40,000 yuan saved in village coffers, but it has no immediate plans for funding any public projects. In 1999, village government revenue came from village taxes of 10,000 yuan, all of which was spent on cadres' wages. Not surprisingly, the following year in 2000, village officials were able to collect only about 20 percent of the taxes assessed on villagers and, as a result, did not receive their salaries.

South Bend's Party secretary complains bitterly about his lack of authority in the village. When I asked him if the villagers had confidence or trust in him (*xinren*), he lamented, "Not a lot! The villagers believe in religion (*xinjiao*), not in me." When asked to elaborate, he continued, "The villagers don't trust me because I never go to church." I then expressed some confusion about the improvised shrine in the room that had a wooden crucifix and posters of Jesus and Mary labeled with Chinese translations of their names, and he explained, "My wife put those up. I'm a Party member and Party members are not supposed to believe in religion. But to tell you the truth, I am a believer. But I'm a bad disciple."[50]

In contrast, the other two villagers serving as village accountant and village committee head, positions that do not require Party membership, are active churchgoers and members of the four-person church management committee as well. The Party secretary lamented, "It's the church management committee that makes all the important decisions (*shuo de suan*)." To counter the power of the church committee, the Party secretary has repeatedly visited and petitioned the township government, the township and county Civil Affairs Bureau, and the county Religious Affairs Bureau for permission to increase the size of the village Party branch. All of these attempts, however, have been fruitless. Although there is no personal enmity between the three village officials – throughout one of my visits to the Party secretary's house, the village accountant noncommittally let the

[50] Interview with male village Party secretary, eastern Hebei province, April 27, 2001.

Party secretary protest without commenting or arguing – the village Party secretary refuses to cooperate with the other two officials. This conflict has essentially paralyzed village administration.

Although South Bend's church is encompassing, it is not embedding. Because the village Party secretary is not allowed by the Party to participate in church activities or be seen as a member of the church, church institutions cannot enable villagers to hold village officials accountable, nor can they offer moral standing as an incentive for the village Party secretary to organize public projects. The village Party secretary feels that no matter what he does or how well he performs, villagers will not regard him very highly. Perhaps as a result, he does not try very hard. Noncompliance with the collection of township and village taxes is very high. Village government is paralyzed with conflict between the village's officials. Village governmental provision of public goods is nonexistent.

The village church does, however, occasionally organize public projects itself. The church management committee (*jiaotang guanli weiyuanhui*) appointed by the priest consists of four male villagers in their forties and fifties who assist the church's priest and divide up responsibilities for church building maintenance, electricity supply, and materials for church activities and masses. Villager donations to the church total about 3,000 yuan per year, an amount exceeding the tax revenue the village government is able to extract. In addition to donations, the church sometimes also receives subsidies from the government Religious Affairs Bureau. In 1997, it received a grant to replace the church's roof and diverted some 20,000 yuan of the grant to pave the village's main road. The grant money went directly to the church, however, completely bypassing the hands of the village government and village public finance.

The village church committee, however, remains studiously apolitical and noncommittal about the performance of village government. Unlike West Gate and Yang Hamlet, South Bend's church does not publicize its accounts or donations or set itself up in direct comparison to the village government.

Conclusion

Even when formal state institutions are weak, village governmental provision of public goods can still be good in places with encompassing and embedding solidary groups. Village temples are one example of how these groups work in rural China. The case studies discussed in this chapter illustrate how temple groups can provide a common framework of moral obligations for the entire community. Villagers can use this framework to reward and sanction officials for their performance. Officials in Yang Hamlet and West Gate who fulfill their obligations to the temple group to provide public goods for the community are rewarded with higher moral standing. If village officials fail to live up to the obligations that they have to contribute to the good of the temple or village community, they lose their standing as both officials and as members of the temple group. In contexts such as rural China, where the standing of local officials in many places is already pretty low, the alternative sources of standing and legitimacy provided by community solidary groups can be extremely valuable.

Ironically, state mores against officials participating in churches prevent village officials from taking advantage of the moral authority and legitimacy that village churches can offer. As encompassing but not embedding solidary groups, village churches in China can mobilize members for collective projects. They may, as we see in the case of South Bend, try to provide the village with public goods on their own, without the help of village officials. But they cannot provide officials with the same incentives to provide public goods that temple groups can, and the public projects they try to organize are not as good as the ones in South Bend and West Gate, which are organized with the benefit of government participation. South Bend's Party secretary fails to make any effort to organize public projects because he believes that it would not make a difference anyway – villagers would still view him with disapproval and suspicion. So although villagers in South Bend are perhaps better off than they would be without a church, they are perhaps not as well off as they could be if relations between the church and the state were different.

6

Lineages and Local Governance

When the boundaries of a solidary group coincide with the boundaries of the local government's jurisdiction, and the group encompasses the entire locality, the group's collective goods become the same thing as public goods. The model of informal accountability thus posits that localities with embedding solidary groups that encompass everyone in a local government's jurisdiction are more likely to have better local governmental provision of public goods than localities without these groups, all other things being equal.

In this chapter, we look at lineage groups, which generally embed village officials in their activities but vary in scale, and whether or not they encompass a local governmental jurisdiction. By looking at a single type of solidary group, we can hold numerous group characteristics constant – lineage groups have similar principles of organization, similar kinds of collective activities, similar types of membership criteria – and see what happens when the scale of the group and its fit with political administrative boundaries vary. If the hypothesis is correct, we should expect villagewide lineages to be more likely to have a positive effect on village governmental provision of public goods. Lineage groups, however, which fragment a village into subvillage groups, should be less likely to have this kind of positive effect.

Lineage Groups in Rural China

Like native-place associations, tribes, and other ethnic groups, lineages organize themselves around claims of common descent. Within this category of groups, lineages have received the most scholarly attention, largely due to Maurice Freedman's 1966 seminal study *Chinese Lineage and Society*.[1]

It is important to note that people with the same surname and related by patrilineal descent are not necessarily organized around this characteristic. Villagers related by patrilineal descent often live in close proximity, but they do not necessarily belong to any well-organized lineage group.[2] Rubie Watson, for example, has estimated that even in Guangdong province, often considered a region dominated by powerful lineages in the pre-Communist period, no more than 30 percent of the rural population belonged to large, organized lineage groups.[3]

How best to distinguish lineage groups from other types of ethnic and kinship groups has been thoroughly debated.[4] Perhaps the most well-known model of lineage organization, Freedman's formulation emphasizes the centrality of corporate property in distinguishing lineage organizations from other kinship groups.[5] Others, such as James Watson, have argued that lineage organizations continue to exist even after collectively owned land disappears. Watson gives the example of a village lineage organization in the New Territories that ceased to be a corporation based on landownership in the late 1950s but provided an organizational framework for migration to Europe and access to the restaurant trade, which became the lineage's shared resource.[6]

Watson proposes a useful model of lineage organization that clearly identifies three distinguishing characteristics.[7] First, like Freedman, Watson defines lineages as corporate groups in which members benefit from group

[1] Maurice Freedman, *Chinese Lineage and Society: Fukien and Kwangtung* (London: Athlone Press, 1971), 20–1.

[2] These cases constituted "residential clusters of agnates" rather than lineage groups. See Watson, "Chinese Kinship Reconsidered," 594. Judith Strauch looks specifically at smaller lineages and multilineage communities. Judith Strauch, "Community and Kinship in Southeastern China: The View from the Multilineage Villages of Hong Kong," *Journal of Asian Studies* 43, no. 1 (November 1983), 21–50. See also Emily Ahern, *The Cult of the Dead in a Chinese Village* (Stanford: Stanford University Press, 1973).

[3] Rubie Watson, "Class Differences and Affinal Relations in South China," *Man* 16, no. 4 (December 1981), 595.

[4] Authors have frequently used the terms "lineage" and "clan" interchangeably. Chinese terms for groups based on descent from a common ancestor (*zu*, *zong*, *shi*, *fang*, and so on) also indicate various and multiple types of kinship groups. Watson, "Chinese Kinship Reconsidered," 597; David Faure, "Lineage as Cultural Invention: The Case of the Pearl River Delta," *Modern China* 15, no. 1 (January 1989), 7.

[5] Freedman, *Chinese Lineage and Society*.

[6] Watson, *Emigration and the Chinese Lineage*.

[7] Idem, "Chinese Kinship Reconsidered," 594.

resources, but Watson argues that these shared resources may be land or other resources such as information, reputation, or job introductions. Lineage organizations were traditionally established with the donation of land and resources to construct an ancestral hall, finance rituals memorializing the benevolence of the donor, and assist the descendants of the donor in material ways.[8] Second, lineage members self-consciously identify themselves as part of a group distinctive from outsiders. Regularly organized rituals and activities reinforce this identity. Important collective rituals included festival celebrations, ceremonies paying respect to ancestral tablets embodying ancestral spirits, ceremonies for entering newborn sons into the lineage's official genealogy, annual communal banquets, and, especially in the north where ancestral halls were less common, collective sweeping of the ancestor's grave.[9]

Third, lineages are based on demonstrated descent from a known common ancestor. Other kinship-based groups such as clans and surname groups are based upon "putative, or fictionalized, descent from historical (or even mythical) figures," though they too may have collectively owned property, communal activities, and ancestral halls.[10] Surname associations (*zongqinhui*) in Taiwan described by Hugh Baker, for example, recruit members on the basis of a shared surname, but members are not descendants of a known common ancestor.[11] Instead, these organizations are voluntary associations with membership dues that individuals join seeking to "create the conditions of agnatic kinship."[12]

Although this chapter generally refers to empirical data about lineage organizations, we can apply the model of informal accountability to any group with norms of group duty and obligation. Any type of ethnic or

8 Ibid., 605.

9 See Strauch, "Community and Kinship in Southeastern China," 21–50; Rubie Watson, "The Creation of a Chinese Lineage: The Teng of Ha Tsuen, 1669–1751," *Modern Asian Studies* 16, no. 1 (1982), 69–100.

10 Watson, "Chinese Kinship Reconsidered," 603, 610. Watson points out that unlike lineages, clans do not focus rituals around graves because not all clan members share the same ancestor. Aside from their principle for determining kinship, clans are similar to what Freedman calls "higher-order lineages," or lineage groups made up of multiple lineage groups, each with its own focal ancestor, but whose focal ancestors all share a common ancestor. Like higher-order lineages, clans are composed of multiple lineage groups, although these groups do not demonstrate descent from a known ancestor and only share the same surname.

11 Hugh Baker, *Extended Kinship in the Traditional City* (Stanford: Stanford University Press, 1977).

12 Watson, "Chinese Kinship Reconsidered," 611.

kinship group that establishes moral obligations for its members constitutes a solidary group with the potential for providing informal institutions of accountability. Although whether a solidary kinship group is based on demonstrated or merely stipulated descent does not matter for this book's analysis, this chapter frequently refers to both lineage and kinship groups simply because lineage groups remain the most common form of kinship group in the countryside.

This chapter discusses the institutions established by lineage groups as simply another set of rural social institutions that – like temple institutions – can substitute for formal state institutions of accountability when imbued with certain characteristics. This approach is consistent with the observations of P. Steven Sangren, who has pointed out that the operational norms for a variety of traditional corporate groups in China – including temple organizations or "deity-cult corporations," chambers of commerce, guilds, and alumni associations – are similar and that these groups should therefore be analyzed in the same context.[13]

In fact, the dividing line between lineage and kinship groups and other types of community groups is not always very clear. Rubie Watson's research in the New Territories finds that lineage organizations often controlled numerous satellite villages of people unrelated to the lineage.[14] Fei Xiaotong observed in pre-1949 rural Yunnan that "local organization is formed in terms of clan which includes even members of different surnames. Functionally these are not strictly kinship groups." As Fei concludes, "kinship is only a means by which social groups are organized for different purposes."[15]

Like temples, lineage and kinship institutions have a long history of integrating rural communities into a framework of state authority. Prasenjit Duara has proposed two ideal types of villages with which to examine state–society relations in the late imperial and Republican periods: "lineage-community" villages and "religious-community" villages. The imperial state actively promoted both lineage and religious institutions as powerful channels for regulating social behavior through moral authority.[16] Duara

13 Sangren, "Traditional Chinese Corporations," 391.

14 Watson, "Class Differences and Affinal Relations in South China," 595.

15 Fei, *Chinese Village Close-Up*, 132–4.

16 James Watson gives examples of state officials actively supporting the establishment and development of lineage organizations. For one lineage organization, state officials arranged for the lineage's estate to be exempt from land taxes, and the founder's son petitioned the throne for the authority to discipline uncooperative lineage members. Watson, "Chinese Kinship Reconsidered," 616.

argues that the political organization of villages located near cities was more likely to be based on temple organizations, whereas villages located far from cities were more likely to be organized in lineage groups, although in most villages, both religious and lineage ideology reinforced the power of the state. For lineage-community villages, the state utilized existing lineage institutions to organize local administration. When villages were divided into smaller units for administrative purposes, these divisions often fell along lineage cleavages. Representation in village councils was often apportioned to the various lineage groups – either different branches of the same lineage or different lineages entirely – that would each select a representative to the council. The moral authority of lineage organizations thus reinforced the legitimacy of state administration.[17]

As with temples, the new Communist state endeavored to stamp out the traditional authority of lineage organizations and replace them with modern state institutions and the all-encompassing authority of the Communist Party. The Cultural Revolution targeted both ancestral halls and village temples alike for destruction, but for much of the Maoist period, the state tolerated (or at least did not notice) kinship-related activities as long as they were practiced within the household rather than collectively. Reinforced as kinship institutions were by affective relationships, villagers often maintained these institutions and communal identities even when material symbols of the institutions no longer existed.[18] Michael Frolic quotes a Henan peasant describing the problems arising from the consolidation of two production teams in 1971:

> We are two separate branches of a [lineage], and for as long as anyone can remember, we haven't gotten along. We don't intermarry, we don't even drink tea together if we can help it. We've lived in our separate parts of the village for so long that no one

[17] Duara, *Culture, Power, and the State*. See also Huaiyin Li, "Village Regulations at Work: Local Taxation in Huailu County, 1900–1936," *Modern China* 26, no. 1 (January 2000), 85; Kevin O'Brien and Lianjiang Li, "Accommodating Democracy in a One-Party State: Introducing Village Elections in China," *China Quarterly*, no. 162 (June 2000), 465–89. During the imperial period, lineage organizations were often involved in tax collection and prompted members to pay their taxes on time, or directly collected them and remitted them to the government. Huaiyin Li notes: "It was not uncommon in such cases for strict 'clan regulations' (*zugui*) to be formulated and enforced to ensure full and prompt tax payment or repayment. Those who failed to fulfill their tax duties were often excluded from sharing the sacrifices to clan ancestors by these clan regulations." Li, "Village Regulations at Work," 80.

[18] On the impact of lineages in rural politics in the Maoist period, see Burns, *Political Participation in Rural China*; Chan et al., *Chen Village under Mao and Deng*.

could imagine it otherwise. During that one year that we were joined, remember all the problems? People wouldn't speak to each other; no cooperation; each team was suspicious of the other. I say that we are two separate units – we are all called Li, but we are two separate families and people from separate families can't form one family. You can't wipe away the facts of the past – ancestral tablets can be destroyed, but they stay in our minds.[19]

Governance became more difficult, as the preceding case illustrates, when administrative institutions did not coincide with existing kinship institutions.

With the start of reforms in 1978, collective lineage groups have again appeared throughout the countryside. Myron Cohen's 1986–7 fieldwork in a Hebei village led him to note:

These lineages are still major reference groups in village life, although they no longer possess corporate holdings or display solidarity by feasting together or through worship at the lineage cemetery.... the contemporary social significance of lineage ties is apparent in many ritual contexts such as weddings, funerals, the lunar New Year, and with respect to various kinds of cooperative relationships.[20]

Clashes between clan groups, sometimes violent and sometimes even organized by local officials, have become a matter of increasing concern to the state.[21] Researchers as well as government officials have linked increased lineage and clan activity to the implementation of democratic reforms and elections at the village level.[22]

Formal state institutions no longer incorporate kinship institutions into village governance as they did in the imperial period. When township governments appoint village officials, they sometimes try to allocate positions to different lineage groups if the village is divided by clear lineage cleavages, but no formal regulations require them to do so. Nor is there any guarantee that village elections will result in a village government composed of representatives from different lineage groups. Since few villages have groups of equal size, and candidates are required to achieve an absolute majority, minority lineage groups may very well experience the "tyranny of the majority" and find themselves perpetually blocked from government office.

19 Michael Frolic, *Mao's People* (Cambridge: Harvard University Press, 1980), 29.

20 Cohen, "Lineage Organization in North China," 511.

21 Perry, "Rural Violence in Socialist China," 756–83.

22 See, for example, Daniel Kelliher, "The Chinese Debate over Village Self-Government," *China Journal*, no. 37 (January 1997), 79; O'Brien, "Implementing Political Reform in China's Villages," 56. Kelliher cites one national survey finding that lineages influence 40 percent of all village elections.

Table 6.1. *Number of Villages with Only Household Kinship Institutions, by Province*

Village	Number of Villages
Shanxi	33
Hebei	12
Jiangxi	3
Fujian	3
Total	*51 villages*

Sample size: 316 villages.

Findings from the Survey Data

Data from my survey in 2000 show that lineage activities and kinship institutions are indeed widespread. Overall, 66 percent of villages in the survey reported kinship activities or institutions in their village. In some places, kinship activities are primarily household-based. Many villagers have small family shrines for paying respect to ancestors. Out of the 316 villages in the survey, 42 percent of villages reported that villagers observed rituals of ancestral respect either within their home or in an ancestral hall, and 16 percent of villages reported that villagers practiced ancestral rituals of respect within the household but that they had no collective kinship activities. Villages with only household-based kinship activity were most common in Shanxi province (see Table 6.1). In some villages, interested individuals also compile genealogies as personal projects without organizing group activity. Nearly half of the villages reported that at least one genealogy had been compiled in their village, and a quarter of villages reported that old genealogies had been updated or new ones created since 1978.

Collective lineage activities and institutions, however, were also common. Out of the 316 villages in the survey, 139 villages (44 percent) reported some form of collective lineage or kinship institution. The vast majority of these villages were located in Jiangxi and Fujian provinces. Among the most common collective lineage and kinship institutions were lineage or clan heads (17 percent of villages in the survey), sweeping of ancestral graves (27 percent), mediation of disputes among lineage members (19 percent), and welfare assistance to the poor (17 percent) (see Tables 6.2 through 6.4).

The clearest and most easily observed indication of collective kinship activities, however, is the existence of an ancestral hall in the village. About

Table 6.2. *Distribution of Villages with Collective Lineage Ritual Activities*

Activity	Percentage of Villages
Collective rituals of respect to ancestor spirits	11
Collective sweeping of ancestral graves	27
Ritual opera performances on holidays	4
Other lineage or clan rituals	13

Note: The sample consists of 316 villages.

Table 6.3. *Distribution of Villages with Lineage-Organized Services*

Service	Percentage of Villages
Mutual aid farming arrangements	13
Welfare assistance	17
Dispute mediation within lineage	19
Protection or advocacy against nonlineage actors	9
Public projects such as road construction	15
Management of collective resources such as forests or ponds	7
Lineage-organized association for the elderly*	4
Lineage-organized weddings and funerals*	21

Note:*In some places, these activities are mandated by government regulations and sometimes organized by village officials. On the other hand, just as frequently these organizations are true lineage organizations that are simply masquerading as state-approved social organizations, just as private enterprises operated under the guise of collective enterprises before they were approved.

Table 6.4. *Distribution of Villages with Specific Lineage Institutions*

Institution	Percentage of Villages
Lineage or clan head	17
Ancestral hall management organization	8
Genealogy organization	16
Lineage dragon-boat association	1

Note: The sample consists of 316 villages.

one-third of the villages reported they had at least one ancestral hall building. The mere existence of an ancestral hall building, however, does not guarantee active lineage institutions. Many villages stopped using their ancestral halls for ritual activities during the Cultural Revolution and never reinstituted kinship practices. Ancestral halls that were not destroyed were

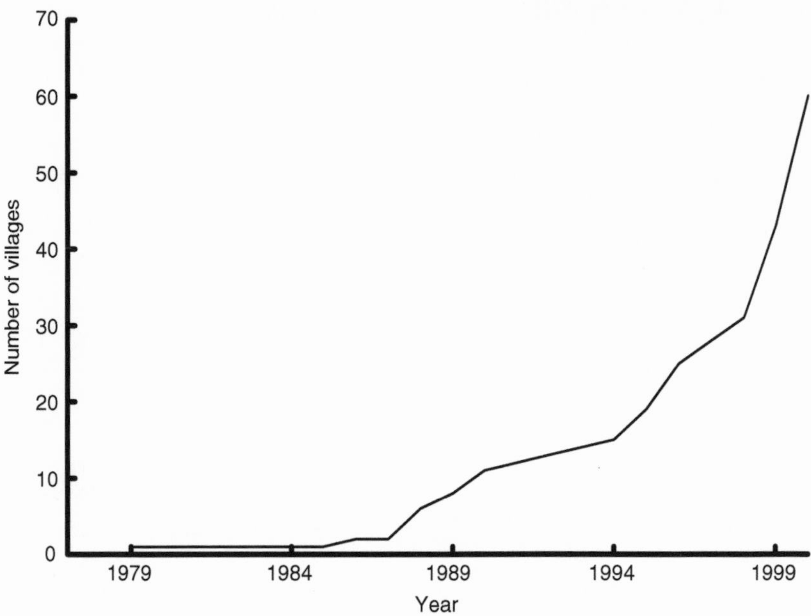

Figure 6.1. Number of villages with ancestral hall reconstruction since 1979.

sometimes converted into granaries or storehouses or left to fall into disrepair.

Many villages, however, have recently refurbished or rebuilt their ancestral halls. Figure 6.1 shows the rise over time in the number of villages that have carried out reconstruction projects since 1979. Ancestral hall reconstruction projects became increasingly common in the late 1980s and showed a steep increase in the late 1990s. In 2000, 19 percent of villages in the survey reported that at least one ancestral hall in their village had been refurbished since 1979.

The scale of these projects is often impressive. Among the sixty villages that reported ancestral hall reconstruction projects, the average cost of the project was about 18,000 yuan, more than ten times the average income per capita for the sample, although project costs varied a great deal from village to village. In some villages, villagers simply donated labor and materials without spending any money, while lineage members in one village spent 400,000 yuan (about U.S.$50,000).

Participation in reconstruction projects is generally very high. When these projects are announced, most lineage members make some sort of donation. As with temple reconstruction projects, lineage members feel a strong sense of obligation as well as considerable social pressure to contribute. In 73 percent of the villages that reported ancestral hall reconstruction, the majority of households belonging to the relevant lineage donated to the project. On average, households donated 17 percent of their village's income per capita, or about 160 yuan, to ancestral hall reconstruction projects, a sizable amount considering that official village and township levies are not supposed to exceed 5 percent of local income per capita. The average household donation exceeded 5 percent of village income per capita in 42 percent of the villages that carried out ancestral hall reconstruction projects. In almost one-fifth of the villages, the average household donation exceeded 20 percent of village income per capita.

Ancestral hall reconstruction projects indicate that lineage institutions are strong enough to mobilize considerable resources from group members. These projects generally involve a relatively short period of concentrated activity. Once construction of the ancestral hall is completed, group activity often subsides. In contrast to village temples, which are usually open to visitors year-round, organize activities according to a ritual calendar with a number of festival holidays, and often double as village community centers, many ancestral halls in villages I visited were locked for most of the year and opened only during the Spring Festival.

Measuring the Explanatory Variable

In this chapter, however, we want to assess the impact of *active* lineage groups in which members have shared moral obligations and collective activities. To identify villages with consistently active collective lineage institutions, I look at whether the village reports the existence of an ancestral hall with ancestor tablets (*paiwei*). Ancestor or spirit tablets are thought to contain the spirits (*hun*) of the deceased, and tablets may represent an individual or a collectivity of ancestors.[23] Ancestral halls with ancestor tablets indicate that people gather at the hall to pay their respects collectively on particular holidays. Fourteen percent of the 316 villages in the survey have ancestral halls with spirit tablets.

[23] Maurice Freedman, *Family and Kinship in Chinese Society* (Stanford: Stanford University Press, 1970), 165; John P. Burns, "China's Nomenklatura," *Problems of Communism* 36, no. 5 (1987), 36–51; Emile Durkheim, *The Division of Labor in Society*, trans. W. D. Halls (New York: Free Press, 1984).

This measure of solidary lineage groups is relatively coarse, but it also has several advantages. First, it does not rely on the accuracy of reports by village officials, the survey's main respondents, of lineage activities and institutions. From a practical standpoint, the existence of ancestral halls with ancestor tablets is a particularly reliable indicator for active kinship institutions because unlike reported activities, survey enumerators could see and personally verify the existence of ancestral halls and tablets. Second, this measure reflects the existence of strong collective rituals and obligations in contrast to lineage and kinship activities such as poverty assistance and dispute mediation, which are sometimes informally organized by villagers on an ad hoc basis without the existence of strong lineage institutions and obligations. Another possible measure would be the reported existence of a lineage head. During survey pretesting, however, potential survey respondents sometimes interpreted this term to mean the oldest male member of an extended family rather than the leader of a solidary group.

Analysis and Findings

So do villages with solidary lineage groups have better village governmental public goods provision than villages without these groups? Again, I use six measures of village governmental public goods provision: per capita village government investment in public projects, the existence of paved roads, the existence of paved paths, the percentage of classrooms usable in rainy weather, the newness of the school building, and the existence of running water.[24] To distinguish the effects of solidary lineage groups from the effects of other factors, the statistical analysis again controls for three sets of variables: geographic and demographic factors, economic development, and the implementation of bureaucratic and democratic institutions.[25]

[24] These same six measures of public goods provision are discussed in Chapter 3 and used in all of the book's statistical analyses (specifically in Chapters 5 through 8).

[25] These same control variables are used in all of the book's statistical analyses (specifically in Chapters 5 through 8). Descriptive statistics for these controls are presented in Appendix Table A5.1. Specifically, I control for the following geographic and demographic factors that may cause variation in the demand for specific public goods as well as variation in costs for the same goods in different places: distance from county seat, village terrain (flat or not flat), the number of natural villages (a proxy for the spatial dispersion of village residents), and village population. Dummy variables for the eight counties from which the villages were randomly sampled were also included. The analysis also controls for the following economic factors: 1997 village income per capita, 1997 village government assets, 1997 village government tax revenue per capita, the existence of village government enterprises (*cunban qiye*) in 1995, and the existence of private enterprises (*siying qiye*) in

No Distinction I first evaluate the effect of lineage groups on village governmental provision of public goods without distinguishing whether or not they encompass the entire village. In this analysis, I assess whether villages with one or more lineage halls with ancestor tablets are more likely to have better governmental provision of public goods than villages without any of these lineage halls.[26]

When we do not distinguish between villagewide and subvillage lineage groups, the estimated effect of lineage groups is unclear. Like village temple groups, village lineage groups are embedding solidary groups in which village officials almost always participate. Lineage groups, however, had a statistically significant effect on only one of the six public goods provision outcomes: the existence of paved paths. The estimated relationship between lineage groups and village governmental provision of public goods was negative for three outcomes (investment, classrooms, and newness of school) and positive for three outcomes (roads, paths, and water) – but except for paths, the uncertainty of these estimates was very high. In sum, it is difficult to conclude much of anything from these results.[27]

Villagewide Versus Subvillage Groups The lack of a clear relationship, however, between village lineage groups and village governmental provision of public goods is not surprising if we go back to the hypothesis suggested by

1995. Economic data from 1995 and 1997 are used instead of data from 2000 to reduce problems with identifying the direction of causality. Following the original official definition used in China, private enterprises are defined as enterprises with eight or more people. I also include the following controls for formal bureaucratic and democratic institutions of accountability: the Party membership of the village head, the percentage of village officials who are Party members, the existence of performance contracts with public project targets that village officials must sign with higher-level officials, and the implementation of village elections and villagers' representative assemblies. The construction of the index for the implementation of village democratic reforms is discussed in greater detail in Chapter 7. But even when the implementation of democratic reforms is measured in different ways, the findings here remain the same.

26 Specifically, I use a dichotomous variable coded one when a village reported the existence of one or more lineage halls with ancestor tablets and zero when it reported that it did not have any lineage halls with ancestor tablets. As noted in the previous section, 14 percent of villages in the survey reported that they had solidary lineage groups as measured by lineage halls with ancestor tablets, whereas 86 percent reported that they did not.

27 The coefficient estimate on paved paths was positive, sizable, and statistically significant, but this result did not hold for the other five public goods provision outcomes. Using the seemingly unrelated regression method, we could not reject the hypothesis that the coefficient estimate on the existence of solidary lineage groups as measured by the existence of one or more ancestral halls with spirit tablets is equal to zero at a 90 percent confidence level. See Appendix Table A6.1 for full model results.

a model of informal accountability. Based on this model, we would expect only those lineage groups that encompass the entire village to have a positive effect on village governmental performance and public goods provision. Unlike village temples and churches, which tend to have boundaries that are coextensive with the political administrative boundaries of the village, lineage groups vary widely in their scale and overlap with administrative boundaries. Lineage group boundaries can be villagewide or fragment villagers into different subvillage lineage groups. When a villagewide lineage group encompasses everyone in the village, and membership in the lineage means the same as membership in the village, lineages should function in the same way as temple groups and enhance village governmental provision of public goods. The members of a subvillage lineage also feel obligations to their group, but in this case group obligations are narrower than obligations to the village community as a whole. Subvillage lineage groups may confer moral standing on their group members, but this standing carries weight only within the group and not with villagers outside of the group.

When we separate villages with villagewide lineage groups from villages with multiple subvillage lineage groups, we find that villages with a single dominant group are more likely to have better public goods provision than either villages with multiple groups or villages without any groups at all.[28] Seven percent of villages reported that they had only one ancestral hall with spirit tablets. Another 7 percent of villages reported that they had multiple ancestral halls with spirit tablets.

Statistical analysis indicated that villages with villagewide lineage groups were likely to have higher levels of government investment in public projects, better roads, better paths, and better water infrastructure than villages with subvillage lineage groups or villages without any lineage groups.[29] We can conclude that villagewide lineage groups have a definite effect on village governmental provision of public goods with a high level of

[28] In this analysis, I use two different dichotomous measures: one for villagewide lineage groups and one for subvillage lineage groups. One variable is coded one when a village reported the presence of only one lineage hall with spirit tablets (and zero otherwise). The second variable was coded one when a village reported multiple subvillage lineage groups as measured by the presence of multiple lineage halls with spirit tablets (and zero otherwise). When one of these variables is coded one, the other is coded zero. When both are coded zero, the village did not report any active lineage groups as measured by the existence of lineage halls with spirit tablets.

[29] As with the statistical analysis assessing the effects of village temples and village churches in Chapter 5, I used seemingly unrelated regression (SUR). See the appendix for a more detailed discussion of the SUR method.

confidence.[30] The estimated relationship between village governmental provision of public goods and villagewide lineage groups as measured by the existence of a single lineage hall with spirit tablets was positive for four public goods outcomes (investment, roads, paths, and water). For two outcomes, classrooms and newness of school, the estimated relationship was negative but also highly uncertain and very small in magnitude. Similar results were obtained regardless of what control variables were included or excluded or how missing data were treated.[31]

The estimated relationship between village governmental provision of public goods and the existence of multiple subvillage lineage groups as measured by the existence of multiple lineage halls with spirit tablets was negative for five out of the six public goods measures (investment, roads, classrooms, school building, and water).[32] For one outcome, the existence

[30] Using SUR, we can reject the null hypothesis that the coefficient estimate on villagewide lineage groups is jointly equal to zero across all six outcomes at a 95 percent confidence level (p-value = 0.04). The full model results are presented in Appendix Table A6.2. The estimated relationship between village provision of public goods and villagewide lineage groups was positive for four outcomes and statistically significant or close to statistically significant for two outcomes (roads and paths). Missing data were deleted listwise, and Huber heteroskedasticity-robust standard errors are reported.

[31] The full model results when missing data are multiply imputed are presented in Appendix Table A6.3. In general, the results are similar to analysis with listwise deletion of missing data, although the coefficient estimate of villagewide lineage groups on investment is larger and the standard error is much smaller. The estimated relationship between village governmental provision of public goods and villagewide lineage groups is again positive for four outcomes and statistically significant or close to statistically significant for three outcomes (investment, roads, and paths). The estimated effect of villagewide lineage groups jointly across outcomes is close enough to statistical significance to be substantively noteworthy (p-value = 0.13). Again, missing data are multiply imputed using the EMis algorithm developed by King et al., "Analyzing Incomplete Political Science Data," 49–69. In this model, robust standard errors are not reported because the existing software program for combining multiply imputed datasets for analysis does not support seemingly unrelated regression with robust standard errors. See Tomz et al., CLARIFY. Results for models using different sets of control variables are in general similar to the results presented here with the exception of the coefficient estimate of villagewide lineage groups on newness of school buildings, which becomes positive and statistically significant when some control variables are dropped. These results are available online at http://www.cambridge.org/9780521871976. Findings from bivariate SUR regression for the six public goods provision measures as well as logit models for the three dichotomous measures of public goods provision (existence of paved roads, existence of paved paths, and existence of running water infrastructure) were generally similar to the multivariate SUR estimates. These results can be viewed online at http://www.cambridge.org/9780521871976.

[32] The full model results are presented in Appendix Table A6.2. The estimated relationship between village provision of public goods and subvillage lineage groups as measured by

of paved paths, the estimated effect was positive.[33] These results were also similar regardless of what control variables were included or excluded or how missing data were treated.[34]

But what if a village's lineage group structure is an effect of village governmental provision of public goods as well as a contributing cause? It seems plausible that villages that have good governmental provision of public goods might be more likely to form villagewide lineage groups rather than fragment into subvillage lineage groups. To examine this possibility, we can use instrumental variables (IV) estimation, a statistical technique that enables us to isolate and estimate the effect of villagewide lineage groups on village governmental provision of public goods even when lineage groups are endogenous.[35] To use this technique, we need an instrument, a variable that is correlated with villagewide lineage groups (the endogenous explanatory variable) and that affects only village governmental provision of public goods through its effect on lineage groups.[36]

the existence of multiple lineage halls with spirit tablets was negative for five outcomes and statistically significant for investment. Missing data were deleted listwise, and Huber heteroskedasticity-robust standard errors are reported.

33 A possible explanation for a positive relationship between the existence of multiple lineage halls and the existence of paved paths is that paved footpaths are generally more common in villages with more building construction because leftover concrete from the construction project is often used to pave surrounding paths. The more lineage halls that a village has, the more likely paths are to be paved with concrete left over from building the halls.

34 The full model results when missing data are multiply imputed are presented in Appendix Table A6.3. Coefficient estimates and standard errors are generally similar to results when missing data are deleted listwise. Again, the estimated relationship between village governmental provision of public goods and subvillage lineage groups is negative for five outcomes (investment, roads, classrooms, school building, and water). None of these relationships are statistically significant, although the level of uncertainty around the estimated effect is relatively low for three outcomes (investment, roads, and newness of school building). The estimated effect on paths is again positive and statistically significant. Again, missing data are multiply imputed using the EMis algorithm developed by ibid. Robust standard errors are not calculated. Results for models using different sets of control variables are in general similar to the results presented here. These results are available online at http://www.cambridge.org/9780521871976. Findings from bivariate SUR regression for the six public goods provision measures as well as logit models for the three dichotomous measures of public goods provision (existence of paved roads, existence of paved paths, and existence of running water infrastructure) were similar to the multivariate SUR estimates. These results can be viewed online at http://www.cambridge.org/9780521871976.

35 IV estimation gives us estimates of the effects of endogenous explanatory variables that are consistent. These estimates converge in probability to the actual effect as the sample size grows without bound.

36 In other words, the variable being used as an instrument must be partially correlated with the endogenous explanatory variable as well as uncorrelated with the error term of the

With these requirements in mind, I designed the survey to collect data on the number of households in each surname group. In this analysis, we can use a simple index of surname fragmentation as an instrument for the current existence of villagewide lineage groups.[37] Surname groups should not be confused with lineage groups, since people with the same surname do not necessarily identify as being in the same lineage or behave collectively as one lineage group. In the Chinese context, surname patterns make a good instrument because they were largely determined exogenously in the pre-Communist period. These patterns were then frozen during the Maoist period, when the state instituted strict policies against internal migration.[38] There is of course no guarantee that villages in which the vast majority of households share the same surname will definitely establish an active villagewide lineage group. But surname patterns and the existence of villagewide lineage groups are correlated since the possibility of a villagewide lineage group requires that a village be dominated by one surname group.

Results from IV estimation also indicated that the estimated effect of villagewide lineage groups on village governmental provision of public goods was positive.[39] In fact, the estimates produced by IV estimation were generally even larger in magnitude. Statistical tests indicated, moreover, that this technique was not necessarily warranted since the differences between these estimates and those produced without using an instrument were not significant enough to suggest that village temple groups were endogenous.

In short, even when we control for economic factors, bureaucratic and democratic institutions, and geographic and demographic factors,

structural equation. See Wooldridge, *Econometric Analysis of Cross Section and Panel Data*, 484–514.

[37] This index was calculated by subtracting the percentage of households in the largest surname group from one.

[38] Dorothy Solinger, *Contesting Citizenship in Urban China: Peasant Migrants, the State, and the Logic of the Market* (Berkeley: University of California Press, 1999).

[39] The bivariate IV model results are available online at http://www.cambridge.org/9780521871976. The estimated relationship between village governmental provision of public goods and villagewide lineage groups was not only positive for all six outcomes but statistically significant for two outcomes (investment and school building). In general, IV estimation produced coefficient estimates much greater in magnitude, which provides even stronger support for the main hypothesis. Hausman tests indicated, however, that the differences between IV estimates and OLS estimates (which in this case are the same as the SUR estimates discussed previously) were not different enough to suggest that OLS or SUR estimates were inconsistent and that village temple groups were endogenous. For one outcome, a Hausman test indicated that OLS or SUR estimates may be inconsistent, but again, the effect estimated by IV regression was still positive and of a much greater magnitude than the effect estimated by OLS or SUR.

villagewide lineage groups have a significant positive effect on village governmental provision of public goods. (These findings also remain the same when we control for the effects of temples and churches.[40]) But just how sizable is this effect? Figure 6.2 compares the mean level or likelihood of different public goods in an average village with a villagewide lineage group to an average village without a villagewide lineage group (average in the sense that all the control variables are set at their means).[41] (These graphs are scaled to match those presented in other chapters in order to facilitate comparison.) The mean per capita investment for a village with a villagewide lineage group as measured by a single lineage hall with spirit tablets was 137 yuan (about U.S.$17), more than double that of villages without any lineage groups and far higher than that of villages with multiple subvillage lineage groups. Villages with villagewide lineages also had a 76 percent mean probability of having paved roads, much higher than villages without lineage groups and more than twice as high as villages fragmented by subvillage lineage groups. They may also be slightly more likely to have running water infrastructure. In terms of paved paths and usable classrooms, villages with different lineage group structures did not differ very much (although villages fragmented by multiple subvillage groups have, on average, school buildings that have gone longer without renovation or reconstruction than villages with villagewide groups or villages without any groups). The uncertainty around some of these estimates (indicated by the gray lines showing 95 percent confidence intervals) was somewhat high, but the fact that we see the same pattern across multiple public goods provision measures makes us more confident that villagewide lineage groups have a notable positive effect and that subvillage lineage groups have a notable negative effect.

Villages with Multiple Types of Solidary Groups

What happens when villages with villagewide lineage groups also have village temples or village churches? Without additional case study research, it is impossible to evaluate how these groups really interact with one another. For statistical analysis of possible interactions, we again run into the problem of small numbers. Only eight villages had a villagewide lineage and a

[40] Full model results when measures of village churches, villagewide lineages, and subvillage lineages are estimated in the same model are presented in Appendix Tables A5.5 (where missing data are deleted listwise) and A5.6 (in which missing data are multiply imputed).

[41] These fitted values are calculated using the model results presented in Appendix Table A6.3.

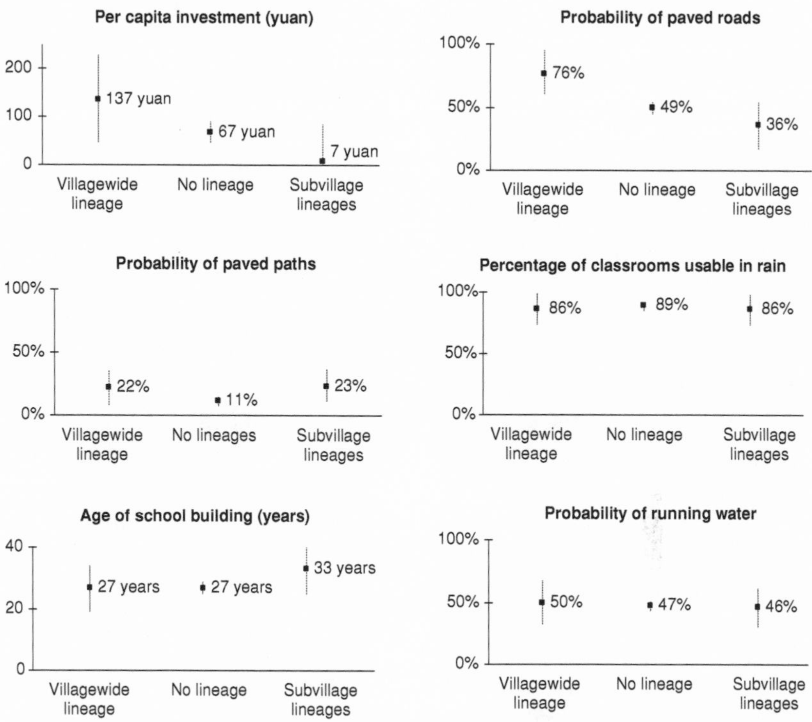

Figure 6.2. Provision of public goods in villages with and without lineage groups.

village temple group (but no church). Results from statistical analysis suggested a possible positive interaction effect between villagewide lineages and village temples, although this interaction effect was not statistically significant in terms of the conventional levels of confidence.[42] Only three villages had both a villagewide lineage and a village church (but no temple), and only one village had all three kinds of solidary groups. With such small numbers, more extensive research is necessary to ascertain whether there are notable interaction effects between villagewide lineages and village churches or among all three types of solidary groups.

[42] When a multiplicative interaction variable for villages' temples as measured by a village temple manager and a villagewide lineage as measured by the existence of a single ancestral hall with spirit tablets was included in the SUR analysis with all controls and missing data multiply imputed, the interaction effect was positive but statistically insignificant for five outcomes. For one outcome, running water, the interaction effect was negative and close to statistically significant, but it is unclear why there would be a negative interaction effect on water only. Full model results are presented in Appendix Table A6.4.

Causal Mechanisms

The rest of this chapter examines the causal mechanisms through which lineage institutions affect village public goods provision. Data from the village-level survey suggest that solidary villagewide lineage groups have a positive effect on public goods provision, but is it because they establish informal institutions of accountability?

I examine the causal mechanisms behind these empirical patterns in two stages. First, I present preliminary data from the individual-level survey suggesting that villagewide lineage institutions improve village provision of public goods by increasing mutual accountability between villagers and officials, not through other causal mechanisms such as increasing social trust or by homogenizing tastes and preferences for public goods and services. These data, however, are based on only a few survey questions and are not conclusive. A series of structured comparative case studies, however, lend further support to a model of informal accountability that emphasizes the importance of villagewide solidary institutions that establish moral obligations for officials and villagers. Data from these case studies corroborate the statistical findings and illustrate the causal processes more concretely.

Evaluating Alternative Causal Mechanisms

Alternative theories suggest two types of causal mechanisms linking lineage identity to public goods provision.[43] One group of theories focuses on differences in *tastes* or *preferences*. These theories posit that communities with multiple ethnic groups experience worse public goods provision because different groups with different preferences clash with each other, making any collective action or decision difficult. Alberto Alesina and his associates argue, for example, that school funding in the United States is lower in ethnically diverse areas because different ethnic groups prefer different languages for school instruction.[44] Others in this category argue that people care less about people from other ethnic groups and prefer to contribute to the good of their own ethnic group.[45] Individuals in ethnically diverse areas will thus be less willing to fund a public project in ethnically

43 See discussion in Miguel and Gugerty, "Ethnic Divisions, Social Sanctions, and Public Goods in Kenya."

44 Alesina and Baqir, "Public Goods and Ethnic Divisions," 1284.

45 Miguel and Gugerty, "Ethnic Divisions, Social Sanctions, and Public Goods in Kenya," 5.

diverse areas because a larger proportion of the benefits from the public project go to people outside their ethnic group.

A second group of theories focuses on the importance of social capital and social sanctions in overcoming the free-rider problem in collective action. Robert Putnam argues that communities with dense social networks and norms of trust and reciprocity are more likely to coordinate and cooperate with each other.[46] Edward Miguel and Mary Kay Gugerty find that in Kenya, ethnically diverse villages threaten fewer sanctions against parents who have not contributed to community fundraisers, paid fees, or participated in school projects than ethnically homogenous villages do. Because sanctioning within groups is less costly and more effective than sanctioning across groups, ethnically homogeneous villages are able to impose stronger sanctions on free-riders and can therefore raise higher levels of funding for education and other public services.[47]

Findings from my survey of 947 villagers in four provinces, however, question whether changes among citizens in preferences for collective utility and in the barriers to collective action are the causal mechanisms by which lineage identities affect village governance in China. If different lineage groups prefer different types of public goods, prefer not to fund public goods that benefit people in other groups, or trust each other less, then people who live in villages with multiple lineage groups should be less willing to contribute to village public projects than people who live in villages with single lineage groups. This does not, however, seem to be the case. The survey asked villagers, "If contributing to a public project benefited the village but did not necessarily have too much benefit for a particular individual, would most people in the village still be willing to contribute labor or money?" Respondents were given a four-point scale ranging from one, for "very willing," to four, for "not willing at all." As Table 6.5 shows, the average score among people in villages with a single lineage group was 2.15 while the average score among people in villages with multiple groups was 2.05. A statistical test showed the differences in these two scores to be statistically insignificant.

Villagers were also asked two questions about trust. The first was, "Do you generally trust people in the village?" As Table 6.6 shows, there was no difference at all in responses from people living in villages with a single

[46] Putnam, *Making Democracy Work*; idem., *Bowling Alone* (New York: Simon and Schuster, 2000).

[47] Miguel and Gugerty, "Ethnic Divisions, Social Sanctions, and Public Goods in Kenya."

Table 6.5. *Comparison of Willingness to Contribute to Public Projects*

	Residents of Villages with Solidary Lineage Groups	Residents of Villages with Subvillage Lineage Groups	Difference between Two Groups (Standard Error Reported)	H_0: No Difference between Two Groups, p-value (t test)
How willing are people in the village to contribute labor or money to projects that do not benefit them directly? 1 = very willing 2 = willing 3 = not very willing 4 = not willing at all	2.15	2.05	0.10 (0.10)	0.33 (H_o cannot be rejected)

Note: Virtually identical results are obtained when variances are not assumed to be equal in the two groups. The total number living in villages with lineage groups is 135 people. Missing data: eight people.

Table 6.6. *Comparison of Social Trust*

	Residents of Villages with Solidary Lineage Groups	Residents of Villages with Subvillage Lineage Groups	Difference between Two Groups (Standard Error Reported)	H_0: No Difference between Two Groups, p-value (t test)
Percentage who say they "generally trust other people in the village"	89 percent	89 percent	0 percent (0.06)	0.95 (H_o cannot be rejected)
Mean score of change in trust in last three years 1 = increased 2 = stayed the same 3 = decreased	1.82	1.88	0.06 (0.11)	0.59 (H_o cannot be rejected)

Note: Virtually identical results are obtained when variances are not assumed to be equal in the two groups. Missing data: five people.

lineage group and people living in villages with multiple lineage groups. About 89 percent of respondents in each group said that they generally trusted other people living in the village. The second question asked villagers, "Do you feel that trust among villagers has declined, stayed the same, or increased in the last three years?" Answers were turned into a simple three-point scale. Among villagers living in villages with a single lineage group, the average score was 1.82. Among villagers living in villages with multiple lineage groups, the average score was 1.88. Again, a statistical test showed the differences in scores to be statistically insignificant.

More survey research with better measures and a larger number of measures of trust, preferences, and social capital that are appropriate to the case of rural China is needed to evaluate the applicability of these theories, but this preliminary evidence suggests that collective action and free-rider problems among villagers are not the causal mechanisms by which lineage diversity affects governmental performance and public goods provision.

Informal Accountability and Confidence in Officials

Data from the individual-level survey are consistent with the implications of an informal accountability model of lineage groups and public goods provision, although again these findings are merely preliminary given the limitations of the survey measures. An informal accountability model posits that solidary lineage groups have a positive effect on public goods provision by increasing accountability between villagers and officials and providing officials with ways to bolster their standing in the village. Preliminary data from the villager survey suggest that villages with single lineage groups differ greatly from villages with multiple lineage groups in terms of villager confidence in village officials. The villager survey asked people: "Does the village government represent the interests of all the villagers in the village?" Ninety-one percent of the people living in villages with single lineage groups responded that yes, the village government represented the interests of all the villagers in the village (see Table 6.7). In contrast, only 66 percent of the people living in villages with multiple lineage groups believed that the village government represented the interests of all in the village. A statistical test indicated that this difference in percentages was statistically significant at a 99 percent confidence level (p-value: 0.0005).

In other words, people living in villages with single lineage groups show much higher levels of confidence in the intentions of their government

Table 6.7. *Comparison of Confidence in and Relevance of Village Government*

	Residents of Villages with Solidary Lineage Groups	Residents of Villages with Subvillage Lineage Groups	Difference between Two Groups (Standard Error Reported)	H_0: No Difference between Two Groups, p-value (t test)
Percentage who believe that "the village government represents the interests of all the people in the village"	91 percent	66 percent	25 percent (7 percent)	0.0005 (H_0 can be rejected)
Percentage who believe that "the village government is important for them"	76 percent	60 percent	15 percent (8 percent)	0.06 (H_0 can be rejected)
1 = increased				
2 = stayed the same				
3 = decreased				

Note: Virtually identical results are obtained when variances are not assumed to be equal in the two groups. Missing data: five people.

officials than people living in villages with multiple lineage groups. They are also more likely to believe that the village government is relevant to their lives. The survey also asked: "Do you feel that the village government is important?" Seventy-six percent of people living in villages with single lineage groups felt that the village government was important, whereas only 60 percent of people living in villages with multiple lineage groups felt the same way (see Table 6.7). This difference in percentages was statistically significant at a 90 percent confidence level (p-value: 0.06).

In sum, data from the survey of villagers suggest that solidary villagewide lineage institutions do not improve village governmental performance and public goods provision by increasing levels of social trust or preferences for collective utility, but by establishing civic obligations for citizens and officials, which makes citizens more confident of government intentions. These groups encourage better governmental provision of public services by offering moral standing and citizen compliance with state policies as incentives for village officials to fulfill their part of the governance bargain conscientiously and carry out their public duties.

Table 6.8. *Comparison of Jiangxi Villages by Key Variables*

Variable	High Mountain Village	Li Settlement
Income per capita	1,100 yuan (estimated through villager interviews)	1,200 yuan (estimated through villager interviews)
Population	3,000 people	4,000 people
Local taxes	126 yuan per person	150 yuan per person
Implementation of democratic reforms	Nonexistent	Nonexistent
Structure of lineage institutions	No lineage institutions	Villagewide lineage institutions
Governmental performance and public goods provision	Poor	Good

Structured Comparison of Case Studies

In this section, structured comparisons of "most similar" cases and "most different cases" are used to corroborate the statistical findings and illustrate the causal processes more concretely, further clarifying the importance of lineage identity and obligation in village governance.

Villagewide Lineage Groups and Governmental Performance

In this section we return to High Mountain and Li Settlement, the two villages introduced at the beginning of this book. High Mountain and Li Settlement constitute two "most similar cases" and illustrate the positive effect that villagewide lineage groups can have on village provision of public goods. Both High Mountain Village and Li Settlement, two villages in Jiangxi province, are extremely similar along most key dimensions, but only Li Settlement has a villagewide lineage group that makes obligations to contribute to the lineage that are equal to its obligations to contribute to the village as a whole.

High Mountain Village and Li Settlement are located 7 kilometers apart in a mountainous district about 70 kilometers southwest of Ganzhou, Jiangxi's only major city in the south. They are located in two townships where relatively high township-mandated taxes are extracted from villagers: 126 yuan per person in High Mountain and 150 yuan per person in Li Settlement. These tax rates constitute more than 10 percent of per capita income. Table 6.8 compares High Mountain and Li Settlement.

The per capita income of these two villages, 1,100 and 1,200 yuan, was well below the national average in 1999 of 2,210 yuan.[48] The residents of both villages rely on income from farming and remittances from migrant labor. Practically every household has at least one family member working in Guangdong. A well-paved road that leads into Guangdong, 50 kilometers away, is the economic lifeline for these villages.

The village governments in both High Mountain and Li Settlement possess few public assets. Neither village has developed any industrial enterprises – collective or private. The only source of annual revenue is a village tax that officials collect on top of the taxes they collect for the township.[49] Like many villages in China that have not industrialized, High Mountain has been selling off village assets in an ad hoc manner to pay for expenditures. Local officials refer to villages that desperately sell off all of their marketable assets as "empty shell" (*kong ke*) villages. In 1998, village officials sold a few parcels of roadside land to villagers who wanted to build small storefronts. The proceeds did not, however, go toward public services. A total of 80,000 yuan out of the 200,000 yuan from the sale paid for the construction of an office building for the village government. Village officials claimed that the remainder of the money had to go to pay back taxes and fees that the village owed to the township and county, but villagers believe the officials pocketed at least some of the money.

In both villages, elections for village officials are poorly implemented, and villagers' representative assemblies exist in name only and meet once a year or not at all. Villagers report that township officials visit households personally to try to pressure voters to choose the candidates favored by the township government. Illiterate villagers reported that there was no way to confirm that their votes were being recorded properly.

The key difference between High Mountain and Li Settlement lies in the social organization of the two communities. Although neither village has temple or church groups, the two villages differ in terms of lineage organization. High Mountain, a multisurname village, lacks active lineage groups. Li Settlement, however, is a single-surname village and has an active lineage organization that exerts moral authority over the entire village. Village officials in Li Settlement actively promote lineage activities and lineage unity,

[48] *Zhongguo Jingji Nianjian (China Economic Yearbook)* (Beijing: Zhongguo Jingji Nianjian She, 2000), 920.

[49] According to one villager's receipt for local taxes collected in 1994, township levies totaled 66 yuan, whereas village levies totaled 30 yuan.

while relations between officials and residents in High Mountain are characterized by distrust and conflict.

In High Mountain Village, the current Party secretary, Chen, and the village head, Li, were both appointed to their positions in 1998 after visiting the township government on their own initiative and convincing officials that they were willing to use any means necessary to force villagers to comply with family planning and tax collection. Li was easily "elected" in the 1998 elections, as township officials took him and the ballot box around to each household. Both Li and Chen have a reputation among villagers for fiercely enforcing tasks set by higher levels of government.

Villagers in High Mountain say that "the county, township, and village all band together to dredge up (*lao*) money from villagers."[50] In a group, sometimes accompanied by police, they visit each household to collect local levies. In 1999, provincial officials visited the village to put up posters saying that local taxes would be limited to 30 yuan per person. The day after they left, township officials tore down the posters and ignored the directive. According to villagers, village officials each "eat up" 8,000 to 9,000 yuan a year in public funds by reimbursing themselves for expenses ostensibly incurred while carrying out village business when in reality the funds are spent for personal purposes such as sugar and wood. If these rumors are true, 90,000 yuan per year goes to High Mountain's nine officials in addition to their 18,000 yuan in annual wages.

Villagers are disgusted with the village officials, and groups of them have repeatedly visited township, county, and city governments to protest. In 2000, after a group of more than fifty villagers demonstrated at township and county governments, it was agreed that they were to be allowed to audit the village accounts. One farmer noted this concession did not amount to much since the accounts are falsified, "but at least we caused them some trouble."[51] When village officials in High Mountain are compelled to organize a public project, as they were when the county directed the village to rebuild the village primary school a few years ago, they imposed levies of 20 yuan on each individual. As they cannot mobilize voluntary donations from villagers who do not trust them, and have no public funds at their disposal, they therefore resort to using the coercive resources that the township makes available to them.

[50] Interview with male villager, southern Jiangxi province, February 8, 2001.
[51] Interview with male villager, southern Jiangxi province, February 4, 2001.

Relations between village officials and villagers in Li Settlement contrast dramatically with those in High Mountain. Li Settlement officials actively try to reinforce village solidarity. Like many single-surname villages, Li Settlement had been grouped loosely into six different sublineages (*fang*), but divisions among the sublineage groups were flexible and blurry. In the past, ritual prayers to ancestors on holidays had been mostly carried out by individual households rather than the *fang* as a whole.[52] Different *fang*, moreover, were in the habit of sharing the same ancestral hall. Over the past century, when political conditions permitted, members of the first, second, and third *fang* visited the ancestral hall at the north end of the village to pay their respects, while members of the fourth, fifth, and sixth *fang* visited the ancestral hall at the south end of the village.

In 1998, village officials helped to renovate the village auditorium into a unified villagewide ancestral hall. Instead of replacing individual spirit tablets, they set up a communal tablet to represent the deceased elders of all the villagers, thus emphasizing the common origin and unity of the village's households rather than sublineage divisions. Now there is an altar set up on the auditorium stage where the communal spirit tablet rests. Another wooden tablet, embossed in gold, implores ancestors to bestow upon their descendants in the village prosperity as well as wisdom and government positions. Two red banners painted with the characters that particular generations of the lineage are supposed to use when naming children ripple on the wall.

Officials demonstrate their commitment to the lineage and the village by participating in lineage rituals, organizing public projects, and managing public funds responsibly. Unlike the officials in High Mountain, they have not used up scarce resources to build themselves a new office building. Instead, they work out of their houses or meet in the new lineage hall. To pave the main village road, they used their personal connections with higher-level officials to secure a bank loan of 90,000 yuan (about U.S.$11,000).[53] They then held a lineage banquet to solicit donations from lineage members, but only after they had built up their moral standing by showing that they themselves were willing to invest their reputations

52 On a village in north China where norms of maintaining communitywide relations are stronger than the distinctiveness or separation of lineage and sublineage groupings within the village, see Ellen R. Judd, *Gender and Power in Rural North China* (Stanford: Stanford University Press, 1994), 54–5.

53 These measures are an example of what Margaret Levi has called "precommitment strategies." Levi, *Of Rule and Revenue*, 61.

and resources to fulfill their obligations to the lineage. When I visited, red banners from the banquet were still hanging on the lineage hall with messages like "Eat together," "Don't forget your brothers and sisters," and "Help take care of each other." Village officials succeeded in collecting over 20,000 yuan in voluntary contributions. In interviews, villagers explained their willingness to donate by referring to their responsibility to the lineage and the village community and by rationalizing that the road would help improve the life of everyone in the village. Village officials used the 20,000 yuan contributed by the villagers to begin paying back the loan. They paid back another 60,000 yuan using donations from nearby township enterprises and profits from the village's forests. A fundraising banquet on the first day of the lunar calendar in 2000 provided sufficient voluntary contributions to pay back the rest of the loan.

Village officials in Li Settlement feel proud of the work they have done for the village and genuinely seem to feel an obligation to work for the good of the community. The moral authority that village officials in Li Settlement have earned through organizing public projects and supporting the creation of a villagewide lineage group has also been invaluable for implementing state tasks such as birth control and tax collection. Villagers in Li Settlement say they know that officials are just doing their jobs. They generally comply with birth control quotas and state tax collection and do not fault village officials for fining the three couples in the last year who violated the family policy.

Li Settlement is a particularly interesting case because unlike previous cases, village officials are not only subject to the village lineage group's moral obligations but they have also helped to create or at least reinforce them. Does that mean that the real reason for good governmental public goods provision in this case is that the officials happen to be good people? Not necessarily. Places with well-intentioned officials are likely to have better governance and public goods provision. Places with well-intentioned officials may also be more likely to have villagewide solidary groups. But this does not necessarily mean that the existence of villagewide solidary groups has no independent effect on governmental provision of public goods and that good governmental provision of public goods is purely a result of officials who happen to be well intentioned. First, the existence of villagewide solidary groups is not simply epiphenomenal. Well-intentioned officials may want to create villagewide solidary groups, but the successful creation of these groups depends on many other factors. Li Settlement has a historical legacy of lineage institutions and activities, and other villagers have also actively helped to renovate the new lineage hall and organize lineage activities. As we have seen in previous cases, there are also plenty of villages with encompassing and embedding solidary groups where officials seem to be somewhat reluctant to provide public goods.

Second, not all well-intentioned officials, as other village case studies have indicated, succeed in good governance and public goods provision. The norms and obligations of a villagewide solidary group help overcome the collective action problem with public goods provision. Solidary institutions can be intervening mechanisms that translate good intentions into results by helping officials mobilize resources from citizens. Third, once the norms and obligations of the lineage group have been established, they have a force of their own. Li Settlement's officials may have had a hand in promoting these obligations, but this simply means that they have made it harder for themselves to misbehave. Villagers can now use lineage norms and obligations as informal institutions for holding them, as well as future people in their positions, accountable.

What other reasons would officials have for promoting encompassing and embedding solidary groups other than being naturally nice people? One important factor is the set of political resources available to them. In the case of High Mountain, officials had few preexisting community institutions upon which they could draw, so taking advantage of the coercive resources offered by the township government was an attractive option. In the case of Li Settlement, village officials had few economic resources, but saw that they could draw upon the village's lineage institutions to mobilize political and economic support – a more attractive option than ruling through coercion and becoming dependent on the township government. By reinforcing loyalties to the lineage group defined to include everyone in the village, Li Settlement's officials not only elicited funding for public projects from within the village but also strengthened appeals to county government officials who grew up in the village. By demonstrating that members of the village see themselves as a villagewide lineage group and donate money to village projects in order to fulfill their group obligations, village officials were also in a better position to claim that higher-level officials originally from the village are still members of the community and still have obligations to it. The fact that the lineage institutions incorporate the whole village community rather than just a portion also makes it easier for both village and county officials to claim that any state subsidies given to the village are being allocated for needed public services, not private patronage. Officials in a similar village with weak kinship institutions at multiple levels would not have the same impetus to engage in institutional entrepreneurship if no one from their village had attained a position as a higher-level government official. Alternatively, officials in a similar village where a villager had attained office in a higher level of government might still not choose to utilize village kinship institutions as a political strategy if they already have plentiful access to other economic or political resources from village enterprises or other personal connections to higher levels of government.

Subvillage Lineage Institutions and Governmental Performance

Returning to our comparative analysis of actual village case studies, the previous set of "most similar" cases illustrated the positive effects of villagewide lineage groups on village provision of public goods. In this section, we compare another pair of "most similar cases." One village has subvillage lineage groups, whereas the other village does not have any lineage groups at all. This comparison suggests that subvillage lineage groups can have a negative effect on village governance and public goods provision. Located right next to each other, Chen Settlement and Pan Settlement in Hebei province look like a single village with all of its houses massed together in a single group. From within the cluster of houses, however, the dividing line between the two villages is clear. The general layout within the residential cluster is the same – one-story adobe houses with small courtyards surrounded by high adobe walls, narrow footpaths winding through the village between the high walls, and a few roads wide enough for cars leading out to larger roads on the perimeters of the villages. Moving into Pan Settlement, the footpaths narrow. More litter is scattered across them, and the walls lining the paths become less well kept. Table 6.9 compares Chen Settlement and Pan Settlement along key dimensions.

When I visited in 2000, both villages were carrying out road-paving projects, but Pan Settlement's efforts were clearly less organized. In both villages, the general process was the same. The dirt roads to be paved are first cleared and flattened by a bulldozer. Workers then lay bricks in a herringbone pattern across the dirt to create a foundation and then pour and smooth concrete across the foundation. The care with which village officials supervised road-paving projects differed significantly. Paved roads in Pan Settlement were narrow, rough, and covered only with reeds. Pan Settlement's officials explained that it was extremely difficult to get villagers to agree to cede even small strips of their land in order to make the roads

Table 6.9. *Comparison of Hebei Single-Surname Villages by Key Variables*

Variable	Pan Settlement	Chen Settlement
Income per capita	3,200 yuan	4,000 yuan
Population	1,400 people	1,300 people
Local taxes	30 yuan per person	30 yuan per person
Implementation of democratic reforms	Incomplete	Incomplete
Structure of lineage	Strong subvillage lineage institutions	Only household-oriented lineage institutions
Governmental performance and public goods provision	Variable	Excellent

wider. They also commented that they had banned cars and motorcycles until the new road had completely hardened but could not get everyone to observe the ban. In contrast, Chen Settlement's roads were wider, and the village officials monitored the project attentively, laying plastic sheets across the road after concrete was poured and then covering the plastic sheets with reeds for additional protection.

Why are governance and the management of public projects in these two villages so different? In many ways, the villages seem like twins. Both are approximately the same size with between 1,300 and 1,400 residents. In both villages, dozens of households operate small enterprises at home, which churn out plastic packaging and thousands of plastic bags a day. These household businesses have boomed, due to the villages' auspicious location between the cities of Beijing and Baoding, and income per capita in the villages is very high – 4,000 yuan in Chen Settlement and 3,200 yuan in Pan Settlement. Township and village taxes in both villages are low – about 30 yuan per person – and significantly less than the standard 50 yuan for other villages in the township.

Neither village has completely implemented the grassroots democratic reforms mandated by the central government. In Chen Settlement, the position of village head had been unfilled for the three years before the 2000 election, after none of the candidates in the previous election were able to achieve an absolute majority. In 2000, unauthorized proxy voting and floating ballot boxes were still commonplace in both villages, and neither village used a secret ballot. The township government reserves the right to appoint village officials and override election outcomes. In both villages, incumbent village officials select at least some of the candidates for village government and villagers' representative assembly (VRA) elections. In Chen Settlement, the village head selects sixty candidates for the VRA and allows villagers to elect forty-three of these candidates. In Pan Settlement, the village Party branch selects the members of the election supervisory committee as well as the election candidates themselves. By their own admission, Pan Settlement's officials select candidates who are in their own faction. They say that if they allowed village representatives to nominate candidates for village elections, it would be "too much trouble" (*tai mafan*) and disorderly (*luan*), and they would have to deal with problems between clans (*jiazu wenti*). Instead, they pressure the VRA to approve their choice of candidates by "doing a lot of thought work" (*da liang de sixiang gongzuo*), or talking individually and extensively with each representative.[54]

Again the central difference between these two villages is in their social institutions. Like the villages previously discussed, these two villages do not have temples or churches, but they do differ in their lineage organization. Even though the vast majority of people in Pan Settlement share the same surname, the village is fragmented into three distinct sublineage groups that villagers call "gates" (*men*).[55] According to local history, Pan Settlement was established by a group of Pans forced by the imperial state during the Ming dynasty (1368–1644) to relocate from a township in Shanxi province and develop this area of central Hebei. Pan Settlement was subsequently divided into three "gates": east, west, and central. The west gate was further divided into six "courtyards" (*yuan*), each of which defined a "clan" (*jiazu*). However, neither the central gate, which had the least people, nor the east gate, which had the most people, organized themselves into courtyards.

Since at least the Maoist period, villagers of the east gate have been rivals of villagers of the west gate. During the Cultural Revolution, Pan Xiaofang of the east gate, skillful at political maneuvering, became village Party secretary. Until eight or nine years ago, the Pans of the west gate

54 Interviews with village officials, central Hebei province, November 26, 2000.

55 Other scholars working in central Hebei have also reported that sublineage branches are referred to as *men* or "gates." Huaiyin Li finds that people in south-central Hebei refer to sublineage branches within the village as either *pai* or *men*. Myron Cohen reports that in a village 75 kilometers south of Beijing, villagers used the phrase *si damenr*, or "four great gates," to describe the four subdivisions of a lineage, each subdivision tracing descent from one of four brothers who originally settled the village. Li, "Village Regulations at Work," 98; Cohen, "Lineage Organization in North China," 511.

considered themselves the "opposition faction" (*fandui pai*), but then they "stood up" (*zhan qi laile*) and gained control of the village government. Now in economic matters and village affairs, the west gate Pans proudly note that "what they say goes" (*shuo de suan*). They have become the largest of the three gates. All three village officials are west gate Pans, a source of considerable satisfaction to Pan Yudong, the father of the deputy village Party secretary. Pan, a university-trained engineer, had been labeled a "bad element" during the Cultural Revolution and had applied unsuccessfully for membership in the Communist Party nine times.

The east gate Pans, now out of power, continue to battle against the west gate Pans, and village officials admit that their relations with many villagers are strained. After failing to win back their positions in village government in the 1997 elections, east gate Pans printed small white cards with the message "Oppose the village officials" and scattered them all over the village. The west gate Pans refer to them as a bunch of old retired cadres (*xiatai de lao ganbu*), but the east gate Pans continue to lodge informal and formal complaints against the west gate Pans with the township and county governments. East gate Pans accuse the west gate Pans of wasting the village's public funds on wining and dining guests, violating government regulations in selling land owned by the village collective, and pocketing money from the land sale for themselves. In 1998, east gate Pans succeeded in mobilizing villagers to protest at the county government every two or three days until higher-level officials consented to visit the village and audit the village government's accounts. Villagers claim that the current officials could not possibly have used all the money from the sale of collective land on public projects. The officials counterattack by pointing out that the only ones who benefited from the audit were the higher-level officials who were banqueted at the village's expense.

East gate Pans also accuse the west gate officials of nepotism in illegally favoring west gate Pans when contracting out land and other village collective assets. In one example, they noted that the fee for contracting the use of the village fish pond had previously been 15,000 yuan. When the existing contract expired, the new contract was not only given to a west gate villager, but the contracting fee was reduced to 10,000 yuan.

Tensions between village officials and villagers also emerge in the administration of state tasks and the implementation of village public projects. East gate Pans castigate the village officials for implementing the birth control program even though they know that the central government sets the policy. They also berate village officials for moving property lines unfairly as village roads have expanded. Despite these conflicts, Pan Settlement's officials have managed to carry out some public projects. The villagers are fairly wealthy, and the current village officials have extensive connections outside the village (the village head's younger brother even lives in Hong Kong). But the projects they organize are not as well administered as the ones in Chen Settlement. It is also clear that officials in Pan Settlement cannot rely, as officials in Chen Settlement do, on voluntary donations from a majority of villagers. They are spending between 200,000 and 300,000 yuan – about half the cost of Chen Settlement's project – and funding the project primarily through the sale of village land. Officials say that through their connections, they have also secured some money from the county and provincial governments, and that enterprises in the village have contributed 20,000 yuan. Although they have tried to get villagers to donate money to the road project by suggesting that donations would increase their chance of obtaining Party membership, only a small percentage of the funding came from voluntary contributions, and villagers have also complained that village officials could not possibly have used all the money from the sale of village land on public projects.

Unlike Pan Settlement, Chen Settlement is not fragmented by lineage cleavages. Despite the fact that villagers all share the same surname, Chen Settlement lacks strong lineage institutions that prescribe group-oriented behavior. People who share a common ancestor five generations back are considered part of the same "clan" (*jiazu*) and visit the same ancestral grave to pay their respects on major holidays. These rituals, however, are carried out on a household basis, not as a group. On a holiday, each family simply makes sure to go at some point during the day. Although villagers may see fellow clan members as part of their extended family, loosely defined, villagers report that during elections they do not vote in blocs along clan cleavages.[56] Compared to the chaos in Pan Settlement, Chen Settlement

[56] Cohen reports the same kind of household-based kinship institutions existed in the village he visited in central Hebei:

> The ritual activities of Qingming might be carried out by an individual family or as a group. Indeed, the basic grave rituals are still practiced in present-day Yangmansa, but only as an expression of lineal ties between near ancestors and their descendants. In the past, however, these rituals were placed in a communal setting when entire lineages were organized as Qingming associations (*Qingming hui*) (ibid., 521–2).

is relatively stable and well governed by the village head, Chen Wenhua, a successful private entrepreneur.

The preceding cases show that when communities are defined by lineage groups that do not include everyone in the village community, lineage institutions do not facilitate public goods provision by acting as informal institutions of accountability. In the case of Pan Settlement, subvillage lineage institutions have moral authority, but because they do not exercise moral authority over the entire village community, villagers cannot use them to hold village officials accountable for providing public goods, and officials cannot use them to elicit compliance from villagers with state regulations. Instead, subvillage lineage institutions in Pan Settlement are used to mobilize villagers into political factions that impede village governance.

Both Pan Settlement and Chen Settlement are single-surname villages, but Pan Settlement has strong subvillage lineage groups whereas Chen Settlement lacks any lineage groups at all. Comparing these two villages makes two things clear. First, subvillage institutions can also be an effective resource for political mobilization, but the type of political mobilization that they facilitate has a negative impact on village governance. Second, single-*surname* villages are not necessarily single-*lineage* villages. Many single-surname villages do not have strong lineage institutions and are simply residential clusters of agnates or people with the same surname.[57] Other single-surname villages, as we see with the case of Pan Settlement, are organized not into a villagewide lineage but into clearly defined subvillage, sublineage groups.[58] Sublineage conflict can be just as intense as conflict between different lineages.[59]

Intervillage Lineage Institutions

Lineage institutions can also link people in one village with people in other villages. Intervillage lineage groups are, however, far less common than

[57] Watson, "Chinese Kinship Reconsidered," 605.

[58] Watson also points out the importance of sublineage rivalry: "Segmentary rivalries are often very pronounced in larger lineages and can cause serious trouble." See ibid., 608. See also Frolic, *Mao's People*, 29.

[59] Strauch has argued that multilineage communities are not necessarily more conflictive than single-lineage communities. She describes the case of a Hong Kong village in which residents established a villagewide solidary institution that was stronger than the subvillage lineage institutions in the village. She hypothesizes that multilineage villages are more likely to suffer from lineage conflict when they are located in an area dominated by powerful lineage organizations. Strauch, "Community and Kinship in Southeastern China," 23.

lineage groups within villages because of the state's wariness that social organizations can form the basis for widespread collective action and protest.[60] The intervillage lineage groups that do exist typically link subvillage groups with other subvillage groups of people rather than entire villages, because coalitions of entire villages would certainly attract attention and almost certain prohibition by the state. By reinforcing subvillage solidary groups, intervillage lineage groups may also have a negative impact on village governmental public goods provision – although provision of collective goods *within* subvillage groups may be quite good.

Take, for example, the case of the Sun Lineage Association in the Xiamen area of Fujian province. The Sun Lineage Association has members in more than a dozen villages scattered across the county-level districts of Huli, Tongan, and Jimei. In the early 1980s, a few Sun elders from one village in Jimei started contacting Sun elders in villages all around the area. Eventually, a group of elders proposed rebuilding two ancestral halls – or ancestral temples (*zu miao*), as local residents call them – honoring their ancestral patriarch and matriarch. They set up a temple reconstruction committee (*chongjian weiyuanhui*). The hall for the lineage's founding patriarch was built first, near the purported site of his grave in Three Forks Village, one of the Fujian villages that I introduced in Chapter 1. Sun elders in Three Forks Village oversaw the ancestral hall's ritual activities and maintenance. The rebuilding committee evolved into a permanent committee of twenty elders, one or two from each village in the area, with a large number of Suns. This committee meets once or twice a year to plan for activities and ceremonies on the major holidays, when members of the lineage are supposed to congregate at the ancestral hall in Three Forks Village. Sun elders in Three Forks hold leadership positions in the lineage committee.

In December 2000, the temple for the lineage's matriarch, located in a mountainous area of Tongan district, was completed. A two-day opening ceremony drew hundreds of lineage members from all over the region. Early in the morning on the first day of the ceremony, Suns from villages in Huli district gathered in Three Forks Village to board several large buses rented to transport everyone to the new ancestral temple two hours away.

The ancestral hall in Three Forks Village is a center of gravity for the entire organization. Not surprisingly, the Suns who reside in Three Forks

[60] Elizabeth Perry makes this observation in her examination of government responses to Falun Gong. Elizabeth Perry, "Challenging the Mandate of Heaven: Popular Protest in Modern China," *Critical Asian Studies* 33, no. 2 (2001), 170–1.

are a tight-knit group. Geographically, they are concentrated in the largest of Three Forks' four "natural villages" (*ziran cun*) or residential clusters. Although not the original chair, Mr. Sun, a retired official and businessman from Three Forks Village in Huli district, currently heads the committee and research society. For more than twenty years, Mr. Sun held various positions in the village government, including village head and village Party secretary, but in the early 1990s he turned to business and eventually worked for three or four years in Indonesia.

In addition to organizing lineage rituals, the Sun lineage committee organizes an array of other services, including welfare provision and the provision of basic social services for lineage members. These services, however, are limited to members of the lineage. The committee organizes financial assistance for lineage members who are sick or impoverished. Lineage members report that roads, school repairs, even the new public toilets within the Sun natural village are organized and funded by lineage elders. A subset of the committee also engages in other nonreligious activities such as the association's research society (*yanjiuhui*), a group of more educated members who research and write on the lineage's history. The research society is officially registered with the district's Lineage Origins Research Association (*xingshi yuanliu yanjiuhui*), a quasigovernmental organization with an office manned by one person in the Jimei county seat. The associations of two other lineages are registered with the Lineage Origins Research Association, and the three lineage societies hold one or two conferences a year during which they report on new findings.

Over the last few years, Suns and non-Suns have clashed over numerous issues. In 2000, Sun elders mobilized their natural village and tried to secede from the rest of the village, accusing the village government of giving preferential treatment to other natural villages. Throughout 2000, tensions were high, and numerous fist fights broke out between members of different natural villages. The township government sent down work teams to canvass every household and meet with the elders of the various natural villages about the possibility of dividing the administrative village in two. Ultimately, township officials determined that it would be impossible to agree on how to split up the village's collective assets – factory buildings, land, debt – and announced that most residents did not want to split up the village. By the end of 2000, township officials had succeeded in suppressing discontent and persuaded residents to stop agitating.

Again, we can see from the case of Three Forks that lineage institutions can be important resources for political activity. In the case of Three Forks, lineage institutions help mobilize resources to provide members of the Sun lineage with roads and other public projects that Three Forks' village government fails to fund. Solidary groups that are neither encompassing nor embedding can still, to some extent, substitute for local government. But the collective goods provided by these groups are enjoyed only by a subset of the locality. In sum, when lineage institutions define a community that differs from the jurisdiction of the local government, they may have a positive impact on the provision of collective goods for the community but a *negative* impact on village governmental performance and *governmental* provision of public goods.

Conclusion

Like village temples and other villagewide community groups, villagewide lineage groups can help citizens and officials hold each other accountable for their duties as citizens and officials. When lineages incorporate everyone in the village, and membership in the lineage means the same as membership in the village, lineages function in the same way as temple and festival groups do. All of these groups promote norms of civic solidarity that help establish and enforce moral obligations to contribute to the community.

There are some differences between villagewide lineage groups and village temple and festival groups. Lineage groups may be easier to organize than temple institutions because they can draw on norms of kinship obligation, which remained more active during the Maoist period. Lineage groups may also be more prevalent than temples because the Chinese state is now less strict about the participation of village officials in lineage activities, although such participation is discouraged. Few officials would admit to being the head of a village temple organization, much less a village church council. But, as we see in the case of Li Settlement, village officials can be active leaders within lineage groups. On the other hand, the informal institutions of accountability provided by solidary groups in which local officials are part of the leadership may be less stable. In solidary groups where village officials are ordinary members, poor performance by the officials may result in group sanctions but does not endanger the existence of the group. In solidary groups where village officials are part of the leadership, poor performance by the officials may delegitimize the group itself, causing it to disintegrate.

Villagers and officials may find it easier to organize lineage groups rather than temple or festival groups, but this can be a double-edged sword if they organize fragmenting subvillage groups instead of solidary villagewide groups. Conflict between subvillage factions can paralyze village governance and lead to violence or the pursuit of patronage for one's own faction. Subvillage lineage institutions can also replace government and provide services for their members that the government is supposed to provide.

Social institutions such as lineage rules can substitute for formal state institutions, but from the state's point of view, substitution may not always be a good thing. In some cases, informal institutions can improve governmental accountability and public goods provision. In other cases, it may allow villagers to do away with ineffective formal state administration entirely. In places such as Three Forks, village organizations no longer work *with* the village government, they work *instead* of the village government.

7

Accountability and Village Democratic Reforms

Previous chapters have shown how encompassing and embedding solidary groups can provide informal institutions that increase the accountability of village officials to citizens. Informal institutions, however, may have limitations. Officials may decide not to participate in these institutions when they have other political resources. Dependence on informal institutions may also be dangerous. They may come to replace the state, rather than just reinforcing it. They may reduce incentives for the central government, local officials, and citizens to invest in strengthening formal state institutions for local public goods provision, thereby limiting the level of provision to lower than it would be under different arrangements that enable localities to take full advantage of the state's resources.

If informal institutions of accountability have potential pitfalls, what about the implementation of democratic institutions for village governance? Many see free and fair elections as at least a partial solution for unresponsive and corrupt governments. If only citizens had the power to choose their own candidates for office and vote them out of power for poor performance, then there would be accountability and better governance. It was with these hopes that the Chinese central government, faced with the deteriorating quality of rural governance, introduced a series of grassroots democratic reforms in 1988 that included elections for village officials.

Since then, much of the research on rural China has focused on these village elections – figuring out how democratic they are, what makes villages more likely to implement them, and how likely they are to extend to higher levels of government.[1] Until recently, however, researchers have devoted

[1] A small sampling includes O'Brien, "Implementing Political Reform in China's Villages," 33–59; Lianjiang Li and Kevin O'Brien, "The Struggle over Village Elections," in *The*

little attention to evaluating the *effects* of these democratic reforms. Are village elections and other participatory institutions such as popular village assemblies having any effect on the decisions that are made by village governments? More in-depth research is needed, but case study and survey data gathered during this project suggest that any positive impact that village democratic reforms have had on village governmental provision of public goods has been limited, at least so far.

Grassroots Democratic Reforms in Rural China

In 1988, hoping to arrest the downward slide of village governmental performance, the central government promulgated the Organization Law of Villagers' Committees, which established villagers' committees as mass organizations of self-government. This law, in conjunction with subsequent drives by the Ministry of Civil Affairs to improve the performance of village governments and restore citizen confidence in the state, gave villagers the opportunity to elect village officials as well as participate in a variety of new democratic institutions. Localities were encouraged to experiment with different arrangements; institutions such as villagers' representative assemblies and various electoral procedures emerged.

In November 1998, the National People's Congress passed a revised version of the Organization Law. In contrast to the original law, which permitted but did not mandate direct election of village officials, the revised law required direct village elections conducted by villagers. Elections had to offer voters a choice between candidates, so regulations required that the number of candidates exceed the number of positions. Voting was required to be by secret ballot, and winning candidates had to obtain an absolute majority. Subsequent directives also mandated the formation of an election

Paradox of Post-Mao Reforms, ed. Merle Goldman and Roderick MacFarquhar (Cambridge: Harvard University Press, 1999); Tianjian Shi, "Village Committee Elections in China: Institutionalist Tactics for Democracy," *World Politics* 51, no. 3 (April 1999), 385–412; O'Brien and Li, "Accommodating Democracy in a One-Party State," 465–89; Robert Pastor and Qingshan Tan, "The Meaning of China's Village Elections," *China Quarterly*, no. 162 (June 2000), 490–512. On the extension of grassroots elections to higher levels, see Li, "The Politics of Introducing Direct Township Elections in China"; Melanie Manion, "Chinese Democratization in Perspective: Electorates and Selectorates at the Township Level," *China Quarterly*, no. 163 (September 2000), 764–82; Jean C. Oi and Scott Rozelle, "Elections and Power: The Locus of Decision-Making in Chinese Villages," *China Quarterly*, no. 162 (2000), 513–39.

committee elected by villagers or villager representatives, the publication of a voter registration list twenty days before the election, final candidates determined by some form of primary elections, a public vote count, and immediate announcement of election results.[2] Outside of these requirements, provincial governments were allowed to determine the specifics of electoral procedures.[3]

Following the promulgation of directives from the central government, provincial governments formulated their own regulations for implementing the revised law. In some cases, provincial regulations specified further requirements. Fujian's regulations, for example, set out a strict timeline for the election process. They required the date for voter registration to be set twenty-five days before the final election. The voter registration list was to be announced twenty days before the final election, in time for villagers to raise objections and correct mistakes with the election committee. Candidates for the final election were to be announced fifteen days before the final election, and final candidates were to be elected by villagers or villager representatives in some form of primary election.[4] Some provincial regulations also spelled out some of the grounds for invalidating ballots and elections and for calling new elections.[5]

But to what extent are these laws and regulations actually enforced? In 2000, officials in the Ministry of Civil Affairs estimated that only 30 to 60 percent of villages had started to implement democratic reforms, and they acknowledged that this estimate was an optimistic one.[6] All 316 villages

[2] "Circular Concerning Improving Villager Committee Election," Reference No. 14, General Office of the CPC Central Committee and General Office of the State Council, 2002. Available online at http://www.chinaelections.org/Eng/readnews.asp?newsid={A8769297-13E5-45EB-96EA-FB3E7671B6D5}.

[3] See Article 13, The Organization Law of Villagers' Committees. The Fifth Meeting of the Standing Committee of the Ninth NPC, November 4, 1998.

[4] "Fujian Province's Measures for the Election of Villager Committees." Twentieth Session of the Standing Committee of the Ninth Fujian Provincial People's Congress, July 28, 2000. Available online at http://www.chinaelections.org/Eng/readnews.asp?newsid={33CECB5D-1E5A-4171-93A5-33F384DD603A}.

[5] For provincial regulations promulgated in Anhui, Fujian, Guangdong, Guizhou, Hainan, Hebei, Heilongjiang, Hubei, Jiangsu, Yunnan, and Zhejiang, see http://www.chinaelections.org/Eng/318.asp.

[6] Interview with officials in the Department of Basic-Level Governance, and community development official, Ministry of Civil Affairs, Beijing, November 28. 2000. Since elections are supposed to be held every three years, villages which instituted elections in 1988, when the first Organization Law was passed, would have held four rounds of elections by 2001. Yet 31 percent of villages in the survey reported that they had held three or fewer rounds.

in the survey reported that they had held at least one round of village elections. But about one-third of villages reported that they did not hold their first competitive election until 1996 or later, and about one-quarter of villages reported that they did not have formal printed ballots until 1996 or later.

Perhaps even more problematic than uneven implementation is that even in villages with extremely good implementation of democratic reforms, citizens do not necessarily have a great deal of leverage over officials, accurate information about their activities, or a particularly strong sense of civic duty. In the next section, we look at a "most likely" case for the argument that democracy improves accountability. When even this most likely case raises reservations about the efficacy of democratic reforms, we need to adjust our expectations for reforms in the rest of rural China accordingly.

The Case of River Bridge Village

Elections in rural China do not get much better than the ones administered in River Bridge, a wealthy suburban village located on Xiamen Island on the outskirts of the Xiamen Special Economic Zone in Fujian province. Fujian has long been hailed as one of the frontrunner provinces in the implementation of grassroots democratic reforms.[7] Within the province, the Xiamen local government has given the reforms an especially high priority – not least because the International Republican Institute has repeatedly sent American election observation teams to Houpu, one of its villages, to monitor the three rounds of elections between 1994 and 2000.[8] If there is a place where democratic institutions should improve governmental accountability, River Bridge would be the place.

From October 2000 to December 2000, I tracked the election process in River Bridge and surrounding villages from the initial stages of preparation at the township and county levels to the actual elections. From March

Fourteen percent reported that they had held only one or two rounds. But 97 percent reported that they had held at least one round of competitive elections (with more than one candidate per position) by 2000.

7 See, for example, Kelliher, "The Chinese Debate over Village Self-Government," 74.

8 See "IRI Election Observation Report, Fujian Province, People's Republic of China," October 2000. Report available online at http://www.iri.org/pdfs/fujianreport.pdf; Becky Shelley, "Political Globalization and the Politics of International Non-Governmental Organization: The Case of Village Democracy in China," *Australian Journal of Political Science* 35, no. 2 (July 2000), 225–38.

to May 2001, I followed up with an investigation of the aftereffects of elections on village politics and administration. When I first started visiting the villages in October 2000, the township and county governments were just regrouping after staging a massive production of model elections a few kilometers away in Houpu for a team of observers from the International Republican Institute. Township officials explained that they had decided to hold the elections in Houpu before all the other village elections in the township because they wanted to focus on orchestrating Houpu's elections smoothly in front of American observers and avoid exposing the observers to all the potential villager complaints and unrest stirred up by elections in neighboring villages. Numerous officials at the county, township, and village levels also highlighted the irony of U.S. observers coming to offer them feedback and suggestions for improving their village elections when authorities in the United States seemed to be doing a far worse job than they with the irregularities in the administration of the 2000 U.S. presidential election, a source of considerable merriment to them all.

Both the township and county governments have been awarded model status for the implementation of grassroots democratic reforms (*cunmin zizhi mofan*). In River Bridge, detailed manuals outlining electoral procedures are distributed to village officials and members of the election administration committee. The township government sets a schedule with fixed deadlines for each stage of the election process. Lists of candidates and registered voters are publicly posted.

Election guidelines allow any villager to nominate someone as a candidate for a position in the village government, and villagers take full advantage of this opportunity. For the October 2000 primary elections, people submitted 179 names. Out of these 179 nominations, 16 people were nominated to run for village head, 53 people were nominated to run for the two deputy head positions, and 110 people were nominated to run for the other two generalist positions. Those who wanted to decline their nomination were required to file a withdrawal form (*ci tui biao*) by October 24. If no withdrawal form is filed, the candidate automatically appears on the slate for the primary elections. Three sets of people were allowed to vote in the primary elections that would determine the candidates for the final election: members of the villagers' representative assembly, Party members, and the current village officials in the Party branch and village committee.

Considerable fanfare marked October 30, the day of the primaries. At around nine o'clock in the morning, the 140 representatives in the villagers' representative assembly filed into one of the village government's large conference rooms to the sound of loud patriotic music blaring from the speakers. Bottles of mineral water were distributed to each voter in anticipation of a long meeting. Across the front of the room hung a red velvet banner with gold characters announcing "River Bridge Village's Election Speeches and Primary Election Assembly." A small banner across the top of the doorway into the next room read "Voting Room," and two wooden ballot boxes, both painted red and labeled "River Bridge Village Election Ballot Box," waited at the front of the room. Members of the village administration committee rushed around, displaying badges of various colors indicating their position: red for "Head Voting Official," green for "Vote Tabulator," and yellow for "Vote Recorder."

The meeting followed a detailed preset agenda. Two deputy village heads who were retiring after the election ran the meeting. One first read the primary election procedures out loud and then asked for a show of hands to approve the procedures. Another show of hands approved the vote tabulators and vote recorders on the election administration committee. The village Party secretary delivered a thirty-minute report on the implementation of village elections in River Bridge, and then the other deputy head announced the list of candidates.

After these preliminaries, each of the three candidates for village head gave a campaign speech lasting about fifteen minutes, but villagers did not seem terribly interested in this stage of the electoral process. Up until then, the village representatives voting in the primary had been seated quietly in rows of wooden school desks. During the campaign speeches, however, people started chatting to one another. By the middle of the first speech, given by the incumbent Village Head Yang, the noise had completely drowned him out, and the village's deputy head had to take the microphone and reprimand the village representatives, telling them that this concerned them and that it was important to listen now so they would know about the candidates for whom they would be voting. People quieted down for a few moments but continued to talk through the second and third campaign speeches.

Voters were given an opportunity to ask questions of the candidates, but officials running the meeting cut the question-and-answer period short after only two people, saying they had to move on because they still had a lot of procedures to execute. The head vote tabulator showed the assembled voters the insides of the ballot boxes, sealed them shut with red tape, and set them down in the "Voting Room" established to allow voters to vote secretly. Election officials counted the number of voters and the number of ballots. Ballots were handed out to voters in their seats, and the eleven extra ballots were torn in half. Despite the availability of a secret ballot booth, most voters proceeded to mark their ballots in their seats and chat about their selections with their neighbors, although some folded over their ballots after marking their choice for village head. After everyone had deposited his or her ballot, the ballot boxes were opened, and the ballots were counted publicly to make sure the number corresponded to the number of voters.

On the face of it, River Bridge had extremely well-implemented preelection institutions. Technically, nominations could only be made by villagers, and villagers were free to nominate whomever they wanted. Procedures for primary elections enabled village representatives to vote for the final candidates who would stand for election, and officials and the election administration committee adhered to these procedures rigorously. Although there was some intervention by the village Party branch in the selection of members for the election administration committee – the committee was selected by a group consisting of five village Party branch officials and a subcommittee of thirteen people from the villagers' representative assembly – on balance, River Bridge had extremely well-implemented elections compared to villages in the survey sample.

Further inquiry, however, revealed that the nomination process was not as free from government intervention as it seemed. First, almost all the popularly nominated villagers applied to withdraw their candidacy. Out of the 179 people nominated, 154 of them declined to run. As noted in the previous section, the rewards of being a village official are not always very clear. In wealthy areas such as River Bridge, individuals often benefit more from pursuing their own businesses or economic activities than from taking office. People also fear that they will lose face if they stand for election and lose. As one villager in River Bridge told his son, who was preparing to run against an incumbent official: "You don't know what it takes. You think it's really easy but it's not, and if you do a bad job, you'll embarrass me and yourself."[9]

Reluctance to run, while problematic, does not itself make the nomination procedures less democratic. A more significant issue was that the election oversight committee made a point of asking particular nominees to stay in the race and not others – or, perhaps more precisely, some nominees

9 Interview with male villager, eastern Fujian province, December 3, 2000.

were allowed to withdraw and some were not. Those requesting to be discharged from their candidacy had to get approval from the election administration committee, which approved requests from most of the nominees but required certain people to remain in the primary. According to River Bridge's Party secretary, the election committee asked people they thought were more capable and public service–oriented to remain in the race, but they could just as easily have targeted their favorites or people who did not pose a serious threat to their favored candidates.

Looking behind the scenes of the nomination process also suggests the low level of political interest and weakness of civic values among villagers – even in a village where villagers would benefit a lot from better infrastructure, relatively few have migrated out of the village, and election procedures are relatively well implemented. Most villagers were not only uninterested in running in the election, they were uninterested in participating in the electoral process at all. I spoke to several dozen villagers during the final election, and they did not think that democratic reforms had generated a great deal of civic interest in village issues and public affairs. Only a few said anything about the provision of public goods and services, and even they were relatively vague, saying that they would vote for the candidate who would do good things for the village. Most were relatively disengaged. One villager commented, "Nobody would vote if they didn't get the 10 yuan per election."[10] Other villagers standing nearby nodded in agreement and laughed when the villager continued, "I myself go to vote early in the day and am very diligent about picking up the ten yuan." One middle-aged woman commented, "We just care about getting three full meals and playing cards."[11] Many simply vote for the incumbent. I spoke to one village representative during the primary election meeting and asked her what she thought of the campaign speeches. She replied that the second candidate definitely made the best speech – he seemed more educated and addressed issues more comprehensively. But when I then asked her who would probably win, she looked surprised and responded that most people will just vote for the incumbent.

One reason for the lack of active interest in the election was a prevailing belief that the incumbent Party branch and village committee officials basically had control over the election. When I told one woman

[10] Interview with female villager, eastern Fujian province, December 2, 2000.
[11] Interview with female villager, eastern Fujian province, December 2, 2000.

that my understanding was that candidates were popularly nominated, she retorted:

> How could villagers have the power to decide on candidates? Who says that villagers themselves select candidates? It's the Party members who decide, and then we choose from what they present us with. We just get a piece of paper with the candidates that the Party members have chosen.[12]

Still, people in the village were not completely disengaged. One village official reported that villagers were becoming more attentive to how incumbent village officials recruit election candidates: "To be honest, they are right to be concerned. Some villagers criticize the village committee for being a retirement home for the elderly (*yang lao yuan*), and they definitely have a point (*you yiding de daoli*)."[13]

But when people did have specific reasons for how they voted, the vast majority did not name ones that had to do with the public interest. One college student, home for the weekend, noted: "People do not consider what is in their direct interest necessarily. People tend to vote for people they are more familiar with."[14] Another middle-aged woman commented: "Candidates are not elected to be cadres because of the things they do. It just matters how many of your relatives and friends are behind you."[15] Many highlighted the importance of informal networks and private interest. People reported that they would vote either for their friends and relatives or for people they thought would be easy to find when they needed the village government to solve a personal problem for them. Political power in the village is so much a function of one's personal networks that villagers actually scorn candidates who visit people they do not already know to ask for their vote (*women kan buqi zhe xie ren*). In an environment where one's social networks reflect how capable and powerful one is, the general attitude is that people who do not already have personal networks sufficiently extensive to win an election do not deserve to win an election.

Looking behind the scenes of River Bridge's 2000 election also illustrates how elite machinations rather than civic outrage may motivate seemingly popular protests and "rightful resistance" to election irregularities.[16]

[12] Interview with female villager, eastern Fujian province, December 2, 2000.
[13] Interview with male village official, eastern Fujian province, December 7, 2000.
[14] Interview with female villager, eastern Fujian province, December 2, 2000.
[15] Interview with female villager, eastern Fujian province, December 2, 2000.
[16] See Kevin O'Brien, "Rightful Resistance," *World Politics* 49, no. 1 (1996), 38.

Upholding state regulations can give elites out of office the perfect excuse to topple those currently in power. An incident during the fall 2000 primaries in River Bridge provides a typical example. After the primary election on October 30, the date for the final election in which all villagers would vote was set for November 6, but on November 5 the final slate of candidates had still not been publicized. On November 6, villagers discovered that the final election had been postponed while the township and village governments figured out how to resolve complaints that there had been procedural violations during the primaries.

What had happened was that Chen Huijiang, a prominent village entrepreneur and a candidate for a general village committee position, had received thirty-six votes in the primary and come in fourth. Only the top three, however, could run in the final election. The problem was that the election committee had invalidated all ballots in which people voted for more than the allowed number of candidates per category. In other words, voters were allowed to choose one out of the three primary candidates in the category of village head to run in the final election. Ballots in which people had voted for two people in the category of village head were discarded. This procedure had technically been approved by a show of hands before voting in the primaries commenced, but was actually at odds with township regulations and the procedures instituted by neighboring villages. Other villages had invalidated the votes in that category but preserved and counted the votes in the rest of the categories on the ballot. If this kind of procedure had been followed, Chen Huijiang would have received eight more votes, putting him in third place.

After the primaries, several villagers visited Chen at home after the election and convinced him that this result was unfair. Chen then contacted township and city officials as well as the village election administration committee (headed by the village Party secretary, He Zhenghuan). All agreed with him in principle, but township and city civil affairs officials said that the village had to convene a special session of all the primary voters in order to approve him as a candidate for the final election.

The special session was called, but the incumbent village head, Yang Hongbin, used the session as an opportunity to increase his own power. Although relations between Party Secretary He and Village Head Yang had been good in the past, a personal feud had developed in recent years. Yang organized a group of villagers to crash the meeting and accuse Party Secretary He of corruption and nepotism. The group of protesters put forward three main demands. First, primary voters should consist only of members of the villagers' representative assembly and exclude Party members. Second, Chen should not be permitted to run in the final election; instead, their candidate, a villager named Li Xiaoguang, should be permitted to run. Third, one of the candidates for deputy village head, He Fuquan, should be disqualified because of his close ties to the village Party secretary. The meeting ran on for hours, and in the end, nothing was resolved.

These events also suggest that embezzlement and corruption are regularly and relatively successfully kept hidden from ordinary villagers. Well-implemented democratic reforms in River Bridge have done little to increase the transparency of village governance. The village Party secretary wanted Chen to continue to challenge Village Head Yang's faction. According to Chen, on November 10, the village Party secretary visited him at home and stayed until midnight, trying to persuade him to continue the appeal process. In the course of their conversation, Party Secretary He provided Chen with ammunition against Village Head Yang's faction, describing instances where Yang had illegally benefited from his official position. Most recently, Yang had purportedly pocketed 30,000 yuan from the sale of a piece of valuable village land next to the road leading into the city of Xiamen. According to Chen, He's intention was to give him information that could get Village Head Yang arrested.

Chen, however, decided to stay out of the conflict. Township and city officials decided that preventing social instability was more important than observing election regulations and encouraged Chen to withdraw his candidacy. In the end, he bowed to pressure from the township Party committee and withdrew his complaint on November 12. Final elections were finally held on November 17, 2000. Chen reasoned that he was already a representative to the township people's congress, so there was no need to compete for a lower position. He was nevertheless appointed a head election supervisor in order to save face.

In this case, the implementation of village elections has done little to improve the provision of village public goods and services. With plenty of public funds at their disposal, River Bridge's village officials are willing to finance public services, but they do so only in an ad hoc and reactive manner. Village officials follow a "squeaky wheel gets the grease" policy. Funds for road repairs or equipment for the village primary school are provided on an as-needed basis. There is no organized plan for road paving or maintenance. Village officials seek to do the minimum possible to get reelected. By providing services only when a large number of villagers demand them, the village government keeps the total amount spent on public projects to less than one-quarter of the village's annual revenue. This amount funds a high level of public services relative to other villages in China, although less industrialized villages often actually spend a higher proportion of their revenue than River Bridge does. Residents of River Bridge note that there are always further improvements that can be made to the village's roads, drainage gutters, and school, and that it is not as though the village government could not afford them. Developing the village's industries, however, takes first priority in the eyes of River Bridge's officials, especially since the township does not give them any concrete targets for the provision of public services.

It may take more time for elections and democratic reforms to foster political interest and civic values, as Shelley Rigger has argued,[17] but after a decade of elections in River Bridge, many villagers are not interested in politics and still prefer to interact with the village government through existing informal channels and social networks. Few are willing to run against the entrenched political elite, and even popular protest during the electoral period reflected not necessarily increased civic consciousness but elite conflict. Many villagers look down on candidates who try to campaign in an election. Rather than seeing it as a healthy effort to articulate citizens' interests and hold existing officials accountable for their performance, campaigning in the form of candidate visits to individual households is interpreted as an indication that the candidate does not have enough social networks through which she can mobilize votes discreetly through her supporters.

The case of River Bridge illustrates how well-implemented electoral procedures do not necessarily increase accountability. Both the ability and the will of villagers to monitor village officials remain limited. Village officials generally succeed in hiding improper behavior and embezzlement from the public. Although village officials publicly post figures for village revenues and expenditures that are internally consistent, the general consensus among villagers is that these are unlikely to be completely accurate.

Structured Comparisons of Case Studies

Comparative analyses of paired case studies in this section also cast doubt on the positive effects of democratic reforms on accountability and governmental provision of public goods.

[17] Shelley Rigger, *Politics in Taiwan: Voting for Democracy* (London: Routledge, 1999).

Table 7.1. *Comparison of Fujian Villages by Key Variables*

Variable	River Bridge Village	West Gate Village
Income per capita	8,600 yuan (official)	6,712 yuan (official)
Population	3,200 people	3,900 people
2000 government revenue	4.6 million yuan	1 million yuan
Implementation of democratic reforms	Excellent	Excellent
Active villagewide solidary institutions	No	Yes; village temple institutions
Governmental performance and public goods provision	Fair; invested 26 percent of 2000 government revenue	Excellent; invested 60 percent of 2000 government revenue

Fujian Village Case Studies: River Bridge and West Gate

As previously mentioned, the village of West Gate (a case introduced in Chapter 1 and discussed in Chapter 5) is located just next door to River Bridge. Along many dimensions, these villages are very similar (see Table 7.1). Like River Bridge and other villages in the same township, West Gate also has outstanding elections and well-implemented democratic reforms relative to the rest of rural China. Both River Bridge and West Gate are large villages, and relative to other villages that this book has discussed, both are extremely wealthy. Although neither village was able to develop enterprises during the collective era, both have benefited more recently from the industrialization and foreign investment that Xiamen has attracted. Although neither is poor, River Bridge is far wealthier, with 4.6 million yuan in public assets compared to West Gate's 16 million yuan.

Given the millions of yuan in revenue pouring in each year, River Bridge could be doing more in the way of providing public services. Village lanes and residential walkways are still unpaved. Where they exist, drainage gutters are shallow dirt ditches, easily clogged with trash and stagnant water. When it comes to public services, village officials have a policy of doing the bare minimum (*keyi jiu tingle*). Out of the 4.6 million in government revenues that they reported for 2000, River Bridge's officials invested about 1.2 million in public projects, or 26 percent. Despite having far less money than River Bridge, West Gate spends a far greater percentage of its public funds on public projects. In 2000, out of its total revenues of 1.6 million yuan, it spent 956,000 yuan – 60 percent – on public services provision. Numerous roads and footpaths in the village are paved, including roads connecting housing settlements to the village's fields in order to make it easier for villagers to transport their fresh vegetables to market every day. The village government also provides neighborhood dumpsters for villagers to deposit their trash and employs seven people to cart the trash from these dumpsters to main pickup points for trucks on the outskirts of the village.

Why are West Gate's officials more conscientious about providing public services? Although village elections may have some impact on holding officials in River Bridge and West Gate accountable for public services provision, West Gate's officials invest a greater percentage of their public funds in public services than River Bridge's officials do, in large part because West Gate's temple community organizations help West Gate's village government provide public services as well as assist villagers to hold officials responsible for providing public services. River Bridge also has a number of lineage and temple organizations, but these are primarily small committees of a few elderly villagers who focus on organizing religious activities within their small hamlet or for villagers of the same lineage. In West Gate, the temple council takes the lead (*dai tou*) on road-paving projects and repairs of the village primary school by collecting donations from villagers to get the project off the ground and then invoking the obligations of the village government to fund the rest.

West Gate's officials seem to be getting a good deal. To plan a public project themselves, they would have to call numerous meetings of the villagers' representative assembly, which would then canvass their neighborhoods for input from villagers. They would have to secure formal permission from the villagers' representative assembly and collect either voluntary contributions or levies from each household. Relying on the authority of the community council and allowing the council to take over these activities is much easier than going through formal democratic institutions to make village policies. The council keeps West Gate's officials informed about its activities and asks for subsidies on an as-needed basis. In exchange for funding the public projects that the council requests, the council also helps West Gate's officials secure compliance from citizens with tax collection and state regulations.

Village democratic reforms may also have limited impact in River Bridge and West Gate because officials in these villages do not necessarily lose much by giving up their government positions. Officials in both villages have extensive personal business investments. In River Bridge, the Party secretary runs the village's property management company (*wuye gongsi*) that oversees the village's various rental properties – 35 million yuan in factory buildings, apartment buildings, ongoing construction projects, and land zoned by the city of Xiamen for industrial use. Not surprisingly, village officials in River Bridge have leveraged their experience in land development to become real estate moguls themselves. A number of officials have invested their own money to construct factory buildings. The Party secretary, for example, made an agreement with his small group (a former production team) to rent a piece of land for 3,000 to 4,000 yuan per mu a year, on which he constructed a factory building that he rents to an outside company.[18] In West Gate, all the village officials operate their own businesses in addition to administering the village. The Party secretary and his brothers invest in factory buildings to rent out to enterprises, while the deputy Party secretary draws on his connections in the city of Xiamen for the exclusive rights to sell coal gas in the village.

Although getting elected may be very desirable, given these lucrative business ventures, losing reelection may not be a very effective sanction against misbehavior while in office. Serving as a government official for a period of time can help private entrepreneurs to establish valuable connections, but they often prefer to step down after they have taken advantage of their positions and resume private business full-time. In River Bridge, two previous deputy village heads refused to run for reelection in the 2000 elections so as to focus on their own businesses. One has contracted an old brick factory from the village that he is now turning into an industrial complex for rental. Another former village official runs the second largest taxicab company serving the Xiamen area.

We can see from this comparison of River Bridge and West Gate villages that while it is possible that democratic reforms may have some positive effect on governmental accountability and public goods provision, any effect they have is likely to be much smaller than the positive effect of the solidary temple group in West Gate.

Hebei Village Case Studies: Yang Hamlet and South Bend

The comparison of Yang Hamlet and South Bend, two neighboring villages in Hebei province discussed in Chapter 5, suggests, moreover, that implementing village democratic reforms may not be sufficient to guarantee accountability and good governance. In both Yang Hamlet and South Bend, elections were reasonably well implemented (Table 7.2 reviews the

[18] A *mu* is a unit of area approximately equal to 667 square meters.

Table 7.2. *Comparison of Hebei Villages by Key Variables*

Variable	Yang Hamlet	South Bend
Income per capita	1,500 yuan	1,300 yuan
Population	367 people	352 people
2000 government revenue	10,000 yuan	10,000 yuan
Implementation of democratic reforms	Good	Good
Encompassing and embedding solidary groups	Yes; villagewide festival association	No
Government performance and public goods provision	Good; modest but regular investment in public projects	Poor; no investment in public projects

villages' basic conditions). The two villages are located in a county designated a model for the implementation of village democratic reforms. If village elections and popular assemblies had some positive effect on governmental accountability, we might expect to see at least some public goods provision in South Bend, although perhaps not as much as we see in Yang Hamlet. Yet only one of the villages, Yang Hamlet, which had a solidary village festival association, experienced good public goods provision. Despite having well-implemented elections, the village government in South Bend has not funded any public goods or services at all.

Jiangxi Village Case Studies: High Mountain and Li Settlement

Good elections and well-implemented democratic reforms do not seem to be necessary for good governmental performance either. We have also seen that even when the implementation of elections and other reforms is weak, governmental provision of public goods and services may still be good. Neither High Mountain nor Li Settlement in Jiangxi province – villages that were introduced in Chapter 1 and discussed earlier in this chapter – had implemented elections or popular villagers' assemblies (Table 7.3 reviews the villages' basic conditions). Township officials bring the ballot box to each household and tell voters which candidate they favor. Villagers' assemblies exist only in name. Yet Li Settlement, which had a villagewide lineage group, still experienced extremely good governance and public goods provision.

We can see from these case studies that democratic institutions are neither necessary nor sufficient for governmental accountability and

Table 7.3. *Comparison of Jiangxi Villages by Key Variables*

Variable	High Mountain	Li Settlement
Income per capita	1,100 yuan	1,200 yuan
Population	3,000 people	4,000 people
2000 government revenue	126 yuan per person	150 yuan per person
Implementation of democratic reforms	Nonexistent	Nonexistent
Encompassing and embedding solidary groups	No	Yes; villagewide lineage group
Government performance and public goods provision	Poor; no investment in public projects	Good; modest but regular investment in public projects

responsible provision of public goods. But are places with better implementation of democratic institutions at least more *likely* to have better governmental provision of public goods? The evaluates this hypothesis.

Measuring the Implementation of Democratic Institutions

In this section, we look at three categories of democratic reforms: preelection procedures, election procedures, and popular villagers' assemblies. Preelection and election procedures help to ensure that people are really able to elect the people they think will perform well (and vote the people who do not perform well out of office).

Voting procedures help to ensure that all candidates have a fair chance of winning and that there is meaningful contestation.[19] The use of secret ballot, carefully regulated use of proxy voting, ballot boxes impervious to tampering, public vote counting – all of these institutions help to ensure that voters will not be coerced into voting for a particular candidate and that their choices will be accurately represented and reported. As we will see, however, villages vary widely in their implementation of these procedures.[20]

[19] Robert A. Dahl, *Polyarchy: Participation and Opposition* (New Haven: Yale University Press, 1971).

[20] According to Article Three of the Election Law, revised on October 27, 2004, "all citizens of the People's Republic of China aged 18 or older are enfranchised regardless of their ethnicity, race, sex, occupation, class, religion, education, wealth or the duration of residence. People who have been deprived of political rights according to law are not enfranchised."

We must also look at the preelection process – whether the election is administered by an impartial group of people, how candidates are nominated, and whether higher-level officials or incumbents interfere in the nomination process. Even when electoral procedures seem free and fair, sometimes the real decisions are made behind the scenes before election day. Free competition requires institutions that ensure incumbent officials permit their opponents to run for office and that prevent unfair intervention in the nomination of candidates. Ideally, independent third parties exist to enforce electoral regulations and monitor the electoral process.

The survey also evaluates the implementation of popular assemblies composed of representatives selected or elected by villagers. Formally, the 1998 Organization Law requires village committee officials to report to either an assembly of villagers or an assembly of villagers' representatives.[21] In practice, few villages can convene a villager assembly with the mandated quorum of more than half the adult villagers, or representatives from more than two-thirds of households, so villagers' representative assemblies (VRA) are the dominant forum for citizen participation in village decision making. Elections, after all, occur infrequently. A greater variety of institutions for citizen participation is also likely to engage larger portions of the population in the political process and the assessment of governmental performance.[22] If we are concerned about the effect of democratic institutions on government accountability, it is also important to assess the effectiveness of institutions such as villagers' representative assemblies.

It is again worth noting that although the respondents of the survey were village officials, many of them were comfortable reporting interference (even by themselves personally) in the implementation of nomination and election procedures even though such interference goes against official state regulations. This high level of frankness was also evident in their responses

[21] Articles 17 through 20 require village committee officials to report to an assembly of which all adult villagers are a member. The assembly must have more than half of all the adults or representatives from more than two-thirds of households for a quorum. In villages that are big or scattered, Article 21 permits in lieu of the village assembly the formation of villagers' representative assemblies with one representative selected by groups of five to ten households, or by a villager small group. The Organization Law of Villagers' Committees. The Fifth Meeting of the Standing Committee of the Ninth NPC, November 4, 1998. Available online at http://www.ptlib.com/law/fagui246.htm.

[22] Larry Diamond, "Is the Third Wave Over?" *Journal of Democracy* 7, no. 3 (1996), 22; also Guillermo O'Donnell, "Delegative Democracy," *Journal of Democracy* 5, no. 5 (January 1994), 60–2.

Table 7.4. *Descriptive Statistics on Interference in the Preelection Process*

	Percentage of Villages	Standard Deviation	Number of Villages
No interference in determination of primary candidates by			
Township government	95%	21%	311
Village Party branch	85%	36%	312
Incumbent village committee	90%	30%	312
No interference in determination of final candidates by			
Township government	82%	39%	314
Village Party branch	90%	29%	315
Incumbent village committee	97%	17%	312
No interference in election oversight committee membership by			
Township government	87%	33%	310
Village Party branch	68%	47%	313
Incumbent village committee	92%	27%	310

to other potentially sensitive survey questions and is largely due to the highly skilled administration of the survey by Chinese undergraduate and graduate students in agricultural economics, sociology, and related disciplines, most of whom had grown up in villages themselves.

Preelection Institutions

To evaluate the preelection phase of the electoral process, the survey asked each village whether there was interference from township government officials, village Party officials, or incumbent village committee officials in each of the following three areas: determination of candidates for the primary election, determination of candidates for the final election, and determination of people serving on the election oversight committee. Table 7.4 summarizes their responses.

Table 7.5 breaks down the same information by the source of interference and the stage of the preelection process in which interference takes place. Most villages – 59 percent – reported that there was some interference. Interference was most frequent in the formation of the election oversight committees, which supervise and administer the election process. Villages were slightly more likely to experience interference in the determination

Table 7.5. *Summary Statistics on Interference in the Preelection Process*

Variable	Percentage of Villages
No interference at all	41%
No interference in primary nominations	81%
No interference in final nominations	75%
No interference in election oversight committee	56%
No interference by the township government	69%
No interference by the village Party branch	55%
No interference by the incumbent village committee	81%

Table 7.6. *Descriptive Statistics on Implementation of Voting Institutions*

Variable	Percentage of Villages	Standard Deviation	Number of Villages
Contested election*	98%	14%	316
Public vote count*	87%	33%	316
Secret ballot booth*	77%	42%	316
Campaign speeches	54%	50%	316
Regulated proxy voting*	40%	49%	314
Fixed ballot boxes	30%	46%	314
Immediate announcement of election results*	99%	11%	316

Note: * Mandated by the 1998 revised Organization Law.

of final candidates than in the determination of primary candidates. Village Party officials were the group most likely to interfere in the preelection process, followed by township officials.

Voting Institutions

To evaluate the actual voting process, the survey asked villages whether they announced the results of their elections immediately after polls closed; whether there were more candidates than offices; whether they counted votes publicly; whether there was a secret ballot; whether candidates gave campaign speeches about their intentions and plans for the village; whether proxy voting was regulated; and whether the ballot box was fixed in a designated polling place rather than brought around to each household, which increases the chances of fraud.

Accountability and Village Democratic Reforms

As we can see from Table 7.6, voting procedures varied substantially in the degree to which they were implemented. (For each of these procedures, I created a dichotomous variable with a value of one when the village reported that the procedure was used in their most recent election and zero otherwise.) Again, we can see that many village officials responding to the survey were willing to report that officially required procedures were not implemented in their village. Nearly all of the surveyed villages reported that their most recent election had been contested by multiple candidates and that the vote count had been announced immediately after the election. In contrast, only about half of the villages in the survey reported the use of campaign speeches to communicate the views of candidates to voters. Less than half of the village officials interviewed for the survey reported that they used ballot boxes that were fixed in a given spot and that they regulated proxy voting on behalf of another person.

Unregulated proxy voting has been a major problem in the implementation of democratic reforms. The revised Organization Law says nothing about proxy voting, although a subsequent state circular states, "Procedures of proxy voting shall be handled according to laws."[23] Since provincial governments are responsible for formulating the specific electoral procedures, laws governing proxy voting are made at the provincial level.[24] Most provincial regulations allow village residents who are absent for the elections to designate someone else, usually a family member, to vote on their behalf. In practice, one family member often casts votes for everyone in the family even if they are present for the election. The following exchange that took place in a northern Zhejiang village with a woman in her thirties recounts a typical example:

> Question: Have there been elections held in your village?
> Answer: Yes, there have probably already been three or four.
> Question: Who have you voted for in these elections?
> Answer: Oh! I don't know. My father usually just fills them [the ballots] all out for us. I have never seen a ballot.[25]

[23] "Circular Concerning Improving Villager Committee Election," Reference No. 14, General Office of the CPC Central Committee and General Office of the State Council, 2002.

[24] Article 29 allows provincial governments to formulate measures for implementing the law in accordance with "actual conditions" in the province. The Organization Law of Villagers' Committees. The Fifth Meeting of the Standing Committee of the Ninth NPC, November 4, 1998.

[25] Interview with female villager, northern Zhejiang province, August 14, 1999.

Other researchers have also observed that there are no clear rules to regulate the scope of proxy voting.[26] Without strict regulations, residents can claim to be voting for one or more absentee villagers, but there is no assurance that proxy voters are faithfully representing the choices of absentee voters. In some areas, proxy voting accounts for more than 20 percent of the total votes cast.[27] The measure I use takes on a value of one only if documentation was required from a villager claiming to vote on behalf of an absentee voter in the last election.

Cases of election fraud have also frequently involved the use of mobile ballot boxes. Instead of clearly designated, fixed ballot boxes at polling stations that are open for a predesignated time period, mobile ballot boxes are brought from door to door, and villagers are asked to vote on the spot. While officials often argue that mobile ballot boxes are more convenient in villages where residences are geographically dispersed, villages with better implemented institutions install multiple, fixed ballot boxes in a variety of locations. Not only is it easier to tamper with mobile ballot boxes since it is more difficult for people to keep track of them, but they also make it easier for officials to pressure people into voting for people whom they may not prefer. In the two Jiangxi villages that I described in Chapter 1, township officials personally brought the ballot box to each house together with the candidates they favored.

As with proxy voting, the central government allows provincial and local governments to set the specific regulations governing the use of mobile ballot boxes.[28] This flexibility is intended to allow the use of mobile ballot boxes for voters who might be elderly or disabled. It can, however, be easy to expand the use of mobile ballot boxes. In one village, for example, officials claimed that they needed mobile boxes for fishermen who took their boats out early in the morning. Unless fixed ballot boxes are used exclusively, it is impossible to prevent abuses. In this analysis, I thus assess the effect of the exclusive use of fixed ballot boxes in the election.

26 See Kevin O'Brien, "Villagers, Elections, and Citizenship in Contemporary China," *Modern China* 27, no. 4 (October 2001), 417; Loren Brandt and Matthew A. Turner, *The Usefulness of Corruptible Elections* (Toronto: University of Toronto, Department of Economics, June 2003), 6.

27 Pastor and Tan, "The Meaning of China's Village Elections," 498.

28 State directives say only that "the use of mobile ballot boxes shall be rigorously controlled." "Circular Concerning Improving Villager Committee Election."

Villagers' Representative Assemblies

In this assessment of village democratic institutions, I also evaluate the implementation of VRAs, popular assemblies composed of representatives selected or elected by villagers. The 1998 Organization Law gives villages two options: elected village committee officials can either report to an assembly open to all adult villagers or to an assembly of villager representatives.[29] In practice, of course, few villages can convene a villager assembly with the mandated quorum of more than half the adult villagers, or representatives from more than two-thirds of households. Villagers' representative assemblies are thus the primary formal institution for direct citizen participation in village decision making. The central government stipulates that one representative should be selected by every five to ten households or by villager small groups. In some localities, representatives are selected through small group discussions and consensus. In other places, representatives may be elected by a show of hands or even secret ballot.

As we can see from Table 7.7, 94 percent of villages in the survey reported the existence of a VRA – but they varied a great deal in the degree to which they have implemented particular institutions enabling villagers to participate in village decision making through VRAs. Most villages reported that their VRA had the formal power to inspect village government expenditures and audit past accounts. But less than half reported that the VRA had the power to recall the elected village head or that they had formal guidelines specifying when the VRA should be convened. Only 13 percent reported that the VRA had actually overturned a village government decision in the past year. In most villages, VRA representatives were not chosen through competitive elections. Only one-quarter reported that their VRA representatives were elected through secret ballot.

Measuring Democratic Institutions in Multiple Ways

This analysis assesses the overall effect of the implementation of village democratic institutions on village governmental provision of public goods as well as the effects of each type of democratic institution. I construct an index summarizing the implementation of preelection procedures, voting

[29] See Organization Law of Villagers' Committees. The Fifth Meeting of the Standing Committee of the Ninth NPC, November 4, 1998. Available online at http://www.ptlib.com/law/fagui246.htm.

Table 7.7. *Descriptive Statistics on Implementation of VRA Institutions*

	Percentage of Villages	Standard Deviation	Number of Villages
Existence of a VRA	94%	24%	316
Measures of VRA institutions			
Elections with secret ballot for VRA seats	25%	44%	307
Formal regulation on when VRA is convened	21%	41%	307
Formal power to recall village head	45%	50%	306
Formal power to inspect village expenditures	91%	29%	309
Formal power to audit village accounts	85%	35%	307
VRA veto of village government decision in the last year	13%	34%	307
Competition for VRA seats	37%	48%	295

procedures, and the VRA, as well as separate indices measuring the implementation of institutions within each category. To increase confidence in the findings, I also construct these indices in two different ways. The first way is to give each village a simple additive score reflecting the number of democratic institutions it has implemented. Using this method, a village that bars intervention from the township government, village Party branch, and incumbent village committee in the nomination of preliminary election candidates but has not barred their intervention in the nomination of final candidates or the election oversight committee would receive a score of three. A village that bars their intervention in the nomination of preliminary candidates, final candidates, and the election oversight committee would receive a score of nine (each of the nine variables in this category would equal one, which adds up to nine). Likewise, a village that implements all seven of the aforementioned voting procedures would receive a score of seven, whereas a village that had implemented none of these procedures would receive a score of zero. In terms of overall implementation of democratic institutions, a village that had implemented all of the aforementioned twenty-three preelection, voting, and VRA institutions would receive a perfect score of twenty-three.

A better way to construct an index is through principal components analysis. Simple additive scores can give us a very rough idea of which villages are "more democratic," but the problem is that they make us assume that villages that score a twenty using this method are twice as democratic as villages that score a ten. Using principal components analysis to construct an index has several advantages. First, it standardizes each of the variables on the same scale.[30] Second, it calculates how each variable should be weighted so that after the variables are weighted and added together, they account for the highest possible percentage of variance or information in the original variables.[31] I report the results both when simple additive scores of the implementation of democratic institutions are used and when indices constructed through principal components are used.

Analysis and Findings

So do villages with better democratic institutions actually have better village governmental provision of public goods? Again, we evaluate such provision using six measures: per capita village government investment in public projects, the existence of paved roads, the existence of paved paths, the percentage of classrooms usable in rainy weather, the newness of the school building, and the existence of running water.[32] To distinguish the effects of democratic institutions from the effects of other factors, the statistical analysis also controls for geographic and demographic factors, economic factors, the implementation of bureaucratic and Party institutions of accountability,

30 Variables are scaled to have a mean of zero and a standard deviation of one.

31 Thus, to measure the implementation of preelection institutions, I created a dichotomous variable for each of the institutions listed in Table 7.4. Each variable took a value of one when the village reported that it did not experience that particular kind of interference in their most recent election. Based on these nine variables, I then constructed a composite index reflecting the implementation of democratic institutions in the preelection stage using principal components analysis. Similarly, to measure the implementation of voting procedures, I created seven dichotomous variables, one for each procedure, and then constructed a composite index using principal components analysis. A similar procedure was used to construct a composite index for the implementation of VRA institutions that was based on the seven dichotomous variables measuring the implementation of seven VRA institutions. To evaluate the overall degree to which democratic institutions were implemented in a village, I combined the indices that measure the implementation of each category of democratic institution into a single composite index of the implementation of formal democratic institutions. The factor loadings for these indices are available online at http://www.cambridge.org/9780521871976.

32 These same six measures of public goods provision are discussed in Chapter 3 and used in all of the book's statistical analyses (specifically in Chapters 5 through 8).

and the existence of village solidary groups such as temples, churches, and lineages.[33]

In short, there is little evidence to suggest that democratic institutions have a strong positive effect on village governmental provision of public goods. When the implementation of village democratic institutions was measured by a simple additive score, its estimated effect on village governmental provision of public goods was small and relatively uncertain for all six public goods provision measures.[34] When we switched to an index of the implementation of village democratic institutions constructed through principal components analysis, the magnitude of the estimated effect on investment increased somewhat. But this modest positive estimated effect on investment was still *not* accompanied by a sizable positive effect on the actual provision of roads, paths, classrooms, school buildings, and water. The estimated effect of the implementation of democratic institutions on these public goods provision measures was again extremely small.[35]

33 Descriptive statistics for these controls are presented in Appendix Table A5.1. Specifically, I control for distance from county seat, village terrain (flat or not flat), the number of natural villages (a proxy for the spatial dispersion of village residents), village population, 1997 village income per capita, 1997 village government assets, 1997 village government tax revenue per capita, the existence of village government enterprises (*cunban qiye*) in 1995, the existence of private enterprises (*siying qiye*) in 1995, the Party membership of the village head, the percentage of village officials who are Party members, the existence of performance contracts with public project targets that village officials must sign with higher-level officials, village temple groups as measured by the existence of a temple manager, village church groups as measured by the existence of an active village pastor, villagewide lineages as measured by the existence of a single ancestral hall with spirit tablets, and subvillage lineages as measured by the existence of multiple ancestral halls with spirit tablets.

34 Full model results using a simple additive score are presented in Appendix Table A7.1. As with previous analyses in Chapters 3, 5, and 6, I use seemingly unrelated regression to estimate the effects. The estimated relationship between village governmental provision of public goods and the implementation of village democratic institutions as measured by a simple additive score was negative and statistically insignificant for two outcomes (roads and newness of school). The estimated relationship was positive and statistically insignificant for four outcomes (investment, paths, classrooms, and water). Using SUR, we cannot reject the null hypothesis that the coefficient estimate on the implementation of democratic institutions is jointly equal to zero across all six outcomes (p-value = 0.51).

35 The full model results are presented in Appendix Table A5.5. The estimated relationship between village provision of public goods and the implementation of democratic institutions was positive but statistically insignificant for five outcomes (investment, roads, paths, classrooms, and water) and negative and statistically insignificant for one outcome (newness of school). Moreover, the magnitude of the estimated effect on the provision of roads, paths, classrooms, and water was very small. Using SUR, we cannot reject the null hypothesis that the coefficient estimate on the implementation of democratic institutions is jointly equal

Regardless of what control variables were included, how missing data were treated, or whether the implementation of village democratic institutions was estimated as an endogenous or exogenous variable, the data do not provide strong evidence that the implementation of village democratic institutions had a major positive effect on village governmental provision of public goods.[36]

It is easier to see the lack of impact that village democratic institutions have when we compare the average village with relatively good implementation of democratic institutions (in the sense of having an index score at the 75th percentile of the sample) to the average village with relatively poor implementation of democratic institutions (in the sense of having an index

to zero across all six outcomes (p-value = 0.41). Missing data were deleted listwise, and Huber heteroskedasticity-robust standard errors are reported.

36 The full model results when missing data are multiply imputed are presented in Appendix Table A5.6. The estimated relationship between village provision of public goods and the implementation of democratic institutions was again positive for five outcomes (investment, roads, paths, classrooms, and water). For one outcome (paths), the estimated effect became statistically significant. The estimated relationship was again negative and statistically insignificant for one outcome (newness of school). The estimated effect of democratic institutions jointly across outcomes also became statistically significant at a 90 percent confidence level (p-value = 0.09). However, because the modest positive effect on investment was not matched by any sizable positive effects on the other public goods provision outcomes, we cannot conclude that democratic institutions had a positive effect on the provision of actual public goods. Findings from bivariate SUR regression for the six public goods provision measures as well as logit models for the three dichotomous measures of public goods provision (existence of paved roads, existence of paved paths, and existence of running water infrastructure) were similar to multivariate SUR estimates. These results can be viewed online at http://www.cambridge.org/9780521871976. When two-stage least squares (2SLS) is used to estimate the effects of democratic institutions, there is still little indication of a substantively interesting effect. As an instrument for the implementation of village democratic institutions, a county's status as an experimental county for the implementation of village democratic reforms is used. Experimental counties receive more resources, attention, and pressure to implement village democratic reforms. Experimental county status is an appropriate instrument because a county's status is determined without regard to conditions at the village level and is causal prior to the implementation of village democratic institutions. The instrumental variable method imposes the condition that designation of the county as a model for democratic reforms affects a village's public goods provision only through its impact on the implementation of democratic reforms at the village level. Hausman tests comparing the differences between the 2SLS estimates and the OLS estimates (which in this case are identical to the SUR estimates) indicate that the differences are not statistically significant. We cannot therefore reject the null hypothesis that the implementation of democratic reforms is exogenous, suggesting that the SUR estimates are more efficient than 2SLS estimates. Wooldridge, *Econometric Analysis of Cross Section and Panel Data*, 506. These results can be viewed online at http://www.cambridge.org/9780521871976.

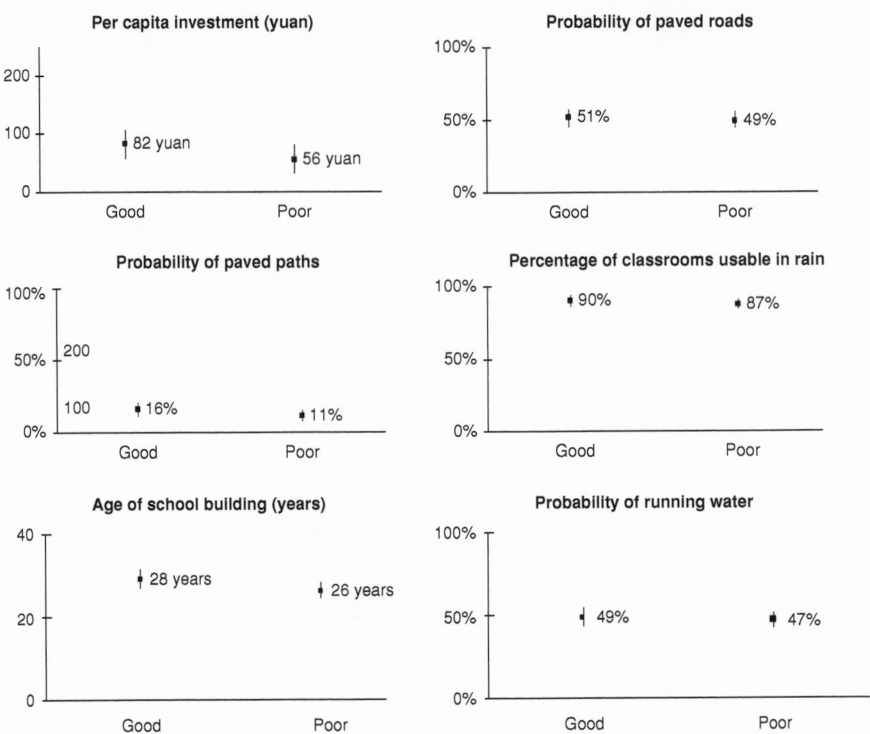

Figure 7.1. Provision of public goods in villages with good and poor implementation of grassroots democratic institutions.

score at the 25th percentile of the sample). As we can see from Figure 7.1, there is little difference in the probability of paved roads, the probability of paved paths, the percentage of classrooms usable in rain, the newness of the village school building, or the probability of running water between villages with good implementation of democratic institutions and villages with poor implementation of democratic institutions. On average, the differences are only a few percentage points.[37] (These graphs are scaled to match those presented in other chapters in order to facilitate comparison.) Villages with good implementation of democratic institutions do have higher investment – about 26 yuan higher – but this increase is markedly smaller than the increase of 48 yuan associated with the existence of a village

[37] These fitted values are calculated using the model results presented in Appendix Table A5.6.

temple group or the increase of 71 yuan associated with the existence of a villagewide lineage group. Moreover, this increase in investment is not accompanied by similar increases in the quality of actual public goods.

Looking at Preelection, Voting, and Representative Assemblies Separately

The implementation of village democratic institutions does not seem to have a clear positive effect on village governmental provision of public goods, at least not when it is measured by a composite index that reflects overall implementation of three categories of democratic institutions. But what about a particular category on its own? Is it possible, for example, that how well voting procedures are implemented really does have an impact on how much villagers can hold officials accountable for public goods provision, but that this effect is submerged when we subsume the implementation of voting procedures into the implementation of village democratic institutions more generally? I thus assessed the effects of each of the three categories of democratic institutions – preelection institutions, voting procedures, and villagers' representative assemblies – separately. For each category, an individual index was constructed through principal components analysis to measure the implementation of institutions in that category.

But even when we looked at preelection institutions, voting procedures, and villagers' representative assemblies individually, none of these individual indices of different kinds of democratic institutions had a sizable positive effect on village governmental provision of public goods. All of the estimated effects were very small in magnitude.[38] The change associated

[38] The full model results for preelection institutions are presented in Appendix Table A7.2. Missing data were deleted listwise, and robust standard errors are calculated. The estimated relationship between village provision of public goods and the implementation of preelection institutions was statistically insignificant for three outcomes (investment, roads, and paths). The estimated relationship was statistically significant or close to significant for classrooms, newness of school, and water. Using SUR, we could reject the null hypothesis that the coefficient estimate on preelection institutions was equal to zero at a 95 percent confidence level (p-value = 0.05), but again, because the magnitudes of the estimated effects are so small, this result simply means that we are fairly certain that preelection institutions have a small effect on village governmental provision of public goods. The full model results for voting institutions are presented in Appendix Table A7.3. The estimated relationship between village provision of public goods and the implementation of voting procedures was statistically insignificant for all six public goods provision outcomes, and we could not reject the null hypothesis that the coefficient estimate on voting institutions was equal to zero (p-value = 0.56). The full model results for VRA institutions are presented

with an increase from the 25th percentile to the 75th percentile for any of the three implementation indices was no more than a few percentage points for the percentage of classrooms usable in rain and the likelihood of paved roads, paths, and water, and no more than 12 yuan for per capita investment (the average per capita investment for the sample being 67 yuan).[39] Moreover, many of these estimates had very high levels of uncertainty associated with them. Results were similar regardless of whether I used a simple additive score or an index constructed through principal components, what control variables were included or excluded, or whether missing data were deleted listwise or multiply imputed.[40]

Why might democratic reforms have only a limited impact on governmental performance and public goods provision? An obvious explanation might be that villagers can only elect the officials on the village committee portion of the village government. The rest of the officials in village government belong to the village Party branch and are generally appointed by Party officials from the township. Although both the village committee and the village Party generally have three to five positions available, officials frequently hold positions in both simultaneously. The percentage of village officials in the village government who are elected can therefore vary quite a bit. In the villages surveyed, the percentage of elected officials in the village government varied from 25 percent to 100 percent, with an average of 74 percent and a standard deviation of 19 percent. It seems plausible that village governments in which most of the officials are elected would be more representative and thus have better provision of public goods and services than village governments in which most officials are appointed by the township.

Findings from my survey, however, do not show any significant correlation between a greater proportion of elected officials in village government and better public goods provision. Even when villages are governed by mostly elected officials, they do not have better public goods provision than

in Appendix Table A7.4. Again, the estimated relationship between village provision of public goods and the implementation of VRA institutions was statistically insignificant for all six public goods provision outcomes, and we could not reject the null hypothesis that the coefficient estimate on VRA institutions was equal to zero (p-value = 0.22), although this estimate was closer to statistical significance than the estimate on voting institutions. Even so, the magnitude of every single one of these estimates was minute.

39 These fitted values are calculated using the results presented in Appendix Tables A7.2 through A7.4.

40 Results are available online at http://www.cambridge.org/9780521871976.

villages that are governed mostly by unelected officials. Nor is there any discernible interaction effect between the proportion of elected officials and the implementation of democratic institutions. In other words, the implementation of democratic reforms does not have a stronger positive effect when more of the village government's officials are elected.

Interactions between Village Democratic Institutions and Village Solidary Groups

There is no evidence that village democratic institutions have a sizable positive effect on village governmental provision of public goods, but what about when they exist in conjunction with encompassing and embedding solidary groups that do have a positive effect? Perhaps democratic institutions have a positive impact only on village governmental provision of public goods when they work in conjunction with the informal institutions of accountability of a village temple group or villagewide lineage. Perhaps when villagers already use temple or lineage norms of obligation to hold village officials accountable for public goods provision, they are also more likely to use elections and representative assemblies to hold officials accountable.

Findings from statistical analysis, however, did not support this hypothesis. Democratic institutions still had no significant positive effect even when the village also had a village temple, and better implementation of democratic institutions did not help temple groups become even more effective at encouraging village governmental provision of public goods.[41] Similarly,

[41] When a multiplicative interaction variable for democratic institutions (as measured by an overall index constructed through principal components) and village temple groups (as measured by the existence of a temple manager) was included in the SUR analysis, we could not reject the null hypothesis that the coefficient estimate on the interaction variable was equal to zero (p-value = 0.30). The coefficient estimate was positive but statistically insignificant for three outcomes (investment, classrooms, and water). The estimate was negative and statistically insignificant for three outcomes (roads, paths, and newness of school). Again, we could not reject the hypothesis that there was really no interaction effect across all six public goods provision outcomes. Full model results are presented in Appendix Table A7.5. Missing data were deleted listwise, and robust standard errors were calculated. When the interaction effect was included, temples on their own still had a positive and statistically significant effect jointly across public goods provision outcomes at a 99 percent confidence level (p-value = 0.0009), and coefficient estimates on both temples and democratic institutions were similar to those produced when an interaction effect was not included.

democratic institutions still did not have a sizable positive effect when the village also had a villagewide lineage, nor did villagewide lineages show a sizable increase in their effectiveness at holding officials responsible for public goods provision. Some evidence suggested a positive interaction for roads and newness of school, but the magnitude of this interaction was small.[42] It is not entirely clear whether combining village democratic institutions with nonencompassing or nonembedding solidary groups such as village churches or subvillage lineages should make village governments better or worse at providing public goods. Findings from the statistical analysis suggested that combining good implementation of democratic institutions with these solidary groups had little impact as well.[43]

Why do democratic reforms have little or no impact on the quality of governmental provision of public goods? This draws on qualitative evidence from interviews and case study research to examine the implementation of democratic reforms in more detail. If villages with better elections are not performing better than villages with worse elections, then perhaps the institutions themselves are flawed. It may be that regardless of how well elections are implemented, they will not have a major positive effect on governmental performance and public goods provision in the current political context.

42 When a multiplicative interaction variable for democratic institutions and villagewide lineage groups (as measured by the existence of a single ancestral hall with spirit tablets) was included in the SUR analysis, we could not reject the null hypothesis that the coefficient estimate on the interaction effect was equal to zero (p-value = 0.19). The coefficient estimate was negative and statistically insignificant for two outcomes (paths and classrooms). The estimate was positive for four outcomes (investment, roads, newness of school, and water) and statistically significant for newness of school. The magnitude of the effect, however, was modest for roads and small for newness of school. Although there is some indication that there may be a positive interaction between democratic institutions and villagewide lineages, any such effect that exists was only small to modest for the provision of actual roads, schools, and water infrastructure. Full model results are presented in Appendix Table A7.6. Missing data were deleted listwise, and robust standard errors were calculated. When the interaction effect was included, villagewide lineages on their own still had a positive and statistically significant effect jointly across public goods provision outcomes at a 90 percent confidence level (p-value = 0.065), and coefficient estimates on both temples and democratic institutions were similar to those produced when an interaction effect was not included, with the exception of the estimated effect of villagewide lineages on investment, which became much larger in magnitude (though still statistically insignificant).

43 The interaction effects did not have a statistically significant effect jointly across the six public goods provision outcomes, and coefficient estimates were generally similar regardless of whether an interaction variable was included.

The Limitations of Village Democratic Reforms

Why might competitive elections and villagers' representative assemblies have little effect on village governmental provision of public goods? Interviews with villagers and officials at various levels of government suggest a number of factors.

Lack of Leverage

For elections to give villagers leverage over village officials, such officials have to care about getting voted out of office. But in many places, the rewards of holding office can be low. In less-developed areas, one of the main incentives for becoming a village official includes wages that are often relatively high and supposedly guaranteed by the state. Village governments, however, are expected to be self-financing, which means that funds to pay for village government expenditures – including wages for village officials – must come from within the village. Although officials in some places are paid exorbitant salaries that are two to four times the village income per capita, officials in 48 percent of surveyed villages received wages in 2000 that were below the village income per capita. One or more officials in 40 percent of the surveyed villages did not receive any wages. In one Hebei village, where both the village Party secretary and accountant had "had enough" (*gan goule*) and quit in order to focus on selling fruit, the remaining two village officials reported that they had not been paid since they took office two years ago. The deputy village head reflected, "I don't even know how much I'm supposed to get."[44]

For private entrepreneurs in richer areas, where the wages of village officials often pale in comparison to what they make in the private sector, the prospect of expanding one's personal networks and making government connections may still be a powerful inducement to *take* office but not necessarily to *stay* in office. Once new business connections are made, it often makes sense to step down and return to one's business. In a village near Xiamen, one villager observed: "One kind of person who wants to be a village cadre is the kind of person who is happy to benefit – at least for three years – from the economic opportunities and connections that you make when you become a cadre."[45]

[44] Interview with male village official, eastern Hebei province, May 4, 2002.
[45] Interview with male villager, eastern Fujian province, October 30, 2000.

Private entrepreneurs often complain that their incomes and businesses suffer while they are in office. In one western Fujian village, for example, the last two village heads quit in the middle of their terms because their bamboo bead-making enterprises started to fail without their undivided attention. In desperation, officials in the township government asked one of the village's highly successful businesspeople who ran a profitable medicinal herb shop in the township seat next to the government office building to do them a favor and fill in. When I visited, this village head noted that "when a village cadre's personal [that is, business] and public responsibilities conflict, they choose the personal interest."[46] He went on to say that he was constantly joking with villagers about the likelihood that he himself would finish his term given the fact that his herb shop was being run into the ground under his wife's management.

Once in office, rather than initiating a variety of ambitious community projects, village officials in some places may actually find that it is in their personal best interests to do as little as possible. The village community council head in West Gate village in Fujian province explained:

> The more issues you deal with, the fewer supporters you have. For example, in building houses, if you are called upon to mediate a dispute, once you fix things between two people, you will offend at least one person. So it's really hard to be a grassroots cadre. It can be better for the cadre who just sits in his office, drinking tea all day, saying, okay, okay, I'll take care of it tomorrow when someone comes to him with a problem.[47]

In these places, the personal satisfaction that comes with performing well and successfully organizing public projects is unlikely to be a reason for anyone to desire a position in the village government.

One potential reason for becoming a village official is control over public funds. In some places, villages enjoy a steady stream of revenue from rental properties or the use of publicly owned land. In these villages, officials may indeed have a strong incentive to hold on to their positions. As a former villager in a western Fujian township observed, "Cadres have to maintain a balance between embezzling money and developing the village economy."[48] Near Xiamen, one village official noted: "Village cadres benefit from being the people in the middle (*zhongjian ren*). For example, companies can't start

[46] Interview with male village head, western Fujian province, February 23, 2001.

[47] Interview with village community council head, eastern Fujian province, November 6, 2000.

[48] Interview with male township resident, western Fujian province, February 21, 2001.

construction in the village without my approval. If I say where they have to buy their sand or stones, they have to follow what I say."[49]

But these places are increasingly rare. Most villages lack land or other public assets that are valuable enough to generate revenue streams. Over three-quarters of the villages in the survey had some governmental debt, and about 40 percent had debts that exceeded the amount of their total revenue in 2000. In many places, any revenue that the village government can generate has to go toward servicing the debt or paying village officials' wages. Over dinner in one such village, also in Fujian, one of the officials commented, "If there were any money to embezzle, we might embezzle it too – but there's just no money."[50] In other villages that lack a stable source of yearly revenue, village officials who are primarily motivated by the chance to line their own pockets have a strong incentive to do so within a couple of terms since, as both villagers and local officials report, it is much harder to hold village officials responsible for fiscal mismanagement after they step down from office.[51]

Lack of Information

Another obstacle to electoral accountability is that villagers sometimes find it difficult to distinguish between village officials who fail to provide needed public goods because there is no money in the village coffers and those who fail to provide public goods because they are bad officials. Although the state has tried to promote improvements in financial transparency by requiring village officials to publicize the village accounts on a regular basis and establishing public financial transparency bulletin boards, little can be done to ensure that village officials are publicizing the true figures. Villagers everywhere said that the figures posted in their village were fabricated. At

[49] Interview with male village official, eastern Fujian province, December 3, 2000.

[50] Interview with male village official, western Fujian province, February 23, 2001.

[51] For ordinary villagers who might otherwise consider stepping up and trying to do something for the community, one major concern is the loss of face in losing an election. During election season in one Fujian township, officials from various villages appeared almost every day at the township government offices to ask what they should do when every single one of the nominated candidates declined to stand for election. One township official commented, "People don't feel confident that they have a chance – because of their abilities or whatever – and they don't want to go through and stand for election, lose, and leave that kind of impression on other villagers. You know if you lose, then people will always think, oh, that's that person who lost in the last election." Interview with female township official, eastern Fujian province, October 27, 2001.

times, the figures posted on bulletin boards did not even add up correctly. In other villages, the bulletin boards existed but nothing had been posted on them since they were first built. Even where villagers' representative assemblies had the authority to audit village accounts, VRA members had no way of ensuring that the account books they reviewed were the real ones. Rural protests about fiscal mismanagement are common, but in many cases, audits of village accounts by higher levels provide little evidence. Financial irregularities are often not discovered until new people take office and find that previous officials had secretly run up large debts or that the village account books did not make sense.

One protest I observed in a Shanxi county illustrates how democratic accountability requires more than the implementation of elections and villagers' representative assemblies. While I was interviewing county civil affairs officials in charge of implementing village democratic reforms one morning, thirty or forty villagers barged into the county government offices to complain about corruption in their village. Elections for village government had been called five times in the village in an attempt to achieve a majority vote, but with no success. The problem, however, was not election fraud. Instead, people were furious because the township electricity bureau was threatening to cut off their electricity. According to the township government, villagers owed four years of unpaid township and village taxes, and until they started paying, the township would withhold electricity. The village fractured into one group that contended that they had paid the taxes and that village officials had embezzled the funds, and another group that supported the village officials. As a result, no candidate could secure a majority vote in village elections. One villager commented, "Without financial transparency, how do we know if it is the collective that owes the villagers, or the villagers who owe the collective?" Another noted, "It's not that we don't have money. We have money! But we're not going to pay until the village accounts are made transparent."[52] As this example makes clear, regulations on public access to information and financial transparency must be enforced from above by the state to enable the monitoring of village officials by the villagers themselves.[53] Bottom-up democratic institutions

52 Interview with villagers, southern Shanxi province, April 19, 2001.

53 Su and Yang also make this point. See Fubing Su and Dali Yang, "Elections, Governance, and Accountability in Rural China" (unpublished manuscript, 2001).

of accountability may require top-down enforcement of supplementary institutions.[54]

Elections and Civic Values

So far elections and village democratic reforms have had limited effects on monitoring and sanctioning village officials. But, as Rigger has argued, they may still increase accountability by promoting a stronger sense of civic duty among citizens and officials that motivates them to contribute to the good of the community. Is it possible that democratic institutions have not yet improved village governmental provision of public goods but that they are helping to create or strengthen community obligations? If so, we might expect people in villages with more democratic elections to be more willing to contribute to village public projects. Nineteen percent of villagers in the survey reported that they thought the last election in their village was only pro forma or rigged by the existing officials, whereas 81 percent thought that the election administration was so-so or good. The survey also asked villagers, "If contributing to a public project benefited the village but did not necessarily have too much benefit for a particular individual, would most people in the village still be willing to contribute labor or money?" Respondents were given a four-point scale ranging from one for "very willing" to four for "not willing at all." As Table 7.8 shows, the average score among people who thought the election was rigged or pro forma was 2.30, whereas the average score of willingness to contribute among people who thought the election administration was average or very good was 2.34. A statistical test shows that the difference between the two groups is statistically insignificant.

In other words, villagers who felt that the last election in their village had been administered fairly without manipulation from above were not more likely to report that people in the village have a stronger sense of civic obligation to the community.

What about villagers' representative assemblies and other institutions that are intended to foster discussion about community issues among

[54] Robert Dahl, Guillermo O'Donnell, and Susan Rose-Ackerman have also emphasized the need for auxiliary institutions to reinforce electoral institutions. See Dahl, *Polyarchy*; Guillermo O'Donnell, "Illusions about Consolidation," *Journal of Democracy* 7, no. 2 (1996), 55–69; Susan Rose-Ackerman, *From Elections to Democracy: Building Accountable Government in Hungary and Poland* (Cambridge: Cambridge University Press, 2005).

Table 7.8. *Comparison of Willingness to Contribute to Public Projects Among People with Different Assessments of Elections in their Village*

	People Who Thought the Last Election Was Rigged or Pro Forma (170 People)	People Who Thought the Implementation Was So-So or Good (724 People)	Difference between Two Groups (Standard Error Reported)	H_0: No Difference between Two Groups, p-value (t test)
How willing are people in the village to contribute labor or money to public projects that do not benefit them directly? 1 = very willing 2 = willing 3 = not very willing 4 = not willing at all	2.30	2.34	0.04 (0.06)	0.55 (H_0 cannot be rejected)

Note: Virtually identical results are obtained when variances are not assumed to be equal in the two groups. N = 894 households. Missing data: fifty-three households.

citizens? Perhaps people who live in villages where VRAs are better implemented are more likely to develop a sense of collective identity and obligation. To assess this possibility, the survey asked villagers whether they thought villager representatives had a larger impact in village governance than village officials did. Fifteen percent of respondents thought that villager representative institutions had a larger impact than officials in their village.[55]

Levels of willingness to contribute to public projects were almost the same between villagers who thought villager representative groups were more important in village governance and villagers who thought village officials were more important in village governance.[56] As Table 7.9 shows, the average score among people who thought villager representative

[55] The number of respondents was 858.

[56] The correlation between strength of villager representative groups and willingness to contribute was negligible ($r = 0.04$).

Table 7.9. *Comparison of Willingness to Contribute to Public Projects Among People with Different Assessments of the Importance of Villagers' Representative Institutions*

	People Who Thought Villager Representative Institutions Were More Important Than Village Officials (132 People)	People Who Thought Village Officials Were More Important Than Villager Representative Institutions (754 People)	Difference between Two Groups (Standard Error Reported)	H_0: No Difference Between Two Groups, p-value (t test)
How willing are people in the village to contribute labor or money to public projects that do not benefit them directly? 1 = very willing 2 = willing 3 = not very willing 4 = not willing at all	2.23	2.35	0.12 (0.07)	0.09 (H_0 can be rejected)

Note: Virtually identical results are obtained when variances are not assumed to be equal in the two groups. N = 886 households. Missing data: sixty-one households.

institutions had a bigger impact than village officials was 2.23, while the average score among people who thought village officials had a bigger impact was 2.35.

Elections may allow people to select the individuals they want in office, but if they do not strengthen civic values and norms, even well-implemented elections may not result in better public goods provision. In some places, elections have spurred new forms of political participation and activity.[57] But in the villages I visited, the view voiced by one villager in Xiamen whom the township had recruited to be a candidate in the village primary election seemed to be more representative:

[57] See, for example, Li and O'Brien, "Villagers and Popular Resistance in Contemporary China," 43–50.

To be honest, I haven't been interested at all in this "democratization" since it began. I haven't even voted in the last elections. I'm too busy running around and traveling outside the village for my petroleum business, and it's too hard to know what's going on both outside and inside the village. I would have withdrawn from the election, but the day before yesterday, village cadres visited and said that everyone else had already withdrawn. I thought, well, I'll just help out and stay in, but I have no real interest in being elected. Elections haven't really changed anything in the village. There's not much difference between when cadres were appointed and now that they are elected.[58]

We need more research and data on the levels of civic interest among villagers and their motivations for voting, especially over time, in order to assess the impact of democratic reforms on the development of civic values accurately. It may simply be that democratic reforms have not had enough time to change how people think and behave. But at least currently, a lot of anecdotal evidence suggests that people are motivated at least in part by private benefits and patronage. One young villager, for example, noted that "people need village cadres in order to get permits and licenses so they give them bribes. Just the day before yesterday, my family went to get a land permit for our factory building in the village."[59] A former village official observed that "the people who get elected are not necessarily the people who do well and those who don't get elected are not necessarily the people who do poorly. Sometimes doing well or doing poorly doesn't come into it (*you shihou tan bu shang zuo hao, zuohuai*). Sometimes the people who go out drinking more (*jiu he de bijiao duo*) get elected." One reason for the lack of civic duty among citizens is that many do not believe that village officials have any sense of civic duty either. The general opinion of people in his village, according to a villager in Fujian, was that "no one would be a village cadre if he or she didn't have an interest in it (*li yi*), if he or she didn't get something out of it (*de dao liyi*)."[60]

Conclusion

Informal institutions provided by solidary groups may work too well. Villages like West Gate and Yang Hamlet are better off than they would be without the villagewide solidary groups that provide informal institutions enabling villagers to hold their officials accountable. But they may not be

58 Interview with male villager, eastern Fujian province, October 30, 2000.
59 Interview with female villager, eastern Fujian province, December 10, 2000.
60 Interview with male villager, western Fujian province, February 21, 2001.

as well off as they would be with a well-implemented democratic system backed by the rule of law guaranteeing their ability to monitor and sanction officials through formal institutions such as elections accompanied by public disclosure laws and freedom of press.

The case of West Gate even suggests that strong community solidary institutions may inhibit the development of formal democratic institutions. When village officials need input from villagers, or when villagers want village officials to do something for them, both go to the community council. Neither village officials nor villagers have much reason to strengthen the role of the formal villagers' representative assembly in village policy making as long as existing informal institutions work perfectly well. Ironically, informal institutions that enhance village governance may actually make it harder to implement the formal democratic reforms intended to enhance village governance.

8

The Limitations of Formal Party and Bureaucratic Institutions

In this chapter, we turn to formal bureaucratic institutions of accountability. As we will see, serious problems of bureaucratic monitoring and accountability plague local governance. Current bureaucratic institutions intended to enable higher-level officials to hold lower-level officials accountable have little impact on the village governmental provision of public goods and services. Evidence from my fieldwork suggests that reforming these formal institutions of accountability will be very difficult without simultaneously creating effective new systems for intergovernmental transfers and information flow within the state.

Formal Accountability at the Village Level

State elites have two key formal institutions they can use to secure compliance from village officials: village Party organizations and the bureaucratic cadre responsibility system.

Formal Party Institutions of Accountability

In terms of formal Party institutions, higher-level Party officials at the township level and above exercise authority over village officials and over officials in the village Party branch. A more detailed description of the structure of village government is presented at the beginning of Chapter 2, but as a brief review, the village government is formally composed of two organizations: the village committee and the village Party branch. Each organization typically has three to five positions, depending on the population of the village. A village head chairs the village committee. State regulations require village committee members to be elected through direct, competitive popular elections, although, as we saw in the last chapter, the implementation of these elections varies a great deal across localities. A village Party secretary chairs the village Party branch. Members of the village Party branch are appointed by the Party committee at the township level. Recently, some localities have experimented with pilot reforms for internal Party democratization. In these places, village Party branch members have to be approved through a vote by the village Party members in addition to township Party approval.

Despite these formal distinctions, in practice village officials often hold concurrent positions in both organizations, especially since the state has increasingly encouraged local governments not to burden villagers with salaries for superfluous officials. Thus Party institutions potentially have a direct influence not only on the village Party branch but on the elected village committee.

Higher-level Party officials elicit compliance from village officials by activating norms emphasizing corporate identity, duty, and loyalty to the Party.[1] The township Party committee inculcates these organizations' norms through selective recruitment and Party indoctrination or "study" (*xuexi*) meetings. Village officials who are Party members typically attend monthly meetings in the township during which they are supposed to learn about and study central Party directives. Village officials are then expected to convene meetings of Party members within the village to disseminate this information and to enlist the help of village Party members in implementation.

Formal Bureaucratic Institutions of Accountability

In terms of the cadre responsibility system, the heads of one level of government (such as the village) sign a performance contract with the level above them (the township) guaranteeing that they will meet certain policy targets and performance standards by the end of the year (or some fixed

[1] At the township level and higher, the Party keeps official lists of positions over which it exerts control as well as lists of reserve officials who are approved to fill vacancies. All reserve officials are investigated and reevaluated (*kaohe*) annually. See Burns, "China's Nomenklatura," 36–51; John P. Burns, *The Chinese Communist Party's Nomenclatura System: A Documentary Study of Party Control of Leadership Selection, 1979–1984* (Armonk: M. E. Sharpe, 1989); idem, "Strengthening CCP Control of Leadership Selection: The 1990 Nomenclatura," *China Quarterly*, no. 138 (1994), 458–91. See also Melanie Manion, "The Cadre Management System, Post-Mao: The Appointment, Promotion, Transfer, and Removal of Party and State Leaders," *China Quarterly*, no. 102 (1985), 203–33.

time). In exchange for meeting these targets, local governments enjoy a high degree of autonomy. They have discretion over how to meet targets and over other activities that are not covered by targets. This system grew out of the administrative guarantee system (*baogan zhidu*), originally promoted by Liu Shaoqi in the 1960s and resurrected in 1979 after the start of reforms. As Audrey Donnithorne notes, the administrative guarantee system gave each level of government "wide latitude in the conduct of its own affairs" in exchange for guaranteeing "a certain level of performance to the level above it."[2] The state made each level of government responsible only for evaluating the level immediately below it. The rationale was that proximate levels of government were in the best position to acquire information about each other. Constructing multiple channels for acquiring information about performance that would allow checks on the accuracy of performance evaluations would also be too costly, both politically and financially.[3] A series of central directives between 1986 and 1989 mandated a yearly comprehensive performance evaluation for local officials, which included the preparation of a performance summary (*gongzuo zongjie*) and a poll soliciting evaluations from colleagues.[4] In 1988, the first countywide implementation of performance contracts between township leaders and county governments took place in Henan province.[5] Procedures varied widely from region to region. In some places I visited, performance evaluations took place two, three, or even four times a year; others had none at all.

Different performance contracts exist for different types of officials and different policy areas. Top officials in a locality (the Party secretary and government head) sign contracts with the level of government above them. Ordinary cadres sign contracts with the top officials in the same level of

[2] Donnithorne argued that this concept was the only way the central government could govern a country as large as China, since supervising everything done by subordinate levels was impossible. Audrey Donnithorne, "Aspects of Neo-Liuist Economic Policy," *Australian Journal of Chinese Affairs*, no. 3 (January 1980), 28.

[3] For an overview of formal and informal modes of communication within the bureaucracy developed during the Maoist period, see Michel Oksenberg, "Methods of Communication within the Chinese Bureaucracy," *China Quarterly*, no. 57 (January–March 1974), 1–39.

[4] Yasheng Huang, "Administrative Monitoring in China," *China Quarterly*, no. 143 (September 1995), 830–1. In some cases, local officials are evaluated more frequently.

[5] See Ministry of Organization, "Notice Regarding Implementation of the Annual Job Evaluation System for Leading Cadres of Local Party and Government Organs (*Guanyu shixing difang dangzheng lingdao ganbu niandu gongzuo kaohe zhidu de tongzhi*)," June 6, 1988; Saich, "The Blind Man and the Elephant"; Latham, "Rural Reforms and Grassroots Cadres," 69.

government and are supervised by the personnel department at that level.[6] Different contracts may be drawn up for different policy areas such as industrial development, agricultural development, tax collection, or social order; alternatively, a single contract may encompass multiple types of targets.[7] Specific targets vary across localities. For the villages I visited in grain-producing areas, contracts frequently encouraged officials to change the structure of agricultural production (*nongye jiegou tiaozheng*) by setting targets for the amount of land devoted to cash crops, whereas for areas threatened by desertification, contracts for officials often set targets for reforestation.

Contracts also prioritize targets.[8] Mandatory targets (*yipiao fojue*, literally "targets with veto power") must be achieved. Targets for social order and birth control often fall into this category.[9] If they are not met, officials may forfeit their bonuses or even lose their jobs. In one Hebei village, for example, officials reported that their basic wages are 1,000 yuan per month. They are then awarded points based on the targets they fulfill on their performance contracts for a maximum score of one hundred points. For each point, they receive another 20 yuan in bonuses with a possible maximum bonus of 2,000 yuan. If there is, however, even one birth over the village's quota, they receive only their basic wage of 1,000 yuan, regardless of how well they have performed in other areas.

After mandatory targets come "hard" targets, usually centered on economic development and tax collection. Easily quantifiable, hard targets have a major impact on prospects for bonuses and, for officials at the township level and higher, for promotion. Last in priority are "soft" targets such as "cultural and social development," which is where the provision of village roads and basic infrastructure usually falls. Soft targets are typically hard to measure and often optional. As one provincial official in Jiangxi noted, if mandatory and economic targets are achieved, local governments are not

[6] National regulations on the evaluations of civil servants in 1993 separated "leading cadres" (*lingdao ganbu*) from ordinary cadres. See also Pierre F. Landry, "Controlling Decentralization: The Party and Local Elites in Post-Mao Jiangsu" (Ph.D. Diss., University of Michigan, 2000).

[7] Maria Edin, "Remaking the Communist Party-State: The Cadre Responsibility System at the Local Level in China," *China: An International Journal* 1, no. 1 (March 2003), 7–8.

[8] Ibid., 10; Edin argues that only veto targets on performance contracts have an impact on the decisions of local officials.

[9] O'Brien and Li, "Selective Policy Implementation in Rural China," 172.

heavily penalized even if they fail to meet the rest of the targets on their contracts.

The Limitations of Top-Down Control

In theory, formal Party and bureaucratic institutions should enable higher-level officials to exercise a substantial amount of control over the behavior of village officials. But theory does not seem to have translated into practice. Part of the problem, some scholars have suggested, may have to do with declining confidence in Party authority and ideology. Minxin Pei has argued that Maoist-era policies and the subsequent adoption of reforms in the late 1970s discredited the Party's self-proclaimed goal of "serving the people." The Party's organizational penetration, appeal to the masses, and internal discipline have thus decayed in the reform period.[10] Avery Goldstein notes that Party efforts to deal with corruption are no longer seen as "part of a healthy process of rejuvenation" but as results of "perverse incentives of a half-reformed system."[11] Interviews, however, with officials at various levels of government also suggest another set of reasons for the weakness of top-down institutions of accountability: the lack of leverage, incentives, and information at higher levels.

Decentralization and Lack of Leverage

The first problem is that higher-level officials often have no bite. As one village head in Fujian noted of the township government above him, "If the father has no money, the children aren't going to listen to him."[12] Though a trend toward recentralization may be starting, over the past two decades, fiscal decentralization (as Chapters 2 and 3 outline) made each locality responsible for financing its own expenditures. The central government minimized interregional transfers and subsidies to lower levels. As a result, higher levels generally had fewer state funds to dispense to lower levels, and their leverage over lower levels of government decreased. Without the prospect of state subsidies as a reward for good behavior, village officials are less likely

[10] Minxin Pei, "Will China Become Another Indonesia?" *Foreign Policy*, no. 116 (Autumn 1999), 94–109. See also Cao, *Huanghebian De Zhongguo: Yige Xuezhe Dui Xiangcun Shehui De Guancha Yu Sikao*, 448.

[11] Avery Goldstein, "State of the Field: Trends in the Study of Political Elites and Institutions in the PRC," *China Quarterly*, no. 139 (September 1994), 723–4.

[12] Interview with male village head, western Fujian province, February 23, 2001.

to comply with demands from the township government, especially if these demands are unfunded mandates for village public goods provision. A village Party secretary explained: "The township has never allocated any funds to us for public projects (*genben meiyou bo guo qian xialai*). They don't give us guidance or targets, and they don't give us funding (*meiyou zhidao, meiyou mubiao, meiyou bokuan*)."[13]

To make matters worse, not only did fiscal decentralization reduce the funds that higher levels could dispense to lower levels, but because each region was expected to be self-financing, higher regional governments became more dependent on the localities within their jurisdiction to deliver tax revenue upward. As a result, township governments are less likely to enforce public goods provision in both rich and poor villages. Regional governments dependent on the localities below them naturally had little wish to alienate officials heading the more prosperous localities by making too many demands and had little reason to care what officials in the rest of the localities were doing.

So the state had little in the way of subsidies with which to induce good performance from village officials, but what about more straightforward inducements, such as bonuses and promotions? Village officials are almost never promoted to higher levels, so their performance contracts work by docking their wages or increasing their bonuses.[14] But as we discussed in the last chapter in regard to getting elected out of office, in many places the loss of wages is not a powerful sanction. According to the survey data, the effect of higher wages on the behavior of officials is quite small. In a typical village, officials who earn relatively high wages in the 75th percentile of the survey (2,727 yuan) are only 3 percent more likely to report that performance contracts have an effect on their decision making than officials who are paid at the 25th percentile (857 yuan). Village officials in Fujian acknowledged that the township penalizes them for birth control violations, but they shrug it off: "If they penalize, then they penalize. It's not much money anyway (*kou jiu koule, fanzheng mei duoshao qian*)."[15] In wealthier places

[13] Interview with male village Party secretary, western Fujian province, February 22, 2001.

[14] One former township Party secretary commented: "Whoever heard of a peasant with a rural registration becoming the head of a township? Peasants are, after all, outside the political sphere (*benlai jiu zai zhengzhi kuangkuang de waimian*)." Former deputy township leader, western Fujian province, February 21, 2001. See also Scott Rozelle, "Decision-Making in China's Rural Economy: The Linkages between Village Leaders and Farm Households," *China Quarterly*, no. 137 (March 1994), 99–124.

[15] Interview with male village official, northern Fujian province, October 15, 2001.

where village officials often own their own businesses, village official wages are often not high enough to motivate them. In poorer places where wages could be a powerful incentive, many localities do not have sufficient funds to pay them.[16]

Decentralization and Lack of Incentives

The second problem is will. Do township governments even *want* to hold village officials accountable for public goods provision? In many cases, the answer is no. A combination of three factors discourages township governments from making sure that village officials provide public goods and services. First, policy makers at the top continue to prioritize economic development and industrialization over public goods provision. Second, fiscal decentralization gives local officials strong incentives to invest in industrialization and short-term revenue growth *instead of* in public services and long-term economic growth. In other words, village officials lack positive incentives to invest in public goods and services, and township officials lack positive incentives to make sure that they do. Third, administrative decentralization hampers the ability of higher levels to make sure that township officials are diligently supervising village officials. Village officials are not punished for failing to provide public goods, and township officials are not punished for failing to punish village officials.

State Priorities All performance contracts signed by officials at the township level and above prioritize economic development, industrialization, and revenue generation, not the provision of public goods and services.[17]

16 Before 2000, village officials' salaries were paid through village levies (*cun tiliu*), which the village government collected and retained for village expenditures, including public goods provision and village government administration, according to the "Regulations on the Management of Peasants' Fees and Labor" issued by the State Council on December 7, 1991. The number of village officials on the village government payroll and the amount of salaries were decided according to the township government according to the size of the village and the level of village economic development. As of March 2, 2000, the "Notice of the Work on the Tax-for-Fee Pilot Reform in the Rural Areas," issued by the Central Party Committee and the State Council mandated that village levies (*cun tiliu*) would be collected in the form of agricultural surtaxes (not to exceed 20 percent of the agricultural tax). Such levies would be designated for village government expenditures but managed by the township government.

17 Edin, "Remaking the Communist Party-State," 11. See also Susan Whiting, *Power and Wealth in Rural China: The Political Economy of Institutional Change* (Cambridge: Cambridge University Press, 2001).

Performance contracts are also likely to have a larger impact on township officials than they do on village officials. Unlike village officials who are rarely promoted to higher levels of government, township officials who perform well are often promoted to higher levels, raised to a higher rank in the Party hierarchy, or awarded a concurrent post at a higher level of government.[18] One village official in Fujian commented: "The township Party secretary has only visited the village twice and the township head once. They [Party officials] don't care about what goes on at the village level. They just care about getting promoted (*sheng guan*)."[19]

Lack of Rewards Rather than spending time and money monitoring the performance of village governments, township officials often find more benefit in using township resources on developing local enterprises, constructing rental buildings, or investing in real estate – activities that generate income quickly. Township officials may also conserve collective funds in order to pay for administrative expenses. Numerous townships spend much of their revenue on administrative expenses such as salaries, official cars, and banquets for visiting officials or businesspeople.[20] These kinds of expenditures please business contacts and higher-level officials and can thus result in greater payoffs for township officials than monitoring village governmental performance and public goods provision.

To maximize expenditures on "productive" investments, township governments also try to minimize the resources spent on supervising village officials. One way of minimizing the costs of supervision is to monitor village governmental performance only in the areas that directly benefit the township government and overlook performance in other areas. Public goods provision is not only less important to them, but it takes more time and effort to assess. In contrast to total output and other indicators of economic development that are easy to quantify, the quality of public services provision usually falls into the category of soft targets that "are not deemed important" and difficult to measure.[21] One village Party secretary explained:

[18] Edin, "Remaking the Communist Party-State," 13.

[19] Interview with male village Party secretary, western Fujian province, February 22, 2001.

[20] Lu also finds that in many townships, most revenues are spent for administrative purposes, such as payroll. In one Liaoning county, he finds that welfare and other public expenditures by local governments were only 5.5 percent of total expenditures. X. Lu, "The Politics of Peasant Burden in Reform China," *Journal of Peasant Studies* 25, no. 1 (1997), 120.

[21] Edin, "Remaking the Communist Party-State," 10; O'Brien and Li, "Selective Policy Implementation in Rural China," 167–86.

> [As far as the township is concerned,] if you organize public projects, that's good. If you don't, that's fine too (*zuo ye hao, bu zuo ye hao*). In actuality, if you have some money, they prefer you to invest it in something profitable, not to use it up on public projects. . . . Things like roads, there's no way to measure or quantify them, so the township thinks they're not worth it (*bu hesuan*). The township emphasizes production output, how much grain is produced, how many pigs or chickens there are, how much you can make per *mu* if you change to cash crops. They just think about how you can sell flowers for 60 yuan per pot, and then how many pots you can have per *mu*. . . ."[22]

Even when public project targets are included in their contracts, village officials report that the township often disregards them except when the central government launches the occasional campaign specifically to improve rural public services, such as the central directives promoting "well-off villages" (*xiaokang cun*) from 1996 to 1998. One village in Fujian reports that the province focused efforts on "five accesses" (*wutong*): access to telephones, roads, cable TV, running water, and electricity. However, even during this period of heightened political will, only telephones and roads saw any significant development. By 1999, the state's priority on improving these public services had petered out. Now, village officials say, "higher levels just say to take it slowly if you can't achieve anything this year."[23] Another strategy that township governments use to minimize resources spent on supervising village officials is to focus on monitoring only the villages that are economically significant to them in terms of economic growth and the generation of tax revenue. Most resources that townships spend on monitoring village officials are focused on the villages that generate the most output and tax revenue,[24] although they may occasionally have to spend time and effort in villages where social stability is a problem. Township heads and Party secretaries visit villages with higher levels of economic development more frequently than they do villages with lower levels of economic development. Villages at the 75th percentile in terms of 1997 income per capita experience, on average, 1.5 more visits than villages at the 25th percentile in terms of 1997 income per capita. Distance from the township seat is also important. Villages that are 7 kilometers from the township (the 75th percentile in terms of distance)

22 Interview with male village Party secretary, western Fujian province, February 22, 2001.

23 Interview with male village official, northern Fujian province, October 20, 2001.

24 Pierre Landry finds, however, that village economic performance has little impact on a village Party secretary's prospects of promotion. See Landry, "Controlling Decentralization," 13.

experience, on average, 1.6 visits less than villages that are two kilometers from the township (the 25th percentile in terms of distance).[25]

In villages that are far away or insignificant for the township's plans for economic development, officials frequently report that the township does not bother to enforce any of the targets on their performance contracts at all. One village official in a removed area of western Fujian said of the targets on his contract: "It's all fake. It's not very realistic. What the township says is, if you don't do it, we're not going to do anything (*ni bu gao, women ye bu guan ni*). It's all empty words (*kong hua*)."[26] Village officials in Hebei reported that township officials only carried out cursory examinations of their performance: "We basically always get perfect scores with a little taken off."[27] Township officials corroborate these observations. A former township Party secretary explained: "Village officials get targets, like how much grain their village has to produce, but if they don't reach the target, the township just meets with them and tells them to do better next year. It doesn't affect their wages – they only get a little over 100 yuan a month anyway – and it only affects their bonuses in a small way."[28] Another village Party secretary noted that he signed a contract, but "there are no consequences – none [of the targets] can be accomplished anyway (*dou meiyou shenme houguo, dou buneng wancheng*)."[29] Officials in one village even reported that although township officials are supposed to visit the village and evaluate their performance twice a year, they didn't even receive a copy of the performance contract from the township in the previous year and had to ask for one.[30] When villages are paralyzed by internal conflict, townships simply write them off and excuse them from signing any contract at all. One Party secretary in a Hebei village that previous village officials had divided into factions, resulting in fights between the factions that had almost resulted in visits to the hospital, commented that he had never personally signed a performance contract but that he had heard of them.[31]

[25] Distance from township seat, terrain of village, village population, number of natural villages, and county dummies are included as controls.

[26] Interview with male village official, western Fujian province, February 22, 2001.

[27] Interview with male village official, eastern Hebei province, May 4, 2002.

[28] Interview with former deputy township head, western Fujian province, February 21, 2001.

[29] Interview with male village Party secretary, eastern Hebei province, April 27, 2001.

[30] Interview with village officials, eastern Hebei province, April 30, 2002.

[31] Interview with male village Party secretary, eastern Hebei province, May 2, 2002.

Another way in which township governments conserve resources spent on supervising villages is by relying on village officials themselves to report on their own performance.[32] Village officials compile statistics on village production, economic growth, government revenue and expenditures, and other data necessary for evaluating their performance. Village officials also put together a written or oral summary of their accomplishments over the past year. Incorporating feedback from citizens is officially encouraged, but often neglected. Even in places where citizen feedback is institutionalized, at best representatives from the township visit the village and randomly solicit the opinions of three or four villagers. But with such a small sample, village officials say, there's nothing you can do if one of the individuals has a personal grievance and seeks revenge against you (*geren baofu*). One village official noted: "There aren't any officials who don't offend someone. If [the township] comes across someone like this, you're out of luck (*dang ganbu meiyou bu shangren, yu dao zhege ren jiu daomei*)."[33] Township governments, as another Hebei village official noted, "just care about whether you have fulfilled state tasks, they don't care about the opinions of villagers or villagers' representative assemblies."[34] In the rare case that levels above the township actually do investigate village-level data they believe to be false, self-reporting by village officials allows township governments to pass the buck and deny responsibility for the false information.[35]

Lack of Information

A third reason for the weakness of bureaucratic performance contracts is that it is hard to monitor the monitors. In general, higher-level governments have few ways of obtaining accurate information about what goes on at the bottom. As a result, it is very difficult for higher-level officials to know how closely the township is monitoring village governmental performance and whether the township is sanctioning village officials for poor performance. Misreporting and collusion between any two levels of government are possible because almost all information transmitted within the

32 Elizabeth Remick points out, however, that there is considerable variation in local state institutions. Elizabeth Remick, *Building Local States: China during the Republican and Post-Mao Eras* (Cambridge: Harvard University Press, 2004).

33 Interview with male village official, eastern Hebei province, May 2, 2002.

34 Interview with male village official, eastern Hebei province, May 4, 2002.

35 See Yongshun Cai, "Between State and Peasant: Local Cadres and Statistical Reporting in Rural China," *China Quarterly*, no. 163 (September 2000), 783–805.

state passes sequentially from one level of government to the next. When a provincial government, for example, decides how much money to allocate to rural poverty alleviation programs in the coming year, it relies largely on information that villages have reported to townships, townships have reported to counties, counties to municipalities, and ultimately, municipalities to the provincial government. There are virtually no institutionalized mechanisms, for example, for the county to obtain information directly from villages. As a result, it is very difficult to verify or discredit information about the activities of one level of government if the level of government above it corroborates the information.

Data from the survey confirm that misreporting continues to be a chronic problem. Not only do township governments have incentives to minimize the resources spent on monitoring village officials, but they often have incentives to *promote* misreporting by village officials. As we mentioned in the previous section, township officials have their own performance contracts to fulfill, and ambitious targets on their contracts lead them to put pressure on village officials to meet or at least report that they meet the targets that have been set.

Data from both case studies and my village survey indicate that misreporting by village officials is rampant. The survey asked village officials how much "the village income per capita (figure reported to higher levels)" was as well as how much "the real (*shiji*) village income per capita" was approximately. Only 14 percent of the villages in the survey reported the same number for both the "reported" income per capita and the "real" income per capita.[36] The average discrepancy between the real and reported income per capita was 601 yuan in 1997 (28 percent of the reported income per capita) and 668 yuan in 2000 (31 percent of the reported income per capita). On average, village officials overstated their income per capita by 630 yuan. In 2000, the mean "real" income per capita for the sample was 1,535 yuan, and the mean reported income per capita was 2,165 yuan, which was very close to the official rural income per capita published by the National Bureau of Statistics (NBS) for 2000: 2,263 yuan.

Some researchers have hypothesized that village officials simply increase their income per capita by one-third to arrive at the figure they report to

[36] The survey questionnaire asked the following two questions: (1) "How much is your village's net income per capita (figure reported to higher levels)?" (*Ni cun renjun chunshouru shi duoshao [shangbao shu]*?); and (2) "About how much is your village's net income per capita in reality?" (*Ni cun renjun chunshouru shijishang dagai duoshao?*).

the township.[37] Data from my survey, however, show considerable variation in the size of the discrepancy between real and reported income per capita. Officials in poorer villages tend to exaggerate village income per capita more than officials in richer villages. For villages that had a real income per capita above 2,263 yuan, the official figure for rural income per capita in 2000, the average discrepancy between real and reported income per capita was only 303 yuan. For villages that had not achieved an income per capita of 2,263 yuan, the average discrepancy between real and reported income per capita was 733 yuan.

The Case of West Field Township The case of West Field Township vividly illustrates how the structure of information transmission and data collection can make it difficult for higher levels of government to hold local officials accountable. In 1993, the township government started a rural credit cooperative that promised an interest rate of 22 percent to people who deposited money in the fund and charged an interest rate of 28 percent to people who borrowed from the fund. In 1994, Zhu Rongji announced that it was illegal for government organs to operate these financial institutions, but the township successfully convinced the county government to allow it to keep operating the credit cooperative. Subsequently, when the local branch of the People's Bank of China came to audit the township government's activities, the county government suppressed the audit. When the fund eventually ran out of money and people who had deposited their savings could not withdraw their funds, the township government decided to arrest individuals and enterprise owners who had taken out loans and then detain them at the township government's offices until they agreed to pay their debts immediately. Township government officials claimed that these measures had been approved by the county Party committee. One former township official wryly explained to me:

> The problems start at the township and county levels. For example, if the township wants to do something illegitimate, such as using earmarked funds for something else, it first goes to the county Party secretary. The county Party secretary doesn't have any spare time to figure out what's going on in the townships, and he thinks the township Party secretary is *my* Party secretary so he decides to trust him and gives him permission. Then when mismanagement of funds comes to light, the township can say that the county Party secretary agreed to the arrangement and it knows that the county court or inspection bureau will stop its investigation right there. No

[37] See ibid., 789.

leader at the county level ever gets into trouble – at most a county deputy head will be publicly reprimanded. The lowest levels get permission and then they are able to blame their mistakes on the middle level. The higher levels always support those right beneath them. Not to do so would be like slapping your own mouth (*da ni ziji de zuiba*).[38]

In short, township governments fail to hold village officials accountable for public goods provision in large part because county governments often fail to hold township governments accountable for anything.

Improving Information Transmission Improving information transmission and data collection has consistently headed the political agenda. In 1996, the NBS promulgated a revised version of the 1983 Statistics Law that emphasized improvements in data collection methodology and criminalization of statistical fraud. Previously, the NBS relied on compulsory self-reporting and periodic surveys of "keypoint" sites for statistical data.[39] The Revised Statistics Law now requires the NBS to rely primarily on census data and frequent surveys of randomly sampled data points.[40] Subsequent statutes made statistical misreporting a punishable criminal offense.[41] These statutes led to a widespread crackdown on falsified statistics in 1997, although the state focused primarily on falsification of statistics related to industrial production. In 2003, the NBS again reiterated the state's commitment to punishing fraud and announced new measures to improve output statistics at the local level. Noting that more than ten thousand illegal activities in statistical reporting had been discovered annually, it equated misreporting to corruption: "We will beef up inspections to punish unlawful activities in statistical work such as fraud and deception. Fraud and deception are not only serious political issues, but a kind of corruption in and of themselves."[42]

38 Interview with former deputy township head, western Fujian province, February 22, 2001.
39 See ibid.
40 Article 10, Revised Statistics Law, May 15, 1996.
41 The "Detailed Rules for Implementation of the Statistics Law of the PRC" states that state organs, public organizations, enterprises, institutions, and self-employed industrialists and businesspeople that are under statistical investigation "must provide the true statistical data and information according to the stipulations of Statistical Law and must not make falsified, concealed reports, refuse or delay to report or forge or tamper with records." Article 4, "Detailed Rules for Implementation of the Statistics Law of the PRC," March 31, 2002. See also Article 3, "Statistics Law of the People's Republic of China," May 15, 1996.
42 *Renmin Ribao*, December 24, 2003.

New laws and regulations, however, have not altered the basic level-by-level structure of pipeline information transmission. Multiple channels for collecting the same data that could potentially constitute ways of checking data accuracy are actively discouraged. Although many individual ministries collect their own statistics, there is no institutionalized system for cross-checking figures.[43] Not only do ministries often measure the same variable in different ways, but they often keep their own data classified. Furthermore, the Statistics Law makes it technically illegal for government departments to collect statistics already collected by the NBS or by another department: "State, departmental, and local statistical investigations must be explicitly divided in their functions. They shall be made to dovetail with each other and not overlap."[44]

Nor have reforms released local statistical bureaus from the control of local governments.[45] Although the Ministry of Finance directly funds administrative expenditures of statistical bureaus at higher levels, administrative expenditures at lower levels and salaries at all levels continue to come from local government budgets.[46] Without the establishment of an independent statistics organization funded from above, local governments are still in essence reporting on themselves.

Similar shortcomings plague the government offices charged with monitoring and auditing the bureaucracy. The General Auditing Administration (GAA), created in 1983, audits the economic affairs of state enterprises and government offices. At the time of its inception, some argued for making the GAA completely independent of local levels of government but were overruled by others who countered that without cooperation from local governments, local auditors would be unable to do anything. As a result, local governments fund the budgets of local auditing bureaus and appoint their staff members. In many townships, the auditing office is actually a section of the

43 Sean Dougherty, *The Reliability of Chinese Statistics* (Beijing: U.S. Department of Commerce, 2001).

44 Article 9, "Statistics Law of the People's Republic of China," May 15, 1996.

45 At the central level, the NBS is a bureau-level organization directly subordinate to the State Council. Its administrative rank is therefore somewhere in between a ministry and a bureau within a ministry, which means that it cannot directly issue orders to ministry officials. Local government control over local statistical bureaus has lessened somewhat over the years, but remains high. In 1981, the State Council gave the NBS control over personnel appointments in local bureaus. Huang, "Administrative Monitoring in China," 839–40.

46 Articles 23 and 24, "Detailed Rules for Implementation of the Statistics Law of the PRC," ibid., 839–40.

township financial office, making the monitors subordinate to those they are monitoring.[47]

Likewise, local governments pay the salaries of staff members in local offices of the Ministry of Supervision (MOS). Originally established in 1949, abolished in 1959, and re-established in 1987, the MOS monitors government administration. In addition to local MOS offices, there are also MOS staff members working within specific government departments who are paid through MOS budgets, but the departments that they monitor control their administrative expenditures.[48] Not surprisingly, research suggests that local governments do not allocate much funding to offices with supervisory and auditing responsibilities. While discussing relationships between villages and higher-level government offices, one village Party secretary noted: "The *tuanwei*, supervision bureau, planning committee, or the general office of the county Party committee, however, have no money and no power. All these offices just come down to the village to visit and eat [at the village's expense]."[49]

Findings from the Survey

Not surprisingly, given all of the issues discussed previously, the survey data show little evidence that formal institutions of top-down control have a significant effect on village governmental provision of public goods.

Party Institutions of Accountability

The central government has repeatedly published directives emphasizing the importance of rural public goods provision.[50] If Party institutions are an effective mechanism for holding village officials accountable, Party control

[47] Maria Edin, "Institutional Basis of Developmentalism and Cronyism in China," paper presented at the Annual Meeting of the Association for Asian Studies, Chicago, March 22–5, 2001.

[48] Huang, "Administrative Monitoring in China," 836–8.

[49] Interview with male village Party secretary, northern Fujian province, October 18, 2001.

[50] See, for example, "Ideas on Several Policies on Further Strengthening the Work in the Countryside and Improving Comprehensive Productive Capacities of Agriculture by the Central Committee of the CCP and the State Council (*Zhonggong zhongyang guowuyuan guanyu jinyibu jiaqiang nongcun gongzuo tigao nongye zonghe shengchan nengli ruogan zhengce de yijian*)," approved December 31, 2004. In recent years, the most systematic and comprehensive central document concerning public goods provision and infrastructural development is "Several Ideas on Promoting the Development of the Socialist New Countryside by the Central Committee of the CCP and the State Council (*Zhonggong zhongyang guowuyuan*

should be especially strong when both of the leading officials in the village government, the village head and the village Party secretary, are Party members. The township Party committee should find it easier to control the village government, and the two leading officials should be more likely to cooperate with each other and hold each other accountable for accomplishing Party objectives. In other words, villages in which the elected head of the village committee is also a member of the Party should have better public goods provision than villages in which the elected head is not a Party member.

Similarly, we might expect villages where a higher percentage of village officials are Party members to have better public goods provision than villages where a lower percentage of village officials are Party members. Again, the township Party committee should find it easier to control the village government when most or all of the village officials are Party members, and village officials should be more likely to cooperate with each other and hold each other accountable.

I thus measure the degree of Party control over a village's officials by using two indicators: the Party membership of the village head and the percentage of village officials who are Party members.[51] Sixty-nine percent of village heads in the survey were Party members, and the mean percentage of village officials with Party membership was 74 percent. As in previous statistical analyses, I evaluate village governmental provision of public goods using per capita village government investment in public projects, the existence of paved roads, the existence of paved paths, the percentage of classrooms usable in rainy weather, the newness of the school building, and the existence of running water. The analysis also controls for geographic and demographic factors, economic factors, the implementation of formal bureaucratic performance contracts as measured in the previous analysis, the implementation of formal democratic institutions, and the existence of village solidary groups such as temples, churches, and lineages.[52]

guanyu tuijin shehui zhuyi xin nongcun jianshe de ruogan yijian)," approved December 31, 2005.

[51] The Party membership of the village head is measured as a dichotomous variable, with a value of one when the village head is a member of the Party and a value of zero when he is not.

[52] Descriptive statistics for these controls are presented in Appendix Table A5.1. Specifically, I control for distance from county seat, village terrain (flat or not flat), the number of natural villages (a proxy for the spatial dispersion of village residents), village population, dummy variables for the eight counties from which the villages were randomly sampled, 1997 village income per capita, 1997 village government assets, 1997 village government tax revenue per

In short, there was no evidence at all suggesting that Party institutions were effective at holding village officials accountable for the provision of public goods and services. Neither the Party members of the village head nor the percentage of village officials had a noteworthy effect of any kind on village governmental provision of public goods. In both cases, the estimated effects were generally small in magnitude and all highly uncertain (in other words, these estimates could have been produced purely by chance).[53] When missing data were multiply imputed rather than deleted listwise, some estimates that had been positive became negative, and some that had been negative became positive, which makes us even more uncertain of what the true effects really are.[54]

capita, the existence of village government enterprises (*cunban qiye*) in 1995, the existence of private enterprises (*siying qiye*) in 1995, the existence of performance contracts with public project targets that village officials must sign with higher-level officials, an index of the implementation of formal democratic institutions, village temple groups as measured by the existence of a temple manager, village church groups as measured by the existence of an active village pastor, villagewide lineages as measured by the existence of a single ancestral hall with spirit tablets, and subvillage lineages as measured by the existence of multiple ancestral halls with spirit tablets.

53 The full model results are presented in Appendix Table A5.5. For each measure of formal Party control, I again used seemingly unrelated regression (SUR). Missing data were deleted listwise, and Huber heteroskedasticity-robust standard errors are reported. Using SUR, we could not reject the null hypothesis that the estimated effect of the Party membership of the village head jointly across public goods provision outcomes was equal to zero (p-value = 0.98). In this specification, the estimated effect of the village head's Party membership status was statistically insignificant for all six public goods provision outcomes. The estimated effect was negative for investment, roads, and paths and positive for classrooms, newness of school, and water, but again the uncertainty around these estimates was very high. The estimated effect of the percentage of village officials with Party membership was statistically insignificant for all six outcomes. The estimated effect was negative for investment, paths, and classrooms, and positive for roads, school, and water. Again, we could not reject the null hypothesis that the estimated effect of the percentage of village officials with Party membership jointly across all of these public goods provision outcomes was actually equal to zero (p-value = 0.50).

54 The full model results when missing data are multiply imputed are presented in Appendix Table A5.6. When missing data are multiply imputed instead of deleted listwise, the signs on the estimated effect of the village head's Party membership for roads, classrooms, and water change, which makes us even more doubtful of these estimates. We could not reject the null hypothesis that the estimated effect of the village head's Party membership was actually equal to zero (p-value = 0.85). Likewise, when missing data are multiply imputed, the direction of the estimated effects of the percentage of village officials in the Party change on investment, roads, and classrooms, which makes us even more doubtful of the accuracy of these estimates. We could not reject the null hypothesis that the estimated effect of the percentage of village officials with Party membership across all public goods provision outcomes was actually equal to zero (p-value = 0.86). Findings from bivariate SUR regression

Bureaucratic Institutions of Accountability

If the bureaucratic cadre responsibility system is an effective institution for holding village officials accountable for their performance, we would then expect villages where officials do sign contracts that mandate public goods provision to have better public goods provision than villages where officials do not sign such contracts. To make the strongest case possible for the importance of bureaucratic accountability, I operationalize the existence of formal bureaucratic institutions that mandate village public goods provision using a dichotomous variable that has a value of one only when officials have signed contracts that both include targets for public goods provision and, in their opinion, have an impact on their decision making. In the survey, 44 percent of villages reported that village officials have signed performance contracts that include public project targets and that contracts had an impact on the decision making of village officials. This measure of bureaucratic accountability for village public goods provision is only a rough one, and a better measure would identify the existence of targets for the particular public goods in which we are interested – roads, school buildings, and water – but it can at least give us a preliminary sense of whether higher levels are successfully holding village officials accountable for public goods provision through formal top-down supervision.

Using the same public goods provision measures and the same control variables, the analysis did not indicate that this measure of bureaucratic performance contracts had a strong positive effect on village governmental provision of public goods. In fact, the results are consistent with the concerns raised by scholars such as Justin Lin who fear that ambitious targets for public goods provision and policy implementation facilitate fiscal mismanagement. Lin argues that targets allow local officials to justify raising local levies on citizens. Local officials then use the revenue on hiring unnecessary staff and on personal consumption.[55]

Findings from the analysis indicated that formal bureaucratic performance contracts could have some positive effect on investment but did not have sizable positive effects on actual roads, schools, and water infrastructure. Although for three public goods provision outcomes (investment,

for the six public goods provision measures as well as logit models for the three dichotomous measures of public goods provision (existence of paved roads, existence of paved paths, and existence of running water infrastructure) were similar to the multivariate SUR estimates. These results can be viewed online at http://www.cambridge.org/9780521871976.

[55] See Lin et al., *The Problem of Taxing Peasants in China*, 29–44.

classrooms, and newness of school) the estimated effect of this measure of performance contracts was positive, in all cases the estimated effect was small or modest in size, and for investment and newness of school the estimate was relatively uncertain.[56] For the other three outcomes (roads, paths, and running water), the estimated effect was negative.[57] Because the positive effect on investment was not accompanied by positive effects on the provision of actual public goods, we have to wonder if all of the increased investment was actually being used on public projects.

In general, these findings did not change when control variables were added or dropped, or when villages with missing data were deleted or data were multiply imputed (although when missing data were multiply imputed rather than deleted listwise, the uncertainty of the positive estimated effect on investment decreased).[58]

Figure 8.1 compares village governmental provision of public goods in villages with contracts and village without contracts.[59] (To facilitate comparison, these graphs are scaled to match those presented in other chapters.) In the first graph, we can see that higher investment is associated with performance contracts, but the following graphs show that this higher investment

[56] The full model results are presented in Appendix Table A5.5. As with previous analyses, SUR was used to estimate the results. The estimated relationship between this measure of performance contracts was individually statistically insignificant for two of these outcomes (investment and newness of school) and significant for one outcome (classrooms) at a 95 percent confidence level.

[57] The estimated relationship between performance contracts was statistically insignificant for all three of these outcomes.

[58] The full model results when missing data are multiply imputed are presented in Appendix Table A5.6. When missing data are multiply imputed instead of deleted listwise, the results are similar, although the magnitude of the estimated effect on investment increases and its standard error decreases. The estimated relationship between village provision of public goods and performance contracts was again negative and statistically insignificant for three outcomes (roads, paths, and running water) and positive for three outcomes (investment, classrooms, and newness of school). Missing data were multiply imputed using the EMis algorithm developed by King et al., "Analyzing Incomplete Political Science Data," 49–69. In this model, robust standard errors are not reported because the existing software program for combining multiply imputed datasets for analysis does not support seemingly unrelated regression with robust standard errors. See Tomz et al., CLARIFY. Findings from bivariate SUR regression for the six public goods provision measures as well as logit models for the three dichotomous measures of public goods provision (existence of paved roads, existence of paved paths, and existence of running water infrastructure) were similar to the findings from the multivariate SUR analysis. These results can be viewed online at http://www.cambridge.org/9780521871976.

[59] These fitted values are calculated using the model results presented in Appendix Table A5.6.

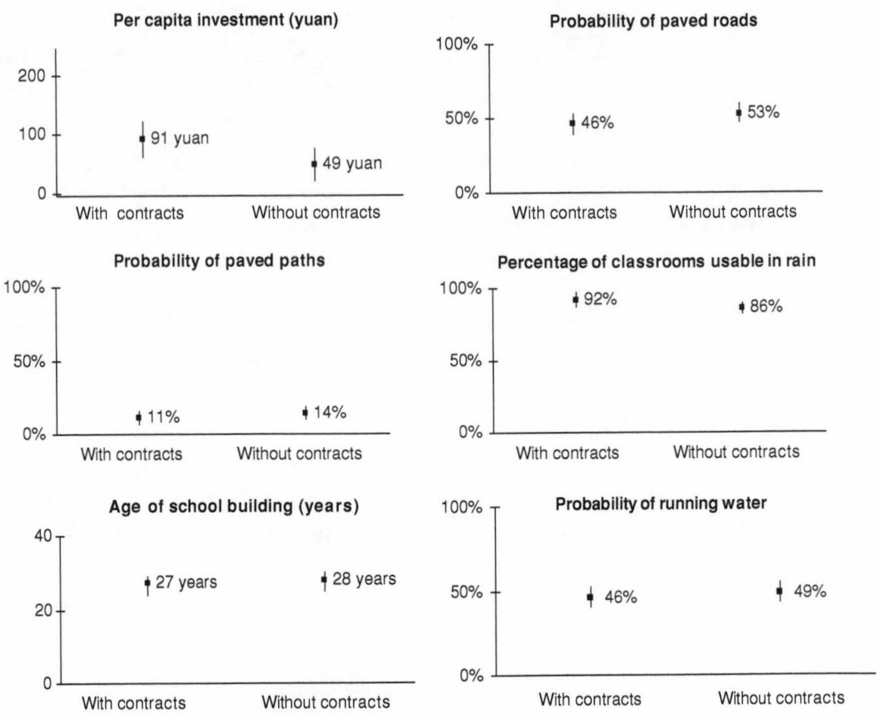

Figure 8.1. *Provision of public goods in villages with and without performance contracts.*

does not translate into significantly higher levels of public goods provision. In the average village where officials have signed contracts (average in the sense that all the control variables are held at their means), the average percentage of classrooms usable in rain is only about 6 percent higher and the average age of the school building is only about one year younger, which is not commensurate with the sizable increase in per capita investment from 49 yuan to 91 yuan. Moreover, the average likelihood of paved roads, paved paths, and running water is actually slightly lower. We cannot therefore conclude that performance contracts have a major positive impact on village governmental provision of public goods. Performance contracts may have a sizable impact on village government spending, but since this increase is not accompanied by better-quality public goods, it may be that the funds are being diverted for expenditures unrelated to public goods provision.

Party and Bureaucratic Institutional Limitations

These findings are not definitive since the survey did not ask specifically about the particular public goods provision targets on the performance contracts of village officials. It may be that contracts have no effect in these analyses because the public project targets for the villages in the sample did not include ones for roads, schools, and water or that these targets were not mandatory targets. Another possibility is that village-level performance contracts are just not very specific. In Jiangxi, for example, one township head explained that the performance contracts ask village officials to make one or two tangible improvements to the village – "things that are visible to the villagers" (*cunmin neng kan de dao*) – but what the officials did was up to them. Another possibility is that contracts were more likely to be instituted for villages where public goods provision was poor. If so, this relationship would mask any positive effect that contracts have on provision. Although the survey did not ask how the contracts were set, anecdotal evidence suggests that at least in some places, the implementation of performance contracts for villages was standardized within each township. Either officials in all the villages received more or less the same contract or no one received anything. If this was the case among most of the villages in the sample, we could be more confident about the findings of this analysis.

In either case, further research with more precise measures is needed, but these findings provide preliminary evidence that higher levels have trouble using performance contracts to sanction officials who do not provide good roads, schools, and water infrastructure.

Conclusion

In sum, both case study and survey data suggest that Party and bureaucratic institutions intended to hold local officials accountable have little impact on village governmental provision of public goods and services. Formal state institutions that set performance standards for local officials can have little impact when the state continues to reward local officials not for good performance but for *reporting* good performance. "Good officials," as one village Party secretary from Fujian pithily observed, "are those who can deceive higher levels and tell lies."[60] Like village elections and bottom-up democratic institutions, performance contracts and Party membership are not enough on their own – they require auxiliary institutions to serve as scaffolding and support them. The problem is not that village democratic

[60] Interview with male village Party secretary, northern Fujian province, October 15, 2001.

and bureaucratic institutions of accountability are being implemented in a system that lacks democracy at the national level. The findings presented in this book suggest that even if the national government were elected through free and fair elections, accountability at the local level would not necessarily increase. For formal bureaucratic and democratic institutions to be more effective at holding grassroots officials accountable for public goods provision, more and better channels for information transmission within the state need to be constructed. Fiscal and administrative institutions need to be restructured so that village officials and the higher-level officials who supervise them have strong incentives to pursue administrative efficiency and performance rather than just revenue maximization and economic growth. Improving formal bureaucratic and democratic accountability at the local level may be less a matter of democratization and more a matter of state building.

9

Conclusion

People everywhere struggle to make sure that government officials provide schools for their children, roads to bring their goods to market, and safe water to drink. Why are some people more successful than others? We have seen in the case of rural China that it is not always because they are richer. Economic growth is not necessarily correlated with better public goods provision and better government. Villages with higher levels of industrialization and economic development do not necessarily provide better roads and schools. Democratic reforms have not been a straightforward solution either. Even officials elected through free and fair procedures may fail to respond to citizens' needs when the rewards of office are low and getting voted out of office is not such a bad prospect.

This book argues that the key to explaining governmental performance and public goods provision when formal democratic and bureaucratic accountability is weak is to look more closely at *informal* institutions of accountability. When neither democratic institutions (such as elections) nor bureaucratic institutions (such as performance reviews) hold officials accountable for public goods provision, local governance may still be good when social groups enmesh local officials in community obligations. When officials are embedded in solidary groups such as temples or villagewide lineages that encompass everyone under their jurisdiction, obligations they have to contribute to the good of the group are synonymous with obligations to contribute to the public good. Under these conditions, social institutions can reinforce or substitute for state institutions. Officials in these communities have an extra incentive to perform well and provide public goods and services because they can earn moral standing by meeting and exceeding their obligations to the solidary group.

Findings

As with other transitional systems in the former Soviet Union, Africa, and Latin America, where local officials are not always closely supervised from above and democratic institutions are still weak or nonexistent, most residents of rural China seem to have little chance of getting the state to invest scarce resources on basic public goods and services that do not immediately result in increased state revenue. State policies of fiscal decentralization over the last two decades have been good for rural industrialization but bad for rural public goods provision. These developments suggest a darker picture of decentralization than has previously been painted by political scientists. Now that localities are allowed to keep any revenues they can generate in excess of a preset amount to be delivered upward, rich localities have strong incentives to promote industrialization and maximize revenue growth rather than invest in basic public goods, such as village schools, that do not immediately increase revenue. Fiscal decentralization has also hurt public goods provision in poor localities. In exchange for allowing localities to keep surplus revenues, the state has shifted responsibilities for funding local public goods and services downward. Poor localities now have increased expenditure responsibilities without increased funding. A long-standing historical legacy of allowing local governments to develop informal and quasilegal sources of revenue to pay for these unfunded mandates – informal local road-paving levies, tuition fees for public education, and illegal bank loans, to name just a few – has compounded the state's difficulties in supervising local officials effectively.

Not surprisingly, findings from the survey data presented in this book indicated that richer areas were not more likely to have better public goods provision than poorer areas, all other things being equal. The Chinese experience shows that while decentralization can generate conditions for rapid economic growth and rural industrialization, it can also contribute to the deterioration of local governance and public goods provision when mechanisms of accountability and resource redistribution have not been formally institutionalized.

Under these conditions – fiscal disincentives against investment in public goods, weak top-down institutions for holding lower-level officials accountable for public goods provision, and weak bottom-up democratic institutions – why would local officials provide more than the minimal level of public goods needed to maintain social stability? This book proposes a model highlighting the importance of informal institutions and how they interact with the formal institutions of local government. I argue that solidary groups – groups such as temples, lineages, or tribes that are based on shared moral obligations and ethical standards – can provide informal rules and norms that were not created or authorized to help citizens hold local officials accountable but do so nevertheless. By prescribing the ways in which people should act in order to maintain and improve their moral standing, groups such as temples or lineage groups enable those who exhibit exemplary behavior – citizens and officials – to acquire moral authority in the community. These groups make the conferral of moral standing possible by providing two critical things. First, these groups provide the criteria that people use to judge whether other members behave in ways that make them worthy of approval, respect, and admiration. Second, the activities, rituals, and dense social networks of these groups provide opportunities for members to express and publicize their exemplary behavior to the rest of the group.

Whether or not a group has a positive impact on local governance and public goods provision depends on how its structure meshes with state structures. When group boundaries overlap with the administrative boundaries of local government and the group embeds local officials in its activities and institutions – like the small-town church and the small-town mayor who is a diligent churchgoer – officials are more likely to carry out their duties and perform well. Under these conditions, officials have a strong incentive to provide public goods and services because doing so earns them moral standing among fellow group members as well as the help of other local elites in implementing state policies.

Comparing the different effects of village temples and village churches on governmental performance showed us the importance of groups that embed local officials. In China, both temples and churches generally encompass the administrative village in which they are located. They differ, however, in their embeddedness of local officials. The Communist Party's deeply ingrained distrust of Christianity and Christian organizations prevents village officials from participating in village churches even when the majority of the people in the village consider themselves part of the congregation. In contrast, village officials often participate in the activities and rituals of temple groups in their community, which are tolerated by the state as long as they limit their activities to within the village. Both survey and case study data indicated that villages with temples were more likely to have better village governmental provision of public goods than villages without temples. Officials in villages with temples were more likely to care about their moral standing within the village, and moral standing was often invaluable in helping them to elicit compliance from villagers with state policies. Villages with churches, however, were not more likely to have better village governmental provision of public goods than villages without churches. Officials in villages with churches typically could not participate in church activities and were thus unable to earn moral standing through church institutions. Churches themselves would sometimes organize public goods provision, but they were generally unable to help improve *governmental* public goods provision. In other words, while churches could *substitute* for village governmental provision of public goods, they could not hold the village government *accountable* for public goods provision.

Comparing different types of lineage groups then illustrated the importance of solidary groups that *encompass* local government jurisdictions. Lineage groups in rural China, like temple groups, usually embed the participation of village officials. In contrast to temple groups, however, lineage groups vary a great deal in scope. Some encompass entire villages like temple groups. Others are much smaller than a village. A single village can have multiple lineage groups that fragment people into subvillage groups. Survey and case study data indicated that villages with villagewide encompassing lineage groups were more likely to have better village governmental provision of public goods than villages without these groups. In these villages, the obligations of embedded officials to contribute to the lineage were the same as obligations to contribute to the village as a whole. Villages with multiple subvillage lineage groups, however, did not have better governance than villages without multiple lineages. In these villages, embedded officials still had obligations to contribute to their lineage group, but their contributions were unlikely to take the form of public goods that benefited villagers outside of their lineage.

Village case studies and survey data also suggested numerous obstacles to constructing effective formal institutions of accountability in rural China. Better implementation of election procedures and villagers' representative assemblies did not have any notable or consistent impact on village governmental provision of public goods. Interviews with officials suggest that the gains associated with public office have declined. Even though village officials often enjoy privileged access to networks and resources, in more developed places it is often more profitable to work in the private sector or serve a single term as an official to boost one's connections and then return to business. In less-developed places, the salary associated with being a village official may be an important incentive, but it is in these same places that the widespread problem of local governmental debt is likely to be most serious and to render local governments unable to pay for salaries. As a result, elections cannot provide effective sanctions because the costs of being voted out of office are relatively low.

Another problem is the issue of monitoring village officials. Because financial transparency remains low despite numerous state directives, villagers still find it difficult to evaluate the performance of village officials and their use of public funds. Without state enforcement of impartial audits and other formal mechanisms in addition to elections and assemblies that enable citizens to obtain accurate information about village finances and the actions of village officials, citizens cannot apply sanctions effectively and in a timely manner.

Because of decentralization and the structure of the state, top-down monitoring of village officials is also weak. In China, each level of government is directly responsible only for supervising the level of government directly below it. Township governments are thus responsible for supervising village governments. Because of fiscal decentralization and the state's emphasis on economic growth, however, township officials generally have few incentives for making sure that village officials invest public funds efficiently and effectively in village public goods provision. Similarly, officials at the county level and higher are unlikely to make sure that township officials are holding village officials accountable for public goods provision because they too have few incentives for doing so and because it is very difficult for them to obtain accurate information about what goes on at the grassroots level since information is generally passed up from level to level.

In short, if we looked only at formal institutions, it would be impossible to explain why some village governments actually provide a reasonably high level of public goods. By paying attention to informal institutions, we can start to make sense of the enormous variation we see in the performance of governments across different localities.

An informal institutional approach can also help illuminate "everyday forms of governance." Over the last twenty years, studies of rural China have taken advantage of newly accessible data to produce empirically rich accounts of village democratic reforms, popular protest, and rural industrialization. But what about everyday local politics and the day-to-day operation of local governments in nondemocratic and transitional systems? What is the relationship between citizens and officials when elections and protests are not occurring? How do citizens "normally" participate in local policy making? Are they at all able to make local officials respond to their needs and demands? When do citizens comply with or ignore state policies? The social institutions that shape accountability relations between citizens and officials may be the same ones that shape popular protest. Elizabeth Perry, for example, has observed that religious, lineage, and communal ties can be an important resource for local officials mobilizing rural protest.[1] A better understanding of the rules that structure the daily give and take between citizens and officials on ordinary issues such as repairing the village school, getting villagers to observe a state-mandated ban on firecrackers, or deciding whose land to appropriate for the village enterprise's wastewater drainage can help to shed new light on the rules and norms that structure more dramatic events such as elections and protests.

Informal Institutions and Governmental Performance

The importance of informal institutions and social networks in explaining political outcomes is of course nothing new to scholars of rural China. In her research on rural politics, Jean Oi has examined the ways in which citizens and officials pursue their private individual interests through informal clientelist relationships. Clientelist norms enable people to subvert formal state regulations and elicit special favors, better jobs, and better land from local officials. During the Maoist period, the state guaranteed villagers a minimum subsistence, so these informal institutions were "interest-maximizing rather than risk-minimizing" – in contrast to the patron-client relationships structuring James Scott's model of a rural moral economy.[2] Xiaobo Lu and Lowell Dittmer have argued that when *guanxi* – which they define as informal social relationships – involves public office and state power, it provides "a mechanism for people to collude for private gain by abusing the power entrusted to agents of the state (*ganbu*). In this mode, *guanxi* violates the formal organizational relationships sanctioned by the regime."[3] Mayfair

[1] Perry, "Rural Violence in Socialist China," 430–6. Roger Petersen has noted the importance of such ties in Lithuania for determining which communities participated in rebellions and protests. See Roger Petersen, *Resistance and Rebellion: Lessons from Eastern Europe* (New York: Cambridge University Press, 2001).

[2] See Oi, "Communism and Clientelism," 252; James C. Scott, *The Moral Economy of the Peasant: Rebellion and Subsistence in Southeast Asia* (New Haven: Yale University Press, 1976).

[3] Lowell Dittmer and Lu Xiaobo, "Personal Politics in the Chinese Danwei under Reform," *Asian Survey* 36, no. 3 (March 1996), 255.

Yang has also looked at *guanxi* networks as a vehicle used by citizens to resist official state power.[4]

These studies highlight the use of informal institutions to circumvent formal institutions for personal gain. But informal institutions can also reinforce formal institutions and facilitate collective projects. David Wank, for example, has found that local government bureaus may develop localistic networks with private firms and informal institutions that support these firms, albeit in "ways of varying legality."[5] Wang Hongying and Pittman Potter have argued that *guanxi* relations complement China's legal reforms rather than simply substituting for formal institutions.[6] In his careful study of gift exchange relationships, Yan Yunxiang describes the morality of such relationships and how they support mutual assistance within village communities.[7]

Informal Accountability and the Structure of Social Groups

One of the main objectives of this book is to identify the conditions under which informal institutions would have positive rather than negative effects on governance and public goods provision. Its key finding is that *we can have accountability without formal democracy if we have the right kinds of social groups: encompassing and embedding solidary groups*. This book highlights the importance of groups that encompass state administrative units. This focus accords with the research of G. William Skinner, whose seminal analysis of rural marketing communities in China also emphasized the interrelationships between political, social, and economic geographies.[8] Skinner argued

[4] See Yang, *Gifts, Favors, and Banquets*, 91–108; Wai Fung Lam, "Institutional Design of Public Agencies and Coproduction: A Study of Irrigation Associations in Taiwan," in *State-Society Synergy: Government and Social Capital in Development*, ed. Peter Evans (Berkeley: International and Area Studies, 1997), 11–47.

[5] David Wank, "Business-State Clientelism in China: Decline or Evolution?" in *Social Connections in China: Institutions, Culture, and the Changing Name of Guanxi*, ed. Thomas Gold, Doug Guthrie, and David Wank (Cambridge: Cambridge University Press, 2002), 113.

[6] See Hongying Wang, "Informal Institutions and Foreign Investment in China," *Pacific Review* 13, no. 4 (2000), 525–56; Pittman Potter, "Guanxi and the PRC Legal System: From Contradiction to Complementarity," in *Social Connections in China*, ed. Gold, Guthrie, and Wank, 183.

[7] Yunxiang Yan, *The Flow of Gifts: Reciprocity and Social Networks in a Chinese Village* (Stanford: Stanford University Press, 1996), 128–31.

[8] See Skinner, "Marketing and Social Structure in Rural China: Part I," 3–43; idem, "Marketing and Social Structure in Rural China: Part II," *Journal of Asian Studies* 24, no. 2 (February 1965), 195–228.

that rural life in the pre-Communist period was structured not around "village communities" but around local markets and the social networks constructed among the villages and villagers who participated in the same market. Skinner hypothesized that lineage ties, for example, were more likely to remain intact when members of a lineage migrated within the area served by their local market than when they migrated (the same physical distance) to a place outside of that area into a different marketing community. Likewise, people's communes during the Maoist period failed largely because the administrative boundaries of the commune drawn by the state did not coincide with preexisting social and economic boundaries defined by rural marketing communities.

Patterns of rural economic activity have changed significantly since Skinner conducted his research in 1948. Although rural markets have reemerged in the post-Mao period, and supravillage networks continue to be important (as we saw in our examination of lineage groups), novel forms of rural enterprise established by local governments have made townships and villages important units of economic activity. The provision of basic public goods and services is now structured around the village, and very few public projects are undertaken collaboratively by multiple villages or localities. Skinner himself noted that the one place where state administrative structures and socioeconomic structures did coincide during the Maoist period was at the level of the production brigade/village community.[9] State and social structures can change, but Skinner's basic insight remains extremely important: formal state institutions are likely to work better when their boundaries overlap with social and economic boundaries and when social groups encompass political administrative jurisdictions.

It is important to note, however, that villages with encompassing solidary groups do not have to be the "closed corporate villages" described by Eric Wolf or the amoral familism that Edward Banfield observed in rural Italy.[10] Closed corporate villages are an example of encompassing solidary groups, but encompassing solidary groups can also exist as one social structure among many others. Solidary villagewide community groups, for example,

[9] Idem, "Marketing and Social Structure in Rural China: Part I"; idem, "Marketing and Social Structure in Rural China: Part III," *Journal of Asian Studies* 24, no. 3 (May 1965), 385–6, 399.

[10] Eric Wolf, "Types of Latin American Peasantry: A Preliminary Discussion," *American Anthropologist*, no. 57 (June 1955), 452–71; Edward C. Banfield, *Moral Basis of a Backward Society* (New York: Simon and Schuster Adult Publishing Group, 1958).

can coexist with regional marketing cooperatives, subvillage rotating credit groups, and national political parties. The villages described in this book are not closed or exclusionary. They are likely to have subvillage groups, patron–client ties, and economic and social networks that extend outside the village in addition to encompassing solidary groups.[11] People in communities with encompassing solidary groups can and usually do have moral obligations to people and groups outside the encompassing solidary group. Governmental performance is better not because of low levels of conflict and consensus decision making but because moral standing becomes an important incentive for good performance.

It is also important to note that "the right kinds of social groups" for enhancing informal accountability in nondemocratic and transitional systems are not necessarily the ones proposed by theories of civil society and social capital. Theories of civil society and social capital typically posit that social groups improve governmental performance and responsiveness by increasing social trust and the political skills of citizens. Increased trust among skilled citizens helps them organize into interest groups to voice their demands more effectively. Autonomy from the state ensures that these groups represent citizen interests accurately and challenge state power in ways that enhance governmental performance and legitimate authority.

But in a political system where group articulation of interests is illegal or repressed, better organizing and voicing may have a significant impact only through the mobilization of popular protest. Autonomous civil society groups such as urban community groups in Chile under the Augusto Pinochet dictatorship and Solidarity in communist Poland can have dramatic effects on regime change.[12] But in the absence of well-implemented formal democratic institutions – whether corporatist or pluralist – that give autonomous civil society groups a guaranteed role in the political decision-making process, it is unclear how these groups can influence government on a day-to-day basis, which is perhaps more relevant than protest for the

[11] Skinner has noted that throughout history Chinese villages were open to social and economic exchanges beyond village boundaries and participated in intervillage marketing networks. G. William Skinner, "Chinese Peasants and the Closed Community: An Open and Shut Case," *Comparative Studies in Society and History* 13, no. 3 (July 1971), 270–81.

[12] Julia Paley, *Marketing Democracy: Power and Social Movements in Post-Dictatorship Chile* (Berkeley: University of California Press, 2001); Grzegorz Ekiert, *The State against Society: Political Crises and Their Aftermath in East Central Europe* (Princeton: Princeton University Press, 1996).

responsible and stable provision of public services by local governments. Protests can sanction officials for extremely poor performance but typically do not offer rewards for exemplary performance. In rural China, we see that village churches have no leverage over village officials because the state draws a sharp line between the activities of church groups and the activities of local officials.

Others have also observed that autonomy is not always a good thing in nondemocratic and transitional systems. Richard Rose has pointed out that a lack of connections between dense social capital at the bottom and at the top makes Russia what he calls an "hour-glass society." At the bottom, people are integrated in dense social networks with their family, friends, and acquaintances. At the top, elites cooperate with each other and use state institutions to pursue their interests. But nothing connects citizens and elites with each other. As a result, governmental performance and public services provision are poor. Citizens are forced to rely on "informal coping systems" that provide what the state fails to provide.[13]

In places where people lack formal political power or economic resources, solidary groups that embed local officials in their institutions can make an enormous difference. In Ecuador and Bolivia, for example, where non-Spanish– speaking indigenous groups have encountered formal and informal barriers to democratic representation, indigenous groups that embed local officials have had a positive effect on local governmental performance. Localities where the mayor and local government officials belong to local indigenous groups are less likely to suffer from patronage systems and misappropriation of public funds.[14] In contrast, indigenous groups in Latin America, Bangladesh, and Kenya that are rich in social capital are handicapped when they lack sufficient linkages with the state. Despite high

[13] Richard Rose, "Russia as an Hour-Glass Society: A Constitution without Citizens," *East European Constitutional Review* 4, no. 3 (1995), 34–42.

[14] See Sarah Radcliffe, "Indigenous Municipalities in Ecuador and Bolivia: Transnational Connections and Exclusionary Political Cultures," paper presented at the conference Beyond the Lost Decade: Indigenous Movements and the Transformation of Development and Democracy in Latin America, Princeton, March 2001. Tanya Korovkin has noted that "the private appropriation of public funds (which reached scandalous proportions nationwide . . .) was not unheard of in indigenous communities, but such practices seemed to occur less frequently in communities with active *cabildos* [councils] and regular general assemblies." Tanya Korovkin, "Reinventing the Communal Tradition: Indigenous Peoples, Civil Society, and Democratization in Andean Ecuador," *Latin American Research Review* 36, no. 3 (2001), 53.

levels of community solidarity, indigenous communities that do not embed local officials in their institutions "remain poor with few connections to the powerful within or outside the community."[15] When government officials are not embedded in encompassing indigenous groups, local governments are more likely to offload the responsibility for public goods provision onto the indigenous communities rather than take responsibility themselves. In these cases, indigenous community councils wind up performing many of the functions of local government.[16]

One important finding of this book is that the kind of social group involved affects whether embeddedness is actually good for governance. Peter Evans demonstrates that embeddedness and informal institutions can be good for governance and does not degenerate into patronage when the state has a high degree of solidarity and corporate coherence.[17] He shows that developmental states differ from predatory states in their ability to generate bureaucracies with corporate coherence and commitment based on meritocratic recruitment and performance-based incentives that prevent their informal connections with powerful business interests from sliding into patron–client relationships.

My research, on the other hand, shows that embeddedness can also be good for governance and will not degenerate into patronage when *social groups* have a high degree of solidarity and corporate coherence. These encompassing and embedding solidary groups can be especially important in authoritarian or transitional systems where states may be fragmented and formal institutions for establishing shared obligations between officials and citizens, such as constitutions and laws, may be weak. Few would describe the Chinese state as having enough corporate coherence to prevent individual officials from using social networks to pursue private objectives. Yet in some places something restrains their pursuit of private gain. A close examination of the micro-interactions between local governments and solidary groups such as temples and lineages suggests that the corporate

[15] Deepa Narayan, *Bonds and Bridges: Social Capital and Poverty* (Washington: World Bank, 1999), 32–3. See also D. Yashar, "Democracy, Indigenous Movements, and the Postliberal Challenge in Latin America," *World Politics* 52, no. 1 (1999), 76; idem, "Contesting Citizenship: Indigenous Movements and Democracy in Latin America," *Comparative Politics* 31, no. 1 (1998), 23; Jonathan Fox, "How Does Civil Society Thicken? The Political Construction of Social Capital in Rural Mexico," in *State-Society Synergy: Government and Social Capital in Development*, 119–49.

[16] Korovkin, "Reinventing the Communal Tradition," 55.

[17] Evans, *Embedded Autonomy*.

solidarity and collective obligations of social groups can also prevent informal networks between officials and citizens from sliding into patron–client ties.

Informal Accountability and Political Transitions

When states are fragmented and formal democratic institutions are weak, moral authority and informal institutions can become an extremely valuable political resource. Richard Sklar and others, for example, have argued that weak and unstable states in Africa could potentially benefit from "new infusions of authority" from chieftaincies, lineage groups, and other traditional institutions. Informal institutions can substitute for formal ones in improving governmental performance and shore up regime stability. Sklar notes that traditional chieftaincy groups in Uganda and Nigeria that embed government officials in their informal institutions are "sources of immense moral authority in everyday life" and may be critical for maintaining "civic morale and social order during the current era of extremely difficult transitions to modern forms of economy and society."[18] Moral standing can also become especially important when local officials lose access to other resources such as funding, coercion, state legitimacy, or support from higher levels due to decentralization programs, regime change, or economic shocks.

Paying more attention to informal institutions might thus help us understand why some so-called "transitional" systems may not be transitional at all. As Jonathan Fox has noted, political systems can stabilize far short of democracy. At least at the micro level, the findings presented in this book confirm this observation – villages with strong solidary institutions can have good governance even without formal democratic institutions.

How might states take advantage of existing solidary groups and informal institutions of accountability? This question is an important one not only for states seeking to bolster their legitimacy but also for the many states in both developed and developing countries seeking to reduce their responsibilities for welfare provision. One possibility is formalizing the informal institutions and transforming them into part of the state apparatus. In Bolivia, a decentralization law created with the 1994 constitution allows indigenous

[18] Richard Sklar, "The Premise of Mixed Government in African Political Studies," in *Tradition and Politics: Indigenous Political Structures in Africa*, ed. Olufemi Vaughan (Trenton: Africa World Press, 2004).

settlements to become subunits of municipal local government through the creation of indigenous municipal districts (DMI).[19] In Uganda, the traditional kingdom of Buganda has been lobbying the government to create a federal system that would transform the kingdom's quasisovereign status into a legitimate part of the state.[20]

Another possibility is formalizing "handover points" or linkages between informal and formal institutions. In Botswana, one of the most successful democratic systems in Africa, chiefs are not formally government officials, but the law authorizes them to adjudicate land disputes and to organize public meetings to elect land boards and village development committees.[21] Chieftaincy thus remains a system of informal authority and accountability, but chiefs interact with the state through legally defined and formally guaranteed channels. In Taiwan, Wai Fung Lam attributes the success of irrigation governance to the fact that the state bureaucracy takes over irrigation administration at the point where community norms and social networks become too weak to hold local authorities accountable informally. Below this handover point, grassroots irrigation officials are held accountable through local social and political ties, and local communities retain a great deal of autonomy over irrigation management. Above this handover point, the next level of irrigation officials is supervised by top-down bureaucratic institutions, which pick up where informal community institutions leave off.[22]

Solidary groups and informal institutions of accountability can be very beneficial to local governmental performance in nondemocratic and transitional systems. But there may also be serious drawbacks to relying on a system of informal accountability. First, this kind of informal system may work only at the local level for towns and villages. In theory, the absolute size of a solidary group should not matter as long as group boundaries coincide with political boundaries and the group is coextensive with the local government jurisdiction. In practice, solidary groups may have

[19] These reforms, however, have had little effect so far since the state does not require municipal governments to allocate funding to these indigenous districts. See Anthony Stocks, "Too Much for Too Few: Problems of Indigenous Land Rights in Latin America," *Annual Review of Anthropology* 34 (2005), 85–104.

[20] See Pierre Engelbert, "Born Again Buganda or the Limits of Traditional Re-Surgence in Africa," *Journal of Modern African Studies* 40, no. 3 (2002), 345–68.

[21] Sklar, "The Premise of Mixed Government in African Political Studies," 11.

[22] Lam, "Institutional Design of Public Agencies and Coproduction: A Study of Irrigation Associations in Taiwan."

a weaker impact in larger towns and cities for two reasons. First, encompassing solidary groups may be less likely to exist because people's interests and identities are likely to be more diverse and thus reaching a consensus on shared obligations may become more difficult. Second, the encompassing solidary groups that do exist may have less extensive obligations for group members since such obligations are costly and deter people from joining. Thus, informal institutions of accountability established by solidary groups may be less effective at substituting for formal institutions at higher levels.

One way of overcoming these limitations of scale may be the confederation of community-level solidary groups. Theda Skocpol has noted that in the United States, voluntary associations have historically been most effective at influencing policy making when they have been structured as translocal federations of local grassroots organizations paralleling the national, state, and local levels of the government.[23] In Ecuador, 70 percent of all indigenous people are represented by a national federation that has accumulated significant political power. The federation unites second-tier indigenous associations, unions, and federations in small towns, which themselves unite community-level communes, cooperatives, and centers based in villages.[24] In Africa, many traditional chieftaincies and kingdoms also have hierarchically arranged levels of authority. The structure of these informal institutions of governance could potentially be a crucial consideration in the structuring of decentralization programs and the creation of new local government units.[25]

A second potential drawback to relying on solidary groups for informal institutions of accountability is that their numbers may be declining as developing countries "modernize." It may be that these groups are not being created as quickly as they are being destroyed by increasing geographical mobility and processes of marketization, urbanization, and globalization. Once destroyed, the state may not be able to create them again. Lauren Morris MacLean, for example, has found that encompassing mutual assistance groups initiated by the state in the Côte d'Ivoire

[23] Theda Skocpol, "How Americans Became Civic," in *Civic Engagement in American Democracy*, ed. Theda Skocpol and Morris P. Fiorina (Washington: Brookings, 1999), 27–80.

[24] Ibid., 27–80.

[25] See, for example, J. Maxwell Assimeng, "Traditional Leaders' Capability and Disposition for Democracy: The Example of Ghana," paper presented at the International Conference on Traditional and Contemporary Forms of Local Participation and Self-Government in Africa, Nairobi, Kenya, October 9–12, 1996.

have failed to generate popular participation among villagers. Villagers continue to rely instead on patrons within their own kinship and ethnic networks. Instead of becoming more accountable to citizens, officials in villages with these groups try to pass on their problems to the next level of government.[26]

Other studies of solidary groups in developing countries, however, suggest that processes of modernization do not necessarily lead directly to the demise of solidary groups. Chieftaincy groups in Africa persist despite increasing integration into the global economy. Some, like those in Nigeria, have even flourished.[27] Such groups have deftly adapted to changing contexts. In many cases, highly educated doctors, lawyers, and civil servants have become chiefs. In recent years, chiefs in Ghana have invented extremely popular "traditional" cultural festivals to reinforce group solidarity. Government officials feel compelled to attend these festivals to show that they respect the institutions of the chieftaincy, but these festivals also give them opportunities to popularize government policies.[28]

Migrant village associations and native-place organizations common in many countries of Asia, Africa, and Latin America are examples of how modernization can also create new types of encompassing and embedding solidary groups. Lane Ryo Hirabayashi's study of Mixtec migrants from Oaxaca living in Mexico City illustrates how solidary groups can be based on territorial attachments and embed grassroots officials, even when members of the group do not reside in that territory.[29] Such associations are shaped by both norms from the home village as well as the new urban environment. Hirabayashi argues in fact that the need for cooperation in the new urban setting helps to sustain and reinforce the sense of moral obligation that migrants have to their home village. Adrian Peace's description of migrant entrepreneurs in the Yoruba town of Agege on the outskirts of Lagos echoes many of the same observations.[30]

[26] Lauren Morris MacLean, "Mediating Ethnic Conflict at the Grassroots: The Role of Local Associational Life in Shaping Political Values in Côte D'Ivoire and Ghana," *Journal of Modern African Studies* 42, no. 4 (December 2004), 607.

[27] See, for example, Axel Harneit-Sievers, "Igbo 'Traditional Rulers': Chieftaincy and the State in Southeastern Nigeria," *Afrika Spectrum* 33, no. 1 (1998), 57–70.

[28] See Carola Lentz, "Local Culture in the National Arena: The Politics of Cultural Festivals in Ghana," *African Studies Review* 44, no. 3 (December 2001), 47–72.

[29] Lane Ryo Hirabayashi, "The Migrant Village Association in Latin America: A Comparative Analysis," *Latin American Research Review* 21, no. 3 (1986), 7–29.

[30] Adrian Peace, "Prestige Power and Legitimacy in a Modern Nigerian Town," *Canadian Journal of African Studies* 13, no. 1/2 (1979), 40.

It may be, however, that the most serious drawback to relying on informal accountability is not a question of supply or scale but the potential costs of their success. Informal accountability can help citizens get more public goods and services than they would get without this kind of informal system – but perhaps not as much as they might get if a system of formal accountability were in place to ensure that higher levels of government contributed resources and took responsibility for providing public goods and services. Vincent Ostrom and Elinor Ostrom have noted that strictly voluntary efforts often "fail to supply a satisfactory level of public goods."[31]

It is also possible that successful, effective informal institutions of accountability may inhibit the development and consolidation of formal institutions. Informal institutions that are good at holding local officials accountable for public goods provision may relieve pressure on the state to make formal institutional reforms a high priority. Citizens may also get used to informal accountability and resist the implementation of formal institutions. Even worse, from the state's point of view, is the prospect that people may start to question the legitimacy and utility of formal state institutions if social institutions take over their functions. Tanya Korovkin, for example, has noted that indigenous citizens in Ecuador often prefer their own informal institutions to formal democratic ones. Indigenous citizens tend to view electoral politics as divisive, manipulative, and dishonest in contrast to indigenous institutions of governance.[32]

Solidary groups that are good for governmental performance and public goods provision at the *local* level may also be bad for democratic consolidation and state building at the *national* level. In the Central Asian republics, clans hold government officials responsible for contributing to the collective good of the clan, but, as Kathleen Collins argues, clan-based politics also makes the state inherently vulnerable to fragmentation and collapse.[33] In Ghana and Nigeria, scholars have noted that mobilization of support from traditional chiefs by political parties may exacerbate political fragmentation and instability.[34]

31 Vincent Ostrom and Elinor Ostrom, "Public Goods and Public Choices," in *Alternatives for Delivering Public Services: Toward Improved Performance*, ed. E. S. Savas (Boulder: Westview Press, 1977), 75.

32 Korovkin, "Reinventing the Communal Tradition," 49.

33 Collins notes that clan elites who are regional governors or village elders are "normatively and rationally-bound to foster the well-being of their clan." K. Collins, "Clans, Pacts, and Politics in Central Asia," *Journal of Democracy* 13, no. 3 (2002), 142–3.

34 See Kwame Boafo-Arthur, "Chieftaincy and Politics in Ghana since 1982," *West Africa Review* 3, no. 1 (2001), 15–18; Olufemi Vaughan, *Nigerian Chiefs: Traditional Power in Modern*

Understanding Governance and Development

What general lessons can we draw from the experiences of citizens and officials in rural China? The first important lesson that emerges from this research is that economic development is not necessarily correlated to political or institutional development. Good governance may foster economic growth and industrialization, but it is not clear that the opposite is also true. In Chapter 1, we saw in the cases of West Gate and Three Forks villages that there is no guarantee that the rich get better roads, schools, and water. Conversely, good government does not have to be a luxury, a finding illustrated by the Jiangxi villages of Li Settlement and High Mountain. As so many have argued, there is no single linear process of modernization or development. The evolution of local state institutions in different political systems does not simply vary in the speed of change; as localities become wealthier, they do not all follow the same trajectory of institutional development.

A second lesson is that we need to move away from the emphasis that scholars and policy makers put on reforming formal institutions and look more systematically at informal institutions. When examining the behavior of government officials, political scientists tend to look first within the formal organization of the state itself at institutions such as constitutions, laws, agency mandates, electoral procedures, and bureaucratic regulations. These formal institutions are the official rules, regulations, and procedures that govern government and keep officials from abusing their power. But just because formal institutions of accountability exist, it does not follow that they will be effective or used. In the case of rural China, there was no indication that localities where officials sign bureaucratic performance contracts or where officials are elected in free and fair elections have better public goods provision. Formal institutions, however detailed and well articulated, cannot facilitate better public goods provision when bureaucrats and citizens do not control resources desired by village officials or when they themselves do not view public goods provision and collective welfare as high priorities. Many people look at China and conclude that governmental performance will improve as soon as the rule of law and other formal institutions are strengthened. But focusing solely on formal institutions does not explain why we observe pockets of good governance

Politics, 1890s–1990s (Rochester: Boydell and Brewer, 2000); Richard Sklar, *Nigerian Political Parties: Power in an Emergent African Nation* (Trenton: Africa World Press, 2004).

in the absence of strong formal institutions or why formal institutions are so difficult to build. Only when we look more closely at the informal institutions that govern state behavior can we account for variation in local state institutions and the unintended effects they can have on the state's capacity to implement its policies, build new institutions, and govern society.

A third lesson from this research is that there are important interaction effects between state structures and social structures. These interaction effects help to explain why not all social capital has a positive effect on governance. This book contributes to existing literature on social institutions by looking very systematically and precisely at the ways in which political processes interact with social structures. To understand governmental performance and the behavior of government officials, we cannot examine attributes of society and attributes of the state as separate explanatory factors that are independent of one another. In the case of rural China, looking at the absolute level of horizontal social capital within a village suggests that social groups and institutions have no effect on village governance. Only when we differentiate between different types of social groups in terms of the extent to which they match local government structures can we see the significant impact of social factors on governmental performance and public goods provision.

As a corollary, we also need to temper the vogue in development studies for social capital research. Treating the social context as important for understanding economic development and governmental performance is an important step forward, but development research frequently employs "catch-all" surveys asking about every social relationship under the sun without also asking about the institutional and political context of these relationships. We must be careful not to leave out important questions on the state's institutional structure and political processes; such questions are necessary to uncover the ways in which social factors interact with these variables.

A final important lesson of this research is that moral authority can be an important political resource. Social groups and networks shape the behavior of individuals not only through trust but also through coercion and moral suasion. Moral authority and other sources of soft power are not always salient, but we need to identify the conditions under which they become important and effective political resources. What are the different specific mechanisms through which social groups, networks, and institutions affect political and economic outcomes? When we ask about individual participation in voluntary associations or churches, are we asking because we believe that such social groups encourage people to trust more or particular people, because we think they improve people's political skills and capacities, or because we think that such groups establish norms and obligations for their members that can affect their political behavior or interactions with the state? Trust, reciprocity, and obligation are not only different from each other, but there are different varieties of each as well. We may find that the same is true for "embeddedness." With more research, it may become clear that it makes a big difference whether local officials are merely participants in a solidary group as opposed to part of the group's leadership, or whether individuals start as solidary group members and then become officials rather than start as officials and then become participants in solidary activities.

In this book I have stressed the importance of informal institutions and social networks that can undergird the state. Solidary groups and institutions can be a critical substitute for weak or nonexistent bureaucratic and democratic institutions. For villagers who have few sources of formal political power, solidary institutions can give citizens leverage over local officials and enable them to obtain public goods and services that would not otherwise have been provided. At the local level, solidary institutions can shore up the local state's performance and stability.

But what about the broader effects of solidary institutions? On one hand, solidary institutions can benefit the state. In a democracy, explicit rules about how to change the rules give the system flexibility. In authoritarian and transitional systems, informality and informal institutions can provide this flexibility and serve as "functional equivalents" to democratic institutions, sometimes at a lower cost to the central government than the building of formal institutions to carry out the same functions. In China, the central government not only economizes on its resources by turning over the financial and organizational responsibilities of local public goods provision to localities, but it also saves on the resources that it would have to expend in order to monitor and sanction all of its grassroots officials effectively by building new bureaucratic institutions or ensuring universal implementation of formal democratic institutions at the village level. Meanwhile, local officials have the freedom to create institutional arrangements that are specific to and appropriate for local conditions. It may be that informal institutions can stabilize states indefinitely.

On the other hand, informal institutions may only be a stopgap measure for the state. What strengthens local state institutions may, at the same time, weaken regional and national state institutions. Informal institutions can decrease pressure on the state to build capacity for rural public administration and public goods provision and to institutionalize democratic reforms. Deepa Narayan has observed that strong social institutions can lead to poorly functioning states. In Latin America, indigenous groups sometimes manage to obtain basic social infrastructure from the government, but they rarely obtain greater access to economic and political opportunities. In Kenya, overuse of the traditional self-help *harambee* group has "left people exhausted and disinclined to participate in any *harambee* initiated by the government."[35] If citizens start to view solidary institutions as sufficient for good governance, they may begin to question the role and legitimacy of higher levels of the state. Stronger local solidarities can weaken national solidarity. The Chinese state may be able to avoid these developments if it has the economic resources and political will to build state capacity for rural administration even in areas that are not in danger of imminent breakdown. Otherwise, we may find that informal institutions that undergird the state in the short term undermine the state in the long term.

[35] Narayan, *Bonds and Bridges*, 33.

References

Ahern, Emily. *The Cult of the Dead in a Chinese Village*. Stanford: Stanford University Press, 1973.

______.*Chinese Ritual and Politics*. New York: Cambridge University Press, 1981.

Alesina, A., and R. Baqir. "Public Goods and Ethnic Divisions." *Quarterly Journal of Economics* 114, no. 4 (1999): 1243–84.

Andreoni, James. "Giving with Impure Altruism: Applications to Charity and Ricardian Equivalence." *Journal of Political Economy* 97, no. 6 (December 1989): 1447–58.

Asian Development Bank. *A Study on Ways to Support Rural Poverty Reduction Projects*. Manila: Asian Development Bank, 2000.

______. *Key Indicators of Developing Asian and Pacific Countries*. Manila: Asian Development Bank, 2002.

Assimeng, J. Maxwell. "Traditional Leaders' Capability and Disposition for Democracy: The Example of Ghana." Paper presented at the Conference on Traditional and Contemporary Forms of Local Participation and Self-Government in Africa, Nairobi, October 9–12, 1996.

Baker, Hugh. *Extended Kinship in the Traditional City*. Stanford: Stanford University Press, 1977.

Banfield, Edward C. *Moral Basis of a Backward Society*. New York: Simon and Schuster Adult Publishing Group, 1958.

Bardhan, P., and D. Mookherjee. "Decentralization, Corruption, and Government Accountability: An Overview," in *Handbook of Economic Corruption*, ed. Susan Rose-Ackerman. Northampton: Edward Elgar, 2005.

Bates, M. Searle. "Churches and Christians in China, 1950–1967: Fragments of Understanding." *Pacific Affairs* 41, no. 2 (Summer 1968): 199–213.

Becker, Jasper. *Hungry Ghosts: Mao's Secret Famine*. New York: Henry Holt, 1998.

Bellah, Robert, Richard Madsen, William Sullivan, Ann Swidler, and Steven Tipton. *Habits of the Heart: Individualism and Commitment in American Life*. Berkeley: University of California Press, 1985.

Benziger, Vincent. "China's Rural Road System during the Reform Period." *China Economic Review* 4, no. 1 (1993): 1–17.

Bernstein, Thomas, and Lu Xiaobo. *Taxation without Representation in Contemporary Rural China*. New York: Cambridge University Press, 2003.

Bhatt, Vikram. *Housing a Billion*.Vol. 2:*Village Upgrading*. Montreal: McGill University, December 1993.

Billings, Dwight B. "Religion as Opposition: A Gramscian Analysis." *American Journal of Sociology* 96, no. 1 (July 1990): 1–31.

Boafo-Arthur, Kwame. "Chieftaincy and Politics in Ghana since 1982." *West Africa Review* 3, no. 1 (2001): 1–25.

Boix, Carles, and Daniel Posner. "Social Capital: Explaining Its Origins and Effects on Government Performance." *British Journal of Political Science* 28, no. 4 (1998): 686–93.

Braithwaite, Valerie, and Margaret Levi, eds. *Trust and Governance*. New York: Russell Sage Foundation, 1998.

Brandt, Loren, and Matthew A. Turner. *The Usefulness of Corruptible Elections*. Toronto: University of Toronto, Department of Economics, 2003.

Brennan, Geoffrey, and James Buchanan. *The Power to Tax: Analytical Foundations of a Fiscal Constitution*. New York: Cambridge University Press, 1980.

Breton, A. *Competitive Governments: An Economic Theory of Politics and Public Finance*. Cambridge: Cambridge University Press, 1998.

Brodsgaard, Kjeld Erik. "Institutional Reform and the Bianzhi System in China." *China Quarterly* no. 170 (June 2002): 361–86.

Buchanan, James. "Federalism as an Ideal Political Order and an Objective for Constitutional Reform." *Publius* 25, no. 2 (1995): 19–81.

Burns, John P. "China's Nomenklatura." *Problems of Communism* 36, no. 5 (1987): 36–51.

———. *Political Participation in Rural China*. Berkeley: University of California Press, 1988.

———. *The Chinese Communist Party's Nomenclatura System: A Documentary Study of Party Control of Leadership Selection, 1979–1984*. Armonk: M. E. Sharpe, 1989.

———. "Strengthening CCP Control of Leadership Selection: The 1990 Nomenclatura." *China Quarterly* no. 138 (1994): 458–91.

Cai, H., and Daniel Treisman. "State-Corroding Federalism." *Journal of Public Economics* 88, no. 3 (2004): 819–43.

Cai, Yongshun. "Between State and Peasant: Local Cadres and Statistical Reporting in Rural China." *China Quarterly* no. 163 (September 2000): 783–805.

Cao, Jinqing. *Huanghebian De Zhongguo: Yige Xuezhe Dui Xiangcun Shehui De Guancha Yu Sikao* (China by the Side of the Yellow River: A Scholar's Observation and Reflections on Rural Society). Shanghai: Wenyi Chubanshe (Shanghai Literary and Arts Press), 2000.

Case, A., J. Hines, and H. Rose. "Budget Spillovers and Fiscal Policy Interdependence: Evidence from the States." *Journal of Public Economics* 52 (1993): 285–307.

Chan, Anita, Richard Madsen, and Jonathan Unger. *Chen Village under Mao and Deng*. Berkeley: University of California Press, 1992.

References

Chau, Adam. "The Politics of Legitimation and the Revival of Popular Religion." *Modern China* 31, no. 2 (2005): 236–78.

Chen, Dong-Hua, Joseph P. H. Fan, and T. J. Wong. "Do Politicians Jeopardize Professionalism? Decentralization and the Structure of Corporate Boards." Unpublished paper, 2002.

Chung, Him. "Some Socio-Economic Impacts of Toll Roads in Rural China." *Journal of Transport Geography* 10, no. 2 (2002): 145–56.

Chwe, Michael. *Rational Ritual: Culture, Coordination, and Common Knowledge*. Princeton: Princeton University Press, 2003.

Cigler, B. "Challenges Facing Fiscal Federalism in the 1990s." *PS: Political Science and Politics* 26, no. 2 (1993): 181–6.

Cohen, Myron. "Lineage Organization in North China." *Journal of Asian Studies* 49, no. 3 (August 1990): 509–34.

Coleman, James. *Foundations of Social Theory*. Cambridge: Harvard University Press, 1990.

Collins, K. "Clans, Pacts, and Politics in Central Asia." *Journal of Democracy* 13, no. 3 (2002): 137–52.

Corbin, David. *Life, Work, and Rebellion in the Coal Fields: The Southern West Virginia Miners, 1880–1922*. Champaign: University of Illinois Press, 1981.

Dahl, Robert A. *Polyarchy: Participation and Opposition*. New Haven: Yale University Press, 1971.

Daunton, Martin. "Trusting Leviathan: British Fiscal Administration from the Napoleonic Wars to the Second World War," in *Trust and Governance*, ed. Valerie Braithwaite and Margaret Levi. New York: Russell Sage Foundation, 1998.

Davis, Deborah. "Chinese Social Welfare: Policies and Outcomes." *China Quarterly* no. 119 (September 1989): 577–97.

de Tocqueville, Alexis. *Democracy in America*. New York: Penguin Classics, 2003.

Deutsch, Karl. "Equity, Equality, and Need." *Journal of Social Issues* 31, no. 3 (1975): 137–50.

Diamond, Larry. "Is the Third Wave Over?" *Journal of Democracy* 7, no. 3 (1996): 20–37.

Dimitrov, Martin. "The Dark Side of Federalism: Decentralization and the Enforcement of Intellectual Property Rights (IPR) Laws." Paper presented at the Annual Meeting of the American Political Science Association, Chicago, 2004.

Dittmer, Lowell, and Lu Xiaobo. "Personal Politics in the Chinese Danwei under Reform." *Asian Survey* 36, no. 3 (March 1996): 246–67.

Donnithorne, Audrey. "China's Cellular Economy: Some Economic Trends since the Cultural Revolution." *China Quarterly* no. 52 (October–December 1972): 605–19.

______. "Aspects of Neo-Liuist Economic Policy." *Australian Journal of Chinese Affairs* no. 3 (January 1980): 27–39.

Dougherty, Sean. *The Reliability of Chinese Statistics*. Beijing: U.S. Department of Commerce, 2001.

Duara, Prasenjit. *Culture, Power, and the State: Rural North China 1900–1942*. Stanford: Stanford University Press, 1988.

Durkheim, Emile. *The Division of Labor in Society*. Translated by W. D. Halls. New York: Free Press, 1984.

Ebrey, Patricia, and James Watson. *Kinship Organization in Late Imperial China*. Berkeley: University of California Press, 1986.

Edin, Maria. "Institutional Basis of Developmentalism and Cronyism in China." Paper presented at the Annual Meeting of the Association for Asian Studies, Chicago, March 22–5, 2001.

———. "Remaking the Communist Party-State: The Cadre Responsibility System at the Local Level in China." *China: An International Journal* 1, no. 1 (March 2003): 1–15.

Ekiert, Grzegorz. *The State against Society: Political Crises and Their Aftermath in East Central Europe*. Princeton: Princeton University Press, 1996.

Elster, Jon, Claus Offe, and Ulrich Preuss. *Institutional Design in Post-Communist Societies*. Cambridge: Cambridge University Press, 1998.

Engelbert, Pierre. "Born Again Buganda or the Limits of Traditional Re-Surgence in Africa." *Journal of Modern African Studies* 40, no. 3 (2002): 345–68.

Esherick, Joseph. *The Origins of the Boxer Uprising*. Berkeley: University of California Press, 1987.

Evans, Peter. *Embedded Autonomy: States and Industrial Transformation*. Princeton: Princeton University Press, 1995.

———, ed. *State-Society Synergy: Government and Social Capital in Development*. Berkeley: International and Area Studies, 1997.

Faure, David. *Structure of Chinese Rural Society*. New York: Oxford University Press, 1986.

———. "Lineage as Cultural Invention: The Case of the Pearl River Delta." *Modern China* 15, no. 1 (January 1989): 4–36.

Faure, David, and Helen Siu, ed. *Down to Earth: The Territorial Bond in South China*. Stanford: Stanford University Press, 1995.

Fei, Xiaotong. *Chinese Village Close-Up (Sanfang Jiangcun)*. Beijing: New World Press (Xinshijie chubanshe), 1983.

Fox, Jonathan. "How Does Civil Society Thicken? The Political Construction of Social Capital in Rural Mexico," in *State-Society Synergy: Government and Social Capital in Developmen*t, ed. Peter Evans. Berkeley: International and Area Studies, 1997.

Freedman, Maurice. *Family and Kinship in Chinese Society*. Stanford: Stanford University Press, 1970.

———. *Chinese Lineage and Society: Fukien and Kwangtung*. London: Athlone Press, 1971.

———. *Lineage Organization in Southeastern China*. Oxfordshire: Berg, 2004.

Fried, Morton. *The Fabric of Chinese Society*. New York: Praeger, 1953.

———. "The Classification of Corporate Unilineal Descent Groups." *Journal of the Royal Anthropological Institute of Great Britain and Ireland* 87, no. 1 (1957): 1–29.

Frolic, Michael. *Mao's People*. Cambridge: Harvard University Press, 1980.

Gao, Gang. "More Rural Residents Ensured Better Quality Potable Water." *Beijing Review*, October 30, 1997.

References

Goldstein, Avery. "State of the Field: Trends in the Study of Political Elites and Institutions in the PRC." *China Quarterly* no. 139 (September 1994): 714–30.

Goode, William J. *The Celebration of Heroes: Prestige as a Control System*. Berkeley: University of California Press, 1979.

Gu, Zhongyang. "Trial on Substitution of Villages by Townships in Fiscal Management in Xingtai (Xingtai 'cuncai Xiangdaiguan' Toushi Wenlu)." *People's Daily (Renmin Ribao)*, October 23, 2005.

Hall, Rodney Bruce. "Moral Authority as a Power Resource." *International Organization* 51, no. 4 (Autumn 1997): 591–622.

Han, Jun, "Public Finance Crisis in Chinese Countries and Towns: Performance, Causes, Impact and Measures: Case Studies of Xiangyang County of Hubei Province, Yanling County of Henan Province, and Taihe County of Jiangxi Province," in International Conference Report on Rural Public Finance, Rural Development Institute, Chinese Academy of Social Sciences, 2002.

Han, Junjie. "Supervision of Villages' Fiscal Issues by Townships: Hindrance or Promotion of Villagers Self-Governance? (Cuncai Xiangjian: Shi Zhangai Haishi Cujin Cunmin Zizhi?)," *China Youth Daily (Zhongguo Qingnianbao)*, October 22, 2003.

Hannum, Emily. "Families, Teachers, and Children's Educational Engagement in Rural Gansu, China." Paper presented at the Annual Meetings of the Population Association of America, Atlanta, March 2002.

Hannum, Emily, and Albert Park. *Children's Educational Engagement in Rural China*. Unpublished manuscript, 2002.

Harneit-Sievers, Axel. "Igbo 'Traditional Rulers': Chieftaincy and the State in Southeastern Nigeria." *Afrika Spectrum* 33, no. 1 (1998): 57–70.

He, Qinglian, and Xiaonong Cheng. "Rural Economy at a Dead End: A Dialogue on Rural China, Peasants, and Agriculture." *Modern China Studies* 74, no. 3 (2001).

Hechter, Michael. *Principles of Group Solidarity*. Berkeley: University of California Press, 1987.

Helmke, Gretchen, and Steven Levitsky, "Informal Institutions and Comparative Politics: A Research Agenda." *Perspective on Politics* 2, no. 4 (2004): 727.

Hinton, William. *Fanshen: A Documentary of Revolution in a Chinese Village*. New York: Random House, 1968, c1966.

Hirabayashi, Lane Ryo. "The Migrant Village Association in Latin America: A Comparative Analysis." *Latin American Research Review* 21, no. 3 (1986): 7–29.

Horne, Christine. "The Enforcement of Norms: Group Cohesion and Meta-Norms." *Social Psychology Quarterly* 64, no. 3 (2001): 253–66.

Hsu, Francis. *Clan, Caste, Club*. Princeton: Van Nostrand, 1963.

Huang, Yasheng. "Administrative Monitoring in China." *China Quarterly* no. 143 (September 1995): 828–43.

Jordan, David K. *Gods, Ghosts and Ancestors*. Berkeley: University of California Press, 1972.

Judd, Ellen R. *Gender and Power in Rural North China*. Stanford: Stanford University Press, 1994.

Kane, John. *The Politics of Moral Capital*. Cambridge: Cambridge University Press, 2001.

Kaufmann, D., and A. Kraay. "Growth without Governance." *Economia* 3, no. 1 (2002): 169–229.

Kelliher, Daniel. "The Chinese Debate over Village Self-Government." *China Journal* no. 37 (January 1997): 63–86.

King, Gary, James Honaker, Anne Joseph, and Kenneth Scheve. "Analyzing Incomplete Political Science Data: An Alternative Algorithm for Multiple Imputation." *American Political Science Review* 95, no. 1 (March 2001): 49–69.

King, Gary, Michael Tomz, and Jason Wittenberg. "Making the Most of Statistical Analyses: Improving Interpretation and Presentation." *American Journal of Political Science* 44, no. 2 (April 2000): 347–61.

Knapp, Ronald G. "Rural Housing and Village Transformation in Taiwan and Fujian." *China Quarterly* no. 147 (September 1996): 779–94.

Korovkin, Tanya. "Reinventing the Communal Tradition: Indigenous Peoples, Civil Society, and Democratization in Andean Ecuador." *Latin American Research Review* 36, no. 3 (2001): 37–67.

Krajewski, M. *Public Services and the Scope of the General Agreement on Trade in Services*. Geneva: Center for International Environmental Law, 2001.

Kratchowil, Friedrich. "Is the Ship of Culture at Sea or Returning?" in *The Return of Identity and Culture in IR Theory*, ed. Yosef Lapid and Friedrich Kratchowil. Boulder: Lynne Rienner, 1996.

Kuran, Timur. "The Provision of Public Goods under Islamic Law." *Law and Society Review* 35, no. 4 (2001): 841–98.

Ladd, H., and J. Yinger. *America's Ailing Cities: Fiscal Health and the Design of Urban Policy*. Baltimore: Johns Hopkins University Press, 1990.

Lam, Wai Fung. "Institutional Design of Public Agencies and Coproduction: A Study of Irrigation Associations in Taiwan," in *State-Society Synergy: Government and Social Capital in Development*, ed. Peter Evans. Berkeley: International and Area Studies, 1997.

Landry, Pierre F. "Controlling Decentralization: The Party and Local Elites in Post-Mao Jiangsu." Ph.D. Diss., University of Michigan, 2000.

Latham, Richard. "Rural Reforms and Grassroots Cadres," in *The Political Economy of Reform in Post-Mao China*, ed. Elizabeth Perry and Christine Wong. Cambridge: Harvard University Press, 1985.

Latourette, Kenneth Scott. *A History of Christian Missions in China*. New York: Macmillan, 1929.

Laumann, Edward, ed. *Social Stratification: Research and Theory for the 1970s*. Indianapolis: Bobbs-Merrill, 1970.

Lawrence, Susan V. "Village Democracy." *Far Eastern Economic Review* 163 (January 27, 2000): 16–17.

Lentz, Carola. "Local Culture in the National Arena: The Politics of Cultural Festivals in Ghana." *African Studies Review* 44, no. 3 (December 2001): 47–72.

Levi, Margaret. *Of Rule and Revenue*. Berkeley: University of California Press, 1988.

———. *Consent, Dissent, and Patriotism*. New York: Cambridge University Press, 1997.

Lewin, Keith, Angela Little, and Jiwei Zheng. *Educational Innovation in China: Tracing the Impact of the 1985 Reforms*. Essex: Long Group Limited, 1994.

Li, Huaiyin. "Village Regulations at Work: Local Taxation in Huailu County, 1900–1936." *Modern China* 26, no. 1 (January 2000): 79–109.

Li, Lianjiang. "The Politics of Introducing Direct Township Elections in China." *China Quarterly* no. 171 (September 2002): 704–23.

Li, Lianjiang, and Kevin O'Brien. "Villagers and Popular Resistance in Contemporary China." *Modern China* 22, no. 1 (1996): 28–61.

———. "The Struggle over Village Elections," in *The Paradox of Post-Mao Reforms*, ed. Merle Goldman and Roderick MacFarquhar. Cambridge: Harvard University Press, 1999.

Li, Xiande. "Rethinking the Peasant Burden: Evidence from a Chinese Village." *Journal of Peasant Studies* 30, no. 5 (2003): 45–74.

Liebman, Benjamin L. "Legal Aid and Public Interest Law in China." *Texas International Law Journal* 34, no. 2 (1999): 211–87.

———. "Lawyers, Legal Aid, and Legitimacy in China," in *Raising the Bar: The Emerging Legal Profession in East Asia*, ed. William P. Alford. Cambridge: Harvard Law School, 2004.

Lin, Justin Yifu. "China's Economy: Boom or Bust?" Paper presented at the National Committee on U.S.–China Relations, Asia Society, New York, January 30, 2004.

Lin, Justin Yifu, and Zhiqiang Liu. "Fiscal Decentralization and Economic Growth in China." *Economic Development and Cultural Change* 49, no. 1 (2000): 1–21.

Lin, Justin, Ran Tao, and Mingxing Liu. *Decentralization and Local Governance in the Context of China's Transition*. Working paper, Center for Chinese Agricultural Policy, Chinese Academy of Social Sciences, 2003.

———. "Decentralization and Local Governments in China's Economic Transition," in *Decentralization and Local Governments in Developing Countries: A Comparative Perspective*, ed. Pranab Bardhan and Dilip Mookherjee. Cambridge: MIT Press, 2005.

Lin, Justin Yifu, Ran Tao, Mingxing Liu, and Qi Zhang. *The Problem of Taxing Peasants in China*. Beijing: Beijing University, China Center for Economic Research, June 2002.

Lipset, S. M. "Some Social Requisites of Democracy: Economic Development and Political Legitimacy." *American Political Science Review* 53 (1959): 69–105.

Lu, Wen. "Problems during the Process of TVE Reforms." *Journal of Agricultural Economy Research* no. 1 (1998): 18–21.

Lu, Xiaobo. "The Politics of Peasant Burden in Reform China." *Journal of Peasant Studies* 25, no. 1 (1997): 113–38.

MacInnis, Donald. *Religious Policy and Practice in Communist China*. New York: Macmillan, 1972.

MacLean, Lauren Morris. "Mediating Ethnic Conflict at the Grassroots: The Role of Local Associational Life in Shaping Political Values in Côte D'Ivoire and Ghana." *Journal of Modern African Studies* 42, no. 4 (December 2004): 589–617.

Madsen, Richard. *Morality and Power in a Chinese Village*. Berkeley: University of California Press, 1984.

———. *China's Catholics: Tragedy and Hope in an Emerging Civil Society*. Berkeley: University of California Press, 1998.

Manion, Melanie. "The Cadre Management System, Post-Mao: The Appointment, Promotion, Transfer, and Removal of Party and State Leaders." *China Quarterly* no. 102 (1985): 203–33.

———. "Chinese Democratization in Perspective: Electorates and Selectorates at the Township Level." *China Quarterly* no. 163 (September 2000): 764–82.

Mauger, Peter. "Changing Policy and Practice in Chinese Rural Education." *China Quarterly* no. 93 (March 1983): 138–48.

Miguel, Edward. "Tribe or Nation? Nation Building and Public Goods in Kenya versus Tanzania." *World Poltics* 56 (April 2004): 327–62.

Miguel, Edward, and Mary Kay Gugerty. "Ethnic Divisions, Social Sanctions, and Public Goods in Kenya." *Journal of Public Economics* 89, no. 11–12 (2005): 2325–68.

Mill, J. S. "Considerations on Representative Government," in *Utilitarianism, Liberalism, and Representative Government*. London: Dart, 1951.

Moe, T. "The New Economics of Organization." *American Journal of Political Science* 28, no. 4 (1984): 739–77.

Montinola, Gabriella, Yingyi Qian, and Barry R. Weingast. "Federalism, Chinese Style: The Political Basis for Economic Success in China." *World Politics* 48, no. 1 (October 1995): 50–81.

Morris, Robert. "Structure, Culture, and Society in British Towns," in *The Cambridge Urban History of Britain*, ed. Martin Daunton. Cambridge: Cambridge University Press, 2000.

Naquin, Susan. *Millenarian Rebellion in China: The Eight Trigrams Uprising of 1813*. New Haven: Yale University Press, 1976.

Narayan, Deepa. *Bonds and Bridges: Social Capital and Poverty*. Washington: World Bank, 1999.

Ng, Pak-Tao. "Open-Door Education in Chinese Communes: Rationale, Problems, and Recent Changes." *Modern China* 6, no. 3 (July 1980): 327–56.

Nye, Joseph. "The Changing Nature of World Power." *Political Science Quarterly* 105, no. 2 (1990): 177–92.

Oates, Wallace. *Fiscal Federalism*. New York: Harcourt Brace Jovanovich, 1972.

———. "An Essay on Fiscal Federalism." *Journal of Economic Literature* 37, no. 3 (1999): 1120–49.

O'Brien, Kevin. "Implementing Political Reform in China's Villages." *Australian Journal of Chinese Affairs* no. 32 (July 1994): 33–59.

———. "Rightful Resistance." *World Politics* 49, no. 1 (1996): 31–55.

———. "Villagers, Elections, and Citizenship in Contemporary China." *Modern China* 27, no. 4 (October 2001): 407–35.

O'Brien, Kevin, and Lianjiang Li. "Selective Policy Implementation in Rural China." *Comparative Politics* 31, no. 2 (January 1999): 167–86.

———. "Accommodating Democracy in a One-Party State: Introducing Village Elections in China." *China Quarterly* no. 162 (June 2000): 465–89.

References

O'Donnell, Guillermo. "Delegative Democracy." *Journal of Democracy* 5, no. 5 (January 1994): 60–2.

———. "Illusions about Consolidation." *Journal of Democracy* 7, no. 2 (1996): 55–69.

Oi, Jean. "Communism and Clientelism: Rural Politics in China." *World Politics* 37, no. 2 (January 1985): 238–66.

———. *State and Peasant in Contemporary China: The Political Economy of Village Government*. Berkeley: University of California Press, 1989.

———. *Rural China Takes Off*. Berkeley: University of California Press, 1999.

———. *State Responses to Rural Discontent in China: Tax-for-Fee Reform and Increased Party Control*. Washington: Woodrow Wilson International Center for Scholars, 2003.

Oi, Jean C., and Scott Rozelle. "Elections and Power: The Locus of Decision-Making in Chinese Villages." *China Quarterly* no. 162 (2000): 513–39.

Oksenberg, Michel. "Methods of Communication within the Chinese Bureaucracy." *China Quarterly* no. 57 (January–March 1974): 1–39.

Olowu, Dele. "Local Institutes and Development: The African Experience." *Canadian Journal of African Studies* 23, no. 2 (1989): 201–31.

Ostrom, Vincent, and Elinor Ostrom. "Public Goods and Public Choices," in *Alternatives for Delivering Public Services: Toward Improved Performance*, ed. E. S. Savas. Boulder: Westview Press, 1977.

Paley, Julia. *Marketing Democracy: Power and Social Movements in Post-Dictatorship Chile*. Berkeley: University of California Press, 2001.

Pan, Philip P. "Cancer-Stricken Chinese Village Tries to Pierce a Wall of Silence." *Washington Post*, November 5, 2001, p. 19.

Park, Albert, Scott Rozelle, Christine Wong, and Changqing Ren. "Distributional Consequences of Reforming Local Public Finance in China." *China Quarterly* no. 147 (1996): 751–78.

Parsons, Talcott. "Equality and Inequality in Modern Society," in *Social Stratification: Research and Theory for the 1970's*, ed. Edward Laumann. Indianapolis: Bobbs-Merrill, 1970.

Pastor, Robert, and Qingshan Tan. "The Meaning of China's Village Elections." *China Quarterly* no. 162 (June 2000): 490–512.

Peace, Adrian. "Prestige Power and Legitimacy in a Modern Nigerian Town." *Canadian Journal of African Studies* 13, no. 1/2 (1979): 25, 27–51.

Pei, Minxin. *From Reform to Revolution: The Demise of Communism in China and the Soviet Union*. Cambridge: Harvard University Press, 1994.

———. "Will China Become Another Indonesia?" *Foreign Policy* no. 116 (Autumn 1999): 94–109.

Peng, Yuan, and Xiaoshan Zhang. "Problems and Challenges Encountered in the Development of TVEs." *Review of Economic Research (Jingji Cankao Yanjiu)* no. 28 (2001): 28–40.

Perkins, Dwight, and Shahid Yusuf. *Rural Development in China*. Baltimore: Johns Hopkins University Press, 1984.

Perry, Elizabeth J. *Rebels and Revolutionaries in North China, 1845–1945*. Stanford: Stanford University Press, 1980.

———. "Rural Violence in Socialist China." *China Quarterly* no. 103 (1985): 414–40.

———. "Challenging the Mandate of Heaven: Popular Protest in Modern China." *Critical Asian Studies* 33, no. 2 (2001): 163–80.

Petersen, Roger. *Resistance and Rebellion: Lessons from Eastern Europe*. New York: Cambridge University Press, 2001.

Peterson, Glen. "State Literacy Ideologies and the Transformation of Rural China." *Australian Journal of Chinese Affairs* no. 32 (July 1994): 95–120.

Pettit, Philip. "Republican Theory and Political Trust," in *Trust and Governance*, ed. Valerie Braithwaite and Margaret Levi. New York: Russell Sage Foundation, 1998.

Poncet, S. "Measuring Chinese Domestic and International Integration." *China Economic Review* 14, no. 1 (2003): 1–21.

Portes, Alejandro. "Social Capital: Its Origins and Applications in Modern Sociology." *Annual Review of Sociology* 24, no. 1 (1998): 1–24.

Potter, Pittman. "Guanxi and the PRC Legal System: From Contradiction to Complementarity," in *Social Connections in China: Institutions, Culture, and the Changing Nature of Guanxi*, ed. Thomas Gold, Doug Guthrie, and David Wank. Cambridge: Cambridge University Press, 2002.

Przeworski, A., and F. Limongi. "Modernization: Theories and Facts." *World Politics* 49, no. 2 (1997): 155–83.

Putnam, Robert D. *Making Democracy Work: Civic Traditions in Modern Italy*. Princeton: Princeton University Press, 1993.

———. *Bowling Along*. New York: Simon and Schuster, 2000.

Radcliffe, Sarah. "Indigenous Municipalities in Ecuador and Bolivia: Transnational Connections and Exclusionary Political Cultures." Paper presented at the conference Beyond the Lost Decade: Indigenous Movements and the Transformation of Development and Democracy in Latin America, Princeton, March 2001.

Reed, Robert Roy. "From Utopian Hopes to Practical Politics: A National Revolution in a Rural Village." *Comparative Studies in Society and History* 37, no. 4 (October 1995): 670–91.

Remick, Elizabeth. *Building Local States: China during the Republican and Post-Mao Eras*. Cambridge: Harvard University Press, 2004.

Riches, David. "Hunting, Herding, and Potlatching: Towards a Sociological Account of Prestige." *Man* 19, no. 2 (June 1984): 234–51.

Rigger, Shelley. *Politics in Taiwan: Voting for Democracy*. London: Routledge, 1999.

Riskin, C. *Rebuilding Effective Government: Local-Level Initiatives in Transition*. Bratislava: United Nations Development Program, 2000.

Rodden, Jonathan. *Hamilton's Paradox: The Promise and Peril of Fiscal Federalism*. Cambridge: Cambridge University Press, 2005.

Rodden, Jonathan, and Susan Rose-Ackerman. "Does Federalism Preserve Markets?" *Virginia Law Review* 83, no. 7 (1997): 1521–72.

Rose, Richard. "Russia as an Hour-Glass Society: A Constitution without Citizens." *East European Constitutional Review* 4, no. 3 (1995): 34–42.

Rose-Ackerman, Susan. *From Elections to Democracy: Building Accountable Government in Hungary and Poland.* Cambridge: Cambridge University Press, 2005.

Rosen, Stanley. "Recentralization, Decentralization, and Rationalization: Deng Xiaoping's Bifurcated Education Policy." *Modern China* 11, no. 3 (July 1985): 301–46.

Rousseau, Jean-Jacques. *The Social Contract.* Book 1, Chapter 3. New York: Penguin Press, 1968.

Rozelle, Scott. "Decision-Making in China's Rural Economy: The Linkages between Village Leaders and Farm Households." *China Quarterly* no. 137 (March 1994): 99–124.

Ruf, G. *Cadres and Kin: Making a Socialist Village in West China, 1921–1991.* Stanford: Stanford University Press, 1998.

Saich, Tony. "The Blind Man and the Elephant: Analysing the Local State in China," in *On the Roots of Growth and Crisis: Capitalism, State, and Society in East Asia*, ed. L. Tomba. Rome: Annale Feltinelli, 2002.

Sangren, P. Steven. "Traditional Chinese Corporations: Beyond Kinship." *Journal of Asian Studies* 43, no. 3 (May 1984): 391–415.

———. *History and Magical Power in a Chinese Community.* Stanford: Stanford University Press, 1987.

Schram, Stuart. *The Scope of State Power.* London: School of Oriental and African Studies, 1985.

Scott, James C. *The Moral Economy of the Peasant: Rebellion and Subsistence in Southeast Asia.* New Haven: Yale University Press, 1976.

———. *Weapons of the Weak: Everyday Forms of Peasant Resistance.* New Haven: Yale University Press, 1985.

Seabright, P. "Accountability and Decentralization in Government: An Incomplete Contracts Model." *European Economic Review* 40, no. 1 (1996): 1–1202.

Shelley, Becky. "Political Globalization and the Politics of International Non-Governmental Organization: The Case of Village Democracy in China." *Australian Journal of Political Science* 35, no. 2 (July 2000): 225–38.

Shi, Tianjian. "Village Committee Elections in China: Institutionalist Tactics for Democracy." *World Politics* 51, no. 3 (April 1999): 385–412.

Siu, Helen. *Agents and Victims in South China: Accomplices in Rural Revolution.* New Haven: Yale University Press, 1989.

Skinner, G. William. "Marketing and Social Structure in Rural China: Part I." *Journal of Asian Studies* 24, no. 1 (November 1964): 3–43.

———. "Marketing and Social Structure in Rural China: Part II." *Journal of Asian Studies* 24, no. 2 (February 1965): 195–228.

———. "Marketing and Social Structure in Rural China: Part III." *Journal of Asian Studies* 24, no. 3 (May 1965): 363–99.

———. "Chinese Peasants and the Closed Community: An Open and Shut Case." *Comparative Studies in Society and History* 13, no. 3 (July 1971): 270–81.

Sklar, Richard. *Nigerian Political Parties: Power in an Emergent African Nation.* Trenton: Africa World Press, 2004a.

______. "The Premise of Mixed Government in African Political Studies," in *Tradition and Politics: Indigenous Political Structures in Africa*, ed. Olufemi Vaughan. Trenton: Africa World Press, 2004b.

Skocpol, Theda. "How Americans Became Civic," in *Civic Engagement in American Democracy*, ed. Theda Skocpol and Morris P. Fiorina. Washington: Brookings, 1999.

______. "Voice and Inequality: The Transformation of American Civic Democracy." *Perspective on Politics* 2, no. 1 (2004): 3–20.

Smith, Arthur H. *Village Life in China*. New York: Kegan Paul, 2002.

Smyth, Russell. "Recent Developments in Rural Enterprise Reform in China: Achievements, Problems, and Prospects." *Asian Survey* 38, no. 8 (August 1998): 784–800.

Smyth, Russell, Jiangguo Wang, and Quek Lee Kiang. "Efficiency, Performance and Changing Corporate Governance in China's Township-Village Enterprises since the 1990s." *Asian-Pacific Economic Literature* 15, no. 1 (May 2001): 30–41.

Solinger, Dorothy. *Contesting Citizenship in Urban China: Peasant Migrants, the State, and the Logic of the Market*. Berkeley: University of California Press, 1999.

Steinfeld, Edward. *Forging Reform in China: The Fate of State-Owned Industry*. Cambridge: Cambridge University Press, 1998.

Stocks, Anthony. "Too Much for Too Few: Problems of Indigenous Land Rights in Latin America." *Annual Review of Anthropology* 34 (2005): 85–104.

Strauch, Judith. "Community and Kinship in Southeastern China: The View from the Multilineage Villages of Hong Kong." *Journal of Asian Studies* 43, no. 1 (November 1983): 21–50.

Su, Fubing, and Dali Yang. "Elections, Governance, and Accountability in Rural China." Paper presented at the International Symposium on Villager Self-Government and Rural Social Movement in China, Beijing, September 2001.

Sun, Lena H. "China's Peasants Hit Back; Rising Rural Unrest Alarms Beijing." *Washington Post*, June 20, 1993.

Sweeten, Alan Richard. *Christianity in Rural China: Conflict and Accommodation in Jiangxi Province, 1860–1900*. Michigan Monographs in Chinese Studies. Vol. 91. Ann Arbor: Center for Chinese Studies, University of Michigan Press, 2001.

Tendler, Judith. *Good Government in the Tropics*. Baltimore: Johns Hopkins University Press, 1997.

Tiebout, Charles. "A Pure Theory of Local Government Expenditures." *Journal of Political Economy* 64, no. 5 (1956): 416–24.

Tilly, Charles. "Reflections on the History of European State-Making," in *The Formation of National States in Western Europe*. Princeton: Princeton University Press, 1975, pp. 3–83.

Tomz, Michael, Jason Wittenberg, and Gary King. CLARIFY: Software for Interpreting and Presenting Statistical Results. Cambridge: Harvard University.

Tsang, Mun C. "Intergovernmental Grants and the Financing of Compulsory Education in China." *Harvard China Review* 3, no. 2 (2002): 1–25.

Tyler, Tom. "Trust and Democratic Governance," in *Trust and Governance*, ed. Valerie Braithwaite and Margaret Levi. New York: Russell Sage Foundation, 1998.

Tyler, Tom, and Peter Degoey. "Trust in Organizational Authorities: The Influence of Motive Attributions on Willingness to Accept Decisions," in *Trust in Organizations*, ed. Roderick Kramer and Tom Tyler. Thousand Oaks: Russell Sage Foundation, 1995.

Vaughan, Olufemy. *Nigerian Chiefs: Traditional Power in Modern Politics, 1890s–1990s*. Rochester: Boydell and Brewer, 2000.

Verdon, Michel. "Kinship, Marriage, and the Family: An Operational Approach." *American Journal of Sociology* 86, no. 4 (1981): 796–818.

Wang, Hongying. "Informal Institutions and Foreign Investment in China." *Pacific Review* 13, no. 4 (2000): 525–56.

Wank, David. "Business-State Clientelism in China: Decline or Evolution?" in *Social Connections in China: Institutions, Culture, and the Changing Name of Guanxi*, ed. Thomas Gold, Doug Guthrie, and David Wank. Cambridge: Cambridge University Press, 2002.

Watson, James. *Emigration and the Chinese Lineage*. Berkeley: University of California Press, 1975.

———. "Chinese Kinship Reconsidered: Anthropological Perspectives on Historical Research." *China Quarterly* no. 92 (December 1982): 589–622.

Watson, Rubie. "Class Differences and Affinal Relations in South China." *Man* 16, no. 4 (December 1981): 593–615.

———. "The Creation of a Chinese Lineage: The Teng of Ha Tsuen, 1669–1751." *Modern Asian Studies* 16, no. 1 (1982): 69–100.

Weber, Max. *Wirtschaft Und Gesellshaft*. Tubingen: Mohr, 1922.

Wedeman, Andrew. "Stealing from the Farmers: Institutional Corruption and the 1992 IOU Crisis." *China Quarterly* no. 152 (December 1997): 805–31.

Weingast, Barry. "The Economic Role of Political Institutions: Market-Preserving Federalism and Economic Development." *Journal of Law, Economics, and Organization* 11, no. 1 (1995): 1–31.

———. *The Theory of Comparative Federalism and the Emergence of Economic Liberalization in Mexico, China, and India*. Stanford: Hoover Institution, 2000.

Weller, Robert P. *Unities and Diversities in Chinese Religion*. Seattle: University of Washington Press, 1987.

———. *Alternate Civilities: Democracy and Culture in China and Taiwan*. Nashville: Westview Press, 2001.

Whiting, Susan. *Power and Wealth in Rural China: The Political Economy of Institutional Change*. Cambridge: Cambridge University Press, 2001.

WHO and UNICEF. *Global Water Supply and Sanitation Assessment 2000 Report*. New York: World Health Organization and UNICEF Joint Monitoring Program for Water Supply and Sanitation, 2000.

Widner, Jennifer. "States and Statelessness in Late Twentieth-Century Africa." *Daedalus* 124, no. 3 (Summer 1995): 129–53.

Will, Pierre-Etienne, and R. Wong. *Nourish the People: The State Civilian Granary System in China, 1650–1850*. Ann Arbor: University of Michigan, Center for Chinese Studies, 1991.

Wolf, Arthur. *Religion and Ritual in Chinese Society*. Stanford: Stanford University Press, 1974.

Wolf, Eric. "Types of Latin American Peasantry: A Preliminary Discussion." *American Anthropologist* no. 57 (June 1955): 452–71.

Wong, Christine. *Financing Local Government in the People's Republic of China*. Hong Kong: Oxford University Press, 1997a.

______. "Rural Public Finance," in *Financing Local Government in the People's Republic of China*, ed. Christine Wong. Hong Kong: Oxford University Press, 1997b.

Wong, Christine, and Richard Bird. "China's Fiscal System," in *The Great Transformation: China's Economy since Reform*, ed. Loren Brandt and Thomas Rawski, New York: Cambridge University Press, Forthcoming.

Wooldridge, Jeffrey. *Econometric Analysis of Cross Section and Panel Data*. Cambridge: MIT Press, 2002.

World Bank. *China: The Transport Sector*. Washington: World Bank, 1985.

______. *China: Provincial Expenditure Review*. Washington: World Bank, 2001.

______. "Making Services Work for Poor People," in *World Bank Development Report 2004*. Washington: World Bank, 2003.

______. *World Development Indicators 2005*. Washington: World Bank, 2005.

World Resources Institute. *China's Health and Environment: Water Scarcity, Water Pollution, and Health*. Washington: World Resources Institute, 1998–9.

Wu, Changhua, Crescencia Maurer, Yi Wang, Zheng Shou, and Devra Lee Davis. "Water Pollution and Human Health in China." *Environmental Health Perspectives* 107, no. 4 (April 1999): 251–6.

Wuthnow, R. *The Restructuring of American Religion*. Princeton: Princeton University Press, 1988.

Yan, Martin. *A Chinese Village*. London: K. Paul, Trench, Trubner, 1948.

Yan, Yunxiang. *The Flow of Gifts: Reciprocity and Social Networks in a Chinese Village*. Stanford: Stanford University Press, 1996.

Yang, C. K. *Religion in Chinese Society: A Study of Contemporary Social Functions of Religion and Some of Their Historical Factors*. Berkeley: University of California Press, 1961.

Yang, Dali L. *Calamity and Reform: State, Rural Society, and Institutional Change since the Great Leap Famine*. Stanford: Stanford University Press, 1996.

Yang, Mayfair Mei-hui. *Gifts, Favors, and Banquets: The Art of Social Relationships in China*. Ithaca: Cornell University Press, 1994.

Yashar, D. "Contesting Citizenship: Indigenous Movements and Democracy in Latin America." *Comparative Politics* 31, no. 1 (1998): 23–42.

______. "Democracy, Indigenous Movements, and the Postliberal Challenge in Latin America." *World Politics* 52, no. 1 (1999): 76–104.

Young, A. "The Razor's Edge: Distortions and Incremental Reform in the People's Republic of China." *Quarterly Journal of Economics* 115, no. 3–4 (2000): 714–1478.

References

Yu, Jianrong. *Township and Village Autonomy: Basis and Path (Xiangzhen Zizhi: Genju He Lujin)*, June 2002.

Zhang, Xiaobo, Shenggen Fan, Linxiu Zhang, and Jikun Huang. "Local Governance and Public Goods Provision in Rural China." *International Food Policy Research Institute* (July 2002): 1–22.

Zhang, Xudong, and Liu Yangyang. "Remarkable Achievement in Pilot Tax and Fee Reform in Rural China – Alleviation of Burdens by 30%." *Xinhua Network*, July 6, 2004.

Zhao, Ling. "Major Shift in the Focus of Farmers' Petition to Rights: From Disputes over Taxes and Fees to Petitioning for the Right to Land." *Nanfang Zhoumo* (Southern Weekend), September 2, 2004.

Zhao, Shukai. "Township and Village Governance: Organization and Conflict (Xiangcun Zhili: Zuzhi Yu Chongtu)." *Strategy and Management* (Zhanlue Yu Guanli) (June 2003).

Zhongguo Jingji Nianjian 2000 (China Economic Yearbook 2000). Beijing: Zhongguo Jingji Nianjian She, 2000.

Zhuravskaya, E. V. "Incentives to Provide Local Public Goods: Fiscal Federalism, Russian Style." Paper presented at the Fifth Nobel Symposium in Economics: The Economics of Transition, Stockholm, September 10–12, 1999.

Appendix

Additional Notes on Survey Sampling and Data Collection

In 2001, I conducted a village-level survey of 316 villages sampled from four provinces: Shanxi, Hebei, Jiangxi, and Fujian. With a team of ten to fifteen Chinese graduate and undergraduate students in each province, the survey took about seven weeks to administer. The selection of these provinces was based both on my network of contacts and on the objective of obtaining a sample that would be roughly representative of the general population. These four provinces varied along two important macro-level dimensions. First, coastal and inland regions differ significantly from each other in terms of economic development and liberalization. Second, north and south China vary greatly in their institutional history and social organization. Shanxi and Hebei provinces in north China are relatively flat and dry, whereas Jiangxi and Fujian provinces in south China are mountainous and humid. Lineage and religious institutions in the north are generally less formalized than in south China. Villages in the north tend to be organized as a single centralized geographical cluster rather than fragmented into numerous settlements, as they often are in the south due to the terrain. Within each pair, one province was coastal and one was inland. Between the two northern provinces, Hebei, which is closer to the coast, has industrialized and developed its infrastructure more than Shanxi has. In the southern provinces, Fujian is on the coast and known for its liberal and successful pursuit of economic and political reforms, whereas Jiangxi is a politically conservative interior province that lags behind Fujian in economic development.

Within each province, I selected two counties. I wanted two counties that would vary in pilot county status for village democratic reforms (pilot counties employ more administrative resources and pressure to implement democratic reforms at the village level) but to have similar economic and geographic characteristics. Out of the possible counties that fit these criteria, I made my final selection based on the kinds of connections that my Chinese colleagues were able to utilize. The rationale for this strategy was to provide me with an instrument for identifying the impact of village democratic reforms on my dependent variable, village governmental provision of public goods.[1] Since the promulgation of reforms in 1988 allowing the implementation of elections for a portion of officials at the village level and the creation of other democratic institutions such as villagers' representative assemblies, most provinces had selected pilot sites for these reforms. Based on a multitude of interviews with officials in Beijing in the Ministry of Civil Affairs, which was responsible for overseeing the implementation of these reforms, as well as interviews with officials in provincial, municipal, county, township, and village governments, the selection of pilot sites seemed to be idiosyncratic. Provinces selected places of all different levels of economic development. Some were in areas that were easy for provincial officials to reach; others were in mountainous areas. As far as I could ascertain from these interviews and from my own field observations, the places that were selected to be pilot sites were not necessarily the places that were already performing well.

Within each county, I used multistage sampling stratified by 2000 income per capita to produce a sample of 316 villages. In each county, I and my team of survey enumerators first visited the county seat and obtained a list of all the townships in the county. We stratified this list by 2000 income per capita and randomly selected eight townships.

We then traveled to each of the township governments. In each township, we obtained a list of all the villages in the township, stratified this list by 2000 income per capita, and randomly selected five villages within each township. This strategy would give us a sample of 40 villages in each county (eight townships multiplied by five villages), which meant that we would survey 80 villages in each province or 320 villages in four provinces. The final sample, however, included 316 villages instead of 320 villages. One village was dropped because no one in the village was working as a village official

[1] Because the implementation of democratic reforms was potentially endogenous in the sense that villages with good governmental provision of public goods might have been more likely to implement democratic reforms well, it was important to find a variable that was exogenous, had an effect on the implementation of democratic reforms, and only had an effect on public goods provision through its effect on democratic reforms. These criteria were necessary for accurately estimating the effect of democratic reforms on public goods provision.

and despite our best efforts to find a qualified respondent, there was no one we could interview. The remaining discrepancy of three villages is due to the fact that two townships had fewer than five villages. In these cases, all of the villages in the township were surveyed.

In each village, two enumerators met with one to three village officials for about three to four hours. Enumerators tried to meet with at least the village accountant and either the Party secretary or the village head. Enumerators filled out the survey questionnaire by interviewing the village officials and looking with them at village account books and other village documents. Our main objective was to obtain data about village-level conditions by interviewing village officials. While in the field administering the survey, I split my time between accompanying teams of enumerators on their visits to villages to evaluate the quality of survey administration, checking over completed questionnaires and trying to obtain answers for accidentally skipped questions while still in the area, visiting villages both in and out of the sample to do more in-depth interviews with both villagers and village officials, and interviewing township and county officials in our research sites.

Coding of Variables for Statistical Analysis

These coding protocols apply to the variables used for the book's statistical analyses. All data are for 2000 unless otherwise indicated.

Per capita government investment in public projects: Total village government investment in village public projects, divided by village population.

Existence of paved roads: Dummy indicating whether the village has one or more paved roads (0 = no; 1 = yes).

Existence of paved footpaths: Dummy indicating whether the village has one or more paved paths (0 = no; 1 = yes).

Percentage of classrooms usable in rainy weather: Number of village primary school classrooms usable in rainy weather, divided by total number of village primary school classrooms.

Newness of school building: Number of years since the village primary school's construction or last major renovation.

Existence of running water infrastructure: Dummy indicating whether the village has household running water taps and/or communal running water taps (0 = no; 1 = yes).

Existence of a temple manager: Dummy indicating whether the village has a temple manager (0 = no; 1 = yes).

Percentage of households engaging in temple reconstruction: Number of households making donations to temple reconstruction divided by total number of households in the village.

Existence of an active village pastor: Dummy indicating whether the village has a village pastor or priest who organizes church services and activities (0 = no; 1 = yes).

Existence of a church reconstruction project: Dummy indicating whether the village has organized a church reconstruction project since the beginning of reforms and the implementation of the household responsibility system in the early 1980s (0 = no; 1 = yes).

Existence of ancestral halls with spirit tablets in village: Dummy indicating whether the village has one or more ancestral halls with spirit tablets (0 = no; 1 = yes).

Existence of a single ancestral hall with spirit tablets: Dummy indicating whether the village has only one ancestral hall with spirit tablets (0 = no; 1 = yes).

Existence of multiple ancestral halls with spirit tablets: Dummy indicating whether the village has two or more ancestral halls with spirit tablets (0 = no; 1 = yes).

Distance from county town: Distance from nearest county town in kilometers.

Number of natural villages: Number of natural villages in the (administrative) village.

Village terrain: Dummy indicating whether the village is located on flat terrain (0 = no; 1 = yes).

County dummies: A series of seven dummy variables indicating the county in which the village was located. The omitted category is County A of Shanxi province.

1997 village income per capita: "Actual" (*shiji*) village income per capita in yuan (as opposed to village income per capita reported to the state [*shang bao shu*]).

1997 village government assets: Village government total current or floating assets.

1997 village tax revenue per capita: Total amount of village levies (*tiliu*) and village apportionments (*jizi*) divided by village population.

Existence of village government enterprises in 1995: Dummy indicating whether the village had one or more village government enterprises in 1995 (0 = no; 1 = yes).

Existence of private enterprises in village in 1995: Dummy indicating whether the village had one or more private enterprises (officially defined as those with eight or more employees) in 1995 (0 = no; 1 = yes).

Party membership of village head: Dummy indicating whether the elected village head is a member of the Communist Party (0 = no; 1 = yes).

Percentage of village officials in Party: Number of village officials (in both the village committee and the village Party branch) who are members of the Communist Party, divided by total number of village officials.

Existence of bureaucratic targets for public projects: Dummy indicating whether the township government requires village officials to sign a performance contract with public project targets, which the officials themselves report as having an impact on their decision making (0 = no; 1 = yes).

Additive index for the implementation of preelection procedures: Nine-item additive scale. Villages are assigned a score from one to nine based on their implementation of nine aspects of preelection procedures: determination of primary candidates free of interference from the township government; determination of primary candidates free of interference from the village Party branch; determination of primary candidates free of interference from the incumbent village committee; determination of final candidates free of interference from the township government; determination of final candidates free of interference from the village Party branch; determination of final candidates free of interference from the incumbent village committee; determination of election oversight committee members free of interference from the township government; determination of election oversight committee members free of interference from the village Party branch; and determination of election oversight committee members free of interference from the incumbent village committee.

Additive index for the implementation of voting procedures: Seven-item additive scale. Villages are assigned a score from one to seven based on their implementation of seven voting procedures: immediate announcement of election results; an election contested or fielding more than one candidate per position; public vote count; secret ballot booth; campaign speeches; regulated proxy voting; and fixed ballot boxes.

Additive index for the implementation of villagers' representative assemblies: Seven-item additive scale. Villages are assigned a score from one to seven based on their implementation of seven procedures: competition for assembly seats; elections with secret ballot for assembly seats; formal regulations on when the assembly is convened; formal power to recall the village head; formal power to inspect village expenditures; formal power to audit village accounts; and veto of a village government decision by the assembly in the last year.

Index for the implementation of preelection procedures: Index created through principal components analysis of nine dummy variables, each indicating the implementation of one of the following nine procedures: determination of primary candidates free of interference from the township government; determination of primary candidates free of interference from the village Party branch; determination of primary candidates free of interference from the incumbent village committee; determination of final candidates free of interference from the township government; determination of final candidates free of interference from the village Party branch; determination of final candidates free of interference from the incumbent village committee; determination of election oversight committee members free of interference from the township government; determination of election oversight committee members free of interference from the village Party branch; and determination of election oversight committee members free of interference from the incumbent village committee (0 = no; 1 = yes).

Index for the implementation of voting procedures: Index created through principal components analysis of seven dummy variables, each indicating the implementation of one of the following seven procedures: immediate announcement of election results; an election contested or fielding more than one candidate per position; public vote count; secret ballot booth; campaign speeches; regulated proxy voting; and fixed ballot boxes (0 = no; 1 = yes).

Index for the implementation of villagers' representative assemblies: Index created through principal components analysis of seven dummy variables, each indicating the implementation of one of the following seven procedures: competition for assembly seats; elections with secret ballot for assembly seats; formal regulations on when the assembly is convened; formal power to recall the village head; formal power to inspect village expenditures; formal power to audit village accounts; and veto of a village government decision by the assembly in the last year (0 = no; 1 = yes).

Index for the implementation of village democratic reforms: Index created through principal components analysis of the three previous indices on the implementation of preelection procedures, voting procedures, and villagers' representative assemblies.

Legacy of village temple activity: Dummy indicating whether the village reported temple activity at the time of the Communist takeover or "liberation" in 1949 (0 = no; 1 = yes).

Surname fragmentation index: The percentage of households in the village that do not belong to the largest surname group.

Pilot county status: Dummy indicating whether the village is located in a county that has been designated a pilot county for the implementation of village democratic reforms (0 = no; 1 = yes).

Seemingly Unrelated Regression Model

The seemingly unrelated regression (SUR) model estimates a system of equations, one for each of the six public goods provision outcomes, and allows the errors in the different equations to be correlated. Because each measure of public goods provision is regressed on the same set of explanatory variables, the coefficients and standard errors produced by SUR are identical to those produced by ordinary least squares regression (OLS). The advantage to using an SUR software routine in this case is that it automatically produces the covariances between estimators from different equations that allow us to test joint hypotheses involving parameters in different equations.[2] As Edward Miguel notes, "[w]hen there is limited correlation in village disturbance terms across the different dependent variables," as there is in this case (see Appendix Table A3.1 for intercorrelations), "this method is equivalent to an increase in sample size – and this explains why statistical significance may be higher for SUR hypothesis tests than for any single OLS coefficient on its own."[3] SUR also enables us to analyze the impact of particular explanatory variables on village governmental provision of public goods without combining the six measures of provision into a single index. Because intercorrelations among the six measures of village governmental provision of public goods are weak, it is inappropriate to combine these measures into a single index of village governmental provision of public goods.

2 Wooldridge, Econometric Analysis of Cross Section and Panel Data.

3 Edward Miguel, "Tribe or Nation? Nation Building and Public Goods in Kenya versus Tanzania," *World Politics* 56 (April 2004): 327–62.

Identifying and Estimating the Effects of Temple and Church Institutions (Chapter 5)

I estimate the effects of village temple institutions and village church institutions on village public goods provision. The empirical specification for temple institutions is presented in Equations 1 and 2. Y_i^k is the public goods provision outcome measure, where k may denote village government investment, existence of paved roads, access to running water, or another provision outcome. X_i is a vector of socioeconomic, geographic, and institutional controls.

$$Y_i^k = a^k + X_i\beta^k + \tau^k TM_i^{kj} + \mu_i^k \tag{1}$$

TM_i^j denotes a temple institutions measure, where i denotes a village and j denotes a measure of village temple institutions: the existence of a temple manager or the village participation rate in temple reconstruction projects. The hypothesis can be restated as $H_0 : \tau^k = 0$, jointly for all outcomes k. Rejecting this hypothesis means that village temple institutions have a significant effect on public goods provision outcomes.

$$Y_i^k = a^k + X_i\beta^k + \tau^k CH_i^{kj} + \mu_i^k \tag{2}$$

In Equation 2, CH_i^j denotes a church institutions measure, where i denotes a village and j denotes a measure of village church institutions: the existence of an active church or the organization of a church reconstruction project. The hypothesis can be restated as $H_0 : \tau^k = 0$, jointly for all outcomes k. Rejecting this hypothesis means that village church institutions have a significant effect on public goods provision outcomes.

Identifying and Estimating the Effect of Active Lineage Groups (Chapter 6)

No Distinction between Types

The empirical specification for active lineage institutions (without distinguishing between subvillage and villagewide lineage institutions) is presented in Equation 1. Y_i^k is the public goods provision outcome measure, where k may denote village government investment, existence of paved roads, access to running water, or another provision outcome. X_i is a vector of socioeconomic, geographic, and institutional controls.

$$Y_i^k = a^k + X_i\beta^k + \tau^k L_i^k + \mu_i^k \tag{1}$$

L_i^k denotes a measure for the existence of a solidary lineage group, where i denotes a village. The hypothesis can be restated as $H_0 : \tau^k = 0$, jointly for all outcomes k. Rejecting this hypothesis means that the existence of functioning lineage institutions has a significant effect on public goods provision outcomes. As in Chapter 6, I use SUR, in which the errors associated with the different outcome variables may be correlated.

Villagewide Lineage Groups versus Subvillage Groups

The empirical specification is presented in Equation 2. Y_i^k is the public goods provision outcome measure, where k may denote village government investment, existence of paved roads, access to running water, or another provision outcome. X_i is a vector of socioeconomic, geographic, and institutional controls.

$$Y_i^k = a^k + X_i\beta^k + \tau^k SL_i^k + \upsilon^k FL_i^k + \mu_i^k(2) \tag{2}$$

SL_i^k denotes a measure for the existence of a solidary lineage group, where i denotes a village. FL_i^k denotes a measure for the existence of multiple fragmenting lineage groups, where i denotes a village. The first hypothesis can be restated as $H_0 : \tau^k = 0$, jointly for all outcomes k. Rejecting this hypothesis means that the existence of a solidary lineage group has a significant effect on public goods provision outcomes. The second hypothesis can be restated as $H_0 : \upsilon^k = 0$, jointly for all outcomes k. Rejecting this hypothesis means that the existence of subvillage fragmenting lineage groups has a significant effect on public goods provision outcomes.

Identifying and Estimating the Effects of Democratic Institutions (Chapter 7)

The empirical specification for the implementation of democratic reforms is presented in Equation 1. Y_i^k is the public goods provision outcome measure, where k may denote village government investment, existence of paved roads, access to running water, or another provision outcome. X_i is a vector of socioeconomic, geographic, and institutional controls.

$$Y_i^k = a^k + X_i\beta^k + \tau^k D_i^k + \mu_i^k(1) \tag{1}$$

D_i denotes a measure of the implementation of democratic reforms, where i denotes a village. The hypothesis can be restated as $H_0 : \tau^k = 0$, jointly for all outcomes k. Rejecting this hypothesis means that the implementation of democratic reforms has a significant effect on public goods provision outcomes.

Identifying and Estimating the Effects of Institutions of Party Control (Chapter 8)

I estimate the effects of Party control on village public goods provision. The empirical specification for institutions of Party control is presented in Equation 1. Y_i^k is the public goods provision outcome measure, where k may denote village government investment, existence of paved roads, access to running water, or another provision outcome. X_i is a vector of socioeconomic, geographic, and institutional controls.

$$Y_i^k = a^k + X_i\beta^k + \tau^k P_i^{kj} + \mu_i^k \tag{1}$$

P_i^j denotes a Party control measure, where i denotes a village and j denotes a measure of Party control: the Party membership status of the village head or the percentage of village officials who are Party members. The hypothesis can be restated as $H_0 : \tau^k = 0$, jointly for all outcomes k. Rejecting this hypothesis means that institutions of Party control have a significant effect on public goods provision outcomes.

Identifying and Estimating the Effects of Bureaucratic Control (Chapter 8)

I estimate the effects of bureaucratic control on village public goods provision. The empirical specification for institutions of bureaucratic control is presented in Equation 1. Y_i^k is the public goods provision outcome measure, where k may denote village government investment, existence of paved roads, access to running water, or another provision outcome. X_i is a vector of socioeconomic, geographic, and institutional controls.

$$Y_i^k = a^k + X_i\beta^k + \tau^k T_i^k + \mu_i^k \tag{1}$$

T_i denotes a Party control measure, where i denotes a village. The hypothesis can be restated as $H_0 : \tau^k = 0$, jointly for all outcomes k. Rejecting this hypothesis means that institutions of bureaucratic control have a significant effect on public goods provision outcomes.

Notes on Survey Sampling and Data Analysis

Appendix Tables

Appendix Tables A3.1 through A7.6 present data referenced in Chapters 3, 5, 6, and 7.

Appendix Table A3.1. *Intercorrelations (r) among Indicators of Village Governmental Provision of Public Goods*

	Per Capita Investment	Existence of Paved Roads	Existence of Paved Paths	Percentage of Classrooms Usable in Rain	Newness of School Building	Existence of Running Water
Per Capita Investment	1.00	0.1396	0.0823	0.0430	0.0920	0.1090
Existence of Paved Roads	0.1396	1.00	0.2541	−0.0657	−0.0097	0.2927
Existence of Paved Paths	0.0823	0.2541	1.00	0.0210	0.0692	0.1316
Percentage of Classrooms Usable in Rain	0.043	−0.0657	0.0210	1.00	−0.1011	−0.0403
Newness of School	0.0920	−0.0097	0.0692	−0.1011	1.00	−0.0934
Existence of Running Water	0.1090	0.2927	0.1316	−0.0403	−0.0934	1.00

Appendix Table A3.2. *Economic Factors and Public Goods Provision in Rural China: All Five Economic Factors in the Same Model with All Controls (SUR). Missing Data Are Multiply Imputed*

	Per Capita Investment	Existence of Paved Roads	Existence of Paved Paths	Percentage of Classrooms Usable in Rain	Newness of School	Existence of Running Water	Ho: B = 0 p-value (SUR)
Economic variables							
1997 income per capita (thousands of yuan)	0.0052 (0.010)	0.000039* (0.000023)	0.000022 (0.000016)	0.000007 (0.000016)	0.00072 (0.0010)	−0.0000024 (0.000020)	0.53
1997 government assets (thousands of yuan)	−0.000012 (0.000027)	0.000000060 (0.000000063)	−0.000000019 (0.000000043)	−0.000000020 (0.000000042)	0.00000072 (0.0000025)	0.00000014 (0.000000054)	0.24
1997 tax revenue per capita	−0.40 (0.43)	0.0012 (0.0010)	−0.0012* (0.00069)	−0.0010 (0.00068)	−0.007 (0.039)	0.0010 (0.00086)	0.16
Existence of village government enterprises in 1995	−9.60 (22.53)	0.0066 (0.052)	0.053 (0.035)	0.011 (0.035)	−1.09 (2.00)	0.052 (0.045)	0.65
Existence of private enterprises in 1995	10.74 (28.53)	0.16** (0.066)	0.12*** (0.045)	0.032 (0.044)	−4.73* (2.55)	0.054 (0.057)	0.019**
Control variables							
Distance from county town	−0.28 (0.60)	−0.005*** (0.0014)	−0.003*** (0. 00093)	−0.00042 (0.00091)	0.070 (0.053)	−0.0011 (0.0012)	
Number of natural villages	−0.97 (3.06)	−0.004 (0.007)	−0.0045 (0.0048)	0.0082 (0.0047)	0.14 (0.27)	−0.0056 (0.0061)	
Village population	−0.016 (0.011)	0.000023 (0.000025)	0.000033 (0.000017)	0.000004 (0.000017)	−0.0011 (0.0010)	0.000012 (0.000022)	
Village terrain	−2.55 (33.41)	0.074 (0.077)	−0.016 (0.053)	−0.014 (0.051)	−1.92 (2.97)	0.005 (0.066)	

Party membership of village head	7.70	0.015	−0.036	−0.00019	2.54	0.012
	(24.91)	(0.057)	(0.039)	(0.038)	(2.23)	(0.049)
Percentage of village officials in Party	31.22	0.15	0.017	0.037	2.75	0.13
	(64.79)	(0.15)	(0.10)	(0.10)	(5.78)	(0.13)
Existence of bureaucratic targets for public projects	42.68	−0.076	−0.031	0.056*	1.13	−0.026
	(22.01)	(0.050)	(0.034)	(0.034)	(1.95)	(0.043)
Existence of a temple manager	45.70	0.091	0.069	0.11**	0.30	0.12*
	(37.28)	(0.081)	(0.055)	(0.053)	(3.19)	(0.070)
Existence of an active church pastor	−67.83	0.12	−0.08	−0.27***	4.19	−0.00021
	(43.07)	(0.10)	(0.068)	(0.066)	(3.85)	(0.085)
Existence of only one ancestral hall with spirit tablets	74.64	0.255**	0.11	−0.016	−0.60	0.019
	(45.82)	(0.11)	(0.072)	(0.070)	(4.15)	(0.090)
Existence of multiple ancestral halls with spirit tablets	−44.69	−0.15	0.14**	0.017	−6.36	−0.016
	(44.12)	(0.10)	(0.069)	(0.067)	(3.93)	(0.087)
Index of the implementation of village democratic reforms	19.31	0.010	0.037**	0.023	−1.30	0.014
	(11.29)	(0.026)	(0.018)	(0.021)	(1.26)	(0.024)
County dummies	Yes	Yes	Yes	Yes	Yes	Yes
Constant term	34.71	0.37***	0.10	0.85***	48.51***	0.71***
	(57.70)	(0.13)	(0.092)	(0.088)	(5.14)	(0.11)

Note: N = 316 villages. Figures in cells are seemingly unrelated regression coefficients. Standard errors are in parentheses. * p = 0.10; ** p = 0.05; *** p = 0.01. The hypothesis that the coefficient estimates on each term are equal to zero across the six outcomes in the table is tested using SUR in the final column.

Appendix Table A5.1. *Descriptive Statistics*

	Mean	Standard Deviation	Number of Observations
Measures of public goods provision			
2000 total village government expenditure on public projects per capita (yuan)	66.76	192.42	312
Existence of paved roads (1 = yes, 0 = no)	0.5	0.5	316
Existence of paved paths (1 = yes, 0 = no)	0.13	0.33	312
Percentage of classrooms unusable in rain	0.11	0.29	310
Average age of school building (years)	27.26	18.26	309
Existence of running water (1 = yes, 0 = no)	0.47	0.5	316
Measures of village temple groups			
Existence of a temple manager (1 = yes, 0 = no)	0.14	0.35	311
Proportion of households in temple reconstruction	0.09	0.29	313
Existence of temple activities at the start of the Communist period (1 = yes, 0 = no)	0.46	0.50	287
Measures of village church groups			
Existence of an active church pastor (1 = yes, 0 = no)	0.07	0.25	316
Existence of church reconstruction project (1 = yes, 0 = no)	0.04	0.21	316
Measures of village lineage groups			
Existence of a single active lineage hall (1 = yes, 0 = no)	0.07	0.26	315
Existence of multiple active lineage halls (1 = yes, 0 = no)	0.07	0.26	315
Surname fragmentation index	0.5	0.26	312
Strength of formal state institutions			
Democratization index	0	1.07	270
Party membership of village head (1 = yes, 0 = no)	0.69	0.46	316
Percentage of village officials with Party membership	0.74	0.19	313
Bureaucratic targets for public projects (1 = yes, 0 = no)	0.44	0.5	316
Model county status (1 = yes, 0 = no)	0.49	0.50	316
Economic controls			
1997 income per capita (yuan)	1,481.36	1,130.07	308
1997 village government assets (yuan)	42,644	393,067	311
1997 village tax revenue per capita (yuan)	21.85	27.37	306

	Mean	Standard Deviation	Number of Observations
Existence of village government enterprises in 1995	0.43	0.50	316
Existence of private enterprises in 1995	0.20	0.40	316
Geographic and demographic controls			
Distance from county seat (km)	26.45	20.97	316
Number of natural villages	3.9	4.53	316
Village population	1,240.1	981.42	315
Village terrain (1 = flat, 0 = not flat)	0.36	0.48	316
County dummies	–	–	316

Appendix Table A5.2. *Village Governmental Provision of Public Goods and the Existence of a Temple Manager, with All Controls (SUR). Missing Data Are Deleted Listwise*

	Per Capita Investment	Existence of Paved Roads	Existence of Paved Paths	Percentage of Classrooms Usable in Rain	Newness of School	Existence of Running Water	Ho: B = 0 p-value (SUR)
Village temples							
Existence of a temple manager	60.77 (71.41)	0.13 (0.10)	0.13* (0.079)	0.13** (0.055)	4.71 (2.87)	0.15* (0.093)	0.0058***
Control variables							
Distance from county town	−0.39 (1.06)	−0.0050*** (0.0013)	−0.0022** (0.0011)	0.00085 (0.0011)	0.080 (0.053)	−0.00061 (0.0014)	
Number of natural villages	−0.74 (3.39)	−0.0020 (0.0093)	−0.0033 (0.0036)	0.0065* (0.0034)	0.20 (0.19)	−0.0040 (0.0055)	
Village population	−0.0173* (0.0096)	0.000021 (0.000038)	0.000031 (0.000027)	0.000005 (0.000009)	−0.0017*** (0.0007)	0.000013 (0.000022)	
Village terrain	−10.29 (25.66)	0.13 (0.093)	0.019 (0.055)	−0.022 (0.058)	−1.60 (3.082)	−0.015 (0.069)	
1997 income per capita (thousands of yuan)	0.029* (0.016)	0.000094** (0.000043)	0.000054* (0.000028)	−0.0000043 (0.000023)	−0.00051 (0.0020)	0.000006 (0.000045)	
1997 government assets (thousands of yuan)	−0.000015** (0.0000061)	0.000000030 (0.000000025)	−0.000000032 (0.000000018)	−0.000000014 (0.000000011)	0.0000015 (0.0000017)	0.00000014*** (0.000000030)	
1997 tax revenue per capita	−0.55 (0.26)	−0.00047 (0.0014)	−0.0014** (0.00063)	−0.0001 (0.00065)	0.025 (0.049)	0.0014 (0.0010)	

Existence of village government enterprises in 1995	−11.57	−0.0078	0.079**	−0.017	−0.66	0.021
	(21.86)	(0.060)	(0.039)	(0.035)	(2.11)	(0.050)
Existence of private enterprises in 1995	−25.44	0.086	0.080	0.074*	−7.29***	−0.0019
	(28.40)	(0.077)	(0.056)	(0.039)	(2.68)	(0.065)
Party membership of village head	−1.79	−0.036	−0.0065	0.024	0.99	0.025
	(27.74)	(0.068)	(0.041)	(0.047)	(2.30)	(0.055)
Percentage of village officials in Party	−14.88	0.036	−0.081	−0.093	1.81	0.24*
	(60.08)	(0.18)	(0.12)	(0.12)	(5.97)	(0.14)
Existence of bureaucratic targets for public projects	27.40	−0.11*	−0.014	0.074*	1.87	−0.051
	(27.66)	(0.064)	(0.041)	(0.038)	(2.24)	(0.052)
Index of the implementation of village democratic reforms	17.52	−0.0036	0.015	0.031	−0.89	0.023
	(14.45)	(0.031)	(0.017)	(0.019)	(1.046)	(0.022)
County dummies	Yes	Yes	Yes	Yes	Yes	Yes
Constant term	64.85	0.37**	0.082	0.92***	53.69***	0.59***
	(61.77)	(0.17)	(0.12)	(0.09)	(6.04)	(0.11)
R-squared	0.1152	0.2620	0.2669	0.1025	0.2757	0.4988

Note: N = 237 villages. Figures in cells are seemingly unrelated regression coefficients. Huber heteroskedasticity-robust standard errors are in parentheses. * $p = 0.10$; ** $p = 0.05$; *** $p = 0.01$. The hypothesis that the coefficient estimates on each term are equal to zero across the six outcomes in the table is tested using SUR in the final column.

Appendix Table A5.3. *Village Governmental Provision of Public Goods and the Existence of a Temple Manager, with All Controls (SUR). Missing Data Are Multiply Imputed*

	Per Capita Investment	Existence of Paved Roads	Existence of Paved Paths	Percentage of Classrooms Usable in Rain	Newness of School	Existence of Running Water	Ho: B = 0 p-value (SUR)
Village temples							
Existence of a temple manager	49.62 (37.77)	0.11 (0.082)	0.069 (0.056)	0.11* (0.055)	0.54 (3.19)	0.12 (0.069)	0.099*
Control variables							
Distance from county town	−0.21 (0.6012)	−0.0053*** (0.0013)	−0.0027** (0.00093)	−0.0002 (0.00093)	0.067 (0.053)	−0.0011 (0.0012)	
Number of natural villages	−1.061 (3.053)	−0.0047 (0.0070)	−0.0062 (0.0048)	0.0084 (0.0047)	0.18 (0.27)	−0.0056 (0.0060)	
Village population	−0.017 (0.011)	0.000028 (0.000026)	0.000035* (0.000017)	−0.00000035 (0.000017)	−0.0011 (0.00099)	0.000012 (0.000022)	
Village terrain	−0.031 (33.71)	0.083 (0.080)	−0.024 (0.053)	−0.016 (0.052)	−1.54 (2.978)	0.0062 (0.066)	
1997 income per capita (thousands of yuan)	0.0071 (0.010)	0.000042 (0.000024)	0.000022 (0.000016)	0.0000093 (0.000016)	0.00074 (0.00098)	−0.0000020 (0.000020)	
1997 government assets (thousands of yuan)	−0.000012 (0.000028)	0.000000063 (0.000000064)	−0.000000019 (0.000000043)	−0.000000022 (0.0000000043)	0.00000077 (0.0000025)	0.00000014* (0.0000000054)	
1997 tax revenue per capita	−0.43 (0.44)	0.0012 (0.001013)	−0.0013 (0.00070)	−0.0010 (0.00070)	−0.0043 (0.039)	0.0010 (0.00086)	

Existence of village government enterprises in 1995	−10.68	0.0077	0.055	0.008	−1.14	0.051
	(22.77)	(0.053)	(0.036)	(0.035)	(2.011)	(0.044)
Existence of private enterprises in 1995	11.66	0.14*	0.12**	0.050	−4.96	0.053
	(28.69)	(0.066)	(0.045)	(0.045)	(2.55)	(0.056)
Party membership of village head	5.48	0.02	−0.038	−0.010	2.66	0.012
	(25.14)	(0.058)	(0.039)	(0.039)	(2.24)	(0.049)
Percentage of village officials in Party	31.70	0.11	0.033	0.070	1.77	0.13
	(65.18)	(0.15)	(0.10)	(0.10)	(5.78)	(0.13)
Existence of bureaucratic targets for public projects	39.77	−0.078	−0.036	0.051	1.27	−0.026
	(22.18)	(0.05)	(0.035)	(0.034)	(2.00)	(0.043)
Index of the implementation of village democratic reforms	16.87	0.0036	0.035	0.022	−1.28	0.014
	(11.39)	(0.026)	(0.018)	(0.022)	(1.25)	(0.024)
County dummies	Yes	Yes	Yes	Yes	Yes	Yes
Constant term	28.95	.382**	0.095	0.82***	49.00***	0.71***
	(58.22)	(0.13)	(0.092)	(0.090)	(5.15)	(0.11)

Note: N = 316 villages. Figures in cells are seemingly unrelated regression coefficients. Standard errors are in parentheses. * $p = 0.10$; ** $p = 0.05$; *** $p = 0.01$. The hypothesis that the coefficient estimates on each term are equal to zero across the six outcomes in the table is tested using SUR in the final column.

Appendix Table A5.4. *Village Governmental Provision of Public Goods and the Percentage of Households Participating in Temple Reconstruction, with all Controls (SUR). Missing Data Are Deleted Listwise*

	Per Capita Investment	Existence of Paved Roads	Existence of Paved Paths	Percentage of Classrooms Usable in Rain	Newness of School	Existence of Running Water	Ho: B = 0 p-value (SUR)
Village temples							
Percentage of households participating in temple reconstruction	45.94	0.039	−0.065	0.17**	−2.49	0.20	0.012**
	(123.26)	(0.11)	(0.12)	(0.058)	(4.014)	(0.12)	
Control variables							
Distance from county town	−0.33	−0.0051***	−0.0024*	0.0008	0.075	−0.00077	
	(1.044)	(0.0013)	(0.0011)	(0.0011)	(0.053)	(0.0014)	
Number of natural villages	−1.96	−0.0030	−0.0045	0.0060	0.16	−0.0040	
	(3.80)	(0.0096)	(0.0038)	(0.0032)	(0.19)	(0.0053)	
Village population	−0.023	0.000021	0.000033	0.0000055	−0.0016*	0.000018	
	(0.013)	(0.000038)	(0.000027)	(0.0000090)	(0.00065)	(0.000024)	
Village terrain	−1.55	0.15	0.026	−0.0030	−1.40	0.0065	
	(22.30)	(0.092)	(0.056)	(0.058)	(3.080)	(0.069)	
1997 income per capita (thousands of yuan)	0.042*	0.00011*	0.000065*	0.0000039	−0.00017	0.000010	
	(0.020)	(0.000042)	(0.000030)	(0.000023)	(0.0020)	(0.000045)	
1997 government assets (thousands of yuan)	−0.000027*	0.000000023	−0.000000041*	−0.000000018	0.0000012	0.00000014***	
	(0.000011)	(0.000000024)	(0.000000018)	(0.000000011)	(0.0000018)	(0.000000030)	

1997 tax revenue per capita	−0.69*	−0.00046	−0.0013*	−0.000078	0.027	0.0016
	(0.31)	(0.0014)	(0.00065)	(0.00064)	(0.048)	(0.0010)
Existence of village government enterprises in 1995	−23.88	−0.022	0.068	−0.029	−1.00	0.012
	(22.60)	(0.061)	(0.040)	(0.035)	(2.096)	(0.049)
Existence of private enterprises in 1995	8.97	0.11	0.11*	0.091*	−6.22*	0.00037
	(34.24)	(0.075)	(0.057)	(0.04)	(2.56)	(0.063)
Party membership of village head	−0.71	−0.035	−0.0046	0.017	1.03	0.015
	(30.69)	(0.069)	(0.041)	(0.048)	(2.32)	(0.055)
Percentage of village officials in Party	29.18	0.039	−0.072	−0.086	1.85	0.22
	(69.99)	(0.18)	(0.12)	(0.12)	(5.93)	(0.14)
Existence of bureaucratic targets for public projects	41.19	−0.11	−0.012	0.0741*	1.84	−0.060
	(29.60)	(0.064)	(0.041)	(0.038)	(2.23)	(0.053)
Index of the implementation of village democratic reforms	22.86	−0.0053	0.012	0.029	−1.02	0.017
	(15.33)	(0.030)	(0.018)	(0.019)	(1.055)	(0.022)
County dummies	Yes	Yes	Yes	Yes	Yes	Yes
Constant term	26.52	0.37*	0.065	.912***	53.32***	0.61***
	(68.49)	(0.17)	(0.12)	(0.087)	(6.05)	(0.15)
R-squared	0.12	0.26	0.27	0.10	0.28	0.49

Note: N = 239 villages. Figures in cells are seemingly unrelated regression coefficients. Huber heteroskedasticity-robust standard errors are in parentheses. * $p = 0.10$; ** $p = 0.05$; *** $p = 0.01$. The hypothesis that the coefficient estimates on each term are equal to zero across the six outcomes in the table is tested using SUR in the final column.

Appendix Table A5.5. *Village Governmental Provision of Public Goods and all Solidary Group Measures, with All Controls (SUR). Missing Data Are Deleted Listwise*

	Per Capita Investment	Existence of Paved Roads	Existence of Paved Paths	Percentage of Classrooms Usable in Rain	Newness of School	Existence of Running Water	H0: B=0 p-value (SUR)
Solidary groups							
Existence of a temple manager	59.40 (67.93)	0.13 (0.093)	0.12 (0.079)	0.12* (0.054)	5.24 (2.90)	0.15 (0.093)	0.0091***
Existence of an active church pastor	−65.26 (44.89)	0.26* (0.12)	−0.095 (0.087)	−0.23* (0.10)	6.37 (4.45)	0.008 (0.10)	0.03**
Existence of only one ancestral hall with spirit tablets	1.62 (83.23)	0.27** (0.10)	0.13 (0.11)	−0.011 (0.082)	−3.40 (3.13)	0.068 (0.12)	0.10*
Existence of multiple ancestral halls with spirit tablets	−64.02* (31.41)	−0.17 (0.10)	0.17 (0.10)	0.027 (0.081)	−5.24 (2.97)	−0.050 (0.10)	0.01***
Control variables							
Distance from county town	−0.50 (1.04)	−.0047*** (0.0013)	−.0024* (0.0011)	0.0052 (0.00)	0.090 (0.052)	−0.00062 (0.0014)	
Number of natural villages	−1.26 (3.31)	−0.0016 (0.0092)	−0.0011 (0.0037)	.0066* (0.0032)	0.13 (0.19)	−0.0039 (0.0055)	
Village population	−0.017 (0.0087)	0.000013 (0.000034)	0.00003 (0.000026)	0.0000077 (0.0000085)	−.0017** (0.00065)	0.000012 (0.000021)	
Village terrain	−15.91 (27.30)	0.12 (0.092)	0.032 (0.053)	−0.021 (0.054)	−1.96 (2.99)	−0.018 (0.070)	
1997 income per capita (thousands of yuan)	0.023 (0.017)	.0000886* (0.000043)	.000055* (0.000028)	−0.000010 (0.000024)	−0.00040 (0.0020)	0.0000020 (0.000046)	

1997 government assets (thousands of yuan)	−0.000014*	0.000000027	−0.000000031	−0.000000010	0.0000014	0.00000014***	
	(0.0000063)	(0.000000025)	(0.000000018)	(0.000000011)	(0.0000017)	(0.000000030)	
1997 tax revenue per capita	−0.60*	−0.00033	−.0013*	−0.00020	0.024	0.0014	
	(0.26)	(0.0014)	(0.00060)	(0.001)	(0.050)	(0.0010)	
Existence of village government enterprises in 1995	−7.46	−0.012	0.073	−0.012	−0.56	0.022	
	(20.77)	(0.059)	(0.040)	(0.035)	(2.08)	(0.050)	
Existence of private enterprises in 1995	−27.01	0.12	0.082	0.064	−7.20**	0.0038	
	(27.55)	(0.077)	(0.055)	(0.038)	(2.68)	(0.066)	
Party membership of village head	−0.93	−0.044	−0.0038	0.029	0.83	0.025	0.98
	(28.01)	(0.064)	(0.041)	(0.044)	(2.28)	(0.054)	
Percentage of village officials in Party	−2.74	0.084	−0.104	−0.098	2.50	0.25	0.50
	(60.62)	(0.17)	(0.11)	(0.11)	(5.97)	(0.14)	
Existence of bureaucratic targets for public projects	30.51	−0.095	−0.0094	.077*	1.69	−0.046	
	(30.01)	(0.063)	(0.041)	(0.037)	(2.24)	(0.054)	
Index of the implementation of village democratic reforms	18.88	0.0045	0.017	0.032	−0.97	0.026	0.41
	(15.16)	(0.029)	(0.017)	(0.020)	(1.04)	(0.023)	
County dummies	Yes	Yes	Yes	Yes	Yes	Yes	
Constant term	68.35	0.35*	0.088	0.93***	53.30***	0.59***	
	(62.53)	(0.16)	(0.11)	(0.082)	(5.95)	(0.15)	
R-squared	0.13	0.30	0.29	0.14	0.29	0.50	

Note: N = 237 villages. Figures in cells are seemingly unrelated regression coefficients. Huber heteroskedasticity-robust standard errors are in parentheses. * p = 0.10; ** p = 0.05; *** p = 0.01. The hypothesis that the coefficient estimates on each term are equal to zero across the six outcomes in the table is tested using SUR in the final column.

Appendix Table A5.6. *Village Governmental Provision of Public Goods and All Solidary Group Measures, with All Controls (SUR). Missing Data Are Multiply Imputed*

	Per Capita Investment	Existence of Paved Roads	Existence of Paved Paths	Percentage of Classrooms Usable in Rain	Newness of School	Existence of Running Water	H0: B = 0 p-value (SUR)
Solidary groups							
Existence of a temple manager	45.70	0.091	0.069	0.11*	0.30	0.12	0.096*
	(37.28)	(0.080)	(0.055)	(0.053)	(3.188)	(0.070)	
Existence of an active church pastor	−67.83	0.12	−0.08	−0.27***	4.19	−0.00021	0.0008***
	(43.07)	(0.099)	(0.068)	(0.066)	(3.85)	(0.085)	
Existence of one and only one ancestral hall with spirit tablets	74.64	0.25*	0.11	−0.02	−0.60	0.019	0.16
	(45.82)	(0.11)	(0.072)	(0.070)	(4.15)	(0.090)	
Existence of multiple ancestral halls with spirit tablets	−44.69	−0.15	0.14*	0.017	−6.36	−0.016	0.08*
	(44.12)	(0.10)	(0.069)	(0.067)	(3.93)	(0.087)	
Control variables							
Distance from county town	−0.28	−0.0053***	−0.0028**	−0.0004	0.070	−0.0011	
	(0.60)	(0.0014)	(0.00093)	(0.00091)	(0.053)	(0.0012)	
Number of natural villages	−0.97	−0.0039	−0.0045	0.0082	0.14	−0.0056	
	(3.06)	(0.0070)	(0.0048)	(0.0047)	(0.27)	(0.0061)	
Village population	−0.016	0.000023	0.000033	0.0000039	−0.0011	0.000012	
	(0.011)	(0.000025)	(0.000017)	(0.000017)	(0.00099)	(0.000022)	
Village terrain	−2.55	0.074	−0.016	−0.014	−1.92	0.005	
	(33.41)	(0.077)	(0.052)	(0.051)	(2.97)	(0.066)	
1997 income per capita (thousands of yuan)	0.0052	0.000039	0.000022	0.0000069	0.00072	−0.0000024	
	(0.010)	(0.000023)	(0.000016)	(0.000016)	(0.00097)	(0.000020)	

1997 government assets (thousands of yuan)	−0.000012	0.000000060	−0.000000019	−0.000000020	0.00000072	0.00000014*	
	(0.000027)	(0.000000063)	(0.000000043)	(0.000000042)	(0.0000025)	(0.000000054)	
1997 tax revenue per capita	−0.40	0.0012	−0.0012	−0.0010	−0.0068	0.0010	
	(0.43)	(0.0010)	(0.00069)	(0.00068)	(0.039)	(0.00086)	
Existence of village government enterprises in 1995	−9.60	0.0066	0.053	0.011	−1.09	0.052	
	(22.53)	(0.052)	(0.035)	(0.035)	(2.00)	(0.045)	
Existence of private enterprises in 1995	10.74	0.16*	0.12**	0.032	−4.73	0.054	
	(28.53)	(0.066)	(0.045)	(0.044)	(2.55)	(0.057)	
Party membership of village head	7.70	0.015	−0.036	−0.00019	2.54	0.012	0.85
	(24.91)	(0.057)	(0.039)	(0.038)	(2.23)	(0.049)	
Percentage of village officials in Party	31.22	0.15	0.017	0.037	2.75	0.13	0.86
	(64.79)	(0.15)	(0.10)	(0.10)	(5.78)	(0.13)	
Existence of bureaucratic targets for public projects	42.68	−0.076	−0.031	0.056	1.13	−0.026	
	(22.01)	(0.050)	(0.034)	(0.034)	(1.95)	(0.04)	
Index of the implementation of village democratic reforms	19.31	0.010	0.037*	0.023	−1.30	0.014	0.088*
	(11.29)	(0.026)	(0.018)	(0.021)	(1.26)	(0.024)	
County dummies	Yes	Yes	Yes	Yes	Yes	Yes	
Constant term	34.71	0.37**	0.10	0.85***	48.51***	0.71***	
	(57.70)	(0.13)	(0.092)	(0.088)	(5.14)	(0.11)	

Note: N = 316 villages. Figures in cells are seemingly unrelated regression coefficients. Standard errors are in parentheses. * $p = 0.10$; ** $p = 0.05$; *** $p = 0.01$. The hypothesis that the coefficient estimates on each term are equal to zero across the six outcomes in the table is tested using SUR in the final column.

Appendix Table A5.7. *Village Governmental Provision of Public Goods and the Existence of a Village Church, with All Controls (SUR). Missing Data Are Deleted Listwise*

	Per Capita Investment	Existence of Paved Roads	Existence of Paved Paths	Percentage of Classrooms Usable in Rain	Newness of School	Existence of Running Water	Ho: B = 0 p-value (SUR)
Village churches							
Existence of an active church pastor	−83.89	0.23*	−0.074	−0.23*	4.79	−0.0025	0.062*
	(44.40)	(0.11)	(0.088)	(0.11)	(4.46)	(0.10)	
Control variables							
Distance from county town	−0.48	−0.0048***	−0.0025*	0.00037	0.083	−0.00080	
	(1.11)	(0.0014)	(0.0011)	(0.0010)	(0.052)	(0.0014)	
Number of natural villages	−2.062	−0.0032	−0.0048	0.0057	0.16	−0.0043	
	(3.87)	(0.0096)	(0.0039)	(0.0031)	(0.18)	(0.0053)	
Village population	−0.021	0.000017	0.000032	0.0000096	−0.0017**	0.000019	
	(0.012)	(0.000036)	(0.000027)	(0.0000085)	(0.00063)	(0.000024)	
Village terrain	−3.97	0.15	0.021	−0.012	−1.40	−0.0035	
	(24.77)	(0.091)	(0.056)	(0.052)	(3.011)	(0.069)	
1997 income per capita (thousands of yuan)	0.039*	0.00012**	0.000076*	−0.0000041	0.00021	0.000014	
	(0.019)	(0.000041)	(0.000032)	(0.000022)	(0.0019)	(0.000045)	
1997 government assets (thousands of yuan)	−0.000026*	0.000000018	−0.000000043*	−0.000000016	0.0000011	0.00000014***	
	(0.000011)	(0.000000024)	(0.000000018)	(0.000000011)	(0.0000018)	(0.000000030)	
1997 tax revenue per capita	−0.72*	−0.00040	−0.0014*	−0.00015	0.028	0.0016	
	(0.32)	(0.0014)	(0.00066)	(0.00060)	(0.048)	(0.0010)	

Existence of village government enterprises in 1995	−20.33	−0.035	0.066	−0.021	−1.36	0.0094
	(20.98)	(0.060)	(0.040)	(0.035)	(2.070)	(0.049)
Existence of private enterprises in 1995	3.71	0.13	0.093	0.085*	−5.95*	0.01
	(33.068)	(0.075)	(0.057)	(0.039)	(2.50)	(0.063)
Percentage of village officials in Party	2.75	−0.036	−0.0027	0.029	0.92	0.025
	(28.82)	(0.067)	(0.042)	(0.044)	(2.29)	(0.055)
Existence of bureaucratic targets for public projects	26.54	0.041	−0.059	−0.095	2.16	0.21
	(73.87)	(0.18)	(0.12)	(0.11)	(5.95)	(0.14)
Index of implementation of village democratic reforms	42.27	−0.12*	−0.019	0.074*	1.55	−0.069
	(31.55)	(0.063)	(0.043)	(0.037)	(2.21)	(0.052)
Party membership of village head	23.39	−0.0060	0.020	0.029	−0.97	0.016
	(14.91)	(0.029)	(0.018)	(0.019)	(1.048)	(0.022)
County dummies	Yes	Yes	Yes	Yes	Yes	Yes
Constant term	32.22	0.35*	0.053	0.93***	52.79***	0.62***
	(73.26)	(0.16)	(0.12)	(0.082)	(5.99)	(0.15)
R-squared	0.13	0.27	0.27	0.12	0.28	0.49

Note: N = 241 villages. Figures in cells are seemingly unrelated regression coefficients. Huber heteroskedasticity-robust standard errors are in parentheses. * $p = 0.10$; ** $p = 0.05$; *** $p = 0.01$. The hypothesis that the coefficient estimates on each term are equal to zero across the six outcomes in the table is tested using SUR in the final column.

Appendix Table A5.8. *Village Governmental Provision of Public Goods and the Existence of a Village Church (SUR). Missing Data Are Multiply Imputed*

	Per Capita Investment	Existence of Paved Roads	Existence of Paved Paths	Percentage of Classrooms Usable in Rain	Newness of School	Existence of Running Water	Ho: B = 0 p-value (SUR)
Village churches							
Existence of an active church pastor	−69.58	0.12	−0.052	−0.26***	3.17	0.0018	
	(42.83)	(0.099)	(0.067)	(0.065)	(3.81)	(0.084)	
Control variables							
Distance from county town	−0.26	−0.0052***	−0.0027**	−0.00044	0.069	−0.0012	
	(0.60)	(0.0014)	(0.00094)	(0.00092)	(0.053)	(0.0012)	
Number of natural villages	−1.30	−0.0049	−0.0065	0.0078	0.19	−0.006	
	(3.048)	(0.0071)	(0.0048)	(0.0047)	(0.27)	(0.0060)	
Village population	−0.014	0.000029	0.000038*	0.0000074	−0.0011	0.000016	
	(0.011)	(0.000026)	(0.000017)	(0.000017)	(0.00098)	(0.000022)	
Village terrain	5.20	0.094	−0.017	−0.0043	−1.51	0.018	
	(33.48)	(0.078)	(0.053)	(0.051)	(2.96)	(0.066)	
1997 income per capita (thousands of yuan)	0.0067	0.000044	0.000022	0.0000072	0.00077	−0.0000020	
	(0.010)	(0.000024)	(0.000016)	(0.000016)	(0.00098)	(0.000020)	
1997 government assets (thousands of yuan)	−0.000010	0.000000059	−0.000000021	−0.000000023	0.00000073	0.00000013*	
	(0.000028)	(0.000000064)	(0.000000043)	(0.000000043)	(0.0000025)	(0.000000054)	
1997 tax revenue per capita	−0.40	0.0012	−0.0012	−0.00094	−0.0049	0.00099	
	(0.44)	(0.0010)	(0.00070)	(0.00069)	(0.039)	(0.00086)	

Existence of village government enterprises in 1995	−11.00 (22.71)	0.0013 (0.052)	0.053 (0.036)	0.0066 (0.035)	−1.20 (2.0034)	0.046 (0.045)
Existence of private enterprises in 1995	13.43 (28.46)	0.16* (0.066)	0.13** (0.045)	0.047 (0.044)	−4.71 (2.54)	0.067 (0.056)
Party membership of village head	7.87 (25.14)	0.016 (0.058)	−0.036 (0.039)	−0.00078 (0.038)	2.54 (2.24)	0.011 (0.049)
Percentage of village officials in Party	24.4 (65.31)	0.13 (0.15)	0.028 (0.10)	0.041 (0.10)	2.14 (5.79)	0.13 (0.13)
Existence of bureaucratic targets for public projects	40.85 (22.18)	−0.082 (0.051)	−0.035 (0.035)	0.055 (0.034)	1.20 (1.96)	−0.028 (0.043)
Index of implementation of village democratic reforms	16.05 (11.42)	0.00018 (0.026)	0.033 (0.018)	0.021 (0.020)	−1.32 (1.25)	0.011 (0.023)
County dummy	yes	yes	yes	yes	yes	yes
Constant term	37.57 (58.34)	0.37** (0.14)	0.10 (0.093)	0.85*** (0.089)	48.66*** (5.16)	0.71*** (0.11)

Note: N = 316 villages. Figures in cells are seemingly unrelated regression coefficients. Standard errors are in parentheses. * p = 0.10; ** p = 0.05; *** p = 0.01. The hypothesis that the coefficient estimates on each term are equal to zero across the six outcomes in the table is tested using SUR in the final column.

Appendix Table A5.9. *Village Governmental Provision of Public Goods and the Existence of Church Reconstruction, with All Controls (SUR). Missing Data Are Multiply Imputed*

	Per Capita Investment	Existence of Paved Roads	Existence of Paved Paths	Percentage of Classrooms Usable in Rain	Newness of School	Existence of Running Water	Ho: B = 0 p-value (SUR)
Village churches							
Existence of church reconstruction	−82.33	0.28*	−0.13	−0.10	4.22	0.16	0.012**
	(51.89)	(0.12)	(0.085)	(0.10)	(5.71)	(0.13)	
Control variables							
Distance from county town	−0.27	−0.0053***	−0.0028**	−0.00048	0.067	−0.0012	
	(0.59)	(0.0014)	(0.00096)	(0.00092)	(0.052)	(0.0012)	
Number of natural villages	−1.20	−0.0032	−0.0044	0.0078	0.14	−0.0056	
	(3.067)	(0.0070)	(0.0049)	(0.0047)	(0.27)	(0.0061)	
Village population	−0.016	0.000023	0.000035*	0.0000092	−0.0010	0.000015	
	(0.011)	(0.000025)	(0.000017)	(0.000017)	(0.00096)	(0.000022)	
Village terrain	0.0052	0.000038	0.000021	0.0000071	0.00077	−0.0000017	
	(0.010)	(0.000023)	(0.000016)	(0.000016)	(0.00089)	(0.000020)	
1997 income per capita (thousands of yuan)	−0.000010	0.000000059	−0.000000015	−0.000000017	0.00000093	0.00000013*	
	(0.000028)	(0.000000063)	(0.000000043)	(0.000000045)	(0.0000024)	(0.000000054)	
1997 government assets (thousands of yuan)	−0.40	0.0011	−0.0011	−0.00078	−0.0057	0.00099	
	(0.43)	(0.0010)	(0.00070)	(0.00068)	(0.038)	(0.00086)	
1997 tax revenue per capita	−7.93	−0.0013	0.056	0.0026	−1.02	0.043	
	(22.79)	(0.051)	(0.037)	(0.036)	(1.00)	(0.045)	
Existence of village government enterprises in 1995	12.37	0.17**	0.13**	0.036	−3.84	0.077	
	(29.15)	(0.066)	(0.045)	(0.045)	(2.57)	(0.056)	

Existence of private enterprises in 1995	−2.35	0.068	−0.012	0.0017	−2.029	0.012
	(33.77)	(0.077)	(0.053)	(0.052)	(2.94)	(0.066)
Party membership of village head	8.20	0.016	−0.037	−0.013	2.74	0.011
	(24.90)	(0.056)	(0.039)	(0.041)	(2.19)	(0.049)
Percentage of village officials in Party	49.08	0.12	0.024	0.076	0.48	0.12
	(63.00)	(0.15)	(0.11)	(0.11)	(5.76)	(0.13)
Existence of bureaucratic targets for public projects	41.64	−0.083	−0.027	0.054	0.81	−0.031
	(22.03)	(0.050)	(0.035)	(0.034)	(1.93)	(0.044)
Index of the implementation of village democratic reforms	18.31	0.00011	0.030	0.0060	−1.40	0.0091
	(11.25)	(0.026)	(0.017)	(0.018)	(1.0016)	(0.023)
Existence of a temple manager	26.71	0.082	0.050	−0.21*	2.24	−0.069
	(40.72)	(0.080)	(0.056)	(0.083)	(4.76)	(0.11)
Existence of only one ancestral hall with spirit tablets	78.16	0.24*	0.13	−0.0082	−1.39	0.018
	(46.09)	(0.11)	(0.073)	(0.071)	(4.047)	(0.091)
Existence of multiple ancestral halls with spirit tablets	−56.73	−0.13	0.13	0.0073	−6.01	−0.011
	(43.40)	(0.099)	(0.069)	(0.068)	(3.88)	(0.088)
County dummies	yes	yes	yes	yes	yes	yes
Constant term	19.10	0.40**	0.093	0.83***	49.86***	0.73***
	(57.76)	(0.13)	(0.095)	(0.092)	(5.17)	(0.12)

Note: N = 316 villages. Figures in cells are seemingly unrelated regression coefficients. Standard errors are in parentheses. * $p = 0.10$; ** $p = 0.05$; *** $p = 0.01$. The hypothesis that the coefficient estimates on each term are equal to zero across the six outcomes in the table is tested using SUR in the final column.

Appendix Table A5.10. *Village Governmental Provision of Public Goods and Interaction between Temple and Church Groups (SUR). Missing Data Are Deleted Listwise*

	Per Capita Investment	Existence of Paved Roads	Existence of Paved Paths	Percentage of Classrooms Usable in Rain	Newness of School	Existence of Running Water	Ho: B = 0 p-value (SUR)
Temple and church variables							
Existence of a temple manager	78.32	0.15	0.16	0.081	5.31	0.17	0.017**
	(75.92)	(0.096)	(0.083)	(0.050)	(3.062)	(0.096)	
Existence of an active church pastor	−28.32	0.30*	−0.019	−0.31**	6.51	0.046	0.053*
	(38.56)	(0.12)	(0.097)	(0.12)	(5.49)	(0.10)	
Interaction of temple manager and church pastor variables	−174.86	−0.21	−0.36*	0.39**	−0.64	−0.18	0.0012***
	(100.17)	(0.31)	(0.15)	(0.13)	(7.20)	(0.28)	
Control variables							
Distance from county town	−0.50	−0.0047***	−0.0024*	0.00052	0.090	−0.00060	
	(1.036)	(0.0013)	(0.0011)	(0.00099)	(0.053)	(0.0014)	
Number of natural villages	−1.51	−0.0019	−0.0016	0.0072*	0.13	−0.0042	
	(3.38)	(0.0093)	(0.0037)	(0.0033)	(0.19)	(0.0055)	
Village population	−0.017	0.000015	0.000028	0.0000097	−0.0017**	0.000011	
	(0.0092)	(0.000034)	(0.000025)	(0.0000084)	(0.00065)	(0.000021)	
Village terrain	−20.17	0.11	0.023	−0.012	−1.97	−0.023	
	(28.59)	(0.093)	(0.052)	(0.053)	(3.016)	(0.070)	
1997 income per capita (thousands of yuan)	0.022	0.000086*	0.000051	−0.0000083	−0.00040	0.000000041	
	(0.017)	(0.000043)	(0.000028)	(0.000023)	(0.0020)	(0.000047)	
1997 government assets (thousands of yuan)	−0.000010	0.000000029	−0.000000028	−0.000000015	0.0000014	0.00000014***	
	(0.0000065)	(0.000000025)	(0.000000017)	(0.000000011)	(0.0000017)	(0.000000030)	
1997 tax revenue per capita	−0.58*	−0.00030	−0.0012*	−0.00024	0.024	0.0015	
	(0.26)	(0.0014)	(0.00063)	(0.00063)	(0.050)	(0.0010)	

Existence of village government enterprises in 1995	−6.32	−0.010	0.075	−0.014	−0.56	0.023
	(20.84)	(0.059)	(0.039)	(0.035)	(2.08)	(0.050)
Existence of private enterprises in 1995	−32.38	0.11	0.071	0.076*	−7.22**	−0.0018
	(29.41)	(0.077)	(0.054)	(0.038)	(2.71)	(0.067)
Party membership of village head	−1.41	−0.045	−0.0047	0.030	0.83	0.024
	(27.94)	(0.064)	(0.041)	(0.042)	(2.28)	(0.054)
Percentage of village officials in Party	−0.026	0.087	−0.098	−0.10	2.51	0.25
	(60.24)	(0.17)	(0.11)	(0.11)	(5.96)	(0.14)
Existence of bureaucratic targets for public projects	28.28	−0.098	−0.014	0.082*	1.68	−0.048
	(29.50)	(0.063)	(0.041)	(0.037)	(2.25)	(0.054)
Index of implementation of village democratic reforms	19.84	0.0056	0.019	0.029	−0.97	0.027
	(15.30)	(0.029)	(0.016)	(0.019)	(1.035)	(0.023)
Existence of only one ancestral hall with spirit tablets	1.63	0.27**	0.13	−0.011	−3.40	0.068
	(82.53)	(0.10)	(0.11)	(0.078)	(3.14)	(0.12)
Existence of multiple ancestral halls with spirit tablets	−64.77*	−0.17	0.17	0.028	−5.25	−0.047
	(31.41)	(0.096)	(0.10)	(0.081)	(2.97)	(0.10)
County dummies	Yes	Yes	Yes	Yes	Yes	Yes
Constant term	72.22	0.35*	0.096	0.92***	53.32***	0.60***
	(63.25)	(0.16)	(0.12)	(0.081)	(5.98)	(0.15)
R-squared	0.14	0.30	0.30	0.16	0.29	0.50

Note: N = 237 villages. Figures in cells are seemingly unrelated regression coefficients. Huber heteroskedasticity-robust standard errors are in parentheses. * p = 0.10; ** p = 0.05; *** p = 0.01. The hypothesis that the coefficient estimates on each term are equal to zero across the six outcomes in the table is tested using SUR in the final column.

Appendix Table A6.1. *Village Governmental Provision of Public Goods and Village Lineage Groups, with All Controls (SUR). Missing Data Are Deleted Listwise*

	Per Capita Investment	Existence of Paved Roads	Existence of Paved Paths	Percentage of Classrooms Usable in Rain	Newness of School	Existence of Running Water	Ho: B = 0 p-value (SUR)
Village lineages							
Existence of one or more ancestral halls with spirit tablets	−10.21	0.075	0.18*	−0.0058	−2.70	0.0037	0.32
	(49.13)	(0.083)	(0.080)	(0.060)	(2.49)	(0.085)	
Control variables							
Distance from county town	−0.35	−0.0051***	−0.0023*	0.00072	0.076	−0.0008	
	(1.099)	(0.0014)	(0.0011)	(0.0011)	(0.053)	(0.0014)	
Number of natural villages	−2.23	−0.002	−0.0019	0.0056	0.12	−0.0043	
	(3.71)	(0.0094)	(0.0038)	(0.0030)	(0.19)	(0.0054)	
Village population	−0.022	0.000018	0.000027	0.0000075	−0.0016*	0.000019	
	(0.012)	(0.000036)	(0.000024)	(0.0000091)	(0.00064)	(0.000024)	
Village terrain	−4.024	0.15	0.035	−0.011	−1.64	−0.0032	
	(26.14)	(0.092)	(0.055)	(0.057)	(3.022)	(0.070)	
1997 income per capita (thousands of yuan)	0.043*	0.00011**	0.000080**	0.0000067	0.000020	0.000014	
	(0.019)	(0.000041)	(0.000031)	(0.000023)	(0.0019)	(0.000044)	
1997 government assets (thousands of yuan)	−0.000027*	0.000000022	−0.000000043*	−0.000000019	0.0000012	0.00000014***	
	(0.000011)	(0.00000024)	(0.000000018)	(0.000000011)	(0.0000018)	(0.000000030)	
1997 tax revenue per capita	−0.70*	−0.0004	−0.0012	−0.000078	0.024	0.0016	
	(0.31)	(0.0014)	(0.00064)	(0.00062)	(0.049)	(0.0010)	

Existence of village government enterprises in 1995	−22.34 (21.43)	−0.032 (0.061)	0.056 (0.040)	−0.028 (0.035)	−1.096 (2.073)	0.0091 (0.050)
Existence of private enterprises in 1995	7.29 (33.50)	0.12 (0.074)	0.11 (0.055)	0.096* (0.040)	−6.32* (2.52)	0.011 (0.063)
Percentage of village officials in Party	27.61 (69.64)	0.032 (0.18)	−0.084 (0.12)	−0.095 (0.12)	2.55 (5.93)	0.21 (0.14)
Existence of bureaucratic targets for public projects	39.99 (31.35)	−0.12 (0.063)	−0.015 (0.041)	0.069 (0.037)	1.57 (2.20)	−0.069 (0.052)
Index of implementation of village democratic reforms	22.62 (14.91)	−0.0033 (0.029)	0.021 (0.017)	0.027 (0.020)	−0.96 (1.036)	0.016 (0.022)
Party membership of village head	1.0058 (28.74)	−0.031 (0.069)	−0.0044 (0.041)	0.024 (0.047)	1.017 (2.30)	0.025 (0.055)
County dummies	Yes	Yes	Yes	Yes	Yes	Yes
Constant term	26.69 (71.67)	0.37* (0.16)	0.053 (0.12)	0.92*** (0.086)	53.013*** (6.021)	0.62*** (0.15)
R-squared	0.12	0.26	0.29	0.08	0.28	0.49

Note: N = 241 villages. Figures in cells are seemingly unrelated regression coefficients. Huber heteroskedasticity-robust standard errors are in parentheses. * p = 0.10; ** p = 0.05; *** p = 0.01. The hypothesis that the coefficient estimates on each term are equal to zero across the six outcomes in the table is tested using SUR in the final column.

Appendix Table A6.2. *Village Governmental Provision of Public Goods and Different Types of Lineage Groups (SUR). Missing Data Are Deleted Listwise*

	Per Capita Investment	Existence of Paved Roads	Existence of Paved Paths	Percentage of Classrooms Usable in Rain	Newness of School	Existence of Running Water	Ho: B = 0 p-value (SUR)
Village lineages							
Existence of only one ancestral hall with spirit tablets	65.54	0.31**	0.19	−0.012	−1.096	0.045	0.037**
	(95.00)	(0.096)	(0.11)	(0.084)	(3.16)	(0.12)	
Existence of multiple ancestral halls with spirit tablets	−78.54*	−0.13	0.17	−0.00054	−4.21	−0.034	0.035**
	(33.090)	(0.10)	(0.10)	(0.075)	(3.12)	(0.10)	
Control variables							
Distance from county town	−0.38	−0.0052***	−0.0024*	0.00072	0.076	−0.00090	
	(1.092)	(0.0013)	(0.0012)	(0.0011)	(0.053)	(0.0014)	
Number of natural villages	−2.16	−0.0018	−0.0019	0.0056	0.12	−0.0043	
	(3.70)	(0.0092)	(0.0038)	(0.0030)	(0.19)	(0.0053)	
Village population	−0.023	0.000014	0.000027	0.0000075	−0.0017**	0.000018	
	(0.012)	(0.000035)	(0.000024)	(0.0000089)	(0.00063)	(0.000024)	
Village terrain	−9.57	0.13	0.034	−0.010	−1.76	−0.0062	
	(26.58)	(0.091)	(0.054)	(0.057)	(3.02)	(0.070)	
1997 income per capita (thousands of yuan)	0.036	0.000089*	0.000078*	0.0000073	−0.00020	0.000010	
	(0.020)	(0.000042)	(0.000031)	(0.000024)	(0.0020)	(0.000045)	
1997 government assets (thousands of yuan)	−0.000026*	0.000000025	−0.000000043*	−0.000000020	0.0000012	0.00000014***	
	(0.000011)	(0.000000024)	(0.000000018)	(0.000000011)	(0.0000018)	(0.000000030)	

1997 tax revenue per capita	−0.68*	−0.00040	−0.0012	−0.000080	0.025	0.0016
	(0.31)	(0.0014)	(0.00064)	(0.00062)	(0.048)	(0.0010)
Existence of village government enterprises in 1995	−19.76	−0.024	0.056	−0.028	−1.04	0.011
	(21.35)	(0.060)	(0.040)	(0.035)	(2.065)	(0.049)
Existence of private enterprises in 1995	12.10	0.13	0.11	0.095*	−6.21*	0.013
	(34.17)	(0.074)	(0.054)	(0.040)	(2.51)	(0.065)
Percentage of village officials in Party	−0.39	−0.035	−0.0046	0.025	0.99	0.024
	(28.76)	(0.066)	(0.041)	(0.047)	(2.31)	(0.055)
Existence of bureaucratic targets for public projects	41.46	0.074	−0.082	−0.096	2.85	0.21
	(72.41)	(0.18)	(0.11)	(0.12)	(5.94)	(0.14)
Index of the implementation of village democratic reforms	45.86	−0.099	−0.014	0.068	1.70	−0.066
	(33.10)	(0.063)	(0.041)	(0.037)	(2.19)	(0.053)
Party membership of village head	24.85	0.0035	0.021	0.027	−0.92	0.017
	(15.47)	(0.028)	(0.017)	(0.020)	(1.047)	(0.022)
County dummies	Yes	Yes	Yes	Yes	Yes	Yes
Constant term	29.93	0.38*	0.054	0.92***	53.083***	0.62***
	(70.78)	(0.16)	(0.12)	(0.087)	(6.023)	(0.15)
R-squared	0.14	0.29	0.29	0.084	0.28	0.49

Note: N = 241 villages. Figures in cells are seemingly unrelated regression coefficients. Huber heteroskedasticity-robust standard errors are in parentheses. * p = 0.10; ** p = 0.05; *** p = 0.01. The hypothesis that the coefficient estimates on each term are equal to zero across the six outcomes in the table is tested using SUR in the final column.

Appendix Table A6.3. *Village Governmental Provision of Public Goods and Different Types of Lineage Groups (SUR). Missing Data Are Multiply Imputed*

	Per Capita Investment	Existence of Paved Roads	Existence of Paved Paths	Percentage of Classrooms Usable in Rain	Newness of School	Existence of Running Water	Ho: B = 0 p-value (SUR)
Village lineages							
Existence of only one ancestral hall with spirit tablets	71.58	0.27**	0.11	−0.034	−0.17	0.028	0.13
	(45.88)	(0.10)	(0.072)	(0.072)	(4.12)	(0.090)	
Existence of multiple ancestral halls with spirit tablets	−58.067	−0.13	0.12*	−0.033	−5.63	−0.019	0.11
	(43.72)	(0.10)	(0.068)	(0.068)	(3.88)	(0.086)	
Control variables							
Distance from county town	−0.24	−0.0054***	−0.0027**	−0.00025	0.067	−0.0012	
	(0.60)	(0.0014)	(0.00093)	(0.00094)	(0.053)	(0.0012)	
Number of natural villages	−1.16	−0.0041	−0.0048	0.0076	0.14	−0.006	
	(3.074)	(0.0071)	(0.0048)	(0.0048)	(0.28)	(0.0061)	
Village population	−0.016	0.000028	0.000034*	0.000004	−0.001	0.000016	
	(0.011)	(0.000025)	(0.000017)	(0.000017)	(0.00098)	(0.000022)	
Village terrain	0.73	0.084	−0.011	−0.0076	−1.83	0.016	
	(33.44)	(0.077)	(0.052)	(0.052)	(2.96)	(0.066)	
1997 income per capita (thousands of yuan)	0.006	0.000038	0.000023	0.0000097	0.00068	−0.000002	
	(0.010)	(0.000023)	(0.000016)	(0.000016)	(0.00097)	(0.000020)	
1997 government assets (thousands of yuan)	−0.000014	0.000000058	−0.000000022	−0.000000025	0.00000075	0.00000013*	
	(0.000028)	(0.000000063)	(0.000000043)	(0.000000044)	(0.0000024)	(0.000000054)	

1997 tax revenue per capita	−0.41	0.0012	−0.0012	−0.001	−0.0055	0.00099
	(0.44)	(0.0010)	(0.00069)	(0.00070)	(0.039)	(0.00086)
Existence of village government enterprises in 1995	−12.23	0.0037	0.049	0.0041	−1.062	0.046
	(22.62)	(0.052)	(0.035)	(0.036)	(1.0)	(0.045)
Existence of private enterprises in 1995	20.28	0.16*	0.14**	0.061	−4.93	0.068
	(28.27)	(0.065)	(0.044)	(0.045)	(2.53)	(0.056)
Party membership of village head	5.16	0.019	−0.039	−0.0099	2.68	0.011
	(25.0015)	(0.057)	(0.039)	(0.039)	(2.23)	(0.049)
Percentage of village officials in Party	40.53	0.14	0.029	0.072	2.23	0.14
	(65.012)	(0.15)	(0.10)	(0.10)	(5.78)	(0.13)
Existence of bureaucratic targets for public projects	40.67	−0.073	−0.033	0.049	1.23	−0.027
	(22.14)	(0.050)	(0.034)	(0.034)	(1.95)	(0.043)
Index of implementation of village democratic reforms	17.76	0.0084	0.035	0.019	−1.27	0.012
	(11.34)	(0.026)	(0.018)	(0.022)	(1.24)	(0.024)
County dummies	Yes	Yes	Yes	Yes	Yes	Yes
Constant term	29.21	0.38**	0.096	0.82***	48.95***	0.71***
	(57.94)	(0.13)	(0.092)	(0.091)	(5.13)	(0.11)

Note: N = 316 villages. Figures in cells are seemingly unrelated regression coefficients. Standard errors are in parentheses. * p = 0.10; ** p = 0.05; *** p = 0.01. The hypothesis that the coefficient estimates on each term are equal to zero across the six outcomes in the table is tested using SUR in the final column.

Appendix Table A6.4. *Village Governmental Provision of Public Goods and Interaction between Villagewide Lineage Groups and Village Temple Groups (SUR), with all Controls. Missing Data Are Multiply Imputed*

	Per Capita Investment	Existence of Paved Roads	Existence of Paved Paths	Percentage of Classrooms Usable in Rain	Newness of School	Existence of Running Water	Ho: B = 0 p-value (SUR)
Solidary group measures							
Existence of only one ancestral hall with spirit tablets	32.85	0.10	0.068	−0.093	−3.19	0.14	0.77
	(70.53)	(0.14)	(0.10)	(0.095)	(5.75)	(0.13)	
Existence of a temple manager	31.36	0.037	0.053	0.087	−0.62	0.16*	0.26
	(37.86)	(0.088)	(0.059)	(0.058)	(3.45)	(0.075)	
Interaction of only one ancestral hall and temple manager variables	90.86	0.34	0.10	0.17	5.69	−0.26	
	(120.33)	(0.21)	(0.15)	(0.14)	(8.35)	(0.19)	0.22
Existence of multiple ancestral halls with spirit tablets	−47.039	−0.16	0.13	0.012	−6.52	−0.0086	
	(44.016)	(0.10)	(0.069)	(0.067)	(3.93)	(0.087)	
Existence of active church pastor	−62.31	0.14	−0.075	−0.25***	4.54	−0.016	
	(43.68)	(0.099)	(0.068)	(0.066)	(3.89)	(0.086)	
Control variables							
Distance from county town	−0.28	−0.0053***	−0.0028**	−0.00042	0.070	−0.0011	
	(0.59)	(0.0014)	(0.00093)	(0.00091)	(0.053)	(0.0012)	
Number of natural villages	−1.03	−0.0042	−0.0046	0.0080	0.13	−0.0054	
	(3.049)	(0.0070)	(0.0048)	(0.0047)	(0.27)	(0.0060)	
Village population	−0.016	0.000023	0.000033	0.0000038	−0.0011	0.000012	
	(0.011)	(0.000025)	(0.000017)	(0.000017)	(0.00098)	(0.000022)	

Village terrain	−4.71	0.066	−0.018	−0.018	−2.047	0.011
	(33.51)	(0.077)	(0.053)	(0.051)	(2.97)	(0.066)
1997 income per capita (thousands of yuan)	0.0053	0.000039	0.000022	0.0000069	0.00072	0.0000024
	(0.010)	(0.000023)	(0.000016)	(0.000016)	(0.00097)	(0.000020)
1997 government assets (thousands of yuan)	−0.000012	0.000000061	−0.000000019	−0.000000019	0.00000075	0.00000013*
	(0.000027)	(0.000000063)	(0.000000043)	(0.000000042)	(0.0000024)	(0.000000054)
1997 tax revenue per capita	−0.41	0.0012	−0.0012	−0.00098	−0.0072	0.00098
	(0.43)	(0.00099)	(0.00069)	(0.00068)	(0.039)	(0.00086)
Existence of village government enterprises in 1995	−10.30	0.0038	0.052	0.010	−1.14	0.05
	(22.47)	(0.051)	(0.035)	(0.035)	(2.0034)	(0.044)
Existence of private enterprises in 1995	9.29	0.15*	0.12**	0.030	−4.80	0.057
	(28.57)	(0.065)	(0.045)	(0.044)	(2.55)	(0.056)
Party membership of village head	10.94	0.027	−0.033	0.0058	2.74	0.0026
	(25.19)	(0.057)	(0.039)	(0.038)	(2.26)	(0.049)
Percentage of village officials in Party	31.86	0.16	0.018	0.039	2.82	0.13
	(64.68)	(0.15)	(0.10)	(0.10)	(5.78)	(0.13)
Existence of bureaucratic targets for public projects	41.41	−0.080	−0.032	0.054	1.063	−0.023
	(21.99)	(0.050)	(0.035)	(0.034)	(1.95)	(0.043)
Index of implementation of village democratic reforms	18.18	0.0057	0.036*	0.021	−1.36	0.017
	(11.48)	(0.026)	(0.018)	(0.021)	(1.27)	(0.024)
Constant term	35.00	0.37**	0.10	0.85***	48.58***	0.70***
	(57.60)	(0.13)	(0.092)	(0.088)	(5.14)	(0.11)

Note: N = 316 villages. Figures in cells are seemingly unrelated regression coefficients. Standard errors are in parentheses. * $p = 0.10$; ** $p = 0.05$; *** $p = 0.01$. The hypothesis that the coefficient estimates on each term are equal to zero across the six outcomes in the table is tested using SUR in the final column.

Appendix Table A7.1. *Village Governmental Provision of Public Goods and the Additive Score of Implementation of Village Democratic Institutions (SUR). Missing Data Are Deleted Listwise*

	Per Capita Investment	Existence of Paved Roads	Existence of Paved Paths	Percentage of Classrooms Usable in Rain	Newness of School	Existence of Running Water	Ho: B = 0 p-value (SUR)
Democratic measures							
Additive score for the implementation of democratic institutions	8.70 (7.011)	−0.0006 (0.012)	0.0041 (0.0077)	0.011 (0.0079)	−0.62 (0.45)	0.0052 (0.011)	0.51
Control variables							
Distance from county town	−0.49 (1.042)	−0.0048*** (0.0013)	−0.0024* (0.0011)	0.00049 (0.0010)	0.088 (0.053)	−0.00070 (0.0014)	
Number of natural villages	−1.098 (3.32)	−0.0015 (0.0092)	−0.00096 (0.0037)	0.0069* (0.0031)	0.13 (0.19)	−0.0037 (0.0055)	
Village population	−0.017 (0.0088)	0.000013 (0.000035)	0.000030 (0.000026)	0.0000085 (0.0000086)	−0.0016* (0.00066)	0.000013 (0.000022)	
Village terrain	−15.99 (27.28)	0.12 (0.092)	0.033 (0.053)	−0.020 (0.055)	−1.91 (2.97)	−0.017 (0.070)	
1997 income per capita (thousands of yuan)	0.023 (0.017)	0.000089* (0.000043)	0.000055* (0.000028)	−0.000012 (0.000024)	−0.0004 (0.0020)	0.0000024 (0.000046)	
1997 government assets (thousands of yuan)	−0.000016* (0.0000066)	0.000000028 (0.000000025)	−0.000000031 (0.000000018)	−0.000000011 (0.000000011)	0.0000016 (0.0000017)	0.00000014*** (0.000000030)	
1997 tax revenue per capita	−0.61* (0.27)	−0.00030 (0.0014)	−0.0013* (0.00063)	−0.00019 (0.00063)	0.026 (0.050)	0.0015 (0.0010)	
Existence of village government enterprises in 1995	−7.61 (20.82)	−0.012 (0.059)	0.073 (0.040)	−0.012 (0.035)	−0.54 (2.077)	0.022 (0.050)	

Existence of private enterprises in 1995	−26.011	0.12	0.083	0.066	−7.24**	0.0056
	(27.10)	(0.077)	(0.056)	(0.038)	(2.66)	(0.066)
Party membership of village head	−0.25	−0.045	−0.0040	0.030	0.75	0.024
	(27.82)	(0.064)	(0.041)	(0.044)	(2.28)	(0.054)
Percentage of village officials in Party	−4.52	0.083	−0.11	−0.10	2.55	0.25
	(60.91)	(0.17)	(0.11)	(0.11)	(5.95)	(0.14)
Existence of bureaucratic targets for public projects	30.43	−0.096	−0.010	0.076*	1.67	−0.047
	(29.93)	(0.063)	(0.041)	(0.037)	(2.23)	(0.054)
Existence of temple manager	58.98	0.13	0.11	0.12*	5.15	0.15
	(67.47)	(0.092)	(0.079)	(0.054)	(2.92)	(0.094)
Existence of active church pastor	−65.89	0.26*	−0.094	−0.23*	6.47	0.0097
	(45.23)	(0.12)	(0.087)	(0.10)	(4.56)	(0.11)
Existence of only one ancestral hall with spirit tablets	0.84	0.27**	0.12	−0.015	−3.51	0.061
	(82.90)	(0.10)	(0.11)	(0.081)	(3.21)	(0.12)
Existence of multiple ancestral halls with spirit tablets	−67.38*	−0.17	0.17	0.023	−4.98	−0.047
	(32.47)	(0.098)	(0.10)	(0.080)	(2.98)	(0.10)
County dummies	yes	yes	yes	yes	yes	yes
Constant term	−69.10	0.36	0.022	0.76***	63.071***	0.51*
	(86.96)	(0.24)	(0.17)	(0.13)	(9.57)	(0.21)
Rsquared	0.13	0.30	0.29	0.13	0.29	0.49

Note: N = 237 villages. Figures in cells are seemingly unrelated regression coefficients. Huber heteroskedasticity-robust standard errors are in parentheses. * p = 0.10; ** p = 0.05; *** p = 0.01. The hypothesis that the coefficient estimates on each term are equal to zero across the six outcomes in the table is tested using SUR in the final column.

Appendix Table A7.2. *Village Governmental Provision of Public Goods and the Index of Implementation of Preelection Institutions (SUR). Missing Data Are Deleted Listwise*

	Per Capita Investment	Existence of Paved Roads	Existence of Paved Paths	Percentage of Classrooms Usable in Rain	Newness of School	Existence of Running Water	Ho: B = 0 p-value (SUR)
Index of implementation of preelection institutions	5.62 (6.65)	−0.016 (0.017)	0.0073 (0.0093)	0.031** (0.017)	−0.86 (0.60)	0.024 (0.015)	0.046**
Control variables							
Distance from county town	−0.41 (1.0061)	−0.0051*** (0.0013)	−0.0026* (0.0010)	0.000040 (0.0010)	0.089 (0.050)	−0.00036 (0.0014)	
Number of natural villages	−0.70 (3.13)	−0.0022 (0.0076)	−0.0018 (0.0034)	0.0093** (0.0033)	0.11 (0.20)	−0.0022 (0.0049)	
Village population	−0.014 (0.0073)	0.000024 (0.000039)	0.000033 (0.000027)	−0.0000010 (0.000011)	−0.0013 (0.00069)	0.000014 (0.000022)	
Village terrain	−9.97 (22.57)	0.086 (0.086)	0.018 (0.048)	0.017 (0.051)	−2.45 (2.93)	−0.0098 (0.067)	
1997 income per capita (thousands of yuan)	0.025 (0.016)	0.000090* (0.000041)	0.000053* (0.000026)	−0.000017 (0.000023)	−0.00080 (0.0019)	−0.00000039 (0.000044)	
1997 government assets (thousands of yuan)	−0.000012 (0.0000066)	0.000000029 (0.000000024)	−0.000000027 (0.000000017)	−0.0000000078 (0.000000011)	0.0000013 (0.0000017)	0.00000013*** (0.000000029)	
1997 tax revenue per capita	−0.39 (0.21)	0.00036 (0.0014)	−0.0012* (0.00055)	−0.00087 (0.00073)	0.035 (0.046)	0.0015 (0.00092)	
Existence of village government enterprises in 1995	−7.91 (18.57)	0.0061 (0.055)	0.071* (0.036)	0.0078 (0.034)	−1.33 (2.03)	0.024 (0.046)	

Existence of private enterprises in 1995	−17.59	0.11	0.082	0.057	−5.95*	0.036
	(24.39)	(0.073)	(0.054)	(0.044)	(2.57)	(0.065)
Party membership of village head	−2.78	−0.015	0.0035	−0.0021	0.43	0.014
	(27.09)	(0.062)	(0.040)	(0.042)	(2.24)	(0.051)
Percentage of village officials in Party	−5.90	0.13	−0.11	0.0059	2.49	0.20
	(55.99)	(0.16)	(0.10)	(0.11)	(5.58)	(0.13)
Existence of bureaucratic targets for public projects	28.71	−0.083	−0.012	0.070	1.69	−0.033
	(25.81)	(0.058)	(0.038)	(0.036)	(2.07)	(0.050)
Existence of temple manager	44.38	0.10	0.13	0.12	2.72	0.096
	(60.03)	(0.087)	(0.073)	(0.061)	(2.94)	(0.097)
Existence of active church pastor	−60.88	0.20	−0.082	−0.28**	5.84	−0.016
	(38.84)	(0.11)	(0.076)	(0.10)	(4.18)	(0.093)
Existence of only one ancestral hall with spirit tablets	14.27	0.27**	0.11	−0.012	−2.54	0.090
	(76.82)	(0.099)	(0.11)	(0.081)	(3.098)	(0.11)
Existence of multiple ancestral halls with spirit tablets	−45.78	−0.16	0.14	0.0055	−5.12	−0.026
	(24.71)	(0.085)	(0.090)	(0.094)	(2.69)	(0.090)
County dummies	yes	yes	yes	yes	yes	yes
Constant term	51.43	0.29	0.076	0.89***	52.52***	0.63***
	(56.81)	(0.15)	(0.10)	(0.079)	(5.59)	(0.13)
R-squared	0.12	0.31	0.30	0.17	0.29	0.51

Note: N = 261 villages. Figures in cells are seemingly unrelated regression coefficients. Huber heteroskedasticity-robust errors are in parentheses. * p = 0.10; ** p = 0.05; *** p = 0.01. The hypothesis that the coefficient estimates on each term are equal to zero across the six outcomes in the table is tested using SUR in the final column.

Appendix Table A7.3. *Village Governmental Provision of Public Goods and the Index of Implementation of Voting Institutions (SUR). Missing Data Are Deleted Listwise*

	Per Capita Investment	Existence of Paved Roads	Existence of Paved Paths	Percentage of Classrooms Usable in Rain	Newness of School	Existence of Running Water	Ho: B = 0 p-value (SUR)
Index for implementation of voting institutions	8.44	0.019	−0.00013	−0.0064	0.93	−0.012	0.56
	(8.38)	(0.022)	(0.012)	(0.011)	(0.81)	(0.017)	
Control variables							
Distance from county town	−0.40	−0.0047***	−0.0027**	−0.00053	0.074	−0.00080	
	(0.96)	(0.0012)	(0.00099)	(0.0011)	(0.048)	(0.0013)	
Number of natural villages	−0.52	−0.00060	−0.0013	0.0087*	0.016	−0.0034	
	(3.13)	(0.0073)	(0.0034)	(0.0039)	(0.23)	(0.0057)	
Village population	−0.013	0.0000019	0.000036	0.0000069	−0.0015*	0.000016	
	(0.0070)	(0.000036)	(0.000028)	(0.000010)	(0.00073)	(0.000024)	
Village terrain	−7.62	0.076	0.012	−0.024	−2.87	0.030	
	(21.63)	(0.086)	(0.047)	(0.048)	(2.93)	(0.070)	
1997 income per capita (thousands of yuan)	0.0028	0.0000027	0.000013	−0.0000043	0.0010	−0.000010	
	(0.0072)	(0.000018)	(0.000014)	(0.0000085)	(0.00070)	(0.000013)	
1997 government assets (thousands of yuan)	−0.00000040	0.0000000048*	−0.0000000063	−0.0000000032	0.00000056	0.00000013***	
	(0.0000066)	(0.0000000023)	(0.000000021)	(0.000000010)	(0.0000017)	(0.000000025)	
1997 tax revenue per capita	−0.36	0.0011	−0.00088	−0.00043	−0.016	0.00063	
	(0.20)	(0.0012)	(0.00047)	(0.00056)	(0.041)	(0.00093)	
Existence of village government enterprises in 1995	−3.06	0.014	0.075*	−0.0016	−0.34	0.03	
	(16.84)	(0.055)	(0.035)	(0.034)	(2.060)	(0.046)	

Existence of private enterprises in 1995	−16.17	0.13	0.099	0.066	−5.83*	0.072
	(24.31)	(0.070)	(0.055)	(0.049)	(2.69)	(0.068)
Party membership of village head	−4.50	−0.002	−0.00034	−0.00089	1.70	0.018
	(25.14)	(0.063)	(0.038)	(0.042)	(2.18)	(0.050)
Percentage of village officials in Party	−8.33	0.15	−0.096	0.0077	1.35	0.17
	(55.072)	(0.16)	(0.099)	(0.11)	(5.42)	(0.13)
Existence of bureaucratic targets for public projects	34.3	−0.055	−0.009	0.073*	−0.014	−0.029
	(24.83)	(0.055)	(0.037)	(0.036)	(1.98)	(0.048)
Existence of temple manager	48.79	0.12	0.12	0.094	1.57	0.081
	(55.48)	(0.082)	(0.067)	(0.058)	(2.67)	(0.088)
Existence of active church pastor	−73.78	0.11	−0.10	−0.27**	3.58	−0.023
	(41.47)	(0.12)	(0.072)	(0.097)	(3.82)	(0.090)
Existence of only one ancestral hall with spirit tablets	19.93	0.32***	0.11	−0.028	−2.38	0.064
	(75.59)	(0.093)	(0.11)	(0.083)	(2.82)	(0.12)
Existence of multiple ancestral halls with spirit tablets	−48.61*	−0.15	0.14	−0.00060	−5.52*	−0.030
	(24.43)	(0.084)	(0.089)	(0.091)	(2.76)	(0.088)
County dummies	yes	yes	yes	yes	yes	yes
Constant term	69.61	0.30*	0.094	0.90***	51.77***	0.65***
	(62.54)	(0.15)	(0.10)	(0.075)	(5.51)	(0.13)
R-squared	0.11	0.31	0.29	0.14	0.26	0.50

Note: N = 275 villages. Figures in cells are seemingly unrelated regression coefficients. Huber heteroskedasticity-robust errors are in parentheses. * $p = 0.10$; ** $p = 0.05$; *** $p = 0.01$. The hypothesis that the coefficient estimates on each term are equal to zero across the six outcomes in the table is tested using SUR in the final column.

Appendix Table A7.4. *Village Governmental Provision of Public Goods and the Index of Implementation of Villagers' Representative Institutions (SUR). Missing Data Are Deleted Listwise*

	Per Capita Investment	Existence of Paved Roads	Existence of Paved Paths	Percentage of Classrooms Usable in Rain	Newness of School	Existence of Running Water	Ho: B = 0 p-value (SUR)
Index for implementation of villagers' representative assemblies	6.64 (7.71)	0.017 (0.021)	0.02 (0.012)	0.022 (0.014)	−0.58 (0.81)	−0.011 (0.017)	0.22
Control variables							
Distance from county town	−0.50 (1.041)	−0.0043** (0.0013)	−0.0025* (0.0011)	0.00073 (0.0010)	0.058 (0.052)	−0.0012 (0.0014)	
Number of natural villages	−1.37 (3.21)	−0.0040 (0.0084)	−0.0017 (0.0035)	0.0080* (0.0032)	−0.036 (0.23)	−0.0033 (0.0054)	
Village population	−0.014 (0.0076)	0.000012 (0.000032)	0.000031 (0.000025)	0.0000065 (0.0000093)	−0.0013 (0.00079)	0.000014 (0.000024)	
Village terrain	−13.95 (25.74)	0.11 (0.090)	0.028 (0.051)	−0.0049 (0.055)	−3.93 (3.0096)	−0.013 (0.068)	
1997 income per capita (thousands of yuan)	0.024 (0.016)	0.000083* (0.000041)	0.000055* (0.000027)	−0.0000025 (0.000023)	−0.00080 (0.0020)	−0.0000074 (0.000044)	
1997 government assets (thousands of yuan)	−0.000010 (0.0000066)	0.000000031 (0.000000025)	−0.000000026 (0.000000022)	−0.000000012 (0.000000014)	0.0000017 (0.0000016)	0.00000014** (0.000000032)	
1997 tax revenue per capita	−0.40 (0.22)	0.0011 (0.0012)	−0.00084 (0.00053)	−0.00058 (0.00067)	−0.000015 (0.042)	0.00062 (0.0010)	
Existence of village government enterprises in 1995	−6.80 (19.037)	−0.0036 (0.057)	0.067 (0.037)	−0.013 (0.035)	−0.72 (2.08)	0.024 (0.048)	

Existence of private enterprises in 1995	−24.16	0.14	0.11	0.077*	−6.71*	0.024
	(25.00	(0.074)	(0.056)	(0.039)	(2.65)	(0.066)
Party membership of village head	−2.32	−0.025	0.00030	0.029	1.75	0.023
	(27.48)	(0.064)	(0.040)	(0.044)	(2.28)	(0.053)
Percentage of village officials in Party	−7.13	0.12	−0.11	−0.094	2.63	0.24
	(59.42)	(0.17)	(0.11)	(0.11)	(5.96)	(0.14)
Existence of bureaucratic targets for public projects	27.79	−0.090	−0.013	0.065	1.47	−0.036
	(28.38)	(0.060)	(0.040)	(0.036)	(2.22)	(0.052)
Existence of temple manager	54.10	0.11	0.099	0.12*	4.24	0.14
	(63.45)	(0.093)	(0.074)	(0.055)	(2.80)	(0.087)
Existence of active church pastor	−58.34	0.23*	−0.089	−0.24*	6.35	0.021
	(39.37)	(0.11)	(0.075)	(0.099)	(4.26)	(0.092)
Existence of only one ancestral hall with spirit tablets	−6.31	0.29**	0.12	−0.025	−3.52	0.055
	(82.22)	(0.10)	(0.11)	(0.079)	(3.21)	(0.12)
Existence of multiple ancestral halls with spirit tablets	−64.92*	−0.17	0.17	0.026	−6.021*	−0.045
	(31.11)	(0.095)	(0.10)	(0.080)	(3.061)	(0.10)
County dummies	yes	yes	yes	yes	yes	yes
Constant term	62.90	0.29	0.077	0.88***	55.36***	0.63***
	(58.36)	(0.16)	(0.11)	(0.083)	(5.87)	(0.14)
R-squared	0.12	0.30	0.29	0.14	0.25	0.50

Note: N = 251 villages. Figures in cells are seemingly unrelated regression coefficients. Huber heteroskedasticity-robust errors are in parentheses. * p = 0.10; ** p = 0.05; *** p = 0.01. The hypothesis that the coefficient estimates on each term are equal to zero across the six outcomes in the table is tested using SUR in the final column.

Appendix Table A7.5. *Village Governmental Provision of Public Goods and Interaction between Village Democratic Institutions and Village Temple Groups (SUR). Missing Data Are Deleted Listwise*

	Per Capita Investment	Existence of Paved Roads	Existence of Paved Paths	Percentage of Classrooms Usable in Rain	Newness of School	Existence of Running Water	Ho: B = 0 p-value (SUR)
Index of implementation of village democratic reforms	2.76	0.032	0.028	0.019	−0.96	0.012	0.28
	(9.52)	(0.031)	(0.015)	(0.019)	(1.21)	(0.023)	
Existence of temple manager	87.23	0.079	0.098	0.15**	5.21	0.17	0.0009***
	(82.70)	(0.096)	(0.080)	(0.052)	(2.91)	(0.098)	
Interaction of democratic reforms index and temple manager variables	79.78	−0.14	−0.055	0.064	−0.074	0.068	0.30
	(64.92)	(0.083)	(0.062)	(0.054)	(2.11)	(0.073)	
Control variables							
Distance from county town	−0.41	−0.0049***	−0.0024*	0.00059	0.090	−0.00054	
	(0.98)	(0.0013)	(0.0011)	(0.0010)	(0.053)	(0.0014)	
Number of natural villages	−1.30	−0.0015	−0.0011	0.0066*	0.13	−0.0039	
	(3.29)	(0.0094)	(0.0036)	(0.0033)	(0.19)	(0.0054)	
Village population	−0.016	0.000012	0.000029	0.0000079	−0.0017**	0.000012	
	(0.0087)	(0.000034)	(0.000026)	(0.0000085)	(0.00065)	(0.000021)	
Village terrain	−31.7	0.14	0.043	−0.034	−1.94	−0.032	
	(34.18)	(0.093)	(0.054)	(0.056)	(3.02)	(0.073)	
1997 income per capita (thousands of yuan)	0.026	0.000083	0.000053	−0.000010	−0.00040	0.0000045	
	(0.018)	(0.000044)	(0.000027)	(0.000024)	(0.0020)	(0.000046)	
1997 government assets (thousands of yuan)	−0.000010	0.000000024	−0.000000033	−0.0000000097	0.00000000014	0.00000014***	
	(0.0000068)	(0.000000026)	(0.000000018)	(0.000000011)	(0.0000017)	(0.000000030)	
1997 tax revenue per capita	−0.57*	−0.00040	−0.0013*	−0.00018	0.024	0.0015	
	(0.26)	(0.0014)	(0.00063)	(0.00064)	(0.050)	(0.0010)	

Existence of village government enterprises in 1995	−6.43	−0.014	0.072	−0.011	−0.56	0.023
	(20.85)	(0.058)	(0.040)	(0.035)	(2.081)	(0.050)
Existence of private enterprises in 1995	−20.62	0.11	0.078	0.069	−7.20**	0.0092
	(23.55)	(0.077)	(0.055)	(0.036)	(2.70)	(0.065)
Party membership of village head	−3.46	−0.040	−0.0020	0.027	0.83	0.022
	(29.099)	(0.063)	(0.042)	(0.043)	(2.28)	(0.054)
Percentage of village officials in Party	−11.11	0.098	−0.098	−0.10	2.51	0.24
	(62.41)	(0.17)	(0.11)	(0.11)	(5.00)	(0.14)
Existence of bureaucratic targets for public projects	38.46	−0.11	−0.015	0.083*	1.68	−0.039
	(32.92)	(0.063)	(0.041)	(0.036)	(2.25)	(0.053)
Existence of active church pastor	−66.57	0.26*	−0.094	−0.23*	6.37	0.0068
	(44.17)	(0.11)	(0.086)	(0.10)	(4.44)	(0.10)
Existence of only one ancestral hall with spirit tablets	−4.04	0.28**	0.13	−0.015	−3.39	0.063
	(80.32)	(0.097)	(0.11)	(0.080)	(3.13)	(0.12)
Existence of multiple ancestral halls with spirit tablets	−61.93*	−0.18	0.17	0.028	−5.25	−0.044
	(30.94)	(0.093)	(0.10)	(0.081)	(2.98)	(0.10)
County dummies	yes	yes	yes	yes	yes	yes
Constant term	79.99	0.33*	0.080	0.94***	53.29***	0.60***
	(67.48)	(0.17)	(0.12)	(0.082)	(5.97)	(0.15)
R-squared	0.15	0.31	0.29	0.15	0.29	0.50

Note: N = 237 villages. Figures in cells are seemingly unrelated regression coefficients. Huber heteroskedasticity-robust errors are in parentheses. * p = 0.10; ** p = 0.05; *** p = 0.01. The hypothesis that the coefficient estimates on each term are equal to zero across the six outcomes in the table is tested using SUR in the final column.

Appendix Table A7.6. *Village Governmental Provision of Public Goods and Interaction between Village Democratic Institutions and Villagewide Lineage Groups (SUR). Missing Data Are Deleted Listwise*

	Per Capita Investment	Existence of Paved Roads	Existence of Paved Paths	Percentage of Classrooms Usable in Rain	Newness of School	Existence of Running Water	Ho: B = 0 p-value (SUR)
Index of implementation of village democratic reforms	15.64 (14.95)	−0.0029 (0.032)	0.022 (0.016)	0.034 (0.021)	−1.35 (1.080)	0.018 (0.024)	0.37
Existence of only one ancestral hall with spirit tablets	24.70 (125.75)	0.32** (0.11)	0.091 (0.14)	−0.027 (0.097)	−0.70 (2.95)	0.12 (0.14)	0.065*
Interaction of democratic reforms index and single ancestral hall variables	31.98 (67.03)	0.073 (0.050)	−0.047 (0.069)	−0.023 (0.048)	3.73* (1.87)	0.073 (0.075)	0.19
Control variables							
Distance from county town	−0.46 (1.081)	−0.0047*** (0.0013)	−0.0024* (0.0011)	0.00049 (0.0010)	0.094 (0.053)	−0.00054 (0.0014)	
Number of natural villages	−1.15 (3.29)	−0.0013 (0.0092)	−0.0013 (0.0037)	0.0066* (0.0032)	0.15 (0.19)	−0.0037 (0.0055)	
Village population	−0.017 (0.0087)	0.000013 (0.000034)	0.000029 (0.000026)	0.0000077 (0.0000084)	−0.0017** (0.00064)	0.000012 (0.000022)	
Village terrain	−17.21 (27.11)	0.11 (0.092)	0.034 (0.053)	−0.020 (0.054)	−2.11 (2.97)	−0.021 (0.071)	
1997 income per capita (thousands of yuan)	0.024 (0.016)	0.000090* (0.000043)	0.000054 (0.000028)	−0.000013 (0.000024)	−0.00030 (0.0020)	0.0000036 (0.000046)	
1997 government assets (thousands of yuan)	−0.000015* (0.0000064)	0.000000026 (0.000000025)	−0.000000031 (0.000000018)	−0.000000011 (0.000000011)	0.0000014 (0.0000017)	0.00000014*** (0.000000030)	

1997 tax revenue per capita	−0.60*	−0.00030	−0.0013*	−0.00020	0.023	0.0014
	(0.27)	(0.0014)	(0.00063)	(0.00063)	(0.049)	(0.0010)
Existence of village government enterprises in 1995	−8.96	−0.015	0.075	−0.011	−0.74	0.018
	(20.28)	(0.059)	(0.040)	(0.035)	(2.08)	(0.049)
Existence of private enterprises in 1995	−25.39	0.12	0.080	0.063	−7.01**	0.0074
	(27.18)	(0.078)	(0.056)	(0.039)	(2.68)	(0.066)
Party membership of village head	−2.21	−0.047	−0.0019	0.030	0.68	0.022
	(29.14)	(0.064)	(0.040)	(0.044)	(2.27)	(0.054)
Percentage of village officials in Party	2.11	0.095	−0.11	−0.10	3.07	0.26
	(65.75)	(0.17)	(0.11)	(0.11)	(5.95)	(0.14)
Existence of bureaucratic targets for public projects	33.15	−0.089	−0.013	0.075*	1.00	−0.040
	(32.40)	(0.064)	(0.042)	(0.038)	(2.27)	(0.054)
Existence of temple manager	57.25	0.12	0.12	0.13*	4.99	0.15
	(65.88)	(0.093)	(0.079)	(0.054)	(2.87)	(0.093)
Existence of active church pastor	−66.42	0.25*	−0.094	−0.23*	6.24	0.0053
	(45.41)	(0.12)	(0.087)	(0.10)	(4.41)	(0.11)
Existence of multiple ancestral halls with spirit tablets	−62.20*	−0.17	0.17	0.026	−5.03	−0.042
	(31.23)	(0.097)	(0.10)	(0.081)	(3.012)	(0.10)
County dummies	yes	yes	yes	yes	yes	yes
Constant term	64.24	0.34*	0.094	0.93***	52.82***	0.58***
	(65.42)	(0.16)	(0.12)	(0.083)	(5.94)	(0.15)
R-squared	0.13	0.30	0.29	0.14	0.29	0.50

Note: N = 237 villages. Figures in cells are seemingly unrelated regression coefficients. Huber heteroskedasticity-robust errors are in parentheses. * p = 0.10; ** p = 0.05; *** p = 0.01. The hypothesis that the coefficient estimates on each term are equal to zero across the six outcomes in the table is tested using SUR in the final column.

Index

accountability, 135, 148. *See also* local government performance
  bureaucratic, 10–12, 15, 52, 58, 88, 228–32, 246–9
  democracy and, 11, 19, 190, 257
  formal, 13, 126, 228–32, 266–7
  incentives and, 18, 234–8
  informal, 13, 16, 19, 88, 99, 160, 169–71, 257–66
  lack of information and, 221–3, 238–41
  solidary groups and, 4, 18–19
  survey data of, 243–5
administrative guarantee system, 230
administrative units, 29
agricultural taxes, 43
Alesina, Alberto, 15, 166
ancestral halls, 154–7, 183
auditing systems, 10, 209, 221, 240, 242

Baker, Hugh, 150
ballot boxes, 1, 136, 173 192, 203, 206, 208. *See also* elections
Banfield, Edward, 258
Bangladesh, 260
baogan zhidu, 230
Bellah, Robert, 89
Benziger, Vincent, 64
Bernstein, Thomas, 39
bianzhi system, 54
Bird, Richard, 38
birth control, 29, 41, 57, 175, 231, 233
Boix, Charles, 16
Bolivia, 260, 262
Botswana, 263
Brazil, 60
Brodsgaard, Kjeld Erik, 54
building permits, 41, 221
Bulgaria, 6
Bureau of Rural Water Conservancy, 72
bureaucracy
  accountability of, 10–12, 15, 52, 58, 88, 228–32, 246–9
  increase of, 52–8
  lack of incentives and, 234–8
  lack of information and, 238–41
  lack of leverage and, 232–4
  personnel costs and, 54
  survey data of, 243–5

Chau, Adam, 113
Chen Settlement, 177–9, 181–2
Chen, Huijiang, 196–7
Chen, Wenhua, 182
Cheng, Xiaonong, 57
Chestnut Village, 108–9
chieftaincies, 262–3, 265
Chile, 259
Chung, Him, 65

churches, 12, 20, 97, 134–6, 145, 253. *See also* temples
British, 14
lineage groups and, 164
lobbying by, 91
public services and, 120, 133
structure of, 120–4
Chwe, Michael, 96
citizen watchdog groups, 14
clans, 14, 17, 94–5, 150, 153, 179, 181
Cohen, Myron, 153, 179, 181
Coleman, James, 15
collective action. *See* free-rider collective action problem
Collins, Kathleen, 266
compliance. *See* noncompliance
Corbin, David, 98
corruption, 15, 38, 52, 54, 180, 197–8, 220, 222, 226, 238–41
Côte d'Ivoire, 264
Cultural Revolution, 66–7, 103, 152, 155
cunban qiye, 126

Daunton, Martin, 91
decentralization, 6, 19
benefits of, 27, 45, 58
governmental debt and, 47–52
lack of incentives and, 234–8
lack of leverage and, 232–4
problems with, 28, 46–7
public goods and, 35–7, 252
Degoey, Peter, 18, 91
democracy. *See also* elections
accountability and, 11, 19, 190, 257
civic values and, 223–6
evaluation of, 211–18
grassroots reforms of, 1, 188–91, 194, 200
implementation of, 203–11
in Fujian province, 199–201
in Hebei province, 202
in Jiangxi province, 202
in River Bridge Village, 190–8
lack of leverage and, 219–21
measures of, 209–11
solidary groups and, 217–18
Deutsch, Karl, 94
Dittmer, Lowell, 256
divorce, 57
Donnithorne, Audrey, 230
downsizing, 57
Duara, Prasenjit, 39
on entrepreneurial state brokers, 101
on lineage groups, 151
on religious groups, 100–1
dundian ganbu, 34

Ecuador, 260, 264, 266
Edin, Maria, 231
education, 32, 66–70, 75. *See also* public goods and services
compulsory, 68
democratic institutions and, 214
during Cultural Revolution, 66–7
ethnically diverse, 166
fees for, 41, 69
GDP and, 60
government funding of, 32
lineage groups and, 164
performance contracts and, 248
reappropriating funds for, 56
reforms of, 69
variation in, 78, 83
village churches and, 133
village temples and, 130
Election Law (2004), 203
elections, 136, 172, 178, 187, 215, 267. *See also* democracy
ballot boxes for, 1, 136, 173, 192, 203, 206, 208
civic values and, 198, 223–6
guidelines for, 188, 191
irregularities with, 206–8
oversight committees for, 205
preliminaries for, 205–6, 215
proxy ballots for, 203, 206–7
withdrawal of candidates from, 193
EMis algorithm, 81, 128, 132, 161, 247

Index

Esherick, Joseph, 122
Evans, Peter, 17, 261

Falun Gong, 183
fang, 174
federalism, 6, 263
  market-preserving, 36, 45, 58
fees and levies, 35, 43, 123, 143
  educational, 41, 69
  for government payroll, 56
  rental, 44, 220
  roadway, 65
Fei, Xiaotong, 151
festival associations, 142
fines, 37, 41, 57, 175
folk dancing, 114, 143
Fox, Jonathan, 262
Freedman, Maurice, 149–50
free-rider collective action problem, 5, 15, 88, 167
Frolic, B. Michael, 152
Fujian province, 1, 25, 87, 136, 139, 183, 200, 236–7
  classrooms in, 78, 82
  governmental investment in, 77
  income per capita in, 82
  lineage groups in, 154
  public goods expenditures by, 62
  roads in, 77, 82
  temples of, 121
  water supply in, 79, 82

gambling, 57
game theory, 96
ganqing, 32, 144
Ganzhou, 1, 171
General Auditing Administration, 242
Georgia, 6
Ghana, 265–6
Goldstein, Avery, 232
gongzuo zongjie, 230
Goode, William, 89, 92
governmental debt, 47–52
governmental levels, 29
Great Leap Forward, 10, 103
Guangdong province, 1, 172
  lineage groups in, 149
  temples of, 121
guanxi, 32, 111, 256
Gugerty, Mary Kay, 167

Haiti, 6
Hamid, Shahid, 66
Han, Jun, 54, 56
Hausman tests, 129
He, Qinglian, 57
He, Zhenghuan, 196
health care, 32
Hebei province, 21–5, 33, 48, 55, 136, 177, 201, 237
  classrooms in, 77, 82
  corruption in, 52
  government investment in, 77
  income per capita in, 82
  lineage groups in, 153–4
  public goods expenditures by, 62
  roads in, 77, 82
  water supply in, 79, 82
Hechter, Michael, 94
Henan province, 51, 56, 152
hepatitis, 73
High Mountain Village, 1–5, 171–7, 202, 267
Hinton, William, 122
Hirabayashi, Lane Ryo, 265
Houpu, 190
Hubei province, 50
Hungary, 6

incentives, 18, 234–8
income per capita, 22, 142
  in Chen Settlement, 178
  in High Mountain, 172, 202
  in Li Settlement, 172, 202
  in Pan Settlement, 178
  in River Bridge Village, 200
  in South Bend, 201
  in West Gate, 139, 200
  in Yang Hamlet, 201
  misreporting of, 24, 40, 239–40

income per capita (*cont.*)
tax rates and, 40, 42
variation in, 82
India, 60
industrialization, 9, 36, 46, 53, 73, 252, 267
instrumental variables (IV) estimation, 23, 129–30, 162–3
International Republican Institute, 190–1

Jiangxi province, 1–2, 12, 21–5, 56, 171, 202, 231
classrooms in, 77, 83
fees in, 43
government debt in, 51
government investment in, 77
income per capita in, 82
lineage groups in, 154
public goods expenditures by, 62
roads in, 77, 83
water supply in, 79, 83
Jimei, 183
Jordan, David, 118
Judd, Ellen, 174

Kane, John, 90
Kaufmann, D., 9
Kenya, 13, 167, 260, 270
King, Gary, 128
kong ke villages, 59, 172
Korovkin, Tanya, 266
Kraay, A., 9
Krajewski, M., 5
Kuran, Timur, 89

Lam, Wai Fung, 263
Landry, Pierre, 236
Latham, Richard, 106
Lawrence, Susan, 30
Levi, Margaret, 90, 98, 174
levies. *See* fees and levies
Li Settlement, 1–5, 9, 12, 171–7, 202, 267
Li, Huaiyin, 152, 179
Lin, Justin, 38, 41, 45, 47, 54, 73, 246
lineage groups, 12, 100, 103, 116, 215, 262
ancestral halls of, 154–7, 183
definition of, 149
donor lists and, 117
embedding, 262
encompassing, 254
intervillage, 20, 183–5
public services and, 158–71
rituals of, 154, 183
subvillage, 20, 148, 158–65, 177–82, 186
surname villages and, 182
survey data of, 154–65
villagewide, 20, 158–65, 186
Lineage Origins Research Association, 184
Lipset, S. M., 8
Liu, Shaoqi, 230
Liu, Zhiqiang, 45
liver cancer, 73
local government performance, 10–12, 27, 60–2, 85. *See also* accountability
debt and, 47–52
lineage groups and, 164, 169–82
measurement of, 74–5
variation in, 76–80
virtuous cycle of, 8
Lu, Xiaobo, 39, 235, 256

MacLean, Lauren Morris, 264
Madsen, Richard, 122
marriage, 41, 57
Mexico, 265
Miguel, Edward, 76, 81, 167
Mill, John Stuart, 11
Ming dynasty, 179
Ministry of Civil Affairs, 188–9
Ministry of Finance, 242
Ministry of Health, 72
Ministry of Supervision (MOS), 243
Ministry of Water Resources, 72

Index

misreporting, 241
Moe, Terry, 10
moral standing, 13–14, 17, 135, 262
  as political resource, 98, 107–12, 268
  as soft power, 18
  awarding of, 92–8, 113–18
  benefits of, 88–91
  status and, 90
Mountain View county, 33, 35

Naquin, Susan, 123
Narayan, Deepa, 270
National Bureau of Statistics (NBS), 239, 241–2
nepotism. *See* corruption
New Brook Village, 48–9
Nicaragua, 6
Nigeria, 262, 265–6
noncompliance, 17, 98, 136, 228

Oi, Jean, 9, 256
  on fiscal decentralization, 45
  on local state corporatism, 59
  on rural industrialization, 36–7, 47
Oksenberg, Michel, 230
opium wars, 122
ordinary least squares regression (OLS), 81, 129
Organization Law of Villagers' Committees, 188, 204, 209
Ostrom, Elinor, 266
Ostrom, Vincent, 266

Pan Settlement, 177–82
Park, Albert, 50, 56
Parsons, Talcott, 94
Patriotic Sanitation Movement, 70
Peace, Adrian, 265
Pei, Minxin, 232
performance contracts, 10, 229–32, 246, 248, 267
  lack of information and, 238–41
  survey data of, 246–9
  targets for, 235–6, 249
performance reviews, 10, 230, 235–8
Perkins, Dwight, 66, 68
Perry, Elizabeth, 103, 105, 183, 256
Pettit, Philip, 92
Pinochet, Augusto, 259
Poland, 259
Portes, Alejandro, 16
Portugal, 91
Posner, Daniel, 16
Potter, Pittman, 257
prestige, 89–90, 113–16, 143
principal-agent models, 10
prostitution, 44, 57
proxy voting, 203, 206–7
Przeworski, A., 8
public finance, 37–45
public goods and services, 5–8, 15, 27, 31–5, 60–2
  bureaucratic wages and, 54
  decentralization and, 35–7, 252
  definition of, 5
  democratic institutions and, 214, 216
  lineage groups and, 158–71
  performance contracts and, 235, 246–9
  survey of, 23, 85
Putnam, Robert, 5, 92, 167

Qing dynasty, 39, 101

Reed, Robert Roy, 91
reforestation, 35, 50
Religious Affairs Bureau, 145
Remick, Elizabeth, 238
Renshou, 65
Rigger, Shelley, 198, 223
Riskin, Carl,
River Bridge Village, 190–8
  West Gate and, 199–201
roads, 60, 75, 178, 198. *See also* public goods and services
  democratic institutions and, 214
  expenditures for, 63–5
  investment in, 236
  lineage groups and, 164

roads (*cont.*)
performance contracts and, 248
reappropriating funds of, 56
variation in, 77, 83
village churches and, 133
village temples and, 130
Roadway Law (1998), 65
Rodden, Jonathan, 58
Rose, Richard, 260
Rousseau, Jean-Jacques, 90
Russia, 7, 60, 260

Saich, Tony, 44
Sangren, P. Steven, 151
Scott, James, 98, 256
seemingly unrelated regression (SUR), 76, 81, 127, 132
SEPA. *See* State Environmental Protection Administration
Shandong province, 55
Shanxi province, 21–5, 56
classrooms in, 77, 83
government investment in, 77
income per capita in, 82
lineage groups in, 154
public goods expenditures by, 62
roads in, 77, 83
water supply in, 79, 83
Sichuan province, 65
siying qiye, 126
Skinner, G. William, 121, 257–8
Sklar, Richard, 262
Skocpol, Theda, 94, 264
social capital, 268
solidary groups, 93–8, 263–5, 269
accountability and, 4, 18–19
definition of, 4, 94
democratic institutions and, 217–18
embedding, 13, 16–17, 93, 96–8, 135, 148
encompassing, 13, 93, 96–8, 120, 135, 146
in early 1900s, 99–102
in Maoist period, 102–4
in reform period, 104–7
types of, 12, 17
village prestige and, 113–16
South Bend Village, 136–9, 145–6, 201
Special Economic Zone (SEZ), 2, 116, 139
State Environmental Protection Administration (SEPA), 72
Statistics Law (1983), 241–2
status, 90. *See also* prestige
Steinfeld, Edward, 36
Strauch, Judith, 149, 182
Su Mountain Grove, 115–16
Sun Lineage Association, 183–5
SUR. *See* seemingly unrelated regression
surname groups, 149–50, 182

Taiwan, 150, 263
Tang Gully, 109–11
temples, 12, 20, 99, 113, 116, 214, 253. *See also* churches
ancestral halls and, 154–7, 183
deity cults and, 151
during Maoist period, 129
festival associations and, 142
lineage groups and, 164
overseas networks of, 121
public services and, 120, 128, 130
structure of, 120–4
suppression of, 102–3
survey data of, 124–36
West Gate, 87, 139–42, 200–1
Three Forks Village, 2–5, 9, 12, 183–6, 267
Tocqueville, Alexis de, 92
township and village enterprises (TVE), 45–7, 50, 59
transparency, 11, 36, 43, 58, 197, 221–3
TVEs. *See* township and village enterprises
two-stage least squares (2SLS), 213
Tyler, Tom, 18, 91, 113

Index

Uganda, 262–3
unfunded mandates, 37–45, 252

vandalism, 111
Verdon, Michel, 94
village committees, 29
villagers' representative assemblies (VRA), 24, 127, 172, 179, 191, 204, 222, 254
  civic values and, 223
  establishment of, 188–90
  evaluation of, 209
villages, *kong ke*, 59, 172
voting. *See* elections

Wang, Hongying, 257
Wank, David, 257
waqfs, 89
water supply, 34, 60, 70–3, 75. *See also* public goods and services
  democratic institutions and, 214
  industrialization and, 73
  lineage groups and, 164
  performance contracts and, 248
  variation in, 80, 83
  village temple groups and, 130
Watson, James, 149–51
Watson, Rubie, 149, 151
Weber, Max, 10, 93
Weingast, Barry, 36, 45
Wen Hamlet, 114–15
Wen, Tiejun, 54, 56
West Field Township, 240–1
West Gate Village, 12, 111–12, 136–42, 267
  elections in, 198
  River Bridge and, 199–201
  temples of, 87, 139–42, 200–1
  Three Fork and, 2–5
West Hu Hamlet, 116–18
White Lotus Societies, 123
Widner, Jennifer, 5
Will, Pierre-Etienne, 38
Wolf, Eric, 258
Wong, Christine, 23, 38
Wuthnow, Robert, 91, 94

Xiamen, 1–2, 12, 21, 183, 219

Yan, Yunxiang, 257
Yang Hamlet, 114–15, 118, 136–9, 142–4, 201
Yang, Dali, 53
Yang, Hongbin, 196
Yang, Mayfair, 257
Yu, Jianrong, 43
Yuan Dwelling, 115–16
Yusuf, Shahid, 68

Zhang, Xiaobo, 23
Zhao, Shukai, 55, 57
Zhu, Rongji, 240
zongqinhui, 150

Other Books in the Series (*continued from page iii*)

Daniele Caramani, *The Nationalization of Politics: The Formation of National Electorates and Party Systems in Europe*

Kanchan Chandra, *Why Ethnic Parties Succeed: Patronage and Ethnic Headcounts in India*

Ruth Berins Collier, *Paths Toward Democracy: The Working Class and Elites in Western Europe and South America*

Christian Davenport, *State Repression and the Domestic Democratic Peace*

Donatella della Porta, *Social Movements, Political Violence, and the State*

Alberto Diaz-Cayeros, *Federalism, Fiscal Authority, and Centralization in Latin America*

Gerald Easter, *Reconstructing the State: Personal Networks and Elite Identity*

M. Steven Fish, *Democracy Derailed in Russia: The Failure of Open Politics*

Robert F. Franzese, *Macroeconomic Policies of Developed Democracies*

Roberto Franzosi, *The Puzzle of Strikes: Class and State Strategies in Postwar Italy*

Geoffrey Garrett, *Partisan Politics in the Global Economy*

Miriam Golden, *Heroic Defeats: The Politics of Job Loss*

Jeff Goodwin, *No Other Way Out: States and Revolutionary Movements*

Merilee Serrill Grindle, *Challenging the State*

Anna Grzymala-Busse, *Redeeming the Communist Past: The Regeneration of Communist Parties in East Central Europe*

Frances Hagopian, *Tradition Politics and Regime Change in Brazil*

Gretchen Helmke, *Courts under Constraints: Judges, Generals, and Presidents in Argentina*

Yoshiko Herrera, *Imagined Economies: The Sources of Russian Regionalism*

J. Rogers Hollingsworth and Robert Boyer, eds., *Contemporary Capitalism: The Embeddedness of Institutions*

John D. Huber and Charles R. Shipan, *Deliberate Discretion? The Institutional Foundations of Bureaucratic Autonomy*

Ellen Immergut, *Health Politics: Interests and Institutions in Western Europe*

Torben Iversen, *Capitalism, Democracy, and Welfare*

Torben Iversen, *Contested Economic Institutions*

Torben Iversen, Jonas Pontussen, and David Soskice, eds., *Unions, Employers, and Central Banks: Macroeconomic Coordination and Institutional Change in Social Market Economies*

Thomas Janoski and Alexander M. Hicks, eds., *The Comparative Political Economy of the Welfare State*

Joseph Jupille, *Procedural Politics: Issues, Influence, and Institutional Choice in the European Union*

Stathis Kalyvas, *The Logic of Violence in Civil War*

David C. Kang, *Crony Capitalism: Corruption and Development in South Korea and the Philippines*

Junko Kato, *Regressive Taxation and the Welfare State*

Robert O. Keohane and Helen B. Milner, eds., *Internationalization and Domestic Politics*

Herbert Kitschelt, *The Transformation of European Social Democracy*

Herbert Kitschelt, Peter Lange, Gary Marks, and John D. Stephens, eds., *Continuity and Change in Contemporary Capitalism*

Herbert Kitschelt, Zdenka Mansfeldova, Radek Markowski, and Gabor Toka, *Post-Communist Party Systems*

David Knoke, Franz Urban Pappi, Jeffrey Broadbent, and Yutaka Tsujinaka, eds., *Comparing Policy Networks*

Allan Kornberg and Harold D. Clarke, *Citizens and Community: Political Support in a Representative Democracy*

Amie Kreppel, *The European Parliament and the Supranational Party System*

David D. Laitin, *Language Repertoires and State Construction in Africa*

Fabrice E. Lehoucq and Ivan Molina, *Stuffing the Ballot Box: Fraud, Electoral Reform, and Democratization in Costa Rica*

Mark Irving Lichbach and Alan S. Zuckerman, eds., *Comparative Politics: Rationality, Culture, and Structure*

Evan Lieberman, *Race and Regionalism in the Politics of Taxation in Brazil and South Africa*

Pauline Jones Luong, *Institutional Change and Political Continuity in Post-Soviet Central Asia*

Julia Lynch, *Age in the Welfare State: The Origins of Social Spending on Pensioners, Workers, and Children*

Doug McAdam, John McCarthy, and Mayer Zald, eds., *Comparative Perspectives on Social Movements*

Beatriz Magaloni, *Voting for Autocracy: Hegemonic Party Survival and Its Demise in Mexico*

James Mahoney and Dietrich Rueschemeyer, eds., *Historical Analysis and the Social Sciences*

Scott Mainwaring and Matthew Soberg Shugart, eds., *Presidentialism and Democracy in Latin America*

Isabela Mares, *The Politics of Social Risk: Business and Welfare State Development*

Isabela Mares, *Taxation, Wage Bargaining, and Unemployment*

Anthony W. Marx, *Making Race, Making Nations: A Comparison of South Africa, the United States, and Brazil*

Joel S. Migdal, *State in Society: Studying How States and Societies Constitute One Another*

Joel S. Migdal, Atul Kohli, and Vivienne Shue, eds., *State Power and Social Forces: Domination and Transformation in the Third World*
Scott Morgenstern and Benito Nacif, eds., *Legislative Politics in Latin America*
Layna Mosley, *Global Capital and National Governments*
Wolfgang C. Müller and Kaare Strøm, *Policy, Office, or Votes?*
Maria Victoria Murillo, *Labor Unions, Partisan Coalitions, and Market Reforms in Latin America*
Ton Notermans, *Money, Markets, and the State: Social Democratic Economic Policies Since 1918*
Roger D. Petersen, *Understanding Ethnic Violence: Fear, Hatred, and Resentment in Twentieth-Century Eastern Europe*
Anìbal Pèrez-Liñan, *Presidential Impeachment and the New Political Instability in Latin America*
Simona Piattoni, ed., *Clientelism, Interests, and Democratic Representation*
Paul Pierson, *Dismantling the Welfare State? Reagan, Thatcher, and the Politics of Retrenchment*
Marino Regini, *Uncertain Boundaries: The Social and Political Construction of European Economies*
Jonathan Rodden, *Hamilton's Paradox: The Promise and Peril of Fiscal Federalism*
Lyle Scruggs, *Sustaining Abundance: Environmental Performance in Industrial Democracies*
Jefferey M. Sellers, *Governing from Below: Urban Regions and the Global Economy*
Yossi Shain and Juan Linz, eds., *Interim Government and Democratic Transitions*
Beverly Silver, *Forces of Labor: Workers' Movements and Globalization since 1870*
Theda Skocpol, *Social Revolutions in the Modern World*
Regina Smyth, *Candidate Strategies and Electoral Competition in the Russian Federation: Democracy without Foundation*
Richard Snyder, *Politics after Neoliberalism: Reregulation in Mexico*
David Stark and László Bruszt, *Postsocialist Pathways: Transforming Politics and Property in East Central Europe*
Sven Steinmo, Kathleen Thelen, and Frank Longstreth, eds., *Structuring Politics: Historical Institutionalism in Comparative Analysis*
Susan C. Stokes, *Mandates and Democracy: Neoliberalism by Surprise in Latin America*
Susan C. Stokes, ed., *Public Support for Market Reforms in New Democracies*
Duane Swank, *Global Capital, Political Institutions, and Policy Change in Developed Welfare States*

Sidney Tarrow, *Power in Movement: Social Movement and Contentious Politics*
Kathleen Thelen, *How Institutions Evolve: The Political Economy of Skills in Germany, Britain, the United States, and Japan*
Charles Tilly, *Trust and Rule*
Daniel Treisman, *The Architecture of Government: Rethinking Political Decentralization*
Joshua Tucker, *Regional Economic Voting: Russia, Poland, Hungary, Slovakia, and the Czech Republic, 1990–1999*
Ashutosh Varshney, *Democracy, Development, and the Countryside*
Stephen I. Wilkinson, *Votes and Violence: Electoral Competition and Ethnic Riots in India*
Jason Wittenberg, *Crucibles of Political Loyalty: Church Institutions and Electoral Continuity in Hungary*
Elisabeth J. Wood, *Forging Democracy from Below: Insurgent Transitions in South Africa and El Salvador*
Elisabeth J. Wood, *Insurgent Collective Action and Civil War in El Salvador*

20180384R00213

Made in the USA
Lexington, KY
23 January 2013